CINEMAS OF THE WORLD

GLOBALITIES
Series editor: Jeremy Black

GLOBALITIES is a series which reinterprets world history in a
concise yet thoughtful way, looking at major issues over large
time-spans and political spaces; such issues can be political,
ecological, scientific, technological or intellectual. Rather than
adopting a narrow chronological or geographical approach,
books in the series are conceptual in focus yet present an array of
historical data to justify their arguments. They often involve a
multi-disciplinary approach, juxtaposing different subject-areas
such as economics and religion or literature and politics.

In the same series

Cinemas of the World

Film and Society from 1895 to the Present

JAMES CHAPMAN

REAKTION BOOKS

This book is dedicated to my father for encouraging my love of film, and to my mother for tolerating it

Published by Reaktion Books Ltd
79 Farringdon Road, London EC1M 3JU, UK

www.reaktionbooks.co.uk

First published 2003
Copyright © James Chapman

Printed and bound in Great Britain by
Bookcraft, Midsomer Norton

British Library Cataloguing in Publication Data

Chapman, James, 1968–
  Cinemas of the world: film and society from 1895 to the present. –
  (Globalities)
  1. Motion pictures - social aspects 2. Motion pictures – History
  I. Title
  306.4'85

ISBN 1 86189 162 8

Contents

Preface

The best way to educate oneself is to write a book. As a historian whose research interests have focused hitherto on the history of British cinema and television, my principal reason for accepting a commission to write a book ambitiously entitled *Cinemas of the World* has been to expand my own knowledge of those areas of cinema that otherwise would have remained unknown to me. I have benefited enormously from reading the work of many scholars whose research into national cinemas from Argentina to Zimbabwe has opened my eyes to the great diversity of film cultures around the world. A book of this sort is inevitably a work of synthesis; the references and bibliography bear witness to the full extent of the scholarly and intellectual debts I owe to the work of others.

It will be useful if, from the outset, I set out precisely what sort of book this is and what sort of book it is not. It is, first and foremost, a work of film *history*. The general reader will find that it is not an exploration of the art of film, nor is it a survey of the 'best' or 'greatest' films ever made. It is concerned not with the work of individual filmmakers but rather with the relationships between films and the societies and cultures in which they have been produced and consumed. It is not a work for the film studies specialist, but is written for undergraduate and graduate historians as well as students in related disciplines in the arts and social sciences. My approach is that of a cultural historian and not that of a film theorist. This book owes nothing to the voguish fads for structuralism and semiotics, psychoanalysis and postmodernism that have been so influential in the study of film within the academy and everything to the tried and proven method of historical empiricism. My interest is not in the minute textual analysis of individual films, but rather with locating film industries, genres and movements within their historical contexts.

There have already been many histories of world cinema; there will undoubtedly be many more. The earliest film histories, such as Terry Ramsaye's *A Million and One Nights* and Paul Rotha's *The Film Till Now*, were written during the middle and late 1920s when the medium had reached its thirtieth birthday – regarded at the time as a point of maturity in its artistic development. More recent works, such as Kristin Thompson and David Bordwell's *Film History: An Introduction* and the encyclopaedic *Oxford History of World Cinema*, edited by Geoffrey Nowell-Smith, cover the first century of cinema – though by this time opinions differed as to whether film was an essentially twentieth century phenomenon now enjoying its dotage or whether it was an exciting new form of cultural practice still in its infancy. As the second century of cinema is now under way, summarizing over a hundred years of film history in one short volume is a somewhat daunting task. This book does not purport to be a comprehensive history of world cinema. Inevitably, for a study of this length, much has been elided and even more has been omitted. I have selected particular themes and issues that seem relevant to me; indeed the book is best read as a series of related critical essays on film and society rather than a pure narrative history of cinemas around the world.

How does this book differ from other film histories? In the first place, and in line with the aims of the series of which this book is a part, it adopts a global perspective on cinema. I have been concerned throughout to consider the geographical spread of cinema across the continents of the world. I have adopted, for the most part, a geographical rather than a chronological structure, with sections focusing on Hollywood, European and world cinemas. This differentiates the book from most other general film histories, which usually follow a chronological structure, an approach best exemplified by the *Oxford History* with its three sections on 'Silent Cinema 1895–1930', 'Sound Cinema 1930–1960' and 'The Modern Cinema 1960–1995'. While few film historians would dispute the significance of those dates in the history of cinema – the first public film shows (1895), the institutionalization of sound cinema (c. 1930) and the almost simultaneous break-up of the Hollywood studio system and the emergence of an international 'new wave' (c. 1960) – I wanted to avoid writing another narrative history. Moreover, the geographical structure allows more space for coverage of less familiar (to Anglo-American and European readers) cinemas from around the world.

Another difference between this and other general histories is that I have opted for a broad-based comparative approach taking account of international trends and developments, rather than writing discrete essays on individual national cinemas. A point that struck me most forcefully whilst preparing this book was the dearth of what could be considered genuinely comparative film history. Most film histories tend to focus on national cinemas, while specialist monographs rightly concentrate on relatively discrete topics, usually within a national context. Yet a comparative perspective is essential even in the study of national cinemas, for only by establishing what one country's cinema has in common with others, as well as how it differs, can its unique characteristics be identified. With the exception of the section on Hollywood, therefore – the dominant model against which all other cinemas are judged and the one national cinema in the world that has a truly global reach – I have tried to adopt throughout a comparative analysis that places film in its global context.

A third difference between this and other histories of world cinema is that my interest focuses on the social and cultural history of cinema as an institution rather than on the aesthetic development of the medium of film. Most single-authored histories – such as David Cook's *A History of Narrative Film*, Jack Ellis's *A History of Film*, David Robinson's *World Cinema* and Basil Wright's *The Long View* – adopt a predominantly aesthetic approach to the subject, discussing film as an art form and analysing its formal and stylistic properties. Eric Rhode's *A History of the Cinema from its Origins to 1970* remains, still, the only thoroughgoing attempt to relate films and filmmakers to the social and political circumstances of their countries of origin. While historians no longer accept uncritically the idea of films as a straightforward 'reflection' of social reality, even the most ardent formalist critic must surely accept that all films, albeit perhaps some to a greater extent than others, are *informed by* and *respond to* the societies in which they were produced. I should make it clear that this is the basic assumption underlying my approach to film history.

A few 'housekeeping' notes are necessary to explain the conventions followed in this book. It is a characteristic of much critical writing that the words 'film' and 'cinema' are often used interchangeably. While there will be examples where the distinction is not straightforward, I have endeavoured to use 'film' when I am referring to the medium itself (comprising bodies of films, genres, styles, trends, movements) and 'cinema' to refer to the wider institutional framework (film industries, studios, organizations).

Academic conventions for citing films tend to interrupt the flow of writing with parenthetical information about dates, directors, production companies, and so forth. In order to maintain the readability of the text, therefore, I have included such information only when I felt it was relevant to the point I was making. Thus I have not habitually included directors' names (except in cases where directors are recognized as important filmmakers in their own right) or dates of films (except in cases where the date is important to the argument or where I am discussing a particular film). I have, however, included directors and dates in the film index. I trust this is an acceptable compromise between providing factual information where it may be of interest to the reader and maintaining the readability of the text.

As far as foreign language terms are concerned, I have maintained the original form wherever possible for film movements (*Nouvelle Vague, Cinéma Vérité, Cinema Nôvo*, etc.), though have used English where the name is one applied by film historians rather than by the practitioners themselves (Poetic Realism, for example). For reasons that would require a separate essay to explain, the Italian movement known by both practitioners and historians as Neo-Realism adopted the English term (it had previously been used in literary criticism; the Italians themselves preferred to call it *neo-verismo* or 'new veracity'). For terms in alphabets other than the Latin, however, I have used the common English term (New Chinese Cinema, New Iranian Cinema). Proper names are presented in their familiar English form (Akira Kurosawa, Zhang Yimou). Where countries or cities have changed their names I have opted for the name used most widely during the historical period under consideration (thus Iran rather than Persia, but Bombay rather than Mumbai and Madras rather than Chennai).

The translation of film titles presents particular problems of its own. For titles in the Latin alphabet I have followed the accepted convention of using the original language title wherever possible, with the familiar English language title in parentheses. Readers should note, however, that the English-language title is not necessarily a literal translation: *Les Enfants du Paradis*, for example, became *Children of Paradise* for the English-speaking market rather than the more literal 'Children of the Gods'. Some films have always been known by their original language titles, even in the English-speaking market: *La Grande Illusion*, *La Dolce Vita* and *Hiroshima, mon amour* are rarely, if ever, referred to as 'The Great Illusion', 'The Sweet Life' or 'Hiroshima, my love'. For other alphabets, however, my opinion is that readability is best maintained through referring to films by their familiar English titles rather than by rendering them in phonetic Latin approximations: thus *Battleship Potemkin* rather than *Bronenosets Potemkin*, *Seven Samurai* rather than *Shichinin No Samurai*, *Farewell My Concubine* rather than *Ba Wang Bie Ji*. Indian cinema is unusual in that some films have accepted English titles (*Mother India*) while others are better known in the original (*Lagaan*).

I have already noted my debts to the work of other scholars. More specific personal acknowledgements are easier to make. My thanks are due in the first instance to Professor Jeremy Black, general editor of the *Globalities* series, for inviting me to write this book, and to Michael Leaman of Reaktion Books for commissioning it. Both made helpful suggestions on content and structure that made the project manageable.

I have been fortunate in working with like-minded colleagues at the Open University, which through the efforts of its founding Professor of History, Arthur Marwick, did much to foster the use of film in historical teaching and research. Friends in the History Department have played a more crucial role than they realize in helping me through the process of writing this book. Particular thanks are due to three fellow members of the course team AA310 *Film and Television History* – Dr Tony Aldgate, Mr Michael Coyne and Dr Annika Mombauer – who will recognize in this book many of the ideas that have taken shape through the writing and discussion of teaching units.

In recent years I have enjoyed the friendship and scholarly community provided by the *Issues in Film History* seminar group at the Institute of Historical Research, including Professor Christine Geraghty, Dr Mark Glancy, Professor Sue Harper, Professor Vincent Porter, Professor Jeffrey Richards, Dr James Robertson, Dr John Sedgwick and Justin Smith. These seminars have proved enormously helpful to me in clarifying my own approach to film history and in engaging with the equally valid and very challenging approaches of other scholars. I am also indebted to numerous colleagues in the film studies and cultural history fields who, in general discussion, have provided me with ideas, information and references, including Mr Jim Hillier, Dr Amy Sargeant, Professor Pierre Sorlin and Professor Philip Taylor. A special note of thanks to Dr Matthew Hilton, who has constantly called me to task for my Anglocentric world view. Needless to say, in acknowledging the intellectual debts I owe to others, I must nevertheless issue the usual disclaimer that I alone am responsible for the content of the book, with all its flaws and omissions.

When I accepted the commission to write this book, it was somewhat in the spirit of Phileas Fogg – the challenge was to travel around the world's cinemas in 80,000 words. Yet for Fogg, the journey was an end in itself – he had little interest in the countries and cultures through which he travelled. As I wrote the book I became more of a Passepartout, enthralled by the sheer diversity of the national cinemas and the film styles that lay waiting to be discovered. It was in watching films to prepare for this book that I first encountered some of the national cinema traditions that recent scholarship has brought to light, including the popular cinema of the Far East, the delirious world of Bollywood and the visually exciting style of the New Chinese Cinema. Films that had been recorded and shelved for viewing at some time in the future were finally watched; FilmFour assumed the status of a research resource. While this book does not cover every national cinema and certainly does not do justice to every significant movement or filmmaker worthy of note, I will be satisfied if it leaves readers wanting to set out on their own journey around the cinemas of the world.

ONE

Film History: Sources, Methods, Approaches

Film history is both like and unlike other types of history. It shares with political, social, economic, military and other forms of history the aim of exploring and, as far as is possible, explaining the past. The film historian is concerned with the historical development of the medium of film and the institution of cinema. To this end, the film historian employs empirically based research methods to establish what has happened, how and why it has happened, and what the consequences have been. Where the film historian differs from other historians is in the nature of the primary sources at his disposal. While the film historian still makes use of traditional types of primary source materials – including production records, scripts, trade journals, the diaries and memoirs of filmmakers, film reviews and surveys of cinema-going habits – his main sources are the films themselves. The film historian may be interested in films as records of the past (actuality and documentary films), films as cultural artefacts (the analysis of film style and aesthetics) or films as social documents (the idea that films reflect the values, attitudes and assumptions of the societies in which they were made). Their analysis, however, from whichever perspective, requires specialist methods and skills that are unique to film history.

A SHORT HISTORY OF FILM HISTORY

While the history of film dates back to the invention of the medium in the 1890s, the study of film history as an academic discipline is a much more recent development. The vast majority of scholarly books and articles that could be described as 'film histories' have been published during the last three decades. This is not to say there were no film histories or film historians before the 1970s. Several pioneering works of film history appeared during the 1920s, 1930s and 1940s. The early history of American cinema was the subject of Terry Ramsaye's *A Million and One Nights* (1926), Benjamin Hampton's *History of the American Film Industry* (1931) and Lewis Jacobs's *The Rise of the American Film* (1939) – three books representing, respectively, the aesthetic, economic and social perspectives on film history that have now become standard approaches to the subject – while the best candidate for the first history of world cinema is the British filmmaker and critic Paul Rotha's *The Film Till Now* (1930). Perhaps the most influential early work of film history, however, was the German sociologist Siegfried Kracauer's *From Caligari to Hitler* (1947), in which he suggested that the cinema of Weimar Germany could be seen as a reflection of the social and psychological condition of the German people – a methodological approach that has been enormously influential on the work of later scholars. The existence of these pioneering works notwithstanding, however, the study of film history was not yet recognized within the academy and research into the history of the medium was the province mainly of cinephiles and film buffs such as Leslie Halliwell in Britain and William K. Everson in America.

It was during the 1960s that the study of film made its first inroads into the academy. In 1960 the British filmmaker Thorold Dickinson took up an appointment at the Slade School of Fine Art in London where he taught courses on film and in 1969 set up the Slade Film History Register as a central record of film material likely to be of interest to historians in the same way as the National Register of Archives had done for manuscript sources. In April 1968 a conference on 'Film and the Historian' was held at University College, London, under the auspices of the British Universities Film Council, providing a forum for historians such as A.J.P. Taylor, J.A.S. Grenville and Nicholas Pronay to discuss the value of filmic evidence to the historian. The outcome of the conference was the establishment of the University Historians' Film Committee 'with the aim of co-ordinating and promoting activities relating to the use of film (together with still photographs and sound recordings) for historical research and teaching'.[1] A series of international conferences on similar themes in the late 1960s and early 1970s – at the universities of Göttingen, Koblenz, Utrecht, Delaware and the Imperial War Museum in London – along with the publication of Paul Smith's edited volume *The Historian and Film* (1976) marked the emergence of the 'film and history' movement, culminating in the foundation of the International Association for Media and History in 1977.

The film and history movement was concerned initially with encouraging the use of archive film, especially newsreels and documentaries, for historical teaching and research. In Britain this cause was taken up in the 1970s by organizations such as the InterUniversity History Film Consortium and the Open University. At the same time, partly developing out of the film and history movement, but also gaining impetus from cultural history and sociology, scholars in Europe and North America were becoming interested in the study of the history of film in its own right. The development from 'film and history' to 'film history' can be traced through the publication of books such as Jeffrey Richards's *Visions of Yesterday* (1973), Robert Sklar's *Movie-made America* (1975), Richard Taylor's *Film Propaganda: Soviet Russia and Nazi Germany* (1979), Pierre Sorlin's *The Film in History* (1979), John O'Connor and Martin Jackson's *American History/American Film* (1979) and K.R.M. Short's *Feature Films as History* (1981), which collectively represented a shift of interest away from newsreel and documentary films towards feature films analysed as cultural artefacts and placed in their historical contexts. It was during the 1970s, too, that the first dedicated courses on 'film history' and 'cinema and society' appeared on the curricula of British and American universities. Initially there was much institutional resistance to this new development. 'Only now is it being realized – and much more tardily in Britain than in the United States – that a study of cinema can reveal much about, for instance, popular attitudes and ideals,' Jeffrey Richards complained in 1973. 'Moribund, Oxbridge-oriented university panjandrums are still to be heard up and down the country chuntering that if Cinema Studies is adopted then the next step will be Football Studies (and why not?).'[2]

The resistance to film history arose largely from ingrained cultural attitudes towards the cinema which regarded a mere entertainment medium as not being a legitimate object of historical enquiry. It may also have been coloured by a misunderstanding of the difference between film history and film studies, which emerged in parallel with film history during the 1970s. While the two disciplines share common ground in terms of their subject matter, their approaches and methods are very different. Film studies grew principally out of English literature, and its agenda was dominated by similar concerns (questions of authorship, genre and narrative) and analytical methods (especially linguistic theories of semiotics and structuralism). Film studies has focused primarily on textual analysis and has been concerned with questions of aesthetics (form and style) and meaning (for which the application of psychoanalytical models derived from the theories of Freud and Lacan became especially voguish in the 1970s). Film history, in contrast, has been more concerned with contextual analysis, exploring the conditions and circumstances under which films have been made, considering their makers' intentions, and, as far as possible, ascertaining how they have been received by both critics and cinema-goers. The institutionalization of the methodological and intellectual differences between the film studies school and the film history school is exemplified in the directions followed by the premier scholarly film journals. Since the early 1970s the pre-eminent film studies journal has been *Screen*, which has been at the vanguard of theoretical developments in the field (psychoanalysis in the 1970s, gender studies in the 1980s, reception theory in the 1990s), whereas the *Historical Journal of Film, Radio and Television*, founded in 1981, has been the leading forum for film historians seeking to place films within their social, political, industrial and cultural contexts.

It has taken several decades for film history to prove that, as a discipline, it has the same scholarly rigour and intellectual validity as other branches of history. Film history now, if still not universally accepted, is no longer regarded as the eccentric upstart that it once was, while the opprobrium of the Oxbridge panjandrums is reserved for more recent and trendy subjects like media and cultural studies.

All history is determined, in the first instance, by the nature of the sources available to the historian. The crucial difference between film studies and film history is that whereas film studies opens up a wider range of possible interpretations (there are different ways of reading films that can elicit all sorts of meanings that may or may not have been intended by the makers and understood by contemporary audiences), film history is an empirical discipline that deals not in speculation but in research. The film historian sets out to assemble, assess and interpret the facts concerning the production and reception of films.

In common with all branches of history, the primary sources for film history are fragmentary and incomplete. For one thing, film is a highly perishable medium. Many films, especially from the early history of cinema, no longer exist. It has been estimated that barely a quarter of all films made during the silent period of cinema (up until the end of the 1920s) still survive. The historian of early cinema, indeed, might be compared to a medievalist in so far as he has to make generalizations based on the relatively small amount of source material that has survived, either by chance or by design, from the period. Little attention was given to film preservation until the 1930s when archives such as the National Film Library in London, the Cinémathèque Française in Paris and the Museum of Modern Art in New York began to collect prints of films for posterity. It was not only the perishability of the raw material that led to a large percentage of early films being lost, but also a failure to appreciate the necessity of film preservation. As Ernest Lindgren, curator of the National Film Library, observed in 1948: 'The word "archive" rings with a deathly sound in the world of cinema, which is so young, vital and dynamic, eager for the future and impatient of the past.'[3] Film companies, moreover, have generally regarded films as commodities first and foremost rather than as cultural artefacts and, until recently, have done little to ensure their preservation.

Even when films survive, furthermore, they are not always available to the researcher. Many films, especially those made in developing countries, do not circulate beyond their national boundaries. Films are sometimes withdrawn from public view by governments and regimes which disapprove of their political or social content. Even in liberal democracies such as Britain and the United States, foreign-language films are generally confined to a minority niche market and are often difficult to see. 'Britain has one of the most restrictive exhibition systems in Europe', the respected film critic Derek Malcolm complained recently, 'and there's little or no hope of seeing an enormous amount of world cinema, even on video or the internet.'[4] Even where viewing prints and videos are available, furthermore, the historian constantly has to be alert to whether the film he sees today is the same film that audiences in the past would have seen, and how the interventions of censors and commercial distributors may have deleted scenes from the film. Sometimes, 'lost' scenes may be rediscovered. The much-vaunted restoration of Abel Gance's epic *Napoléon* by archivist Kevin Brownlow, for example, calls into question the existence of a definitive version of the film.

Film history has also been determined, to a considerable extent, by the attitudes of contemporaries as to which films are deemed significant or important. 'Out of two or three thousand full-length films produced in the world every year, there are perhaps only about fifteen whose titles are worth remembering, a half dozen that are worthy of mention in the future histories of cinema', the influential French film critic André Bazin once remarked.[5] While some films are celebrated and acclaimed, others disappear from view and become invisible to such an extent that they are virtually 'written out' of film history. It is astonishing how often the views of film critics have become received wisdoms that have permeated into film history. Canons exist in film history just as they do in English literature. One of the aims of what has been termed the 'new film history' since the 1980s has been to challenge critical orthodoxies and to reclaim films, genres and cycles, especially of popular cinema, that hitherto had been neglected or marginalized at the expense of more critically respectable art cinema.

The availability of the more traditional manuscript and printed source materials is also highly variable. One of the reasons why American cinema is the most heavily researched in the world is because it is also the best documented: the company papers of the major film studios have been deposited with university libraries, while the Academy of Motion Picture Arts and Sciences houses a large archive of filmmakers' personal papers and collections from bodies such as the Production Code Administration. Other national cinemas have been less well documented – there is a paucity of sources for British cinema in comparison to Hollywood, for example – and in the developing world, especially, where the need for archiving has only recently been recognized and is in any event hampered by lack of proper resources, relatively little material is available. Some archives, notably in Eastern Europe, have only very recently been opened up to scholars; some still remain closed. The type of evidence available is also variable. While it is usually possible to piece together details of the production histories of films from working papers, scripts and trade journals, and while film reviews can provide insights into the critical reception of films, evidence regarding the popular reception of films and the social composition of cinema audiences is scarce.

THE DIFFERENT APPROACHES TO FILM HISTORY

As with other branches of history, film history is open to a variety of different approaches and interpretations. There is much more to film history than just the history of films. 'The cinema', writes David Robinson, 'involves an aesthetic, a technology, an economy and an audience.'[6] The history of cinema has been written from all those perspectives. In their didactic work *Film History: Theory and Practice* – one of the few serious attempts to engage with the historiography of film scholarship – Robert C. Allen and Douglas Gomery identify four approaches to film history, which they label aesthetic, technological, economic and social.[7] Kristin Thompson and David Bordwell, in their *Film History: An Introduction*, add a fifth category – biographical – to those used by Allen and Gomery. 'This sort of inventory', they write, 'helps us understand that there is not *one* history of film but several possible histories, each adopting a different perspective.'[8]

Biographical history is probably the most familiar to the general reader. Biographies of movie stars, film directors, producers and studio heads proliferate; the majority are either hagiographic, anecdotal accounts of their subject or scandalous exposés of a famous individual's private life. Even in the more scholarly biographies, however, there is a tendency to reduce film history to the stories of 'great men'. The 'great man' tradition in film history encompasses both inventors (such as Thomas Edison and the Lumière brothers) and filmmakers to whom important technological and artistic developments in the medium are attributed (the pre-eminent example being D.W. Griffith, often acclaimed as the 'father of film'). The emphasis is very much on the role of individual agency, though it is often reduced to that indefinable quality of 'genius' that certain individuals are supposed to possess.

Aesthetic film history, put simply, is the history of film as an art form. Early works of film history, such as those by Terry Ramsaye and Paul Rotha, set out to claim film as a legitimate artistic practice that could take its place alongside established arts such as music, painting, sculpture, literature, drama and poetry. The orientation of much aesthetic film history has been towards claiming the 'best' films which, due to their special status as works of art, stand apart from the rest. Allen and Gomery term this the 'masterpiece tradition' and it has resulted in the creation of a canon of 'classic' films which are privileged in the writing of film history (examples would include, but are not limited to, *The Birth of a Nation*, *Das Kabinett des Dr Caligari*, *Battleship Potemkin*, *La Grande Illusion*, *The Grapes of Wrath*, *Citizen Kane*, *Brief Encounter*, *Les Enfants du Paradis*, *Bicycle Thieves*, *Tokyo Story*, *Seven Samurai*, *Pather Panchali*, *A bout de souffle* and *Raise the Red Lantern*). It has also resulted in the claiming of certain filmmakers as *auteurs* due to their personal vision and artistry (Robert Bresson, Carl Theodor Dreyer, Federico Fellini, John Ford, Jean-Luc Godard, Alfred Hitchcock, Akira Kurosawa, Yasujiro Ozu, Satyajit Ray, Jean Renoir and Orson Welles are all names familiar to cinephiles around the world). Derek Malcolm believes that 'during its hundred or so years of existence, it [the cinema] has produced as many major artists as any other art form during that time'.[9] The prevalence of aesthetic film history was apparent in the vogue for critics' choices of the 'best' or 'greatest' films ever made that marked the centenary of cinema in 1995. The BBC celebrated the centenary by broadcasting a hundred films throughout the year – beginning, predictably, with *Citizen Kane*, the film which more often than any other attracts the epithet of best film ever made – which purported to represent the best of world cinema. As the BBC's film programmer acknowledged, however, the season was 'not an attempt to represent the history of cinema, only a version of it'.[10] It is only relatively recently that historians interested in questions of film style and aesthetics have looked beyond the canon, realizing that the consequence of privileging certain films and filmmakers within the 'masterpiece tradition' is a history that marginalizes the vast majority of more ordinary, run-of-the-mill films. 'Film historians have not generally acknowledged the place of the *typical* work', observes the American scholar David Bordwell. 'In most film histories, masterworks and innovations rise monumentally out of a hazy terrain whose contours remain unknown.'[11]

Technological film history concerns the invention and development of the mechanical processes necessary for the projection of moving images. Most technological film history focuses on key moments in the development of film technology: the invention of the medium at the end of the nineteenth century, the introduction of talking pictures in the late 1920s and subsequent additions to the basic components of motion pictures such as colour, widescreen and special effects. The technological approach to film history is essentially deterministic in so far as the technology to make films has to exist before the artistic possibilities of the medium can be explored. 'All my work as an historian', declares Raymond Fielding, 'has proceeded from the premise that the history of the motion picture – as an art form, as a medium of communication, and as an industry – has been determined principally by technological innovations and considerations.'[12] Yet, just as aesthetics do not exist in a vacuum (the much-vaunted use of deep-focus photography in *Citizen Kane*, for example, was only made possible by technological developments including a new generation of silent arc lamps and the invention of fast film stock), the history of technology alone does not explain the history of the medium. The availability of technology is only one aspect of a history that is also influenced by economic, social and aesthetic factors. Certain technologies were adopted by the film industry when it became economically viable to do so (sound) or when the industry saw its audience threatened by another medium such as television (colour and widescreen, for example, had been available long before they became industry norms). Technologies were adopted, further-more, only when they were not aesthetically limiting or cumbersome: thus Technicolor and Panavision (a widescreen process) became standard whereas 3-D and Smell-O-Vision were short-lived gimmicks that quickly died.

Economic film history concerns the organization of the film industry as a business practice. 'It must be stressed that no film has ever been created outside of an economic context', Allen and Gomery remark.[13] This is as true of an art or avant-garde film as it is of the latest Hollywood blockbuster. While there are many examples of individual filmmakers for whom the profit motive is not necessarily the prime consideration, film produc-tion companies and the film industry at large operate according to a commercial imperative that films are made to make money. Films are, in the parlance of the industry, 'product' to be sold in the marketplace. The relationship between the film industry and cinema audiences is based on a transaction in which the former provides a commodity which the latter pays to consume. Economic film historians generally fall into one of two schools depending upon how they conceptualize this transaction between producers and audiences. On the one hand there are Marxisant historians who are critical of the film industry as an oligarchy in which economic (and therefore cultural) power resides with a small cartel of major companies which between them account for the majority of films. Kerry Segrave's book *American Films Abroad*, for example, concludes that the eco-nomic might of the US film industry has allowed it to control the market and thus determine the type of films that are made:

Hollywood integrates its consumers from the top down; producing a product for mass consumption, then creating a demand for it. There is no common demand from the bottom up, forcing the cartel to produce certain types of movies. The US industry is not subject to public demand, rather the public is the subject of calculation and manipulation by the industry.[14]

Business historians, on the other hand, argue that the film industry is led entirely by market forces and that film producers are simply responding to popular demand. In his study of the production strategy of the Warner Bros. studio in the 1930s, for example, Nick Roddick asserts: 'This is, after all, a normal industrial pattern: the market determines what is manufactured, and not vice versa.'[15]

Social film history focuses on the place of cinema in the wider society and culture. It involves questions such as who made films and how they were made (modes of production), what sort of films were made (film as a cultural artefact), who watched films (the study of audiences), how films have been evaluated and by whom (critical response), what constraints were placed on the content of films (censorship) and relations between the film industry and other institutions (government agencies, pressure groups and so forth). It also involves the extent to which films can be seen as mirrors of social reality, as reflections of the values, beliefs and concerns of the societies in which they were produced. Social film history, then, is a broad category that includes both the textual analysis of films and the investigation of the various contexts in which they may be placed. It encompasses the production histories of individual films, the investigation of genres and cycles that have been popular at given moments and the study of cinema-going as a social practice. It also includes the use of film as an instrument of propaganda and social control, an area that has provided a fruitful source of historical enquiry over the last twenty years and which shows no signs of abating.

This book belongs principally to the category of social film history. It focuses on themes of 'film and society': the importance of cinema as a social practice, the cultural significance attached to film in different societies, the role of film as a medium of popular entertainment and its use as a vehicle for promoting values and ideologies in both national and international contexts. This is not to say, however, that aesthetic, technological and economic factors are ignored. It would be absurdly reductive to make too rigid a distinction between the different approaches to film history or to assume they exist in isolation. Quite obviously the different approaches intersect and overlap with each other. Allen and Gomery demonstrate the plurality of approaches by explaining how the same film might be placed within different, parallel histories:

> *Citizen Kane*, for example, is often treated by film critics and historians as a work of art, a milestone in the history of American cinema as an art form. To its studio, RKO, however, *Citizen Kane* was primarily an economic product: one unit of the annual output, a capital outlay that had to be recouped at the box office. When the film was released in 1941, many commentators read *Citizen Kane* as a social statement – a thinly disguised account of the life of newspaper magnate William Randolph Hearst and a sermon on the corrupting effects of material and political power. *Citizen Kane* might also be regarded as an illustration of 'state-of-the-art' Hollywood movie technology, with its use of deep-focus photography and elaborate special effects. Which of these definitions of *Citizen Kane* as historical artefact is correct? Clearly, *Citizen Kane* is at one and the same time an artwork, an economic product, a social statement, and a use of technology.[16]

While it is possible to take account of all these factors in a detailed investigation of a single film, however, a general survey such as this cannot hope to cover all approaches in equal depth. The methodological focus of this book, therefore, is on social film history, though I will be referring to aesthetic, technological and economic factors as and where they intersect with the social context.

The notion that film is a reflection of social conditions and pre-occupations received its first sustained expression from the German sociologist Siegfried Kracauer. Films reflected society more accurately than any other medium, Kracauer maintained, because they were made collectively rather than being the work of individuals and because they were produced to satisfy the desires of a mass audience. The cinema of Weimar Germany, he argued, provided a unique insight into the collective mind set and psychological state of the German people. 'What films reflect are not so much explicit credos as psychological disposi-tions – those deep layers of mentality which extend more or less below the dimension of consciousness', he claimed.[17] His con-clusion was that the disturbing themes and violently dislocated imagery in films such as *Das Kabinett des Dr Caligari*, *Nosferatu* and *Dr Mabuse, der Spieler* reflected the psychological trauma of the period following the First World War and revealed the unconscious disposition of the German people towards author-itarianism as the only answer to the social problems of the time, thus, he suggested, anticipating the rise of Nazism.

Kracauer's approach – a form of *Zeitgeist* criticism in which films are seen to reflect the moods, thoughts and feelings of their time – has permeated into much social film history. That said, however, there are aspects of Kracauer's work that have been called into question. Paul Monaco, for example, took Kracauer to task for 'mixing weak history with flimsy psychol-ogy' on the grounds that he 'read too much out of the films through hindsight'.[18] The interpretation that Kracauer, writing immediately after the Second World War, imposed on the films could be made only with knowledge of what had happened under the Nazi regime – a perspective that was not available to audiences in the 1920s. Kristin Thompson pointed out, further-more, that Kracauer 'looks only at German films, ignoring the fact that . . . German audiences attended many American films during this period'.[19] One of the criticisms that has been made of Kracauer's work is that he focused on a relatively narrow selection of films (principally those exhibiting Expressionist characteristics) which were not representative of all the films that audiences saw. He did not take account of the fact that up to 40 per cent of the films exhibited in Weimar Germany were American (and therefore very different in content, theme and style from German films); moreover, the films he selected for detailed analysis were not those that had been most successful at the box-office.

The problem with *Zeitgeist* criticism, of course, is that the *Zeitgeist* that is invoked is dependent upon the films that are chosen. This point is eloquently demonstrated in a debate that took place in the pages of the journal *Hollywood Quarterly* in 1947. The producer John Houseman, noting the vogue for tough thrillers such as *The Big Sleep*, argued that 'whether we like it or not . . . the "tough" movie, currently projected on the seventeen thousand screens of this country, presents a fairly accurate reflection of the neurotic personality of the United States of America in the year 1947'. Houseman found these films 'repugnant' due to 'their lack of moral energy, [and] their listless, fatalistic despair'. 'The moral of our present "tough" picture, if any can be discerned', he maintained, 'is that life in the United States of America in the year 1947 is hardly worth living at all.'[20] Critic Lester Asheim, however, responded to this gloomy prognosis by pointing out that the most successful films at the box-office in the same year as *The Big Sleep* (1946) had also included *The Bells of St Mary's*, *Blue Skies*, *Road to Utopia* and *Easy to Wed*. These films, Asheim observed, were 'pure entertainment, light and gay, preferably with music; yet no claim is made that postwar America is a lighthearted, song-in-its-heart haven of romance and the joys of youth'. Asheim was critical of Houseman for making a broad generalization based not merely on one cycle, but largely on one film, and argued instead that 'a sample should represent the major characteristics of the universe for which it stands – and in this instance the universe is the overwhelming popular preference in film entertainment.'[21]

Yet Asheim's corrective view went largely unheeded by film historians. Like Kracauer, indeed, historians of American cinema have tended to privilege a certain type of film when it comes to reading films as reflections of social and psychological conditions. Robert B. Ray points out that there is often 'an enormous discrepancy between the most commercially successful movies and those that ultimately have been seen as significant'.[22] Thus it is that *film noir* is generally seen as more emblematic of American society in the 1940s than films like *Road to Utopia*, which have been neglected by historians despite being more popular – and arguably, therefore, more responsive to mass desires – at the time. Yet, as Arthur Marwick rightly reminds us: 'There is a law of the market; the bigger its commercial success, the more a film is likely to tell us about the unvoiced assumptions of the people who watched it.'[23]

The social film historian must, therefore, take account of all the films that audiences would have seen, not just those which critics have deemed the most significant. The social film historian thus moves away from the aesthetic orientation of much film history, focusing as it does on the masterpieces of film art, and takes as his objects of study the genre films and star vehicles that, due to their popularity with audiences, are more likely to be representative of their social and cultural contexts. For example, in his book *Visions of Yesterday* – a comparative study of the cinema of Empire, the cinema of Populism and the cinema of National Socialism – Jeffrey Richards averred that 'I have . . . looked at both "good" and "bad" films in search of the themes that concern me. Routine circuit fodder may have little artistic merit but can prove richly rewarding as a reflection of certain ideas and preoccupations.'[24]

The dominant metaphor of much social film history is that of reflection. There is an emphasis on films as sources or documents that provide an insight into the societies and cultures of the past. 'Throughout their history', writes American film historian Robert Sklar, 'the movies have served as a primary source of information about society and human behaviour for large masses of people.'[25] Richards, similarly, asserted that films 'are a still largely untapped source of social history'.[26] Evidence that this assumption is not confined to Anglo-American intellectual culture is provided by the Indian scholar Prem Chowdhry:

> Films, as popular culture, need to be considered as one of the repositories of twentieth-century consciousness in that they reflect and articulate, as well as shape, much of the awareness of the men and women who form that consciousness. Cinema

therefore needs to be recognised as a valid historical archive for the writing of political, social and cultural history, in addition to being a primary object of study in its own right.[27]

Chowdhry thus echoes both Kracauer, through his reference to films as repositories of social consciousness, and historians such as Richards and Sklar, with their insistence upon the value of films as primary sources for the study of the past.

However, this type of film history has been challenged by film theorists who regard it as too simplistic. Concerned with understanding film as a medium in its own right and on its own terms, they attack advocates of the reflectionist model for paying scant regard to the formal properties of the filmic medium itself. Instead of seeing films as reflecting society, film theorists tend to regard them as being 'constructed' through aspects of form and style. Jacques Segond, for instance, was critical of what he described as Richards's 'reductionist historical determinism' and asserted that 'the explicit content of a film (and in particular its plot and dialogue) is only part of the form that expresses the implicit meaning'.[28] 'Film does not reflect or even record reality', agrees Graeme Turner; 'like any other medium of representation it constructs and "re-presents" its pictures of reality by way of the codes, conventions, myths and ideologies of its culture as well as by way of the specific signifying practices of the medium.'[29] The inclination of the film theory school is towards close textual analysis, often applying methods of structuralism and semiotics borrowed from literary criticism, and in its most abstract form tends to detach films from any historical context at all and support what David Bordwell refers to as 'the sterile notion of the self-sufficient text'.[30] The idea of film as a 'self-sufficient text' is supported by some filmmakers, particularly advocates of the *auteur* theory who regard films as expressions of individual creativity rather than products of their social contexts. In her introduction to the published screenplay of her film *The Night Porter*, for example, the director Liliana Cavani declared that a film 'is a thing in itself, because in every case it is an invention'.[31]

The textualist approach, with its emphasis on the formal properties of film (such as *mise-en-scène*, camerawork, editing, sound and music) has been of enormous value to our appreciation of the nature of the medium. However, it has less to offer our understanding of cinema as a social institution and a social practice. Film historians have responded to the challenge of the film theorists by modifying the reflectionist model to one of mediation. This is more than just a metaphorical distinction, but rather an attempt to find a model for conceptualizing the relationship between film and society that accounts for the formal properties of filmic texts while also locating them in their historical contexts. John Belton, for example, accepts that 'the relationship between American film and American social and historical reality is highly mediated and extremely complex'. He elaborates thus:

> Films, quite clearly, cannot be viewed as simple mirrors of cultural reality. As fictional works, they do, however, have a 'use-value'. They can be analyzed – even psychoanalyzed – to reveal something about the cultural conditions that produced them and attracted audiences to them . . . In other words, the films do reflect American reality but in a distorted and displaced way. More often than not, they reflect back what audiences want to see rather than what is really there.[32]

And in a study of the 1930s films of Jean Renoir, Elizabeth Grottle Strebel argues that while 'the historian must still look to the films themselves as the central documents', it is also necessary 'to examine cinematic form and content as an expression of the times'.[33]

A further theoretical intervention in the debate arose as a consequence of the so-called 'turn to Gramsci' that occurred in cultural studies during the 1980s. Drawing upon the concept of hegemony discussed by the Italian Marxist political theorist Antonio Gramsci, cultural studies scholars began to interpret popular culture (including films) as a site for the 'negotiation' and 'contestation' of ideology. Hegemony, in Gramscian terms, refers to the process by which the dominant class in society wins the consent of subordinate groups through the exercise of political, moral and intellectual leadership.[34] This came as no revelation, however, to film historians, who did not require such a theoretical 'turn' to realize that film could be used as a vehicle for promoting ideology. Much of the early research into film history, indeed, had focused on the role of cinema as an instrument of propaganda in totalitarian regimes such as Nazi Germany where film was recognized by the state as a powerful medium of persuasion and control. The hegemonic possibilities of cinema (even if historians rarely used Gramscian terminology themselves) are also apparent in liberal democracies where it has served the interests of governing classes in promoting an ideology of consensus. Tony Aldgate, for example, has convincingly made the case for 'the ideological role of the British cinema in fostering harmony and social integration' during the 1930s and 1940s.[35] And it is quite commonplace to see Hollywood as, in the words of one feminist critic, 'the propaganda arm of the American Dream machine'.[36]

While the relationship between film and society may be more mediated and complex than the reflectionist model allows, films cannot be detached from the contexts in which they were produced and consumed if they are to be understood as anything other than abstract formulations of image and sound. And, while the appropriation of Gramsci's ideas may have overlaid a theoretical dimension onto the debate, the 'hegemonic turn' merely reinforced what historians, in their rigorously empiricist fashion, were already doing anyway. It is my contention that while films may not directly reflect society, they nevertheless are informed by and respond to the societies and circumstances in which they were produced. The formal and stylistic possibilities of film are shared between filmmakers in all societies and cultures. The social and cultural contexts, however, are not. The differences between, say, the classical cinema of Hollywood and the entertainment cinemas of Asia, or between the national cinemas of Europe and the so-called 'Third Cinema' of the developing world, are due essentially to the different social, political and economic contexts in which the filmmakers work. It is the nature of those differences that this book seeks to explore.

TWO

World Cinemas: Theoretical and Historical Perspectives

It is impossible to quantify the total number of films produced since the invention of cinema in the 1890s. For the early history of cinema, especially, many of the films do not survive and production records are incomplete. It is estimated that the average global production of feature films per annum is just short of 4,000. Historically the leading film-producing countries have been the USA, Japan and India. The world's largest film-producing nation since the early 1970s, India, has consistently produced between 700 and 800 films per year. While the American film industry has established itself as the dominant presence in the global marketplace, it accounts for approximately only six per cent of total film production in the world. Asia (including Australasia) provides 50 per cent of the world's film production, Europe (including the USSR/Russian Federation) accounts for approximately one third, while Latin America, Africa and the Middle East between them account for approximately one tenth.[1] Over 100 countries have a film production industry of some sort, however small, while film exhibition extends beyond those countries with their own production sector. Film is, without any question, a genuinely global medium and the cinema a truly global institution.

Quite apart from the practical impossibility of one individual ever being able to view all the films produced around the world, the sheer volume of world film production gives rise to a number of theoretical problems. The most significant of these is whether any general model can adequately account for the many different filmmaking practices, genres, styles and traditions that have arisen in the global context. It is my contention that, contrary to the titles of many general histories, there is in

33

fact no such thing as 'world cinema'. There is, however, a great diversity of world cinemas, each with their own unique set of historical, ideological, social, cultural, industrial and economic circumstances and determinants. These are what film studies has termed 'modes of film practice'.

MODES OF FILM PRACTICE

David Bordwell defines a mode of film practice as 'a set of widely held stylistic norms sustained by and sustaining an integral mode of production'.[2] It encompasses both aesthetic and formal aspects of filmmaking (film style) and industrial conditions of existence (mode of production). It combines both textual analysis of the films themselves and contextual analysis of the circumstances in which they were produced and consumed. It posits, moreover, a close and dynamic relationship between film style and mode of production in which each sustains the other. In other words, the prevalence of a particular style of filmmaking gives rise to a production process geared towards making films of the same sort; the institutionalization of the mode of production in turn helps to standardize film style. A mode of film practice needs to be seen historically because it responds to broader aesthetic, technological, industrial and cultural determinants and is therefore subject to modification and change over time.

The pioneering investigation of any mode of film practice is Bordwell, Staiger and Thompson's *The Classical Hollywood Cinema* (1985), a *magnum opus* that remains the most detailed and systematic piece of film scholarship of its kind. The authors set out to investigate both the stylistic and the production practices that characterized Hollywood cinema between the late 1910s and *c.* 1960. They show how 'style and industry came to be so closely synchronized by 1917': the model of the classical narrative feature film became the dominant style of American filmmaking, while the studio-based mode of production, characterized by a hierarchical management system and a specialized division of labour, was institutionalized.[3] This mode of film practice remained in place for the next forty years.

Later technological developments, such as sound, colour and widescreen, the authors suggest, did not fundamentally alter either the style of films or the way in which they were made. 1960 was chosen as marking the end of this mode of film practice because 'it was widely believed [in the film industry] that at the end of the decade Hollywood had reached the end of its mature existence' and that 'a certain technological state of the art had been reached'.[4] While the classical narrative film did not disappear – the authors suggest that a modified style of classical film has continued to be the norm for American cinema – its dominance was 'reduced somewhat' by structural changes in the American film industry and by the more widespread dissemination of alternative modes of film practice (in the form of various 'art house' and 'new wave' cinemas) from the late 1950s/early 1960s.

'The historical hegemony of Hollywood makes acute and urgent the need to study film styles and modes of production that differ from Hollywood's', Bordwell asserts.[5] It is, perhaps, an indication of the monumental (and intimidating) work of scholarship that is *The Classical Hollywood Cinema* that its methods have not yet been widely applied to other film industries. Colin Crisp's *The Classic French Cinema 1930–1960* (1993), M. Madhava Prasad's *Ideology of the Hindi Film* (1998) and Bordwell's own *Planet Hong Kong* (2000) are perhaps the nearest equivalents. The result is that, in comparison to classical Hollywood, other modes of film practice remain relatively unknown, for, while there is an abundance of aesthetically oriented work on cinemas in Europe, and to a lesser extent on Asia, there is a dearth of scholarship on the film industries and modes of production that sustain them.

As Hollywood has been the dominant mode of film practice in the world, culturally and economically, there has always been a tendency – evident on the part of both filmmakers and film historians – to describe other modes of film practice as 'alternatives' to it.[6] This tendency has had significant implications for the historical mapping of the world's cinemas: those which set out to differentiate themselves from Hollywood have been privileged, while those which modelled themselves on Hollywood have been marginalized. This tendency was evident even in the very early histories of film, such as Rotha's *The Film Till Now*, which exhibited a clear preference for the European avant-garde movements of the 1920s (German Expressionism, Soviet montage and French Surrealism) and was dismissive of other national cinemas, such as the British, which Rotha felt 'has no other aim than that of the imitation of the cinema of other countries', principally America.[7] Seventy years on from Rotha this is still largely the case. Ginette Vincendeau points out that 'the essence of European cinema has been defined as residing in works that are, to various degrees, aesthetically innovative, socially committed and humanist in outlook'. 'To these features', she continues, 'are often added the auteurist notions of originality and personal vision – all characteristics which define, and promote, European art cinema as fundamentally different from the industrially based and generically coded Hollywood.'[8] Thus it is that histories of European cinema have tended to privilege movements such as Italian Neo-Realism and the French *Nouvelle Vague* or the personal 'art cinema' of directors such as Ingmar Bergman and Federico Fellini. And, when western scholars belatedly became interested in the cinemas of the rest of the world, it was the politically committed 'Third Cinema' of Latin America that first attracted attention rather than the commercially oriented entertainment cinemas of India and Asia. It is only very recently, indeed, that scholars have 'rediscovered' or 'reclaimed' other examples of popular cinema such as the classical Japanese cinema of the 1930s, the 'entertainment' cinema of the Third Reich, or mainstream Indian cinema with its star-genre formulas, which have all, to a greater or a lesser degree, imitated or modified the Hollywood mode of production to meet specific cultural and ideological circumstances.

The search for alternatives to Hollywood has been furthered by film theorists who, inspired by Marxisant cultural studies, have been obsessed with exposing the ideological and aesthetic conservatism of classical Hollywood cinema. Thus they have championed those filmmakers (such as Jean-Luc Godard in France, Maya Deren and Stan Brakhage in America, Peter Greenaway and Derek Jarman in Britain) who can be seen to 'deconstruct' or 'subvert' the classical style. This tendency reached *reductio ad absurdum* when theorist Peter Wollen, analysing Godard's *Vent d'est* (1969), advanced the notion of a 'counter cinema' that was the polar opposite of the classical Hollywood style: narrative intransitivity instead of narrative transitivity, estrangement instead of identification, unpleasure instead of pleasure, and so on.[9] Such concepts, however, are merely abstract intellectual exercises that have little application or relevance outside the academy. Wollen's attempt to put the principles of counter-cinema into practice, in collaboration with fellow theorist Laura Mulvey, resulted in the production of *Riddles of the Sphinx* (1977), arguably the most incomprehensible film ever made and one that remains mercifully unseen except on university film studies courses.

Quite apart from their political investment in the avant-garde – which, of course, is worthy of attention as a mode of film practice in its own right, but which bears little or no relation to the role of cinema as a social practice – film theorists have also been culpable of claiming as 'alternative' certain films and filmmakers who were really nothing of the sort. The French theorist Noël Burch, for example, has conceptualized the history of early cinema (up until *c.* 1910) in terms of a 'primitive mode of representation' which he sees as 'a stable system with its own inherent logic and durability'. Yet his suggestion that the early pioneers' experiments with film form 'should appear as strategies in the works of creators seeking explicitly or implicitly to deconstruct classical vision' is an absurd claim in so far as it makes them actors in a process of which they were completely unaware.[10] For all the similarities that might be identified between early cinema and later avant-garde practices, they are not comparable historically for the simple reason that in the early years of cinema there was as yet no dominant model against which an alternative could be constructed.

The fact that most film studies has been written from a perspective that privileges western aesthetics, moreover, accentuates the tendency to construct non-western cinemas as 'alternative' when in their own cultures they are in fact the dominant modes of film practice. Nowhere is this better exemplified than in the case of Hindi cinema in India, which only from a western perspective can be described as alternative. Hindi cinema is the dominant form of popular cinema in India and

Bombay is one of the leading film-producing centres in the world. As one critic rightly points out: 'Bombay filmmakers repeatedly stress that they are aiming to make films which differ in both format and content from Western films, that there is a definite skill to making films for the Indian audience, that this audience has specific needs and expectations, and that to compare Hindi films to those of the West, or of the Indian "art" cinema, is irrelevant.'[11] It is ironic that the two Asian film-makers best known to cinephiles in the West – India's Satyajit Ray and Japan's Akira Kurosawa – are arguably among the least representative filmmakers in their own countries, largely because their films have been seen as more 'western' than most of their contemporaries'.

THE DIFFERENT MODELS OF NATIONAL CINEMAS

The most familiar modes of film practice are national cinemas. Yet a national cinema is also more than just a mode of film practice. Studies of national cinemas, which have provided the mainstay of film history for many years, have traditionally understood a national cinema to refer simply to the films produced within a particular country. More recently, however, this model has been criticized for its failure to take proper account of the full complexity of cinema as a social and cultural practice.

Andrew Higson has advanced a theoretically more rigorous model of national cinema which is posited on the notion that a national cinema involves not only the films produced within a nation state but also the distribution and exhibition of films (including foreign films) and critical discourses around cinema. He suggests that a national cinema can be defined in four main ways: economically, focusing on the organization and political economy of the film industry, its relative economic health, the size of its domestic market and the extent of its penetration of overseas markets; in terms of exhibition, focusing on what sort of films audiences are watching and the relative percentages of indigenous and imported (especially American) films; in evaluative terms, which attempt to privilege the cultural specificity of a national cinema, for example by focusing on particular movements or directors deemed to be culturally significant; and in terms of representation, analysing the content and themes of films and their representations of national (and other) identities. Addressing the debate over whether films reflect national characteristics, or whether films construct such characteristics through their own signifying practices, Higson concludes that it is 'necessary in the end to draw on both these arguments'. 'Yes', he amplifies, 'films will draw on identities and representations already in circulation – and often they will naturalize those identities. But films will also produce new representations of the nation.'[12]

The nature and characteristics of national cinemas are dependent upon a wide range of economic, social, cultural and political determinants. These include, but are not limited to, the size of the production sector, the size of the potential cinemagoing audience, the cultural significance attached to film as an art form in the national culture, the extent of state involvement with the film industry, and the relative popularity of indigenous films against foreign imports. Stephen Crofts suggests that '[the] political, economic and cultural regimes of different nation-states license some seven varieties of "national cinema".'[13] While he adds that his taxonomy is 'highly permeable' in that national cinemas often straddle different categories, his model is worth elaborating upon precisely because of its flexibility.

1. *Asian commercial cinemas.* Perhaps the only national cinemas in the world that are immune to the global economic power of the US film industry are India and Hong Kong. In both cases the size of the domestic market provides the economic base for a self-sustaining indigenous film production industry, while the cultural specificity of the film products has led to their dominance of the home market. India has led the world in the volume of film production since the early 1970s, producing on average four times as many films per year as Hollywood, which feed its massive domestic market and are exported throughout Southeast Asia. The fact that Indian films are produced in different languages for local consumption also helps them maintain their dominance in the home market. Hong Kong, which at the time of writing seems to have maintained enough of its economic and cultural identity following the handover to China in 1997 still to be considered as a national cinema in its own right, produces fewer films than India, but again benefits from a loyal domestic market and from regional exports. Japan, which has also often produced more films than Hollywood, does, however, import more American films than its Asian neighbours.

2. *Anglophone commercial cinemas.* In contrast to the flourishing film industries of India and Hong Kong, English-language cinemas (principally Britain, Canada, Australia and New Zealand) have historically been unable to establish themselves

as the dominant presence in their home and continental markets. The problem was astutely summarized by British film producer Leon Clore: 'If the United States spoke Spanish, we would have a film industry.'[14] The English-speaking countries are more susceptible to Hollywood films than countries where language provides at least some barrier against Americanization. All Anglophone cinemas have suffered, both economically and culturally, from their unequal relationship with Hollywood and, to a lesser extent, with each other. Thus, while Australian cinema has struggled to compete with Hollywood in the Pacific region, New Zealand cinema has suffered even further from being seen as a poor relation of Australian cinema. The proximity of Canada to the United States has almost certainly retarded the development of a national cinema there (Canada even has to endure the indignity of being considered part of the 'domestic' North American market as far as the US film industry is concerned). The particular problem for British cinema was recognized by Lindsay Anderson: 'As, geographically, Britain is poised between continents, not quite Europe, and very far from America, so from certain points of view the British cinema seems to hover between the poles of France and Hollywood.'[15] While Anglophone cinemas sometimes produce films drawn from indigenous cultural traditions that turn out to be international successes (Australia's 'Crocodile' Dundee, Britain's Four Weddings and a Funeral), these invariably turn out to be exceptional rather than commonplace occurrences.

3. *Other commercial cinemas.* This category includes all those national cinemas whose production is based on popular genres (melodramas, thrillers, comedies, musicals and so forth) and which compete, with varying degrees of success, with Hollywood films in their home markets. It includes most European national cinemas, ranging from those with large production sectors such as France (which has often matched Hollywood numerically) to those with small indigenous production industries such as Iceland (which produces on average only four or five films a year, but which has one of the highest rates of cinema-going per head of population in the world). It also includes other commercial cinemas in Asia (Bangladesh, Indonesia, Taiwan) and in the

developing world. The extent of state support for indigenous film industries has varied enormously according to country and historical period, though even in those national cinemas where there is generous subsidy (such as France) the industries are dependent upon private capital investment. These commercial cinemas are often amongst the least well-known outside their own countries, partly because many popular genre films are produced solely for domestic consumption, and partly because they tend to be frowned upon by critics who attach greater cultural significance to the more prestigious 'art cinema' that frequently exists alongside them. With rare exceptions, such as Italian 'spaghetti westerns' and 'peplums', popular genre films are not widely exported. It is generally the case that 'highly popular European films seldom travel well beyond their national boundaries; when they do, as is the case with the recent French successes based on the novels of Marcel Pagnol (*Jean de Florette, Manon des Sources, La Gloire de mon père, Le Château de ma mère*), they are generally repackaged for art cinemas'.[16]

4. *Art cinemas*. The term 'art cinema' entered into critical discourse in the 1970s to describe a tradition of filmmaking that differentiated itself from the commercial mainstream on account of its greater thematic depth and its inclination for experimentation in form and style. It is most commonly associated with European cinemas, where it is manifested in national film movements such as the avant-garde traditions of the 1920s and the 'new wave' cinemas of the 1960s, though it also includes non-European examples such as the Australian period film and the Indian art cinema of Satyajit Ray. It is important to recognize that in the national context art cinema invariably exists alongside a commercial cinema, though it is produced for a different market (a niche audience of cinephiles and film buffs) both in its own country and overseas. In contrast to the commercial cinema of genres and stars, art cinema tends to be seen in terms of *auteurs* (examples would include, but are not limited to, Michelangelo Antonioni, Ingmar Bergman, Robert Bresson, Luis Buñuel, Jean Cocteau, Rainer Werner Fassbinder, Federico Fellini, Peter Greenaway, Krzysztof Kieslowski, Max Ophuls, Pier Paolo Pasolini, Alain Resnais, Jean-Marie Straub and Luchino Visconti) and critical discourse around it tends to focus

on the role and vision of the filmmaker as an artist. Bordwell categorizes art cinema as a mode of film practice that is different from classical cinema due to its looser narrative structure, greater ambiguity, lack of clear causal motivation and multifaceted engagement with external reality in terms of both its themes (especially psychological conditions) and the verisimilitude of its *mise-en-scène*.[17] Steve Neale suggests a different way of understanding art cinema as an institution which 'needs to be conceptualized as a particular and specific space within the commercial institution of cinema as a whole'.[18] In these terms art cinema is understood as much in terms of its exhibition practices (so-called 'art house' cinemas, film clubs and the like) and its audiences (cinephiles and intellectuals) as it is in terms of content. This institutional approach demonstrates that concepts of what art cinema is are culturally specific: thus, films that would be placed within a mainstream entertainment cinema in their own country might cross over into art cinema when they are shown abroad. In Britain and the United States, for instance, foreign-language films tend to have at best a limited distribution on the 'art house' circuit catering for a different sort of audience than the dominant chains of multiplex cinemas.

5. *Totalitarian cinemas*. Examples of totalitarian cinemas would include those of Nazi Germany, Fascist Italy, Stalinist Russia and Communist China. Totalitarian cinemas are generally characterized by state control of film production, a formal or informal nationalization of the film industry, and the restriction, or outright ban, of imported films. It has been in such regimes that the cinema has been most fully exploited as an instrument of propaganda and a device of social control. Lenin, for example, famously declared that 'Of all the arts, for us the cinema is the most important', while Goebbels described the cinema as 'one of the most modern and far-reaching media that there is for influencing the masses'.[19] Yet, as recent research into the nature of Nazi and Soviet cinema has shown, the adoption of film propaganda as a weapon of state was co-dependent with the continuation of a traditional entertainment cinema of popular genres and stars which may have reflected the ideological nature of those regimes only in the most oblique or tangential ways. Goebbels consciously sought to imitate the production values and escapist

fantasies of Hollywood, while filmmakers in the Soviet Union also realized the need to make commercially oriented *kassovye* (cash) entertainment films as well as *klassovye* (class) propaganda films. While most historical examples of totalitarian cinemas are found before, during and immediately after the Second World War, the persistence of this model of national cinema at the start of the twenty-first century is exemplified by North Korea, which has probably the last orthodox, state-sponsored, ideologically committed Marxist cinema in the world.

6. *Third Cinema*. The term 'Third Cinema' was originally used to describe the radical political cinemas that arose in Latin America during the 1960s, such as revolutionary Cuban cinema and the *Cinema Nôvo* movement in Brazil. It was characterized, in the words of Argentinian filmmakers Fernando Solanas and Octavio Getino, as 'a cinema of liberation' from imperialist oppression. 'The anti-imperialist struggle of the peoples of the Third World and of their equivalents inside the imperialist countries constitutes today the axis of the world revolution', they declared in a polemical manifesto of 1969. 'Third Cinema is, in our opinion, the cinema that recognizes in that struggle the most gigantic cultural, scientific, and artistic manifestation of our time, the great possibility of constructing a liberated personality with each people as the starting point – in a word, the decolonization of culture.'[20] Third Cinema should not be seen as synonymous with Third World cinema: its political radicalism differentiates it from the bulk of Third World film production, which has continued to be dominated by popular genres. The notion of Third Cinema was subsequently taken up by theorists who sought to formulate a new approach to film criticism as well as to filmmaking practice. Paul Willemen, for example, has argued that Third Cinema is 'a kind of international cinematic tradition which exceeds the limits of both the national-industrial cinemas and those of Euro-American as well as English cultural theories'.[21] Recent theoretical developments have shifted the focus of debate towards postcolonialism, which emphasizes the politics of cultural representation rather than the sense of revolutionary struggle inherent in the original project of Third Cinema.

7. *Regional, ethnic and sub-state cinemas*. This category encompasses films made by minorities within nation states and,

therefore, tends to be handicapped by a lack of funding and industrial infrastructure. Regional, ethnic and sub-state cinemas exist both within and as alternatives to national cinemas: Québécois cinema in Canada, Catalan cinema in Spain, Welsh and Scottish cinema in Britain, Aboriginal cinema in Australia, Maori cinema in New Zealand. India undoubtedly has the widest range of sub-state cinemas, with Bengali, Punjabi, Assamese, Marathi, Telugu, Tamil, Malayalam and Kannada regional cinemas all recognized alongside the dominant Hindi cinema. Sub-state cinemas range from, on the one hand, those which enjoy some degree of state sanction and support (such as Welsh and Québécois cinema) to, on the other hand, clandestine, underground movements within a nation state. Examples of the latter include the Cine Liberación group in Argentina (founded by Solanas and Getino in opposition to the military government that replaced the nationalist President Juan Perón) and the Chilean documentarist Miguel Littín whose *Acta general de Chile* (1986) was filmed secretly, and on pain of death, during the Pinochet regime.

THE LIMITATIONS OF THE NATIONAL CINEMA MODEL

While the notion of national cinema/s remains the most familiar means of conceptualizing the world's cinemas, it is not without its limitations. For one thing, the taxonomies outlined above are based on modes of production. Yet many states, especially in Africa, have no film production sector of their own but do exhibit films from other countries. A film culture can therefore exist in a country that has no film production industry. The blurring of boundaries between film and other media such as television – exemplified by the likes of Channel 4 in Britain and Canal + in France – raises the question of what precisely constitutes a 'film'. While a generally accepted definition would be that a film has to have been shown in cinemas, it is not unknown for made-for-television 'films' to be released theatrically only outside their country of origin. Should they therefore be included within a national cinema?

Nor is it always possible to locate films unproblematically within a particular national cinema. The term 'Europudding' has recently entered into film journalism to describe an international co-production that draws on funding and personnel from different European nation states. The strategy of combining resources was nothing new in the 1990s, however, and can be seen also in the 'Film Europe' movement of the 1920s and early 1930s which sought to create a pan-European film industry making international co-productions in an attempt to challenge US economic and cultural hegemony in the world film market. Co-productions – which, of course, are not limited to Europe – exemplify the mobility of capital and personnel in film production, and thus pose a fundamental challenge to models of cinematic practice based on narrowly defined concepts of 'the national'.

The process of globalization in the latter part of the twentieth century, furthermore, involving as it does the growth of giant media conglomerates and the consolidation of geographically diverse markets, has weakened, though arguably not to the extent that is often feared, the cultural and economic integrity of nation states. Globalization has also coincided with the most significant geopolitical changes in over half a century – the end of the Cold War and the disintegration of one of the two superpowers that had dominated international politics since 1945 – which has consequently resulted in the fragmentation of old nation states and the emergence of new ones. In a period of flux and transition, the instability of 'the national' has significant implications for both the political economy of the film industry and the nature of cultural representations in films

A COMPARATIVE APPROACH TO FILM HISTORY

The foregrounding of traditions of national cinema in film scholarship is understandable and inevitable. A combination of factors – including linguistic barriers, cultural knowledge, the availability of films and access to archives – means that scholars work within certain defined parameters. The majority of scholarly monographs on film tend to focus not even on one national cinema, but on discrete historical periods and particular genres or cycles. In this respect film history has followed other types of history in adopting the concept of periodization and the principle of subject specialization in order to make the task of research manageable. Indeed, a work of synthesis such as this becomes possible only once a certain body of empirical knowledge has been established through such research.

Yet, for a historical mapping of the world's cinemas in a global context, it becomes necessary to look beyond the geographical and political boundaries of nation states. It is for this reason that I am adopting throughout this book a comparative approach to film history. There is relatively little comparative political, social or economic history; there is hardly any comparative film history. While there are film textbooks and survey histories that are international in scope, the tendency is to treat national cinemas discretely as self-contained entities rather than drawing out comparisons between different countries. This is not to suggest that comparative history should be seen as a better approach than national histories, but simply that it offers a different perspective that is not necessarily apparent from a focus solely on national cinemas.[22]

There are two principal arguments in favour of the comparative approach. The first of these, somewhat paradoxically, is to throw into sharper relief the study of national cinemas. The entire concept of national cinema centres around the question of what is unique to that cinema – how the films of a particular country relate to such concepts as national identity, cultural traditions and values. The question that scholars of national cinemas usually ask is, for instance, what is uniquely 'British' about British cinema, or what is specifically 'German' about German cinema? To take just one example, critical discourse around Spanish national cinema has typically seen it as a reflection of peculiarly Spanish characteristics:

> Fraga's oft-maligned tourist slogan, 'Spain is different', may now be denied by modern Spaniards, but the idiosyncrasies, for better or worse, nonetheless exist. And those idiosyncrasies are what makes the country and its reflection in cinema an eternally fascinating study. Spain is like no other country in

the world. Many of its films bear testimony to this truth, for the films are an expression of an individualism that is deeply rooted in cultural, one might even venture to say, racial pride. Whether we take the historical epics of the 1940s or the zany comedies of Pedro Almódovar, all are merely the varying facets of an unmistakable national identity.[23]

It is of course a truism, though one worth noting nonetheless, that all countries tend to construct their national identities in terms of uniqueness and difference.

However, in a purely theoretical sense, this question of national specificity can be answered only by comparison with other national cinemas. To this extent it becomes necessary to consider both similarities and differences between national cinemas. Thus, Tom O'Regan begins his study of Australian national cinema by asking: 'What does Australian cinema *have in common with other national cinemas* – no matter how diverse?' His point is that the very concept of national cinemas assumes certain similarities: 'Like all national cinemas, the Australian cinema contends with Hollywood dominance, it is simultaneously a local and an international form, it is a producer of festival cinema, it has a significant relation with the nation and the state, and it is constitutionally fuzzy.'[24] This is not to deny the cultural specificity of national cinemas, of course, but it does suggest that many of the issues that concern particular national cinemas are shared with others. In the introduction to their collection on the 'Film Europe' movement, for example, Andrew Higson and Richard Maltby assert 'it is clear that studies of specific national contexts reveal a recurrent pattern, which is not always obvious until they are compared'.[25]

The second reason for adopting a comparative approach is to be able to identify the underlying structures common to different film industries and national cinemas. For all the differences in the content and style of films, national film industries have been organized on remarkably similar principles. Allen and Gomery point out that all film industries since the beginning of the twentieth century have had to devise ways of handling the 'three fundamental tasks' of production, distribution and exhibition.[26] In the US film industry this took the form of a process known as vertical integration, meaning that the largest companies had interests in all sectors of the industry. In the 1930s and 1940s the 'Big Five' companies (MGM/Loew's, Paramount, Warner Bros., Twentieth Century-Fox and RKO Radio Pictures) combined the functions of producers, distributors and exhibitors. Thus, in addition to owning their own production facilities (film studios) they also had their own distribution networks and owned chains of cinemas. While other national film industries have modelled themselves on the American example, they have not usually achieved the same degree of integration. In Britain, only two companies ever achieved full vertical integration (the Rank Organization and the Associated British Picture Corporation). Other countries where some level of vertical integration occurred were Germany during the 1920s (Universum Film Aktiengesellschaft, or Ufa), France during the 1930s (Gaumont-Franco-Film-Aubert and Pathé-Natan) and Japan (Nikkatsu, Shochiku and Toho). India, which represents perhaps the only serious rival to the US film industry due to its dominance of both its own and the Asian diasporic markets, has, in contrast, never achieved any degree of vertical integration, suggesting that this model of economic organization is not always necessary for a thriving film industry.

Structural similarities are not confined to the organization of film industries. They can also be identified in the films themselves through common features such as narrative and genre. A common characteristic of all commercially oriented entertainment cinemas, for example, is that they have adopted the fictional narrative feature film as the mainstay of their production. This type of film has proved remarkably durable across different national cinemas and film cultures. And there are common genres too – the war film, the thriller, the comedy, the musical, the horror film, the historical/costume film – which have proliferated in different national contexts. Even those genres which are nationally specific in terms of their content (the western, for example, is rooted in a specifically American historical experience) have crossed national and cultural boundaries (westerns were also produced in huge numbers in Italy and other European countries during the 1960s and early 1970s).

The utility of the comparative approach is most evident when considering the cinemas of particular regions. A recent study of *Nordic National Cinemas*, for example, highlights the 'high degree of integration and exchange between the countries' (Denmark, Sweden and Norway, especially) that characterizes Scandinavian cinema.[27] It is now quite commonplace to speak of 'Arab cinema' – a diasporic term that ranges geographically from the North African countries of the Maghreb (Morocco, Algeria, Tunisia) to the Persian Gulf (Iraq, Iran) – and 'sub-Saharan cinema', which encompasses most of the African continent.[28] And, while the national cinemas of Europe are arguably the most diverse stylistically, they do share many common themes and concerns. As Pierre Sorlin asks:

> Now, instead of looking separately at the various parts of the Old World, why should we not take Europe as a whole, as a historical entity, a cluster of nations which, at least since the middle of the twentieth century, have been involved in a common experience? Europeans have gone through the same social, economic and mental changes but their cultural backgrounds are far from unified, and it is this gap which seems interesting: how were identical changes interpreted with respect to the cultural habits of the nations?[29]

Sorlin shows how the cinemas of Europe have responded to the shared historical experiences of total war, urbanization and social change. The cinemas of Africa and Asia are perhaps even more linked by common themes such as ethnicity, decolonization and modernization. There is, of course, a danger of over-emphasizing similarity to the extent that it leaves no room for difference. The point of the comparative approach, therefore, is to identify points of both similarity and difference so that the range of cinematic traditions and film cultures around the world can more fully be appreciated.

THREE

Early Cinema

The history of early cinema, which is generally held to mean the period up until *c.* 1910, is as much a job of film archaeology as it is of film history. It is a history based on incomplete records as the majority of films no longer survive and other sources are fragmentary at best. It was, indeed, due principally to the efforts of film archivists that early cinema found its place in the sun as a result of the now legendary Congress of the International Federation of Film Archives held at Brighton in 1978. This conference, which brought together archivists, historians and theorists to see and discuss hundreds of films from the first decade of cinema, many of them seen for the first time in over seventy years, opened up early cinema as an area of scholarly research and debate. That the Brighton conference coincided with the heyday of 'high theory' in film studies has had significant implications for the subsequent directions of research into early cinema. There have been two principal strands which, without wishing to become reductive, are nevertheless grouped around the theoretical and empirical schools of film history. On the one hand, theorists such as Noël Burch, André Gaudreault and Ben Brewster have challenged the notion of 'primitivism' in relation to early cinema and have argued instead that early cinema was a 'system' with its own conventions and signifying practices that was different from, rather than inferior to, the classical cinema that developed out of it. Central to this work is the assertion, contrary to the beliefs of an earlier generation of historians such as Terry Ramsaye and Lewis Jacobs, that the classical narrative film was not necessarily the inevitable form for the evolution of the medium. On the other hand, historians such as Robert C. Allen, Douglas Gomery, Charles Musser and Miriam Hansen have explored the history of cinema as a social institution in its early years, considering its relationship to other forms of popular entertainment such as American vaudeville theatre and researching, as far as evidence exists, the social composition of early cinema audiences.[1] Along with the work of archivist-filmmaker Kevin Brownlow and the comparative statistical analysis of Barry Salt, the results of this research have been to challenge many prevailing orthodoxies in film history and to put early cinema on the map as a subject in its own right rather than merely a precursor to classical Hollywood and the national cinemas of Europe.[2] The history of early cinema, indeed, highlights numerous points of intersection between the different approaches to film history, especially between the aesthetic and the technological, whilst also illuminating the wider social context in which these developments took place.

PATENTS AND PIONEERS

Cinema was the 'last machine' of the Victorian age.[3] It was one of a series of technological discoveries and inventions in the latter part of the nineteenth century that also included the telephone (1876), the internal combustion engine (1876), the cathode ray tube (1878), the phonograph (1878), the electric light bulb (1879) and wireless telegraphy (1894). Histories of the origins of cinema tend, inevitably, to privilege the technological preconditions that were necessary for the projection of moving pictures. These included still photography (perfected by the late 1870s), the invention of celluloid (1870) and of celluloid roll film (patented by George Eastman, who had also invented the Kodak camera, in 1889). Eadweard Muybridge's pioneering experiments involving the still photography of objects in motion in the 1870s are widely regarded as an important landmark in the prehistory of cinema. Culturally, however, cinema can also be placed in a longer-term lineage of visual popular culture during the nineteenth century, including magic lantern shows, dioramas, illustrated books and optical toys which gave the impression of movement such as the Zoetrope and the Praxinoscope.

'To try to chart the origins of the cinema in terms of its inventors and inventions', as Eric Rhode observes, 'is to open up a maze of claims and counter-claims, of parallel discoveries and freakish anticipations.'[4] The problem for the historian is that while there are competing claims for the 'birth' of cinema, evidence to support such claims is often lacking. To attribute the 'invention' of cinema to one individual is a misguided and ultimately futile exercise; it is better understood as an accumulative process in which parallel developments occurred in different countries, sometimes independently of each other. The first intermittent cameras for photographing moving images were developed in the late 1880s by the French inventors Étienne-Jules Marey and Augustin-Louis Le Prince, though a method of projection was still lacking. In 1891 American inventor Thomas Edison (who had already introduced the phonograph and the electric light bulb) patented his Kinetograph camera and Kinetoscope viewing box, though it is now acknowledged that much of the actual development work was done by Edison's British assistant W.K.L. Dickson. The Kinetoscope was a peepshow machine in which a short piece of moving film (less than thirty seconds) could be viewed by one person at a time. The first Kinetoscope parlour opened in New York in 1894 and such parlours were popular for the next few years until they were overtaken by further developments. Most historians agree with Geoffrey Nowell-Smith, who avers that the Kinetoscope 'cannot properly be considered cinema'.[5] It did, nevertheless, have a significant influence on cinema: the 35-millimetre film gauge adopted for the Kinetoscope has remained the norm ever since, while Edison and Dickson were the first to use a purpose-built studio (nicknamed the 'Black Maria') to produce films for showing in the machines.

It was in the winter of 1895–6 that the first public projection of moving pictures on a screen took place. Again there were parallel, and unrelated, developments: the brothers Max and Emil Skladanowsky unveiled their Bioskop at the Wintergarten in Berlin on 1 November 1895, and on 14 January 1896 the British pioneer Birt Acres projected some of his films to the Royal Photographic Society in London. Neither of these, however, quite made the impact achieved by the brothers Auguste and Louis Lumière with their Cinématographe. The Lumières had already shown a film of workers leaving their factory privately to various scientific groups – the first recorded instance was a meeting of the Société d'Encouragement à l'Industrie Nationale on 22 March 1895 – when, on 28 December, at the Grand Café on the Boulevard des Capucines in Paris, they projected a programme of actualité films for a paying audience. It is this event which is widely regarded as the symbolic, if not the actual, beginning of the cinema as a social and cultural practice. It was not the first actual public film show, as is often claimed, but there is a case to argue that the Grand Café was the first semi-permanent cinema in so far as the Cinématographe Lumière remained there for the next five years. What is generally less appreciated, however, is the extent to which the Cinématographe became an international phenomenon. The Lumières, believing that moving pictures would be a short-lived novelty, moved quickly to exploit the commercial potential of their invention by sending operators to tour abroad, showing films in theatres and cafés. If 1895 marks the 'birth' of cinema, then 1896 was the year in which cinema spread around the world as the Cinématographe was exhibited in London (20 February), Brussels (1 March), Vienna (19 March), St Petersburg (4 May), Budapest (10 May), Madrid (15 May), Belgrade (7 June), Helsinki (28 June), New York (29 June), Bombay (7 July), Rio de Janeiro (8 July), Buenos Aires (28 July), Shanghai (11 August), Mexico City (15 August), Sydney (28 September) and Alexandria (10 December).[6]

The two forms of film exhibition – peepshows and projected film shows – existed in parallel for several years. There was considerable overlap between them: the standardization of gauges meant that most films could be shown on different projection systems, while some pioneer filmmakers (such as R. W. Paul in Britain) started out in peepshows before moving over to projection. The attraction of films in the 1890s was undoubtedly the novelty value of seeing moving pictures. Most early films were short 'actualities' that simply recorded scenes of everyday life – the most famous of the Lumières' films was the sensational *Arrivée d'un train en gare* which caused spectators to jump from their seats – while peepshow films often featured dancers and acrobats. The decline in popularity of the peepshow from about 1897, however, signalled the end of what Charles Musser has described as the 'novelty period'.[7] There was a vogue thereafter for 'scenics' (travelogue films which appealed because they offered audiences images of distant, unfamiliar and exotic places) and 'topicals' (short films of newsworthy events). Early examples of such topicals included the coronation of Tsar Nicholas II, Queen Victoria's Diamond Jubilee and the inauguration of President McKinley (all in 1897). By the turn of the century there were already experiments with the size of the image. At the Paris World Exhibition in 1900, the Lumières projected films onto a 400-square metre white canvas; one of the Exhibition's other much-touted attractions – the Cinéorama of Raoul Grimoin-Sanson which projected several films simultaneously onto a curved panoramic screen – was, however, a technical failure.

Most films in the 1890s consisted of a single shot: the camera would be set up in one position and the action would unfold before it in a single take. This is formally the most simple film type; it is also, according to some theorists, the most realistic. 'Photography and the cinema,' wrote André Bazin, 'are discoveries that satisfy, once and for all and in its very essence, our obsession with realism.'[8] But early filmmakers were not content with simply recording pictures of reality. Experiments with camera placement, editing and optical effects opened up new possibilities for the medium that filmmakers were quick to explore. A type of film known as 'phantom rides' involved placing the camera on a moving vehicle such as a motor car or a train and thus giving the spectator the illusion of movement: the Warwick Trading Company's ingenuously titled *View from an Engine Front – Barnstaple* (1898) is an early example of the genre. The 'Brighton School' in England – so-called because they worked in or near the seaside resort – produced some of the first films to experiment with optical subjectivity, such as James Williamson's *The Big Swallow* (1901), in which a man angry at having his photograph taken eats the camera and its operator, and G. A. Smith's *Grandma's Reading Glass* (1900), in which a child sees larger images when looking through a magnifying lens. However, it was the French pioneer Georges Méliès who had perhaps the most significant influence on the future development of the medium. Méliès' achievement was to combine optical effects with narrative in his multiple-shot story films such as *La lune à un mètre* (*The Astronomer's Dream*, 1898), *Cendrillon* (*Cinderella*, 1899) and *Le Voyage dans la lune* (*A Trip to the Moon*, 1902). Méliès used stop-motion photography to create 'magic' effects such as vanishing women and devils appearing from clouds of smoke. They were hugely popular and widely imitated around the turn of the century, to the extent that Méliès had to open a sales office in America in 1903 to licence his films.

It has been argued that all future artistic developments in the medium of film can be traced back to the pioneering efforts of the Lumières and Méliès. David Bordwell, for example, has described 'the fantasy of Méliès and the reportage of Lumière' as 'the two founts of cinema'. 'Since Lumière,' he amplifies, 'motion pictures have been attracted to the detailed reproduction of external reality.' 'From Méliès' theatrical stylization and cinematic sleight-of-hand', in contrast, 'come the distorted décor of Caligari and the camera experimentation of the European avant-garde.'[9] Quite apart from the teleological view of film aesthetics apparent in this argument, however, it rather oversimplifies the differences between the filmmakers, as the Lumières also made dramatized films (*Faust*, *The Life and Passion of Jesus Christ*) and Méliès certainly made his share of *actualités*. In one important respect, furthermore, the Lumières and Méliès had one thing in common: their period of success was short-lived and they were soon overtaken by developments in the medium. The Lumières abandoned film production after the Paris Exhibition of 1900, while bankruptcy later forced Méliès to return to his first profession as a magician.

THE EMERGENCE OF NARRATIVE FILM

It used to be accepted to see the history of early cinema as a story of inevitable progress towards a form of aesthetic perfection represented by classical Hollywood. In this version of events, exemplified in the work of American film historians such as Ramsaye and Jacobs, the classical narrative film is seen as the ideal and the history of the medium until then focuses on the technical and stylistic developments that led to the classical form. It becomes a history of the pioneers who discovered the rudiments of the classical film: linear narrative, continuity editing, seamless narration. The foremost of these pioneers was David Wark Griffith, regarded by many as the 'father of film', to whom the majority of important stylistic breakthroughs were attributed. 'The debt that all film-makers owe to D. W. Griffith defies calculation', the auteurist critic Andrew Sarris later remarked with characteristic hyperbole. 'Even before *The Birth of a Nation*, he had managed to synthesize the dramatic and documentary elements of the modern feature film.'[10]

This history, and the centrality of Griffith to it, has been challenged by film theorists, who, following the example of Noël Burch, have seen early cinema as a 'primitive mode of representation' with its own rules and conventions that was distinct from the 'institutional mode of representation' which followed.[11] The tendency of theorists, excited by the formal difference and unfamiliarity of early cinema, has been to regard it as an 'alternative' to the classical cinema that developed later. Thus, for example, the formal composition of so many early films, usually a tableau or a number of tableaux (staged scenes) filmed from the front, is seen by André Gaudreault as a strategy 'to present the totality of an action unfolding in an homogenous space'.[12] The concept of early cinema suggested by this revisionist work is just as unsatisfactory as that put forward by the old historians. While the old historians regarded early cinema as primitive, the revisionists held it to be formally innovative; while the old historians privileged the role of Griffith, the revisionists simply found others to champion such as Edwin S. Porter; and while the old historians advanced a teleological history which started from the assumption of the classical film as the ideal and worked backwards from there, the revisionists absurdly constructed early cinema as a form of avant-garde practice that provided a coherent alternative to the classical model.

A third way of conceptualizing early cinema has been put forward by Tom Gunning, who identifies a transition from what he terms 'the cinema of attractions' to 'the cinema of narrative integration'. The main value of Gunning's interpretation is that he does not regard one form as being necessarily superior to the other; nor does he assume any inevitability in the process of transition. He argues that 'early cinema was not dominated by the narrative impulse that later asserted its sway over the medium' and that its appeal rested on 'a unique event, whether fictional or documentary, that is of interest in itself'. The genres of early cinema – actualities, scenics, phantom rides, magic films – had more in common with fairground 'attractions' than with stories. This 'cinema of attractions' prevailed, according to Gunning, until *c.* 1906/7, when narrative films finally became dominant. Rather than seeing a sudden shift from one form to the other, however, Gunning identifies the chase film (which proliferated between 1903 and 1906) as 'a synthesis of attractions and narrative'. 'The period from 1907 to about 1913 represents the true narrativization of the cinema', he concludes, 'culminating in the appearance of feature films which radically revised the variety format.'[13]

While the emergence of the narrative film may not have been inevitable, nevertheless its dominance requires explanation. The claims made on behalf of pioneers and visionaries are insufficient as an explanatory framework. For one thing, as with the invention of the medium in the 1890s, the emergence of narrative film in the 1900s was the result of parallel developments taking place in different countries rather than due solely to individual genius. The hubristic claims of some commentators that Porter's *The Great Train Robbery* (1903) was both the first story film and the first western does not stand up to close scrutiny, though it was probably the most successful early story film. Even so, its most memorable moment (a shot of a sheriff pointing a revolver at the camera and firing, which exhibitors could choose to place either at the beginning or the end of the film) was more of an 'attraction' than part of the narrative. The techniques of continuity editing are apparent in the films Porter made between 1903 and 1905 (*Life of an American Fireman, Life of an American Policeman, Life of an American Cowboy*) and also in those of Britain's William Haggar (*Desperate Poaching Affray*, 1903) and Cecil Hepworth (*Rescued by Rover*, 1905). As for Griffith, the consensus among film historians is moving towards the view that, while he certainly did not invent all the techniques he claimed to have done (including close-ups, fades and parallel editing, the practice of cutting between different spatial locations), his importance was

'his ability to combine these techniques in daring ways'.[14] Griffith's place in film history is due not only to the sheer number of films he made – between 1908 and 1913 he directed over 400 one- and two-reelers for the American Biograph Company – but also to their high production values and lively pacing. His most famous short films were those featuring a dramatic last-minute rescue (*The Lonely Villa, The Lonedale Operator, The Battle of Elderbrush Gulch*), though he was equally adept at tragedy (*The Painted Lady*) and social drama (*The Musketeers of Pig Alley*). While Griffith embraced the trend towards longer, multi-reel 'feature' films in the early 1910s, however, he was neither the first nor the only American filmmaker to do so.[15]

Quite apart from privileging the role of 'great men', furthermore, histories attributing the rise of narrative to individuals tend to place film in an aesthetic vacuum that ignores the relationship between film style and social context. One of the reasons for the trend towards narrative, undoubtedly, was the cinema's quest for cultural legitimacy, which saw the adaptation of classics of literature and theatre. As early as 1903 there had been adaptations of *Alice in Wonderland* by Hepworth and *Uncle Tom's Cabin* by Porter. As films became longer in the later 1900s, there were adaptations of Shakespeare, Dickens, Tolstoy, Ibsen and Scott. The cultural significance of these films, suggests American film historian Eileen Bowser, was that 'producers and exhibitors could demonstrate that the motion-picture show was an appropriate place for children and that they were bringing high culture to the masses'.[16] These early adaptations were inevitably much condensed from the originals. Frank Dubrez Fawcett explains how early filmmakers were able to translate a Dickens novel into one or two reels:

> Take the title of a Dickens story; work some of the best-known incidents into a beginning, a middle and an end; then dress up the players to look like the pictures in the novels. The lettering on the screen would do the rest, and the audience could fill in any blanks from their own stores of Dickensian knowledge.[17]

This supposes knowledge of the story on the part of audiences; Bowser suggests, however, that audiences would not necessarily have the sophistication to understand the stories and the presence of a narrator in the auditorium was necessary to make the films intelligible.[18]

It has been argued that the rise of the narrative film was due, in some measure, to early filmmakers adopting the conventions of the nineteenth-century novel and applying them to the new medium. The classic realist novel, like the classical film, is a linear narrative governed by a regime of verisimilitude (seeming to be real). It was the Soviet filmmaker Sergei Eisenstein who, in a seminal essay of 1944, argued brilliantly that the novels of Dickens were possessed of a proto-filmic quality:

> Perhaps the secret lies in Dickens's (as well as cinema's) creation of an extraordinary plasticity. The observation in the novels is extraordinary – as is their optical quality. The characters of Dickens are rounded with means as plastic and slightly exaggerated as are the screen heroes of today. The screen's heroes are engraved on the senses of the spectator with clearly visible traits, its villains are remembered by certain facial expressions, and all are saturated in the peculiar,

slightly unnatural radiant gleam thrown over them by the screen.[19]

Eisenstein went on to compare passages from *Oliver Twist* to the films of D.W. Griffith, arguing that Dickens provided 'a model of parallel montage of two story lines' that was to be the technique for which Griffith 'earned his most glorious laurels'. A sense of narrative and structure had, Eisenstein believed, been 'handed down to the great film-maker of the twentieth century by the great novelist of the nineteenth'. And, if Eisenstein adhered to a great man view of film history, he nevertheless also recognized 'that our cinema is not altogether without parents and without pedigree, without a past, without the traditions and rich cultural heritage of the past epochs'.[20]

EXHIBITION AND AUDIENCES

The audience remains the great unknown factor of film history. Robert C. Allen, one of the first scholars to undertake systematic research into the social history of cinema-going, points out that even in the mid-1970s 'film history still was almost universally taken to mean the history of films'.[21] Little attention was given to questions such as the social composition of the cinema audience or the historical reception of motion pictures. This neglect was partly a consequence of the prominence of aesthetically oriented film histories that were concerned with establishing the canon of film art and, in the case of early cinema, the role of pioneers in the development of the medium. The study of audiences was actually retarded, moreover, by the vogue for 'high theory' in film studies in the 1970s and its assumption that the film text itself 'constructs' the spectator. The absurdity of this theoretical conceit has been exposed by the empirical research of historians whose work over the last two decades reveals an increasingly diverse and complex picture of film exhibition and cinema audiences in which national, regional, class, ethnic, gender and age differences challenge received wisdoms about 'the audience' as a monolithic group. It is the very heterogeneity of cinema audiences, indeed, that makes the social history of cinema-going such a difficult subject for historical research. The cinema audience is what sociologists describe as an 'unstructured group' in that it has no social organization or universally recognized customs and habits (unlike, say, a political party or a religious group). Thus, 'the "audience" for movies in any sociological or historical sense is really only an abstraction generated by the researcher, since the unstructured group that we refer to as the movie audience is constantly being constituted, dissolved, and reconstituted with each film-going experience'.[22]

Research into cinema audiences is handicapped, further, by the absence of reliable empirical data concerning their social composition. This is especially true of early cinema, for which there is a scarcity of even the crude anthropological research undertaken in later decades by individuals such as Margaret Thorp in America and organizations such as Mass-Observation in Britain. Historians of early cinema audiences, therefore, have had to follow a path of deductive reasoning in reconstructing their likely social composition from the clues left by other forms of evidence. Factors such as the location of cinemas, types of programmes, admission prices and exhibition practices help to build up a picture of early cinema audiences that is characterized by diversity and difference.

There is reason to believe, for example, that considerable differences existed between Europe and the United States. During the 'novelty period' of cinema in Europe, film shows tended to take place in theatres and cafés, suggesting they were intended for bourgeois audiences. An early report of the Cinématographe Lumière in Paris described it as a 'fashionable amusement' which was to be found 'in the basement of all the boulevard cafés, in music-hall outbuildings, in theatres where projections are often fitted into variety shows, [and] even in private homes'.[23] When the first permanent cinema in Britain was opened at Mohawks' Hall, Islington, in 1901, the top admission price of three shillings was 'the highest to date'.[24] In the United States, however, where films were exhibited in vaudeville theatres, there is evidence that film shows were angled towards a wider social spectrum. Musser argues that 'the cinema drew its audiences from across the working, middle, and elite classes'.

Admission prices ranged from ten cents to $1.50, suggesting that exhibitors 'offered a scale of prices that accommodated people of diverse financial status'.[25]

Exhibition practices, which both respond to and partly determine the nature of cinema audiences, initially followed similar paths in Europe and America. On both sides of the Atlantic film was incorporated into existing forms of popular culture: music hall and fairgrounds in Britain and France, vaudeville theatre and opera houses in America. Films would be shown as part of a programme of entertainment that also included performers and novelty acts. Travelling showmen also played a role in extending the social reach of film by giving film shows in church halls, tents and in rented shop-fronts. In the days of single-shot films in the 1890s exhibitors had more control over how the films were shown, but the development of longer films with explanatory intertitles in the early 1900s meant this control was weakened as films would have to be shown how their makers had intended. Around this time some film producers even began supplying their own scripts for the lecturers who spoke over films and for the actors who sometimes spoke lines of dialogue from off-stage. As far as the social composition of early cinema audiences is concerned it is probably most appropriate to believe they would have been extremely heterogeneous as the novelty of films appealed to people across the social spectrum. It was the advent of the first purpose-built cinemas a few years later, however, that introduced a more rigid social demarcation into film exhibition practices.

There is some dispute as to where and when the first permanent cinemas appeared: the Vitascope Hall in New Orleans, which opened in June 1896, has probably the best claim. Within less than a year of the first recorded film shows in their respective countries, there were permanent cinemas (or at least cinemas that were intended to be permanent) in Sydney, Rio de Janeiro, Berlin, Brussels and Madrid. It was not for the best part of another decade, however, that permanent exhibition outlets became the norm. The 'nickelodeon boom' took off in America from c. 1905. The nickelodeons were usually converted stores with a small seating capacity (usually fewer than 200) which showed programmes running for between fifteen minutes and one hour. The number of nickelodeons in the United States grew from an estimated 2,500 in 1907 to 10,000 by 1910; New York and Chicago had the greatest concentration with between 500 and 800 each.[26] Several factors help to explain why the nickelodeons displaced other forms of exhibition. They had an advantage over amusement parks because they were permanent rather than seasonal, and they were cheaper than vaudeville houses (the typical admission price was a nickel, or five cents). Several future 'movie moguls' (including Carl Laemmle, Louis B. Mayer, Adolph Zukor and William Fox) began their careers in the film industry as owners or managers of nickelodeons.

The nickelodeons have typically been characterized as rather dingy, spartan places whose patrons were the urban proletariat and immigrant workers. This impression is gained largely from descriptions in the trade press of the time: 'Some of these places are perfectly filthy, with an air so foul and thick that you can almost cut it with a knife. The floor is generally covered with peanut shells, and as there is no stove to spit on everybody spits on the floor.'[27] While this was undoubtedly true of many nickelodeons, local studies, focused principally on New York and Chicago, have revealed that there were considerable variations in location and type of establishment.[28] In Manhattan, for example, nickelodeons were not evenly distributed: there were clusters around some poor and immigrant neighbourhoods (such as the Lower East Side) but there were also large numbers in more affluent areas (such as Harlem, then a middle/lower-middle class neighbourbood). Nor were all nickelodeons the dim and dirty places often assumed; those in more prosperous areas were often quite well appointed. Women and children made up a significant proportion of nickelodeon audiences: it has been suggested that the nickelodeon provided an important 'woman's space' in urban environments.[29] The assumption that nickelodeons catered principally for the entertainment needs of immigrant workers, therefore, needs to be qualified. It seems reasonable to assume, in the big cities at least, that nickelodeons encouraged a more socially demarcated form of exhibition: depending upon location they attracted either predominantly blue-collar or white-collar clientele. In small towns, in contrast, 'a nickelodeon might be the only place showing films, and people from all strata of society would watch movies together'.[30]

In Europe, there was nothing directly comparable to the American nickelodeon boom: the shift towards permanent cinemas came later and was not so rapid. The growth of urban cinemas on a large scale can be dated from *c.* 1907 in France and from *c.* 1909 in Britain. The major difference between French and British cinemas on the one hand, and nickelodeons on the other, would seem to be that whereas nickelodeons differentiated audiences according to location, French and British picture houses differentiated audiences within the auditorium. Thus purpose-built cinemas tended to be modelled on the legitimate theatre with galleries and boxes for the more well-to-do patrons and stalls for the lower classes. Film shows were usually longer than in America and were often still interspersed with song interludes. There is evidence that cinema exhibitors in Britain sought to raise the tone of the 'bijou palaces': the notion of the 'bioscope tea' was introduced in some cinemas 'where in 1908 the lady from the suburbs could pause in her afternoon's shopping, and for a shilling enjoy a "dainty cup of tea and an animated display"'.[31]

The move towards larger and more sumptuously appointed picture palaces also needs to be seen within the context of attempts to raise the social respectability of cinema. This trend actually began earlier in Europe than it did in America. Among the first luxury cinemas in Europe were the Gaumont-Palais in Paris (opened in 1911 with a seating capacity of 5,000), the Alhambra Platz in Berlin (opened in 1911 with 2,000 seats) and the Palads-Teatret in Copenhagen (opened in 1912 with 3,000 seats). The first 'super cinemas' seating over 2,000 in America were the Regent on New York's Seventh Avenue (1913) and the Vitagraph and the Strand on Broadway (1914). The emergence of these larger movie palaces, which charged higher admission prices, coincided with the arrival of the longer, multiple-reel feature film.

It would be misleading, however, to suggest that the cinema, any more than previous forms of popular culture such as musical hall and vaudeville, ever became as gentrified as its exhibitors would have liked. What was initially an attraction intended for élites had become, in the words of British film historian Rachael

Low, 'the drama of the masses'.[32] In America and Britain, at least, cinema was a cheap form of entertainment: admission prices by the time of the First World War were between 10–15 cents and 3d.–6d. respectively. Historical debates about the social make-up of nickelodeon audiences notwithstanding, there is still much truth in Ramsaye's assessment of the appeal of films to the immigrant populations of America: 'The motion picture offered no linguistic barriers. A story on the screen was a picture alike to a Pole, Slovak, Russian, Magyar or Italian. And it was cheap, the price of a glass of beer.'[33] It has been argued that nickelodeons played an important role in the process of assimilation of immigrants into American life and culture. A frequently quoted article by Joseph Medill Paterson in the *Saturday Evening Post* in 1907 is perhaps the first expression of this view: 'In cosmopolitan city districts the foreigners attend in larger proportion than the English speakers. This is doubtless because the foreigners, shut out as they are by their alien tongue from much of the life about them, can yet perfectly understand the pantomime of the moving pictures.'[34]

It was the combination of its cheapness and that fact that it was accessible to large and diverse audiences that accounts for cinema's emergence as the dominant popular art form of the early twentieth century. The primacy of the visual image – especially during the era of the 'silents' – meant that films crossed barriers of language, literacy and culture in a way that other media, such as books and theatre, could not. This also helps to explain why, at a time when film production was concentrated in a handful of countries (mainly France, America, Britain, Italy and Denmark), film exhibition was spreading around the world. Some indication of the speed and extent of this process can be seen in the opening of the first permanent cinemas in China (1903), Japan (1903), Egypt (1904), Portugal (1904), Norway (1904), Denmark (1904), Iran (1905), Iceland (1906), Greece (1907), India (1907), Thailand (1907), South Africa (1908), Bulgaria (1908), Turkey (1908), Tunisia (1908), Lebanon (1909) and Mauritius (1912).[35] As the Russian playwright Leonid Andreyev remarked:

The miraculous Cinema! . . . Having no language, being

equally intelligible to the savages of St Petersburg and the savages of Calcutta, it truly becomes the genius of international contact, brings the ends of the earth and the spheres of souls nearer and gathers the whole of quivering humanity into a single stream.[36]

The cinema spoke an 'international language' that was understood regardless of nationality, race or creed. It was this international language that accounts for the worldwide penetration of films in the period before the First World War.

CENSORSHIP AND CONTROL

The popularity of the cinema as a social institution soon became a cause of concern to legal, social and religious authorities. In the 1900s pressure mounted to 'clean up' the movies. The metaphor is appropriate in two respects: there were concerns over the physical conditions of some movie houses, especially the nickelodeons of popular legend; and there were concerns over the content of movies themselves, which were criticized for their salacious and scandalous nature. Film censorship should be seen as a form of social control in that its advocates were invariably those in positions of legal and social authority (politicians, police, churchmen, moral reformers) who were motivated by a paternalistic assumption that the more impressionable members of society (children, workers, immigrants) needed to be 'protected' from exposure to the corrupting influences of moving pictures. The American theatre critic Walter Eaton exemplified this attitude when, in 1909, he wrote: 'When you reflect that in New York City alone, on a Sunday 500,000 people go to the moving picture shows, a majority of them perhaps children . . . you cannot dismiss canned drama with a shrug of contempt. Here is an industry to be controlled, an influence to be reckoned with.'[37]

'Although the details of censorship procedures varied from nation to nation', Richard Maltby observes, 'there was a striking similarity in the evolution of those mechanisms in the countries of Europe, the Americas, and Australasia.'[38] The history of film censorship during its first decade and a half is one of transition from the local to the national. In most countries film was initially included within established mechanisms of social control developed during the nineteenth century in response to the growth of popular cultural forms and practices. The licensing of theatres, travelling exhibitions, magic shows, marionettes and other types of commercialized entertainment tended to be the responsibility of local authorities. The proliferation of local controls, however, which inevitably gave rise to inconsistencies in decision-making, led to pressure for rationalization at the national level. One of the groups influential in this move was the film distributors, who realized that, as they were probably going to have to accept regulation of film content, they would be better off dealing with national authorities than with a multitude of municipal councils with their own views and prejudices.

The pressure for censorship in the early days of cinema was motivated primarily by moral concerns. The initial targets were films that contained any kind of sexual element. In 1896 the entertainment trade paper *Variety* had complained that 'from the very beginning the Kinetoscope has shown very little delicacy' and cited films of 'enticing dances, vulgar playlets and other lewd exhibitions'. 'According to an increasing number of citizens,' it reported, 'censorship could be the answer.'[39] The first known example of such censorship was the Kinetoscope short *Delorita's Passion Dance*, which was banned by the Mayor of Atlantic City in 1896. Over the next decade the cinema increasingly attracted the wrath of moral campaigners. The targets were violence and sex. A trend for reconstructions of notorious crimes around 1905–6, such as the British-made *The Life of Charles Peace* and Australia's *The Story of Ned Kelly* (ironically the narrative model for these films was the much-admired *The Great Train Robbery*), was followed by sensational 'white slave' films from Denmark ('white slavery' was a euphemism for prostitution). The arguments of those who advocated film censorship were based on the assertion that such films were morally degrading. In 1912, for example, an official of the YMCA in Indianapolis called for the introduction of censorship on the grounds that '[unless] the law steps in and does for moving-picture shows what it has done for meat inspection and pure food, the cinematograph will continue to inject into our social order an element of degrading principle'.[40] An extreme example of moral reaction was the Federation of Businesses Against Pornography, which, meeting in Paris in 1912, described cinema in no uncertain terms as a 'stratagem used by the devil' which 'competes with alcohol for the ruin of the public'.[41]

While the impetus for control of film exhibition came from reformers and pressure groups, the justification offered by civic authorities for regulating exhibition was often that of public safety. Such concerns were undoubtedly genuine – in May 1897 a fire during a film show at the Charity Bazaar in Paris had killed 121 people – though they were in all likelihood a convenient excuse rather than the main reason for regulating exhibition. In 1908 the Mayor of New York, George B. McClellan, temporarily closed down all the city's nickelodeons, ostensibly on the grounds that they represented a safety hazard. It was widely believed, however, that the real reason for the closure was 'the supposedly poor moral condition of the darkened rooms and the kinds of films shown in them'.[42] In Britain the Cinematograph Act of 1909 required local councils to licence cinemas to ensure they met fire safety regulations – cinemas were to have a fire-proof projection box and buckets of sand in the auditorium – though some councils also interpreted this as giving them the authority to licence cinemas on the basis of the films they showed. In 1910, for example, London County Council banned a topical news film of a boxing match between Jack Johnson (the black champion, who won) and James L. Jeffries (the white challenger).

By the eve of the First World War two different mechanisms for censorship at a national level had developed: state censorship and self-regulation. On the one hand, countries that opted for state censors included Sweden (1911), Germany (1912) and France (1916). On the other hand, the two principal adherents of the self-regulatory model were America and Britain where the film industry, realizing that some form of censorship was inevitable, took the initiative in agreeing to censor itself. In America local censorship boards had proliferated since 1907 when Chicago City Council had introduced an ordinance empowering the Chief of Police to ban any film that 'portrays depravity, criminality, or lack of virtue of a class of citizens of any race, colour, creed or religion, and exposes them to contempt, derision or obloquy, or tends to produce a breach of the peace, or riots, or purports to represent any hanging, lynching or burning of a human being'.[43] One of the first films to be banned under this ordinance was a production of *Macbeth* (1908). In New York it was the city's exhibitors themselves who set up the New York Board of Censorship in response to the nickelodeon closure of 1908. With the backing of the newly formed Motion Picture Patents Company, this self-regulatory body evolved into the National Board of Censorship (NBC) in 1915. In Britain representatives of the industry, including filmmaker Cecil Hepworth and exhibitor Colonel A. C. Bromhead, persuaded the government to approve the establishment of the British Board of Film Censors (BBFC), which began operating at the beginning of 1913. Like the NBC in America it had no statutory powers and it did not replace local censorship, as its guidelines were advisory only, though in practice most local councils adhered to its certification system of 'U' (suitable for universal viewing) and 'A' (suitable for adults, which, following the decision of London County Council in 1922, was generally taken to mean those over sixteen). The chief censor from the institution of the BBFC until his retirement in 1948 was Joseph Brooke Williamson, a former journalist regarded as a 'man of Victorian principle and stern moral rectitude' and who has been described as 'arguably the most influential figure in the British film industry during his thirty-six years of office'.[44]

'In the early days', according to Maltby, 'the preoccupations of censors varied: the Dutch and Scandinavian boards were more concerned by violence than by sexual themes, while Australian and South African censors tended to be noticeably more puritanical than the British Board.'[45] In Russia the power of censorship rested with the Orthodox Church, which in 1912 banned Yakov Protazanov's *Departure of a Grand Old Man* as it found the ending of Tolstoy being led into Heaven blasphemous. In 1913, in response to industrial rest, Russia also banned any films showing strikes and 'difficult forms of labour'. It was not until the interwar period, however, that film censorship became overtly political. The BBFC initially prohibited only two subjects – the life of Jesus Christ and nudity – but these were quickly expanded so that by 1917 there were some 43 banned subjects. The first countries to abolish censorship were Russia (under the Provisional Government in March 1917) and Germany (December 1918), though it would quickly be reintroduced in both countries.

THE INSTITUTIONALIZATION OF CINEMA

At the turn of the century cinema was essentially a cottage industry; by the eve of the First World War it had become an international business. The rapid expansion of the film industry was due to a combination of aesthetic, technological, economic and social factors. In aesthetic terms, the experimentation that characterized early cinema had stabilized by the late 1900s and early 1910s: narrative films had established their supremacy and the trend towards feature films was underway. Many aspects of film form and style were international, to the extent that when production spread outside America and Europe there was already an established model. The surviving reels of the first Indian fictional feature film, *Raja Harishchandra* (1913), a mythical fantasy directed by D. G. Phalke, suggest that it adopted the 'current principles of western filmmaking' such as continuity editing and close framing.[46] In addition to the standardization of style, there was also a standardization of film technology, encouraged by the use of patents for film stock, cameras and projection equipment.

The late 1900s and early 1910s saw major changes in the economic structures of the film industry. The largest production industry during this period was the French, and the largest film producer in the world was Pathé Frères, founded in 1896 by the brothers Charles, Émile, Jacques and Théophile Pathé. Pathé Frères was the first company to achieve a significant degree of vertical integration: it built one of the first film studios at Vincennes in 1902 in order to produce films on an assembly-line basis, it began buying its own cinemas in 1906, and in 1907 it began to distribute its own films by renting them to exhibitors rather than selling them outright. Pathé also pursued a strategy of horizontal integration, expanding within one sector: it opened production facilities and distribution offices in other countries, with branches as far afield as London, New York, Budapest, Kiev, Calcutta and Singapore. It specialized in the production of comedies and its biggest star was the comic Max Linder. Pathé's main French rival was Gaumont, which also expanded rapidly under the direction of first Alice Guy and then Louis Feuillade, producing a range of genre films including thrillers, comedies and historical costume pictures.

It is significant to observe, given the later dominance of the international film market by the US film industry, that in the 1900s American producers had not yet achieved any level of dominance even in their home market. It was estimated that in 1908 Pathé accounted for over fifty per cent of all films sold in America. Richard Abel has demonstrated the economic and cultural consequences of this domination: while, initially, Pathé's films were welcomed by exhibitors, their popularity was a cause of concern by the late 1900s when the prominence of 'red rooster' films (so called because of the distinctive symbol used by Pathé) in the nickelodeons led to these films being described as 'alien' and 'foreign' in the press. While American exhibitors turned against Pathé's films ostensibly on the grounds that they were declining in quality and entertainment value, Abel argues persuasively that '[what] made Pathé's very presence, let alone its influence, especially undesirable at this historical moment . . . was a conjunction of concerns about who went to the cinema, and about what and who were being constructed as "American".'[47] The strategies adopted by the US film industry to counter Pathé's influence included the rejection or alteration of its films by the NBC and the decision of the major American producers and distributors to form a cartel that would limit the number of imported films in the domestic market. By 1910 Pathé was already being squeezed out of the American market, and its decision thereafter to concentrate on serials rather than feature films meant that within a few years it was only a marginal influence. 'Once a crucial player in the cinema's expansion and legitimation', Abel remarks, 'the French company now found its moves repeatedly blocked or deflected, stigmatized or appropriated.'[48]

The institutionalization within the US film industry was exemplified by the formation in 1908 of the Motion Picture Patents Company (MPPC). In the mid-1900s American cinema was approaching a state of chaos with a proliferation of production companies and film exchanges. In order to stabilize the industry, the leading producers – including Biograph, Vitagraph, Essanay, Kalem and Selig – agreed to pay a licence fee to Edison in order to purchase patented equipment (including cameras and film stock). As the licensing extended to exhibitors as well (through patents on projectors), the formation of the MPPC is regarded by historians as an attempt by Edison to establish a monopoly over all sectors of the industry. Although the MPPC was successful in the short term – by 1910 it included most distributors through its subsidiary the General Film Company – its position was undermined by a number of factors. A number of independent distributors and exhibitors, led by Carl Laemmle and Thomas Ince, resisted the MPPC. Then, in 1915, the US Supreme Court ruled that the MPPC was an illegal monopoly. Ironically, several of the independents who led the resistance to the MPPC were themselves to form the basis of the oligopoly that brought vertical integration to the industry a decade or so later.[49]

Another significant development that was taking place at this time – and one which had long-term consequences for the institutional structure of the American film industry – was the relocation of the production sector to the West Coast of the United States. The first film studios in America had been built in New York, Chicago and Philadelphia, but weather conditions in those cities were soon realized to be too unpredictable (films were shot either in studios lit by sunlight or outdoors). The first production companies to relocate to the West Coast were the Selig Polyscope Company and the New York Motion Picture Company, both of which built studios there in 1909. Southern California offered several advantages for film production: besides the sunny climate there was a range of different landscapes, including ocean, desert, forests and mountains. The move to California coincided with the emergence of the western as a major genre of American cinema, seen by producers and exhibitors as a genuine 'American' subject that could be differentiated from imported films. The choice of Hollywood, a suburb of Los Angeles, was due largely to the availability of cheap real estate. Los Angeles was a relatively small city of 100,000 inhabitants at the turn of the century. The growth of Hollywood – its population rose from 5,000 in 1910 to 35,000 by 1919 and 130,000 by 1925 – was due principally to the arrival of the motion picture industry.

The production facilities built in Hollywood during the 1910s were the embryonic form of the 'studio system' that became institutionalized in the 1920s. If the first studios were relatively simple affairs, often utilizing converted shops and warehouses, by the middle of the decade they were increasingly coming to resemble small towns with offices, stages, laboratories and extensive backlots where exterior sets could be built. The names of studio complexes – Inceville, Culver City and the like – further emphasized their special status. The production and management structures were transformed during the 1910s, moreover, moving from the 'director-unit system' (whereby individual directors were in charge of their films) to the 'central-producer system' (whereby a producer was in charge of the overall output of a studio and the director's role was downgraded within the studio hierarchy). The central-producer system, which coincided with the emergence of the feature film, brought a new level of efficiency to the production process and remained the dominant model of studio management until the 1930s.[50]

By this stage other changes were afoot that significantly altered the cinema as a form of social practice. One of these was the origin of what came to be known as the 'star system'. Until the early 1910s players in films were rarely billed by their names, being known instead by pseudonyms such as 'the Biograph Girl' (Florence Lawrence), 'the Vitagraph Girl' (Florence Turner) and even 'the Little Girl with the Curls' (Mary Pickford). The practice of naming stars emerged simultaneously in Europe (Asta Nielsen in Denmark, Henny Porten in Germany) and America (where Florence Lawrence's name was revealed as a publicity stunt by Carl Laemmle when he lured her away from Biograph to join his Independent Motion

Pictures). The most prominent early film stars were women, though to see this phenomenon as a reflection of social change as more women entered the workplace in the early twentieth century is a broad generalization that probably applies more to America and less to Europe. The popularity of Mary Pickford, for example, has been attributed to her image as 'a figure of identification for an emerging class of "new woman", which included independent workingwomen, suffragettes, and other nontraditional women who took their place alongside men in the post-Victorian world of modern America'.[51] Yet Pickford's image as 'America's Sweetheart' needs to be contrasted with other star images that were in circulation during the 1910s, including those of Griffith's heroines Lillian and Dorothy Gish, whose fragile beauty made them the embodiment of Victorian respectability, and the exotic Theda Bara, whose image was based on the suggestion of sexual appetite and dangerous allure (according to studio publicity her name was supposedly an anagram of 'Arab Death').

By the eve of the First World War most of the elements that were to characterize cinema as a social institution were already in place in one form or another. Cinema was a mass entertainment medium that reached an audience of millions around the world; the trend towards permanent sites of exhibition that has remained the norm ever since was established; an industry organized on mass-production lines had become institutionalized; fictional films and stars had become the main points of popular appeal; and the first extra-filmic discourses around cinema had emerged in the form of trade journals and fan magazines.[52] Film production was dominated by Western Europe and America, but embryonic production industries were already established in India, Japan, Australia, Brazil, Venezuela and Canada, while the practice of film exhibition spread much wider. Within the space of two decades, cinema had grown from a sideshow attraction to a major industry and popular art form. 'It was an extraordinary metamorphosis', wrote the French historian Edgar Morin. 'For it was not artists or educated men who brought about this transformation but rag merchants, autodidacts, conjurors and clowns.'[53]

FOUR

The Emergence of National Cinemas

For most of its first two decades film was an essentially international medium. Films crossed national boundaries and there was widespread international exchange of ideas and technical developments. Stylistic innovations made in one country were quickly seen and adopted elsewhere. The practice of continuity editing, to take the most important example, had been more or less standardized before the outbreak of war. So, too, had the trend towards longer, or 'feature' films, which were becoming increasingly common by the early 1910s. It was the international success of the Italian costume 'epics' *Quo Vadis?* (1913) and *Cabiria* (1914) that prompted D. W. Griffith in the United States to make his own costume spectaculars such as *Judith of Bethulia* (1913), *The Birth of a Nation* (1915) and *Intolerance* (1916). While these were exceptional rather than typical films, the multi-reeler had become the dominant type of film both in Europe and in America by the eve of the First World War.

The war was to have a decisive impact on the international film industry. Economically, the devastation visited upon European countries left their film industries in a much weaker position by 1918 than they had been in 1914, creating the circumstances in which the American film industry could assume the dominant position in the world market that it has maintained ever since. And culturally, the war disrupted the free flow of films across national boundaries, so that the international exchange in aspects of style and technique that had been such a prominent feature of pre-war cinema was suddenly no longer the case. Some countries, such as Russia and Germany, were partially or completely isolated from film imports. The consequence of these developments was that cinema was transformed in quite significant ways. It is around the time of the First World

War that historians have identified the first genuinely national cinemas that consciously sought to differentiate themselves from the films of other countries. There is, however, some debate as to whether the war was the catalyst for the emergence of national cinemas, or whether it merely accelerated a trend that was already underway by 1914.

THE FIRST WORLD WAR AND ITS CONSEQUENCES

The impact of the First World War on the fledgling film industry cannot be overestimated. For one thing, the financial centre of the film industry shifted from Europe to America. In 1914 the majority of international trade in film was conducted through London; by 1917 New York had become the centre of world distribution. This shift can be attributed to a number of factors, including the increased cost of raw film stock in Britain due to wartime shortages, the imposition of a tariff on luxury goods (which included films) by the British government, and shipping losses caused by unrestricted submarine warfare. At the same time, American distributors were actively building up their international presence, opening subsidiary offices around the world 'and thereby establishing a control which other producing countries would find difficult to erode during the 20s'.[1]

All the belligerent nations of Europe were affected by the war – as, indeed, were non-belligerents such as Denmark and Sweden – but the effects were not uniform across the board. On the one hand, countries which had built up healthy production sectors and exports before the war, such as France, Italy and Britain, experienced a severe decline in levels of domestic production. The reasons included such factors as the redeployment of the labour force, a shortage of raw film stock, and shipping priorities for essential war materials. France actually ceased film production at the outbreak of war, turning studios over to war industries, only resuming production early in 1915 when it became clear the war would not be over quickly. In Britain the number of feature films produced during the war fluctuated between a low of fifteen in 1914 and a high of 107 in 1916, but overall production was down from pre-war levels.[2] On the other hand, however, countries which had not been especially significant before the war, principally Germany and Russia, found that the closure of their borders and, in Germany's case, the banning of all imports from 1916, actually stimulated domestic production. Thus, the number of German-owned film production or distribution companies increased from 25 in 1914 to 130 by 1918; in Russia there were only three Russian producers at the outbreak of war, but by 1916 there were thirty.[3] It was in Russia, furthermore, that a distinctively national style of film arose during the war in the form of the brooding melodramas of directors such as Evgeny Bauer and Yakov Protazanov, characterized by their slow pace, intense acting style and tragic endings.

The war found a new role for cinema as an instrument of propaganda. Both the British and German governments recognized, if somewhat tardily, the potential of film for presenting positive images of the war to the public. Thus it was that cinema acquired a new legitimacy in the eyes of the political classes. 'If anything were needed to justify the existence of the cinematograph, it is to be found in [this] wonderful series of films', *The Times* declared in response to the official British film record of *The Battle of the Somme* (1916).[4] 'The war has demonstrated the paramount power of images and of film as means of enlightenment and influence', declared no less a figure than General Erich Ludendorff, Deputy Chief of the German General Staff, adding that 'it is absolutely imperative that film be employed with the greatest force in all places where German influence is still possible'.[5] In 1917 Alfred Hugenberg of Krupps was put in charge of Ufa (Universum Film Aktiengesellschaft), an amalgamation of several existing production, distribution and exhibition interests that became the first state-supported, vertically integrated film company in Europe. The purpose of creating Ufa, which was partly sponsored by the government, was to make patriotic films in support of the war effort. In the event it had little to show for its efforts before the Armistice in November 1918, but under the post-war Weimar government Ufa would be privatized and become the flagship producer it was always intended to be.[6]

For the neutrals, the effects of war on the development of national cinemas were again mixed. Probably the most distinctive national cinema at the outbreak of war had been that of Denmark. The Nordisk Films Kompagni (Nordisk Film Company), established in 1906 by Copenhagen cinema owner Ole Olsen, was the second largest film company in Europe (after Pathé) by 1914. Nordisk specialized in the production of genre films, farces and thrillers, notable for their naturalistic scenery. The early 1910s were a 'golden age' for Danish cinema, but with the outbreak of war the situation deteriorated. Nordisk's most important foreign market was Germany, and the German ban on all imported films came as a severe blow to the company, which temporarily discontinued production in 1917. When it resumed after the war, Nordisk was effectively starting from scratch and never regained its position in the international film market. In Sweden, by contrast, the process was reversed as the war saw the beginning of a 'golden age' that would last into the 1920s. The success of Nordisk in Denmark had been the inspiration for the formation of Svenska Biografteatern (Swedish Biograph) which soon became the country's leading producer. Sweden became one of the first countries to create a national cinema by drawing on its indigenous culture, with films based on Swedish literature and making striking visual use of natural scenery and landscape. The leading director of this movement was Victor Sjöström, whose films, such as *Terje Vigen* (1916), *The Outlaw and His Wife* (1917) and *The Phantom Chariot* (1920), made a great impact when they were shown abroad after the war. Swedish cinema was recognized as the first major 'alternative' to Hollywood to emerge during the period of us hegemony.

While distinctive national styles emerged in certain European cinemas, however, the dominant international style was American. Why was it that American films were so successful, even after European film industries began to pick themselves up again after the war? Kristin Thompson attributes their dominance to their high level of production values: 'American films were longer and had popular stars, lavish *mise en scène* and skilful cinematography; during the war these changes in the Hollywood film gained for it a definite following and other national industries would have difficulty in creating films as attractive.'[7] The success of American films in the international market, moreover, allowed Hollywood to expend more on film production than other film industries could afford. No country could match the costs of the lavish spectaculars of the early and mid-1920s such as *Robin Hood* ($1,500,000), *The Ten Commandments* ($1,800,000), *The Thief of Bagdad* ($2,000,000) and *Ben-Hur* ($3,900,000).[8] But Hollywood's dominance was more than just economic. It also suggests an acceptance of the 'new' popular culture of America. In France, for example, both the general public and intellectuals lapped up the films of American stars such as Douglas Fairbanks and the 'serial queen' Pearl White. Pathé's greatest success during the war came from distribution of the serial melodrama *The Perils of Pauline*. The French writer Philippe Soupault recalled how intensely this escapist fare affected Parisian audiences:

> Then one day we saw hanging on the walls great posters as long as serpents. At every street-corner a man, his face covered with a red handkerchief, levelled a revolver at the peaceful passerby. We imagined that we heard galloping hooves, the roar of motors, explosions, and cries of death. We rushed into the cinema, and realized immediately that everything had changed. On the screen appeared the smile of Pearl White – that almost ferocious smile which announced the revolution, the beginning of a new world.[9]

It was Charlie Chaplin, however, who, through the persona of his 'Little Tramp', was held to be the most recognizable face in the world during the late 1910s and 1920s. The combination of slapstick (visual comedy that is funny in any culture) and pathos in Chaplin's films such as *The Kid* and *The Gold Rush* made them popular around the world. Chaplin's unique brand of 'innocent utopian socialism' made him one of the richest men in the world, though this did nothing to damage his popularity with cinema audiences even after the arrival of talkies.[10]

There were various attempts during the 1920s to counter American hegemony. These were motivated both by economic considerations (to assist home production) and by cultural concerns (there was a widespread view on the part of European politicians, especially, that American influence was pernicious and harmful). Protectionism took different forms, including restricting the number of imports (Germany from 1925) and imposing a minimum 'quota' of indigenous films on exhibitors (Britain from 1927). At the same time there was an initiative, led by Germany and France, to combine the resources of European film industries so as to compete on equal terms with America. The 'Film Europe' movement, as it became known, can be seen as part of a broader trend in Europe in the 1920s which saw pan-national co-operation in the political and economic spheres as a means of assisting recovery and avoiding another devastating war. On one level this involved a series of reciprocal distribution arrangements, of which the first was a deal between Ufa and the French distributor Establissements Aubert in 1924. On another level it involved – or at least it aspired to – international co-productions. Erich Pommer, head of production at Ufa, was the principal advocate of this strategy: 'It is necessary to create "European films", which will no longer be French, British, Italian, or German films; entirely "continental" films, expanding out into all Europe and amortizing their enormous costs, can be produced easily'.[11] There were, indeed, numerous co-production initiatives, usually involving Germany, which had the most modern and best-equipped production facilities and thus attracted overseas filmmakers. Alfred Hitchcock, for example, worked as a set designer at Ufa, and his first two films as a director (*The Pleasure Garden* and *The Mountain Eagle*) were Anglo-German co-productions shot at the Emelka studios in Munich and on locations in Germany.

The failure of 'Film Europe' to make any lasting challenge to the hegemony of 'Film America' can be explained by several factors. For one thing, 'Film Europe' was a loose, often quite unco-ordinated movement: there was never a formal trade organization on the lines of the Motion Picture Producers and Distributors of America. For another thing, and despite all the talk of 'European' films, the main countries involved were Germany, France and Britain; other major producing nations, such as the Soviet Union, were only tangentially involved. The arrival of talking pictures in the late 1920s undermined efforts to create pan-European films as language differences meant that films were less easily exported. There were attempts to produce versions of the same film simultaneously in different languages –

Atlantic (1929), made by British International Pictures in English, German and French versions was 'possibly the first multiple-language film screened anywhere in the world' – but this strategy proved too expensive and was consequently short-lived.[12] The arrival of sound films, furthermore, coincided with the onset of the Great Depression, which had important consequences for the film industries of Europe: production expenditure was curtailed, thus effectively ruling out ambitious international co-productions, while the widespread introduction of protectionist legislation prevented the sort of free trade in films that had been part of the 'Film Europe' ideal.

EXPRESSIONISM, FORMALISM AND IMPRESSIONISM

It was during the 1920s that cinema began to be taken seriously by intellectuals and that the first recognizable theoretical discourses around film took shape. The work of academicians such as Hugo Münsterberg, Béla Balázs, Rudolf Arnheim and Hans Richter, and the practical film theory of Soviet-Russian filmmakers such as Sergei Eisenstein, Vsevolod Pudovkin and Lev Kuleshov, exemplified, albeit in different ways, what has generally come to be known as the 'formative' tradition in film theory.[13] The formative theorists argued that film could be considered an art form when it went beyond merely reproducing images of the real world, when it used the formal properties of the medium to manipulate the image for aesthetic effect. They privileged film styles and movements that explored the expressive and formal possibilities of the medium. During the 1920s this meant, principally, German, Soviet and French cinema. Three movements in particular – Expressionism in Germany, Formalism in Soviet Russia and Impressionism in France – are usually grouped together as representing the emergence of an avant-garde tradition in cinema that was consciously and deliberately different from the classical style that had become the norm in American cinema by this time. While the focus on a handful of recognized avant-garde classics has resulted in the marginalization of the vast majority of mainstream films (many of which, in any case, no longer survive), there is no denying the importance of the 1920s avant-gardes in the history of film. They are significant in two respects: firstly because they illustrate a remarkable congruence between theory and practice, and secondly because, in the case of German and Soviet film in particular, they had an enormous influence on the international development of the medium.

'Not long ago', Paul Rotha wrote in 1930, 'it was general to look at the German cinema for the real uses of the film medium.'[14] The 'real uses', for Rotha as for others, were the ways in which film form could be used for aesthetic effect. German cinema in the 1920s was described, at the time and since, as Expressionist due to its use of a distorted, displaced, disorienting type of *mise-en-scène*. Expressionism had emerged in other art forms, including painting and theatre, before the First World War, being one of several traditions (Cubism and Impressionism, for instance) that reacted against naturalism. Expressionism came late to the cinema, therefore, with Robert Wiene's *Das Kabinett des Dr Caligari* (*The Cabinet of Dr Caligari*, 1919) generally being recognized as the first Expressionist film. Its use of highly stylized sets, painted backgrounds of distorted, angular buildings and the jerky movements of the actors were consciously modelled on Expressionist theatre. *Caligari* was an international critical success and was followed by a cycle of Expressionist films including Fritz Lang's *Dr Mabuse, der Spieler* (*Dr Mabuse, the Gambler*, 1922), F. W. Murnau's *Nosferatu* (1922) and *Faust* (1926), Artur Robison's *Schatten* (*Warning Shadows*, 1923), G. W. Pabst's *Der Schatz* (*The Treasure*, 1923) and Paul Leni's *Wachsfigurenkabinett* (*Waxworks*, 1924).

The international critical success of some of these films has all too often led critics to describe the entire output of German cinema during the Weimar Republic (1919–33) as being Expressionist. In fact, the canon of Expressionist films is very small and comprises only a fraction of German film production during these years. Yet these films have been privileged both in aesthetic film history (for their highly distinctive visual style which critics have described as 'plastic' due to its manipulation and distortion of the image) and in social film history (where they have been interpreted, *qua* Siegfried Kracauer, as reflecting a *Zeitgeist*). While it is tempting to see the visual style of Expressionist cinema as a response to the social dislocation and economic turmoil of the early Weimar years – Germany was affected by chronic hyper-inflation and mass unemployment in the early 1920s – this interpretation needs to be qualified in so far as Expressionism had been established in other art forms before it emerged in the cinema. And the suggestion that the parade of madmen, master criminals, monsters and mad scientists to be found in Expressionist films can be seen as anticipating the horrors of National Socialism is unconvincing in the extreme.[15]

The Expressionist movement in German cinema had run its course by the mid-1920s. Already, however, intellectuals were finding a new cinema to champion in the Soviet Union. There is an irony, perhaps, in the fact that while the canonical Soviet films of the 1920s were produced as political propaganda – to commemorate the 'revolutionary struggle' of the Bolsheviks against Tsarist tyranny and oppression – the interest of western critics, even those of a generally left-wing disposition, was primarily of an aesthetic nature. Rotha, however, observed that 'however much one may admire their technical excellence and acknowledge their unquestionable superiority over the product of any other film-producing country, it is impossible to ignore their primary social, political, and often anti-religious influence.' 'The whole existence of the Soviet cinema', he went on, 'has come about through the urgent desire to express vividly and with the utmost effect the policy of the Soviet Government and the development of the principles of Marxism.'[16]

The Bolshevik regime had been quick to recognize the possibilities offered by cinema as an instrument of 'revolutionary propaganda'. The first 'agit-prop' trains showing films to the troops had appeared early in 1918. The film industry was nationalized in 1919 and a state film school was established in Moscow. Anatoli Lunacharsky, the People's Commissar for Enlightenment, spoke of 'fostering a completely new spirit in this branch of art and education' and asserted that 'it is impossible to imagine a richer source for cinema than the cultural history of mankind'. The cinema was to be used, moreover, to represent 'all kinds of important events of our recent revolutionary history'.[17] It was in the mid-1920s that a series of technically innovative and formally exciting films were produced to commemorate the achievements of the Bolsheviks and to promote an ideologically acceptable history of the revolutionary struggle to publics at home and abroad. Sergei Eisenstein's *Strike* (1925), about the suppression of industrial unrest in Imperial Russia, applied the principle of 'intellectual montage' that the director was developing through his writings: the juxtaposition of images to create meaning (at the climax of the film, for example, the massacre of the workers by Tsarist troops is cross-cut with images of the slaughter of bulls in an abattoir). Eisenstein's theory of montage was applied to probably its greatest effect in *Battleship Potemkin* (1925), commissioned to commemorate the twentieth anniversary of the 1905 revolution. The film is notable for its striking visual compositions and for its rhythmic editing, most famously in the sequence of the massacre on the Odessa Steps which is often described in terms such as 'one of the most visually electrifying [sequences] ever brought to the screen'.[18] Richard Taylor adds an important caveat that the Odessa Steps not only lays claim to being 'the most famous sequence of images in the history of world cinema', but 'also provides a classic example of poetic licence: a filmic creation of a historical event that in itself never happened but that encapsulates in *microcosm* the *macrocosmic* drama of a more general historical process.'[19]

Eisenstein was interested in representing history in terms of movements and masses rather than as a story of individuals. Vsevolod Pudovkin, in contrast, used individuals who personified the masses, as in *Mother* (1926), based on a novel by Maxim Gorky, which personalized the revolutionary struggle by combining montage with the conventions of the family melodrama (generational difference, conflicting loyalties, personal sacrifice). A series of prestigious and expensive 'Jubilee Films' commemorating the tenth anniversary of the October Revolution of 1917 was commissioned, including Pudovkin's *The End of St Petersburg* (1927), Esther Shub's *The Fall of the Romanov Dynasty* (1927) and Eisenstein's *October* (1928). The latter film, even more ambitious than the director's previous efforts in its application of intellectual montage, was, however, criticized for its excessive 'formalism' and ran foul of political changes following Trotsky's expulsion from the Communist Party and Stalin's consolidation of power.

The historical significance of the Soviet montage cinema of the 1920s is to be found in its international influence rather than in its success as domestic propaganda. *Potemkin*, in particular, was an international critical success, being acclaimed by critics in Berlin and New York. While it was banned from public exhibition in France and Britain due to its ideological content (it was not passed by the censors in either country until the 1950s), it was allowed to be shown privately to members of film societies and cinema clubs, where it was enormously influential on aesthetes and avant-garde filmmakers. At home, however, *Potemkin* suffered a rather different fate. Although it had been premièred at Moscow's prestigious Bolshoi Theatre, it was taken off less than a month after its release in January 1926 and was shown mainly in second-run cinemas throughout Russia. At the box-office *Potemkin* lost out to Hollywood films such as Douglas Fairbanks's *Robin Hood*, which was far more popular with Russian audiences.[20] The lack of commercial success for *Potemkin* and other Soviet montage films prompted the filmmaker and critic Pavel Petrov-Bytov to declare in 1929 that 'We have no Soviet cinema' on the grounds that the films were not reaching the masses. He complained that 'effete directors' were out of touch with the people and that their films were unintelligible. While acknowledging the 'formal virtues' of the films, Petrov-Bytov insisted that Eisenstein and his colleagues did not understand the masses: 'As well as theory we need practice. Before we talk about life we must get to know it. . . . But you have to talk to them [the masses] in their native language and not in the language of the Formalists.'[21] These comments were made in the aftermath of the decision of the first All-Union Party Congress on the Cinema in March 1928 that filmmakers should cease their formalist experimentation and that henceforth 'the basic criterion for evaluating the art qualities of a film is the requirement that it be presented in a form which can be understood by the millions'.[22] This resolution is generally seen as marking the end of the period of Formalism in Soviet cinema and embracing the tenet of Socialist Realism that was to be the officially approved style of filmmaking for the next quarter of a century.

The third of the nationally specific avant-garde movements of the 1920s emerged in France through the work of filmmakers such as Louis Delluc, René Clair, Jean Epstein, Abel Gance and Marcel L'Herbier, whose experiments with form and style have led to their films being seen as part of the Impressionist movement. Whereas Expressionism gained its effect from the arrangement of *mise-en-scène* and Formalism from the relationship between shots (montage), Impressionism involved experimentation with optical subjectivity. Devices such as superimpositions and iris shots were used to foreground the subjective point-of-view and to enhance the *photogénie* of the films. Impressionist films varied from short experiments to Gance's seventeen-reel epic *Napoléon* (1927), which has been described as 'a lexicon of the entire technical grammar of the silent screen' and which combined optical effects (including an early example of a triple-camera widescreen process that predated Cinerama by 25 years) with montage.[23] *Napoléon* was sponsored by the Société Générale de Films, which backed a number of expensive, experimental films in the late 1920s, including Carl Theodor Dreyer's *La passion de Jeanne d'Arc* (*The Passion of Joan of Arc*, 1928), which, like *Napoléon*, was a critical success but a financial failure. 'The market for the French "artistic" production must necessarily remain limited, for the French have not any idea of the entertainment of the masses',

Rotha observed. In terms that anticipated *Cahiers du Cinéma* by several decades, however, he also identified 'the principal characteristic of the French cinema' as being 'the single-minded production with the director or the cameraman, as the case may be, as the sole *metteur-en-scène*'.[24]

To what extent did the avant-garde movements of the 1920s influence the artistic development of the medium of film? Thompson and Bordwell are in no doubt that stylistic influences, at this time, still circulated between countries and thus contributed to the emergence of an 'international style'. 'French Impressionism, German Expressionism, and Soviet Montage began as strictly national trends, but soon filmmakers exploring these styles became aware of each other's work', they write. 'By the mid-1920s, an international avant-garde style blended traits of all three movements.'[25] This is probably overstating the case somewhat, however, for it could equally be argued that the continuing dominance of American movies made Hollywood classicism the true international style. It would be more accurate, perhaps, to say that the avant-garde movements influenced individual filmmakers rather than wider film movements. Alfred Hitchcock is a good example of a director whose films mixed the angular compositions of German Expressionism, the montage principles of the Soviet cinema and the individualistic optical flourishes of the French Impressionists, best exemplified in his first British film *The Lodger: A Story of the London Fog* (1926). When German, and other European filmmakers, left to work in Hollywood in the 1930s and 1940s, the influence of Expressionism, in particular, can be identified in the visual style of particular cycles such as the horror films of the 1930s and *film noir* in the 1940s.

The privileging of avant-gardes, first by contemporary critics and later by historians, has, furthermore, led to a conventional wisdom in which European cinema is associated with 'art' (a term that was increasingly being used in relation to film in the 1920s) and Hollywood with mere 'entertainment'. This critical dichotomy (which invariably also assumes that 'art' is superior to 'entertainment') has tended to obscure some more pertinent factors in the history of film during the 1920s. One of these is that, for all the attention given to the various avant-gardes, they formed only one aspect of their respective national cinemas in which popular genre films and star vehicles were by far the most popular attractions. The most popular star in Russia in the 1920s was the slapstick comedian Igor Ilinsky, serials remained popular in France, while in Germany Expressionist films competed with historical spectacles and chamber dramas (*Kammerspiel*). And Hollywood, of course, provided the biggest star vehicles of the 1920s: the international popularity of Douglas Fairbanks (*The Mark of Zorro, The Three Musketeers, Robin Hood, The Thief of Bagdad*) and Rudolph Valentino (*The Sheik, Blood and Sand, The Eagle*) suggests that heroic spectacle and exotic romanticism crossed national and cultural boundaries.

Nor was Hollywood necessarily the entirely philistine world that was often alleged by its critics. The American cinema was open to 'European' ideas and influences. In the 1920s it lured German filmmakers such as Ernst Lubitsch, Ludwig Berger, Paul Leni, E. A. Dupont and F. W. Murnau to make films in Hollywood. It would later attract the talents of René Clair and Alfred Hitchcock, amongst others; even Eisenstein briefly explored the possibility of working in Hollywood in the 1930s. The reason for Hollywood's recruitment of European talent was essentially a public-relations exercise on the part of the major studios which wanted to create an image of themselves as producers of 'art' as well as just commercial pictures. In the 1920s there was an interest in what Hollywood termed 'highly artistic pictures' intended for more 'high-brow' audiences in the major cities. As the trade journal *Moving Picture World* put it in 1927: 'They are made to satisfy the comparatively limited number who appreciate the best, and produced in the hope that they will help to give tone to the general product through satisfying the minority demand.'[26]

The pre-eminent example of the 'highly artistic picture' was *Sunrise: A Song of Two Humans* (1927), for which the Fox Film Corporation lured F. W. Murnau to Hollywood and gave him a level of artistic licence not to be enjoyed again until Orson Welles made *Citizen Kane* for RKO some fourteen years later. *Sunrise* provides an exemplary instance of how the aesthetic, economic, technological and social approaches to film history intersect. The film tells the story of a farmer who is tempted away from his dutiful wife by a woman from the city; the farmer tries to kill his wife but cannot bring himself to go through with it; they are reconciled, but the wife almost perishes in a storm on the journey home. Murnau combines the narrative codes of American melodrama with the visual style of German Expressionism to create 'a work in which American and European sensibilities blend rather than clash'.[27] The film employs sophisticated narrational techniques to tell its story in visual terms (it uses relatively few intertitles, for instance) and is notable, especially, for its use of deep-focus photography and a mobile camera which gives unusual depth and fluidity to the narration. Its aesthetic qualities aside, however, *Sunrise* also needs to be seen as part of a wider economic and cultural strategy. Robert C. Allen considers it 'an integral part of one of the most carefully orchestrated and ambitious bids for power and prestige in the history of the American cinema'.[28] William Fox invested $1.5 million in the film, which utilized one of the largest sets ever built, including a city section complete with elevated trains and streetcars. In the event, however, *Sunrise* was not to be the prestigious success that Fox had hoped. Its critical reception was mixed and it fared badly at the box-office, its commercial failure due in part to poor publicity (reports in the trade press had suggested that it was 'an unusual picture' and therefore difficult to sell) and in part to the fact that its release coincided, albeit accidentally, with the publicity surrounding the first 'talking picture', *The Jazz Singer*.[29]

THE COMING OF THE TALKIES

Although the beginning of the sound era in cinema is generally dated from the release of *The Jazz Singer* in October 1927, this needs to be nuanced in several ways. Cinema had never in fact been 'silent': narrators in the auditorium had been a feature of the nickelodeon era, while most film shows were accompanied by live music, ranging from a pianist in the smaller movie theatres to full-scale orchestras in the sumptuous picture palaces that had been built during the 1920s. Experiments with synchronous sound had been going on since the early 1900s, but it was not until the 1920s that the technology was perfected. *The Jazz Singer* was not the first film with synchronized sound – *Don Juan* (1926) had used synchronized sound effects and *Sunrise* had used synchronized music – but rather was the first 'part-talking' feature film in that it used some dialogue sequences (largely improvised, such as Al Jolson's prophetic 'You ain't heard nothin' yet') and some song numbers. The first 'all-talking' film, *Lights of New York*, was released in 1928. Many of the 'sound' films that followed *The Jazz Singer* had in fact been shot as silents and had soundtracks added. It took several years for the 'all-talking' feature film to become established and it was not until the end of 1929 that such films had finally displaced the silents.

There are different historical interpretations of the coming of the 'talkies'. The old version of events, which no longer stands up to close scrutiny, is that *The Jazz Singer* had been a desperate gamble by Warner Bros., which stood on the verge of bankruptcy, and took a chance on the new technology that had been turned down by all the other major production companies as being nothing more than a gimmick. In this history – later mythologized by Hollywood itself in the musical *Singin' in the Rain* (1952) – the rest of the industry expected *The Jazz Singer* to be a flop and was taken by surprise when it turned out to be a box-office smash, whereupon all the other studios fell over themselves in the rush to convert to sound.[30] This interpretation has since been challenged by revisionist historians, led by Douglas Gomery, who have argued that, rather than being a gamble, the adoption of sound was in fact part of a planned, long-term strategy on the part of Warner Bros. to secure its place amongst the leading film companies. Warners, which in the 1920s was in a reasonably healthy financial state but which unlike some of its rivals (such as Paramount and MGM) did not own its own movie theatres, saw sound as its entry into Hollywood's major league. Thus, with backing from the investment bankers Goldman Sachs, who were impressed with the studio's strict accounting and budgetary control, Warners embarked upon an ambitious but carefully planned expansion strategy which included the acquisition of the First National theatre chain, and forming, in partnership with Western

Electric, the subsidiary Vitaphone Corporation to produce sound films and market sound equipment. Although Warners had been in the red in 1926, this was not in fact the sign of bankruptcy that earlier commentators had believed, but a deliberate short-term accounting loss to allow corporate restructuring that would bring about profits in the long term. The success of this strategy can be seen in the fact that Warners increased its stock value from $5 million in 1925 to $230 million by 1930.[31]

The most recent account of the arrival of the talkies sees 'the transition to sound as partly rational and partly confused'.[32] While Warners was the first studio to take the plunge, it initially opted for a sound-on-disc system (whereby sound was recorded on phonograph records) which proved technically cumbersome. It was the sound-on-film system (utilizing a photoelectric cell), adopted by the Fox Film Corporation, that was to become the industry's standard. Warners and Fox were the first studios to convert wholesale to the production of sound films; Paramount and MGM followed suit in 1928 when they also entered into agreements with Western Electric. Other companies followed the lead of the industry giants, with the conversion to sound costing the film industry an estimated $500 million, resulting in the formation of alliances between the studios and Wall Street that were to last for years to come. One new major film company was born as a result of the conversion to sound, when the Radio Corporation of America patented its own sound-on-film system (Photophone) and acquired its own chain of cinemas (Keith-Albee-Orpheum) to form RKO Radio Pictures.

The consequences of the conversion to sound were mixed. Industrially, the oligopoly of the major US film corporations was consolidated; the cost of conversion was offset by increased profits in the short term; and, although some cinemas closed, it is difficult to say how far this was due to the cost of being 'wired' for sound or how far it was also affected by the Great Depression which began in 1929 and led to a drop in the number of cinema attendances. Aesthetically, however, the arrival of sound is generally held to have retarded the development of film style. The late silent cinema had been characterized by a highly mobile camera and a consequently fluid style of narration; the technological limitations of early sound cinema (the camera, for example, had to be enclosed in a soundproof box) meant that early talkies were static and cumbersome. Bordwell suggests that these limitations had been overcome by 1933 when the camera had regained its mobility and 'shooting a sound film came to mean shooting a silent film with sound'.[33] Even so, there was initially much resistance to talking pictures from aesthetes, who believed that silent film had been a more expressive and artistic medium. Hitchcock, for example, always believed that 'the silent pictures were the purest form of cinema' and disliked many sound films which he described as 'photographs of people talking'.[34] Sound helped bring an end to the careers of some directors, including the pioneer D. W. Griffith, and stars, especially slapstick comedians such as Buster Keaton and Harold Lloyd. Chaplin continued to resist talkies throughout the 1930s, releasing *City Lights* and *Modern Times* with synchronized sound but without dialogue, finally relenting to the inevitability of speech at the end of the decade with *The Great Dictator*.

The main international consequence of talking pictures, however, was to accelerate the trend towards the emergence of national cinemas. Other film industries quickly followed the lead set by Hollywood: Britain, France and Germany all produced their first full-talking feature films in 1929, with Italy and the Soviet Union following suit in 1930. Sound provided a boost for domestic production industries as audiences were keen to hear films in their own language. The French and German film industries gained a larger percentage share of their home markets in the early 1930s. Italy became the first country to legislate that all films exhibited in cinemas had to be in the native tongue. American films, however, consolidated their hold in English-speaking markets, especially in Britain.[35]

The adoption of sound proceeded less certainly outside America and Europe. In India, for example, which by the mid-1920s had been producing more films annually than Britain, France or the Soviet Union, the advent of sound led to a fragmentation of the market and of the production industry. Indian cinema had been truly 'national' when it was silent, but in the 1930s it was Hindi cinema which became dominant, with other languages (such as Bengali and Marathi) comprising a minority of film production. The case of Japan illustrates a certain resistance to talking pictures, for, while most Japanese cinemas were wired for sound by 1930, the Japanese industry insisted on developing its own sound technology rather than paying the high royalties demanded by the Americans. Thus, in the early 1930s, an unusual situation persisted in which most imported films were talkies but most Japanese films were silent. There was also resistance from the *benshi*, the union of performers whose job it was to explain action orally over the silents. The popular success of the first Japanese talking picture, *Madam and Wife* (1931), indicated that there was a market for talkies, but it was not until the mid-1930s that sound films accounted for half of domestic production. By that time the talkies were well and truly here to stay and silent cinema already seemed a thing of the past.

FIVE

The Dream Factory

'Hollywood' has become a convenient shorthand for the American film industry, even though the label tends to be used imprecisely and often inaccurately. Strictly speaking Hollywood is a suburb of Los Angeles where the majority of American film production facilities have been located. Strictly speaking it refers only to the production sector of the American film industry – the head offices of the distribution networks are located in New York – and strictly speaking it is less accurate a description in the modern era than it was during its so-called 'golden age' of the 1930s and 1940s. For all these caveats, however, the idea of 'Hollywood' has become virtually synonymous with American cinema in all its aspects. Hollywood is more than the geographical location of industrial structures and production plants; it has become a byword for the filmmaking community. It is also a signifier of a particular world-view, a purveyor of fantasy and escapism. 'Hollywood', the anthropologist Hortense Powdermaker remarked in 1951, 'is engaged in the mass production of prefabricated dreams.'[1] The label of Hollywood as a 'dream factory' has stuck, for, despite the contradiction within the phrase (a dream is a spontaneous, personal and unique experience, whereas a factory is a production line turning out identical products for mass consumption), it nevertheless expresses the idea that Hollywood is in some way responding to the hopes and aspirations of the public by providing them with ready-made fantasies. Hollywood itself promotes its own image as the 'Metropolis of Make-Believe' – a description used at the beginning of *A Star is Born* (1937).

This chapter examines the history of the Hollywood 'dream factory' during its heyday of the 1930s and 1940s. This period, often described as Hollywood's 'golden age', is defined, at its outset, by the arrival of talking pictures and the onset of the Great Depression, and, at its end, by the arrival of television and the landmark decision of the US Supreme Court that the major film corporations should relinquish their ownership of movie theatres. On the face of it there is much to recommend the idea of a golden age. Not only was this the time when cinema as a social practice reached its zenith, it was also the time when a particular mode of production – the 'studio system' – was institutionalized in Hollywood. Yet on closer analysis the notion of a golden age is somewhat misleading, as the term might be suggestive of a degree of stability that was not necessarily the case. This was in fact a period of acute crisis and instability for the film industry. It is rather ironic that Hollywood's golden age coincided with a decade of economic and social turmoil in the United States in the wake of the Great Depression and that the cinema's period of greatest popularity in the 1940s came on the back of a war effort that saw the film industry serving the national interest as a vehicle of propaganda. It is even more ironic that Hollywood's role in promoting social unity and patriotism during the Depression and the Second World War was later to result in many of its personnel being branded 'unAmerican' during the anti-communist witch hunts of the late 1940s and early 1950s.

HOLLYWOOD AS A SOCIAL INSTITUTION

In one respect the golden age metaphor is perfectly appropriate: the 1930s and 1940s marked the height of the popularity of cinema as a social institution in America. In 1930 cinema attendances reached a high of approximately 80 million per week (from a total population of some 130 million). While there was to be a sharp decline in the early 1930s as the effects of the Depression were felt – weekly attendances dropped to 70 million in 1931 and 55 million in 1932 – this downturn proved temporary. Attendances began to recover in the mid-1930s and by the end of the decade had once again reached their pre-Depression levels.[2] This upward trend continued during the Second World War, with a peak of around 90 million per week being reached by the mid-1940s. Robert Sklar suggests that it was in 1946, the first full year of peace, that 'American movies attained the highest level of popular appeal in their half century of existence' in that they reached 'nearly three fifths of their "potential audience" – that is, the movie industry's estimate of all the people in the country capable of making their way to a box office, leaving out the very young and very old, the ill, those confined to institutions, and others without access to movie theatres.'[3]

Evidence regarding the social composition of cinema audiences is sketchy to say the least, but according to Margaret Thorp's *America at the Movies* (1939), which historians have generally accepted as the most reliable contemporary survey, the majority of cinema-goers were middle-class whites between the ages of fourteen and 45, of whom a greater proportion were adult women.[4] Although there was a widespread belief that anyone who 'had the price' could visit the cinema – average ticket prices during the 1930s were around 20–25 cents (more for large metropolitan cinemas, less for out-of-town movie houses) – this was not in fact the case. Thorp found that black Americans, who numbered around 13 million, were 'the only considerable section of the population who cannot go to a movie whenever they have the price'.[5] In the South some movie theatres had segregated sections for black patrons; many did not admit them at all.

As to why people went to 'the movies' in such numbers, there seems no reason to depart from the conventional wisdom that it was because cinema provided entertainment and escapism. Garth Jowett asserts that the cinema-going habit was 'a comparative necessity' in times of social and economic hardship such as Depression-era America.[6] This view is also supported by contemporary sources. Thorp believed that 'audiences wanted to be cheered up when they went to the movies; they had no desire to see on the screen the squalor and misery of which there was all too much at home.'[7] While there were examples of social problem films in the 1930s – Warner Bros. was the one studio which explicitly displayed a 'social conscience' in films such as *I am a Fugitive from a Chain Gang* (1932) – they were not representative of Hollywood's total output which tended more towards romantic dramas, sophisticated comedies and Art Deco musicals. The professional ideology of Hollywood filmmakers was that they were producers of 'harmless entertainment' that would appeal to 'the largest possible audience'.[8] That Hollywood itself inclined to this view is eloquently demonstrated in Preston Sturges's wonderful farce *Sullivan's Travels* (1941), in which a film director (Joel McCrea), balking at the suggestion that he should make another musical like *Ants in Your Pants of 1939* (a spoof of 1930s musicals such as MGM's *Broadway Melody* and Warners' *Gold Diggers* films) decides instead to set out on a journey across America in search of material for a film entitled *Oh Brother Where Art Thou?* 'I want this picture to be a commentary on modern ideas – stark realism – the problems that confront the average man', he tells sceptical studio executives. A series of comic and tragic misadventures ends with Sullivan working on a chain gang and attending a church service where the ecstatic reaction to a Mickey Mouse cartoon brings home to him the importance of 'harmless entertainment'. Bosley Crowther, senior film critic of the *New York Times*, called the film 'a beautifully trenchant satire upon "social significance" in pictures . . . and a deftly sardonic apologia for Hollywood make-believe'.[9]

'What was different about the movies in the 1930s', writes Sklar, 'was not that they were beginning to communicate myths and dreams – they had done that from the beginning – but that the moviemakers were aware in a more sophisticated way of their mythmaking powers, responsibilities and opportunities.'[10] It was not only the filmmakers themselves, however, who were aware of the social import of the cinema and of its perceived influence on public morals and behaviour. The Motion Picture Research Council, a quasi-educational pressure group, accused Hollywood of corrupting the minds of the nation's youth through 'academic' studies such as *Motion Pictures and Youth* and *Our Movie-Made Children*. The cinema also came under attack from other pressure groups including the National Congress of Parents and Teachers, the Daughters of the American Revolution and the Catholic Legion of Decency. The Legion of Decency, founded in 1933, was by far the most influential of these organizations, as it signed millions of Catholics to a pledge to boycott movies that were deemed immoral by the

Church. Hollywood was sufficiently concerned about the potential loss of box-office revenues such a boycott would entail that it took the Legion seriously and even invited a Jesuit priest, Father Daniel Lord, to assist in drafting the film industry's own code of practice.[11]

The introduction of self-regulation is usually seen as Hollywood's strategy to prevent the imposition of censorship from external sources. Films were already subject to censorship by state and municipal boards which could deny exhibition following the decision of the US Supreme Court in 1915 that motion pictures were not protected by the First Amendment (free speech). Hollywood, alert to the damage which the scandals of the early 1920s did to its public image – the death of starlet Virginia Rappe, the murder of director William Desmond Taylor and numerous tales of drug-taking and sexual impropriety – had already tried to put its house in order by setting up its own trade organization, the Motion Picture Producers and Distributors of America (MPPDA), with former US Postmaster-General Will H. Hays as its president. In 1924 Hays had introduced a process for vetting source material, but it was ineffective as it was voluntary on the part of producers. In 1927 a self-regulating code was introduced by the MPPDA, known informally as the list of 'Don'ts and Be Carefuls', though again it was largely without effect as the code was advisory only. The arrival of talking pictures, which meant that changing films for local censorship boards would affect sound synchronization, necessitated a more formal arrangement. To this extent the introduction of self-censorship was determined as much by economic factors as it was by social concerns. In 1930 the Production Code was introduced by the MPPDA in order to act as a safeguard for moral standards and to regulate the content of motion pictures.

The introduction of the Code did not, however, immediately result in a 'cleaning up' of the movies. Hollywood films of the early 1930s continued to attract criticism from moral crusaders for their perceived excesses of sex and violence. Paramount's Mae West comedies, *She Done Him Wrong* and *I'm No Angel*, were attacked for their sexual innuendoes – though, unsurprisingly, this did not affect their popularity with audiences – while the gangster cycle of 1930–32 (*Little Caesar, The Public Enemy, Scarface*) became the focus of a debate around screen violence and the representation of gangsters as tragic figures. The MPPDA finally bowed to public pressure in 1934 when the Production Code Administration (PCA) was established to enforce the Code more rigorously. Joseph Breen, a former journalist and a Catholic, was appointed as its chief. The first casualty of the new regime was MGM's *Tarzan and His Mate*, the first sequel to the studio's 1932 hit *Tarzan the Apeman*, from which a nude underwater swimming scene had to be cut.[12]

Breen, who was to remain in office as head of the PCA for twenty years, except for a brief sojourn as a studio executive at RKO Radio Pictures in 1941–2, was later described as the man who 'shaped the moral stature of the American motion picture'.[13] Breen enforced the Production Code with an almost missionary zeal. He was determined to uphold the 'General Principles' of the Code, which were: (1) 'No picture shall be produced which will lower the moral standards of those who see it'; (2) 'Correct standards of life, subject only to the requirements of drama and entertainment, shall be presented'; and (3) 'Law, natural or human, shall not be ridiculed, nor shall sympathy be created for its violation.'[14] There was a list of prohibited subjects and an even longer list of subjects (including sex and crime) that needed to be treated with the utmost caution and restraint. Any form of obscenity, profanity or blasphemy was forbidden. In order to enforce the Code effectively, a PCA seal of approval was introduced: all members of the MPPDA agreed not to distribute or exhibit any film without the seal and a fine of $25,000 was levied on anyone who did. Breen adopted a policy of discussing scripts with producers before they went into production so that any potentially problematic scenes could be removed or revised. He would also inform producers whether their films were likely to run into problems with other censorship bodies in important overseas markets such as Great Britain.

There is no doubt that the implementation of the Code affected the nature and content of American films. The violence of gangster and horror films, for example, was substantially toned down after 1934, while displays of overt sexuality virtually disappeared until Howard Hughes challenged the PCA with *The*

Outlaw (made in 1941 but not released nationally until 1946 when it was shown without a seal of approval and did good business for independent exhibitors). It would be misleading to regard the PCA as a hindrance to film production, even though many commentators have had fun in exposing some of its more patently ridiculous rules such as the requirement that married couples should sleep in separate beds and that a gentleman must always keep one foot on the floor during love scenes. A more useful way of understanding the PCA's role is to see it as a means of negotiating the relationship between Hollywood and those moral watchdogs who were fearful of the social effects of motion pictures. This is not to say there were no more points of controversy – the cycle of 'boy gang' films in 1938–9 (*Dead End, Angels With Dirty Faces*) once again brought concerns about juveniles to the fore – but on the whole the relationship between the PCA and the studios was quite harmonious. Indeed, the PCA came to be so closely associated with the interests of the film industry that when the US Department of Justice filed an anti-trust suit against the major studios in 1938, it implicated the PCA in the film industry's highly restrictive exhibition practices.

THE POLITICAL ECONOMY OF HOLLYWOOD

By 1930 the American film industry had become a mature oligopoly – a state of limited competition in which the market is controlled by a small number of companies. The industry was dominated by eight companies (known as the 'majors') which between them accounted for three quarters of all film production and owned the majority of large 'first run' movie theatres. This cartelization ensured that all sectors of the industry – production, distribution and exhibition – were managed in accordance with the interests of the majors.

The eight majors can themselves be divided into two groups. On the one hand there were the so-called 'Big Five' (MGM/Loew's, Paramount, Warner Bros., Fox – which became Twentieth Century-Fox in 1935 – and RKO) which were fully vertically integrated in the sense that they controlled the production, distribution and exhibition of their own films. On the other hand there were the 'Little Three' (Columbia, Universal and United Artists) which did not own their own movie theatres and so were dependent upon their larger cousins, as well as independent exhibitors, for showing their films. Typically each of the majors would produce around 50 films a year, but the demand for movies was so great that even the Big Five could not fill their own theatres with their own films and so had to show other studios' films too. In practice the majors controlled the market by giving preference to their own and to each other's films. There were few independent producers during the heyday of the studio system – only David O. Selznick, Samuel Goldwyn and Walter Wanger operated successfully as independent producers of major 'prestige films' – and, while numerous small production companies came and went (including Republic, Monogram, Mascot, Reliable, Lone Star, Grand National, First Division and Producers Releasing Corporation), these specialized in the production of cheaply made genre films designed to fill the bottom half of a double bill.

The American film industry had entered the 1930s in a state of good economic health. The financial outlay associated with the conversion to sound, which required both studios and movie theatres being 'wired', was offset in the short term by increased revenues from rising cinema attendances. Weekly cinema attendances rose by almost half between 1926 and 1930. There was a sense of optimism in the industry that was barely dented by the Wall Street Crash of October 1929. The fact that cinema attendances reached a new high in the year following the Crash engendered a belief that Hollywood was Depression-proof. *Variety* reported that 'the film industry's leaders will pass the fiscal period of 1930 to their biggest net profit in history'.[15] Indeed, in that year MGM recorded its highest yet net profits of $15 million, Paramount was even healthier at $18 million, Warner Bros. made $7 million and even the permanently crisis-prone RKO turned a profit of over $3 million.[16]

This buoyancy, however, was to prove short-lived. In 1931 the film industry belatedly felt the effects of the Depression. Attendances slumped, ticket prices were cut in a desperate attempt to attract patrons and consequently revenues were diminished. *Variety* observed at the year's end that the film industry was left 'dizzy from its first real churning in the economic maelstrom'.[17] The economic health of the majors deteriorated throughout the early 1930s: RKO, which recorded losses of $3 million in 1931 and $5 million in 1932, became the first studio to call in the receivers in January 1933. It was followed by Paramount, which suffered losses of $15 million in 1932 and $20 million in 1933, and by Fox, which recorded a deficit of almost $17 million in 1932. Warner Bros. managed to stave off bankruptcy, though it still recorded losses of $8 million in 1931 and $14 million in 1932; MGM was the only one of the Big Five which continued to record profits throughout the 1930s and even then its revenues were severely diminished. The Little Three, who unlike their larger cousins were not burdened with mortgage repayments from the purchase of movie theatres, nevertheless only narrowly survived.[18]

The film industry's response to the Depression was a policy of retrenchment and reorganization. Some less profitable movie theatres were closed, production expenditure was curtailed and salaries were cut. The Big Five sold off some of their exhibition interests in order to focus on the first-run theatres that accounted for the majority of their revenues. The Big Five controlled some 2,600 movie theatres in 1939. While this was a minority (approximately fifteen per cent) of all theatres, it represented over 80 per cent of the first-run houses – the large, showcase, metropolitan cinemas with the largest seating capacities and the highest ticket prices. Their control of this part of the exhibition sector helped to ensure the survival of the Big Five during the economic crisis. 'As a control device, the development of strategic first-run theaters as the showcase of the industry proved remarkably effective', an economic analyst observed in 1944. 'Ownership of these relatively few theaters gave control over access to the market.'[19]

The industry adopted other measures to ensure its survival in the 1930s. The double bill was introduced in an attempt to attract customers by offering two films for the price of one. This move actually boosted independent production, as small companies specializing in supporting features ('B'-pictures) sprang up to meet the demand. The majors also strengthened their position with independent exhibitors through restrictive practices such as zoning and clearance (whereby movie theatres were ranked according to size and location) and blind and block booking (whereby exhibitors were forced to rent films unseen in blocks of between five and fifty rather than being allowed to select individual titles). The majors operated an effective cartel in which they supplied films for each other's theatres and provided screen time for each other's films, thus squeezing out independents and ensuring their own long-term economic health. By the second half of the 1930s there was every indication that these practices were proving successful. Studio finances had been restored to health and only RKO remained in receivership at the end of the decade (the company finally freed itself in January 1940). The year 1939 was widely recognized as an *annus mirabilis* for Hollywood when, for the first time since 1931, all the majors made a profit and the total domestic box-office grosses amounted to a colossal $673 million.[20]

However, the most important factors in the film industry's survival during the 1930s were the collusion of the federal government and the assistance of Wall Street. The economic recovery programme introduced early in Roosevelt's presidency assisted the majors in establishing their control over the industry. The National Recovery Administration (NRA) was established in 1933 to promote fair competition and thereby, it was believed, assist the prosperity of all American businesses. The film industry, through the MPPDA, was required to draft its own code of fair practice. The MPPDA was able, therefore, to codify formally all the monopolistic exhibition practices already in use by the industry. Although the NRA was wound up in 1935, it had effectively strengthened the position of the majors by condoning the cartelization of the film industry.[21]

It has often been suggested that the government's support of the film industry was bought in return for Hollywood's endorsement of the New Deal. The New Deal was a collective term for the social and economic reforms introduced by Roosevelt between 1933 and 1939 which sought to assist financial recovery and relieve unemployment. In 1935 a Marxist critic, F. D. Klingender, commented upon 'the intrusion of the social problem film into the fantastic realm of Hollywood that occurred shortly after Roosevelt was elected president' and argued that film producers supported Roosevelt by promoting 'the deflection of mass indignation, then at its highest, from a criticism of the capitalist system as such to that of particular aspects of that system, such as banking, market speculation, etc.'[22] One does not have to be a Marxist to see that what is at stake in American films of the 1930s are not capitalism or the political system themselves but rather their abuse by self-interested individuals. Thus it is that the villains of 1930s films are often avaricious bankers or corrupt politicians, while their heroes tend to personify the 'little man' or 'ordinary Joe' so beloved of American popular culture. Nowhere is this better exemplified than in Frank Capra's populist hymns to the little man, *Mr Deeds Goes to Town* (1936) and *Mr Smith Goes to Washington* (1939), in which decent, honest, upright, small-town heroes emerge triumphant over greedy lawyers and self-interested politicians. It would be mistaken, however, to make too straightforward a connection between Hollywood and politics in this or any other decade. Contrary to Klingender's assertion, the social problem films of the early 1930s were made and in several cases released before Roosevelt was elected. Nor can the social problem film be considered anything like a staple of Hollywood production throughout the 1930s. It was not until the end of the decade that Hollywood could take a more detached look at the social consequences of the Depression in John Ford's 1940 film of John Steinbeck's dustbowl novel *The Grapes of Wrath*. This film, in the eyes of one commentator, 'brought to a climax all Hollywood's efforts, since the coming of the talkies, to come to terms with the idea of films discussing problems of social progress and social injustice'.[23] While Nunnally Johnson's script waters down some of the more shocking incidents of the novel (due as much to censorship as anything else), the film presents the Joads as tragic figures who are exploited by economic and social institutions: uncaring land companies, unscrupulous labour agents, corrupt police. As a film that affirms faith in basic human dignity in the face of severe social and economic hardship, it is one of the most humane and sincere of all Hollywood films.

The studio which aligned itself most closely with the New Deal was Warner Bros. Indeed, the studio's use of the NRA's

Eagle symbol on the credits of some of its films amounted to nothing less than a wholesale endorsement of New Deal policies. The content of numerous Warner films, moreover, contained direct references to Roosevelt and the New Deal. As Edward Buscombe observes:

> The famous 'Forgotten Man' sequence of *Gold Diggers of 1933* (1933) derives from Roosevelt's use of the phrase in one of his speeches ... Pictures like *I am a Fugitive from a Chain Gang, Black Legion, Heroes for Sale, Black Fury, A Modern Hero, 20,000 Years in Sing Sing, They Won't Forget*, and *Confessions of a Nazi Spy* to mention only the best known, all testify to the vaguely and uncertainly radical yearnings which the studio shared with the New Deal.[24]

In comparison with the other majors, certainly, Warner Bros. was more likely to engage with social issues and to take its stories from the newspaper headlines. Yet the studio's much-vaunted 'social conscience' needs to be qualified. On the one hand, Warners was freer from Wall Street control than most other studios – the Warner brothers themselves still owned a majority of stock in their own company – and therefore in a stronger position to make the sort of films it wanted to make. And the Warners were Democrats, unlike most studio heads. On the other hand, however, social issue films comprised a minority of the studio's production output during the 1930s. Nick Roddick estimates that of the 751 films made by the studio between the Wall Street Crash and Pearl Harbor, only 240 dealt 'more or less seriously with American society' and that the other 511 'bore little or no immediate social message'.[25] The studio's social conscience was, for one thing, influenced by economic considerations (the films made money), and, for another, was only part of an overall production strategy that also included Busby Berkeley musicals, Bette Davis melodramas and Errol Flynn swashbucklers.

Warner Bros. was unusual in not closening its ties with Wall Street during the early 1930s. In general, however, Hollywood turned even more to the East Coast for support during the Depression. New York bankers had been involved with the industry since the late 1920s when they had financed the acquisition of movie theatres and the conversion to sound. Wall Street's involvement increased during the early 1930s as investors bankrolled the studios to survive the Depression and, to the chagrin of the studio heads themselves, became more directly involved in studio management. The result was that some of the pioneers who had effectively founded Hollywood some two decades earlier were forced out of the business. Carl Laemmle Sr, seeking to raise finance from the Standard Capital Company in 1936, allowed the company to buy a majority stock interest in Universal Pictures for $5.5 million, whereupon Standard Capital assumed operating control of the studio and Laemmle retired.

The effects of the involvement of Wall Street on the film industry are disputed. The Marxist view, expressed at the time by F. D. Klingender and Stuart Legg, was that big business had taken control of Hollywood. While they did not detect any significant change in production practices, they did imply an effect on the nature of the films produced: 'Whether the movies will regain their former financial success ultimately depends on whether the Morgans and Rockefellers will find it in their interest . . . to provide the masses with the type of pictures that alone will induce them to flock to their cinemas.'[26] In hindsight, however, the effects on the industry would seem to have been less severe than Klingender and Legg feared. Sklar suggests that 'there is every indication that Wall Street's interest coincided with that of Hollywood's old hands – to make as much money as possible' and asserts that what really matters 'is not who owns the movie companies but who manages them'.[27] This was demonstrated by the case of Paramount, which emerged from receivership in 1935 in the hands of a board consisting of bankers and financiers, but whose new management proved so ineffective that founder Adolph Zukor, kicked upstairs as chairman of the board, was brought back to take charge of production.

What emerged in the film industry during the 1930s was an organizational structure that separated financial and creative control. For economic film historians like Tino Balio, this distinction between ownership and management is the hallmark of a modern business enterprise.[28] The purse strings were held by the bankers and businessmen of the East Coast who raised capital, set budgets and took the key financial decisions. They were also responsible for hiring and firing the studio heads. Creative control, however, was exercised by the studio executives who were in charge of film production. These were the self-styled 'movie moguls' – men like Louis B. Mayer (MGM), Jack Warner (Warner Bros.), Harry Cohn (Columbia) and Darryl F. Zanuck (Twentieth Century-Fox) – who represented the public face of Hollywood.

Many myths have developed around the moguls, most of which were of their own making. As most of them were first or second generation Jewish immigrants of European extraction, their rise to power in Hollywood seemed to represent the American Dream that anyone, through hard work and enterprise, could achieve material wealth and social status. Much has been made of the ethnic and cultural origins of the moguls. Neal Gabler is in no doubt that their Jewishness was a crucial factor in their success:

> The Jews also had a special compatibility with the industry, one that gave them certain advantages over their competitors. For one thing, having come primarily from fashion and retail, they understood public taste and were masters at gauging market swings, at merchandising, at pirating away customers and beating the competition. For another, as immigrants themselves, they had a peculiar sensitivity to the dreams and aspirations of other immigrants and working-class families, two overlapping groups that made up a significant portion of the early moviegoing audience.[29]

While there is surely a kernel of truth in that, it is, however, a less than satisfactory reason for explaining the power of these men in Hollywood. For all their Jewishness and immigrant background, the moguls were passionate supporters of WASPish American culture who themselves became more American than the Americans. Mayer, for example, celebrated his birthday on the Fourth of July. Richard Maltby attributes the success of the moguls less to their ethnicity and more to their qualities of showmanship and flair. The moguls were extroverts who left the business side of the industry to their more conservative colleagues in New York and instead created their own fiefdoms in the sunny climes of southern California. The Hollywood of popular imagination was largely the creation of these men. 'They more or less deliberately set out to create in Hollywood a separate, enclosed world, whose image to the rest of America was as important an ingredient in the product they sold as were the stars or plots of individual films', Maltby writes. It was the moguls' uncanny knack for judging the taste of the public, which pleased distributors and exhibitors because they produced the sort of films audiences wanted, that, in Maltby's view, 'constituted the key to their autonomy from East Coast control'.[30] The highly publicized stories of their autocratic behaviour over stars and other employees was, to some extent at least, a publicity measure designed to create impressions of their power and control. Yet the moguls were not necessarily as secure or as powerful as their own myths would have us – or them – believe. They were frequently involved in bitter internal power struggles and their survival as studio heads was dependent upon their ability to deliver profitable films at economical costs. When the moguls lost their knack for judging public taste, even they were dispensable. The truth of this was vividly illustrated in 1951 when Mayer clashed with Nicholas Schenck, president of MGM's parent company Loew's Inc., and found himself unceremoniously dumped as chief executive of the studio that still bore his name.

THE STUDIO SYSTEM

During the 1930s and 1940s Hollywood institutionalized a mode of production that became known as the 'studio system'. As this mode of production coincided with the stabilization of a particular style of filmmaking that has been labelled 'classical', the term 'classical Hollywood cinema' has been used to describe a mode of film practice that includes both film style and production. David Bordwell asserts that 'the Hollywood mode of film practice constitutes an integral system, including persons and groups, but also rules, films, machinery, documents, institutions, work processes, and theoretical concepts'.[31] There is a dynamic relationship between production and style, which reinforce each other. On the one hand the standardization of production processes is a logical consequence of the desire to make films on a cost-effective basis – to streamline production for maximum profit. On the other hand the adoption of the same production processes across the industry leads to the standardization of product – so that a particular type of film becomes the norm. The typical film produced by the studio system was the 'classical' feature film: a narrative film, linear in construction, its characters existing in a fictional world governed by rules of verisimilitude. The classical film follows a straightforward narrative structure: it is unambiguous, proceeding in a logical cause-and-effect manner to a clear resolution in which goals are achieved and problems are resolved. And the style of a classical film is 'invisible': editing and camera work are seamless; they do not draw attention to themselves for stylistic effect but rather support the story-telling process.

The mode of production that sustained this style of classical cinema throughout the 1930s and 1940s was the studio system. The comparison has often been made between the Hollywood studio system and the mass-production, assembly-line techniques introduced into the motor car industry by Henry Ford. Film studios were production plants which operated according to a strictly demarcated division of labour: producers, screenwriters, art directors, costume designers, actors, directors, cameramen, editors and composers all performed their specific roles within the production process. This compartmentalization of production was due partly to the economic imperative of adopting the most efficient methods and partly to the unionization that occurred during the 1930s which reinforced the subdivision of working procedures. As a corrective to the fashionable *auteur* theory which assigns the prime creative role in filmmaking to the director, it should be noted that the overall control of an individual film within the studio system rested with its producer. In Hollywood's own discourse (as expressed in technical manuals and trade journals) the director was regarded as a technician, albeit an important one. Very few directors during the studio era enjoyed any real autonomy from studio control. For every William Wyler or John Ford (and even Ford regarded himself as a 'hired hand') there were a dozen studio directors such as John Cromwell, Michael Curtiz, Allan Dwan, W.S. Van Dyke, Alfred E. Green, H. Bruce Humberstone, Archie Mayo, Elliott Nugent, Irving Rapper, Richard Thorpe, Raoul Walsh or William Wellman – directors who were regarded as efficient 'journeymen'. (And most directors, incidentally, were men: only two women – Dorothy Arzner, formerly a film editor, and Ida Lupino, formerly an actress – enjoyed fully-fledged directorial careers under the studio system.)

The 1930s saw a change in studio management in which the role of the producer was redefined. At the decade's outset most studios operated a central-producer system with one producer in overall control of their entire output – the foremost example was Irving Thalberg, the 'boy genius' of MGM who died of a heart attack in 1937 – but this was abandoned in favour of a system of several senior producers each responsible for a particular number of films. While this was largely an economy and efficiency measure (one supervising producer could not keep close tabs on up to 50 films in the way that a producer working on two or three films at the same time could), it also had the effect of consolidating the power of the studio heads. At MGM, for example, Mayer had been jealous of Thalberg's influence and was quite happy to see the once all-powerful senior producer become effectively only the first amongst equals.[32] The unit-producer system, which was fully developed by the mid-1930s, would continue until the 1950s. It resulted in the development of production units within the studios that specialized in certain types of films. Examples of such units include that of Busby Berkeley at Warner Bros. during the 1930s, where he established a particular style of musical extravaganza, the Val Lewton Unit at RKO in the 1940s that specialized in the production of psychological horror films, and the famous Arthur Freed Unit at MGM that was responsible for the studio's great musicals of the late 1940s and early 1950s.

The production strategies of the studios were to produce a balanced output of around 50 films per year which, taken together, would guarantee an overall profit. The majors would produce both 'A' and 'B' pictures, though the ratio of 'As' to 'Bs' depended on the resources of the studio and its access to first-run theatres. The bread-and-butter of the majors was the star vehicle and each studio's relative position in the Hollywood hierarchy depended on how many major stars it had under contract. At the top of the hierarchy was MGM, whose publicity boasted 'more stars than in heaven', while further down were studios such as RKO, Columbia and Universal, which had only one or two top stars under contract. Universal's chief asset in the late 1930s was the singer Deanna Durbin, whose films have been credited with saving the studio from bankruptcy.[33] Occasional high-cost, high-risk 'prestige films' began to appear again during the late 1930s as the economic health of the industry improved, but most of these tended to be produced by independents – Walt Disney's *Snow White and the Seven Dwarfs* (1937) and *Fantasia* (1940), David O. Selznick's *Gone With the Wind* (1939) – and were atypical of studio production strategies.

Critical opinion is divided as to whether the studio system provided a creative context for filmmaking. For critics of Hollywood, the standardization of product was an indication of its conservatism. The left-wing intellectuals of the Frankfurt School (a group of academics who had moved to the United States after the Nazis came to power in Germany) argued that all films were the same, irrespective of which studio had produced them: 'That the difference between the Chrysler range and the General Motors products is basically illusory strikes every child with a keen interest in varieties . . . The same applies to the Warner Brothers and Metro Goldwyn Mayer productions.'[34] For its admirers, however, the studio system had raised American film to the level of a classical art. The zenith of the studio system, both commercially and artistically, is by general consent agreed to have been reached in 1939 when Hollywood produced more recognized 'classics' than in any other year. The list includes, but is not limited to, *Stagecoach*, *Wuthering Heights*, *Beau Geste*, *Gunga Din*, *Only Angels Have Wings*, *Mr Smith Goes to Washington*, *The Hunchback of Notre Dame*, *Young Mr Lincoln*, *Destry Rides Again*, *The Cat and the Canary*, *Ninotchka*, *Intermezzo*, *The Wizard of Oz* and *Gone With the Wind*. 'Taken all together', one critic later remarked, 'the films of 1939 are the best argument for the studio system.'[35] The efficacy of the studio system was also recognized by André Bazin: 'The American cinema is a classical art, but why not then admire in it what is most admirable, i.e. not only the talent of this or that filmmaker, but the genius of the system, the richness of its ever-vigorous tradition, and its fertility when it comes into contact with new elements.'[36]

The charge that all Hollywood films are the same is, of course, absurd (what the Frankfurt School objected to was that the underlying ideologies of all films, as they perceived them, were the same). This is where the comparison with the motor industry is not entirely appropriate. While every Model T Ford turned off the production line will be identical, every film has to be different in order to attract the paying public. Conventionally differences between films have been theorized in terms of genre, but there is a strong case to make that there are also differences by studio. 'Each studio has a personality; each studio shows special emphases and values', Leo Rosten observed in 1941.[37] Rosten attributed the differences to the producers involved – again, incidentally, highlighting where creative agency within the studio system rested – but there are other factors, too, which account for differences between studios. Studio style can be observed both visually and generically. Warner Bros., for example, favoured a visual style that was characterized by low-key lighting and bare sets – an economic rather than an aesthetic decision – whereas MGM's films were notable for their glossy sets and high-key lighting, due in large measure to the influence of Cedric Gibbons, the studio's supervising art director from 1927 to 1957. Certain studios also came to be associated with certain genres: Warner Bros. with the gangster film, MGM with the literary adaptation, Universal with the horror film, Paramount with the sophisticated melodrama. And star-genre combinations further differentiated a studio's product: thus RKO produced the Fred Astaire-Ginger Rogers musicals, MGM the William Powell-Myrna Loy comedies, Warner Bros. the James Cagney and Humphrey Bogart crime films. The extent of generic specialization should not be exaggerated for the majors, which each offered a balanced production schedule encompassing a range of genres, but it was very apparent in the case of the studios of 'Poverty Row', such as Republic (associated primarily with series westerns and adventure serials), Monogram (crime films) and PRC (westerns and horror films).

The institutional structures and working practices of the studio system represent a fundamental challenge to any form of film history that privileges the role of the auteur. Yet, paradoxically, some of the acknowledged *auteurs* of American cinema (Howard Hawks, John Ford, Frank Capra, Alfred Hitchcock – the British director who moved to Hollywood in 1939) not only worked within the studio system but also made some of their best films under those conditions. Andrew Sarris, the foremost American auteurist critic, believed that '[there] were (and are) weak and strong directors as there were weak and strong kings . . . The strong director imposes his own personality on a film; the weak director allows the personalities of others to run rampant.'[38] However, this is an imprecise and unsatisfactory explanation. It is only by exploring the production contexts in which directors worked that the extent of authorial possibilities within the studio system can be determined.[39]

The example of Orson Welles and *Citizen Kane* (1941) makes an interesting test case both for the *auteur* theory and for the extent to which the studio system was able to nurture individual creativity. The authorial legend of Welles (promoted by Welles himself and reaffirmed by numerous biographers) is that he was the 'boy genius' who came to Hollywood at the age of 25, made a film that is widely regarded as one of, if not the, best of all time, but then found that his talent could not flourish in the philistine world of Hollywood and was condemned for the rest of his career to wander Europe as a jobbing actor and peripatetic filmmaker constantly trying to raise money to make films outside the studio system. The fact that Welles made his most acclaimed film within the studio system is conveniently overlooked. Welles, who had come to prominence with his Mercury Theater on the radio in the late 1930s, was brought to Hollywood by new RKO president George J. Schaeffer and was given virtually *carte blanche* to develop any project he wished. The unprecedented creative freedom afforded Welles was part of a bid by Schaeffer to bring both artistic and commercial prestige to RKO, which had always been the weakest of the Big Five in terms of both talent and resources. *Citizen Kane*, a biopic of a newspaper magnate consciously modelled on William Randolph Hearst, was a remarkably bold, innovative, multi-layered film that stands out from the norm of classical Hollywood due to its stylistic virtuosity, complex narrative structure and unresolved ending. Yet this film – which Sarris described as 'the work that influenced the cinema more profoundly than any American film since *Birth of a Nation*'[40] – was as much a product of the studio system as any of the 'classics' of 1939. Welles performed the roles of actor, director, producer and co-writer, but he also had to rely on the support of top Hollywood technicians to realize his creative vision. The virtuosity of *Citizen Kane* is due in no small measure to Gregg Toland's cinematography (especially the bravura use of deep-focus), Percy Ferguson's set designs and Vernon Walker's special effects. Thomas Schatz suggests that the significance of *Citizen Kane* is that it illustrates 'the rapid ascent of the producer-director as an industrial and artistic force in prewar Hollywood, as well as of the remarkable range of product differentiation and the licence for stylistic innovation'.[41] In the wake of Welles's triumph other directors, including Capra, Hitchcock and Hawks, would become producers of their own films during the 1940s – a development that, in the long term, would help all directors achieve greater autonomy from studio control. As far as Welles was concerned, however, he never again experienced the level of artistic freedom he had enjoyed with *Citizen Kane*. He also never again made a film that was as thematically rich or as technically accomplished. *Citizen Kane* is rightly regarded as one of the milestones of American cinema, but it was as much a product of 'the genius of the system' as it was of the genius of Orson Welles.[42]

HOLLYWOOD AT WAR

America's entry into the Second World War came as welcome news to many in Hollywood. The US Justice Department, which in 1938 had signalled its intent to challenge monopolistic exhibition practices in the film industry, agreed to drop the pending lawsuit for the duration of the war. In autumn 1941 the film industry was also facing a Senate investigation into whether Hollywood was conducting a propaganda campaign to urge American entry into the war. As the anti-fascist themes of films like *Blockade* (1938), *Confessions of a Nazi Spy* (1939) and *The Great Dictator* (1940) had hardened into the openly pro-interventionist narratives of *Foreign Correspondent* (1940) and *Sergeant York* (1941), the isolationists in Congress had a point – until it was rendered irrelevant by the surprise Japanese attack on Pearl Harbor on 7 December and Hitler's declaration of war on the USA four days later. Hollywood's economic health was strengthened by a wartime boom that saw attendances at motion pictures reach their highest ever levels by 1945–6. This is attributed to the defence industries relocating workers to major urban-industrial centres, which boosted attendance at first-run theatres. The combined profits of the eight majors had already been increasing before the war, from $20 million in 1940 to $35 million in 1941. This upward trend accelerated, reaching $50 million in 1942 and $60 million per year from 1943 to 1945.[43]

The war signalled some changes in industry practices and production strategies. The most significant changes, which were related to one another, were a reduction in the number of films produced by the majors and an increase in production costs. In the five years before Pearl Harbor the eight majors had between them released 1,833 feature films, whereas in the five years after Pearl Harbor they released 1,395 – a reduction of almost 25 per cent.[44] The Big Five cut down their annual production of around 50 films to an average of 30 between 1942 and 1946. This reduction was due partly to wartime shortages and partly to the studios concentrating on top-notch 'A' features in order to exploit the increased attendances at first-run theatres. At the same time, however, the average production costs of feature films increased – from $336,600 in 1942 to $554,386 by 1945 – due partly to wartime inflation but also to the shift to higher production values across the board.[45] By 1945 the Big Five were concentrating almost exclusively on 'A' features for the first-run market.

The demand for movies was such that the majors turned increasingly to independent producers to supply them. Some of the biggest box-office hits of the war and immediate post-war years were made by independent producers: *Sergeant York* (Howard Hawks for Warner Bros.), *Since You Went Away* (David O. Selznick), *Duel in the Sun* (Selznick) and *The Best Years of Our Lives* (Sam Goldwyn). There were different levels and degrees of 'independent' production ranging from in-house units operating within a particular studio (such as Cecil B. De Mille at Paramount and Walter Wanger at Universal) to genuine 'outsider' producers who turned to the majors for distribution and exhibition of their films (such as Goldwyn and Selznick). The bigger studios, such as MGM and Paramount, were more resistant to the trend towards independent production, whereas smaller studios such as RKO depended on outside producers for the majority of their 'A' class product (RKO, for example, distributed films for Goldwyn, Disney, Britain's Rank Organization and Liberty Pictures, a short-lived production company formed at the war's end by Frank Capra, George Stevens and William Wyler).

The war's most immediate impact upon Hollywood was a shortage of manpower and the exodus of a number of top male stars for military service. Clark Gable, James Stewart, Douglas Fairbanks Jr and Robert Montgomery all joined the US military (and all saw active service) – following the example of British actor David Niven, who had been the first to enlist, rejoining the British Army in 1939. While new male stars emerged to fill the gap (Humphrey Bogart, Alan Ladd, Gregory Peck), the most prominent new stars of the 1940s were women (Betty Grable, Ingrid Bergman, Veronica Lake, Lauren Bacall, Rita Hayworth). Several prominent directors also joined the armed services where they went to work making propaganda documentaries, including William Wyler (*The Memphis Belle*), John Ford (*The Battle of Midway*), John Huston (*The Battle of San Pietro*) and Frank Capra (the celebrated *Why We Fight* series made to explain the origins of the war to American servicemen).

The war led to a closening of the ties between Hollywood and Washington as the film industry was co-opted into the national patriotic effort. The government recognized that

Hollywood could be a powerful instrument of propaganda in promoting the American war effort to both domestic and overseas audiences. An Office of War Information (OWI) was set up in June 1942 under the directorship of radio commentator Elmer Davies. The OWI in turn had a Bureau of Motion Pictures, run by newspapermen Lowell Mellett and Nelson Poynter, which advised the film industry on war matters. The relationship between Hollywood and the OWI was not without its points of friction. When the OWI threatened to become interventionist by requesting script approval – motivated by its dissatisfaction with early attempts at war propaganda films – there was an outcry in Hollywood which caused the OWI to back down. By 1943, however, the OWI and the film industry had settled into a more comfortable working relationship that proved mutually beneficial. The OWI was able to see the sort of films it wanted, while the studios realized that working with the OWI could be profitable in that audiences were hungry for war-themed entertainment.[46]

Hollywood responded to the political and social conditions of wartime in various ways. Early in the war there was a vogue for what have been termed 'conversion narratives' which set out to persuade the American people of the necessity for abandoning isolationism and becoming involved in the war. The most successful of these was *Casablanca* (1942), the classic romantic melodrama which has widely been interpreted as an allegory of isolationism and interventionism. Set in a quaintly studio-bound visualization of the North African city, *Casablanca* tells the story of Rick Blaine (memorably played by Humphrey Bogart), a cynical and embittered American expatriate who maintains an emotional detachment from the many refugees who pass through his café ('I stick my neck out for nobody') but who is persuaded to abandon his neutrality in order to help a resistance leader and his wife – who also happens to be Rick's former lover – escape from the Nazis. In this interpretation Rick's acceptance of the need for personal sacrifice and involvement in the war ('I'm no good at being noble, but it doesn't take much to see that the problems of three little people don't amount to a hill of beans in this crazy world') represents the awakening of America's moral conscience. It has even been suggested that the title refers to Roosevelt's decision to enter the war having fought the 1940 presidential election on a neutrality platform: 'casa blanca' means 'white house' in Spanish.[47]

Two new genres, both mandated by the OWI, became prominent in Hollywood's wartime production: the patriotic combat film (*Dive Bomber, Air Force, Bataan, Guadalcanal Diary, The Story of GI Joe, Objective: Burma!*) and the sentimental homefront melodrama (*Since You Went Away, Happy Land, Tender Comrade*). The needs of propaganda were also met with films demonizing the enemy (*Hitler's Children, Behind the Rising Sun*) and promoting favourable images of America's allies, including Britain (*Mrs Miniver, Forever and a Day, The White Cliffs of Dover*), China (*The Keys of the Kingdom*) and – most controversially – the Soviet Union (*Song of Russia, The North Star, Mission to Moscow*). The last of these, made at the personal instigation of Roosevelt, was a part-documentary, part-fictional adaptation of the memoirs of Joseph E. Davies, former US ambassador to the Soviet Union, which adopted a distinctly sympathetic stance towards the Stalinist regime.[48]

The culmination of Hollywood's war effort, both artistically and commercially, came with Sam Goldwyn's 1946 production *The Best Years of Our Lives*, which explores the effects of war on American society from the points of view of three servicemen returning home at the end of the war and facing the problems of adjusting to the peace. Directed by William Wyler, with a screenplay by playwright Robert E. Sherwood, *The Best Years of Our Lives* won seven Academy Awards (including Best Film, Best Director and Best Screenplay), while its box-office grosses of over $10 million made it the most successful film of the 1940s.[49] A film notable for its realism and restraint, *Best Years* addresses the problems faced by many ex-servicemen – physical disability, emotional trauma, unemployment, marital infidelity, alcoholism – and due to the universality of its themes it was well received overseas as well as in the United States. For once, Hollywood was seen as having produced a film that had social relevance rather than being merely a provider of escapism. 'Its touches of human frailty make one realize the almost total lack of that sort of thing in most American films', one critic remarked, 'and it achieves its statements of social criticism

without the edge of bitterness.'[50] There were some voices on the left, however, who thought the narrative was too contrived. Abraham Polonsky, for example, felt that characters in the film were nothing more than 'general stereotypes of the film industry' and criticized the all-too-easy resolution of social problems: 'Fascism is solved with a punch; a bad marriage by the easy disappearance of the wife; the profound emotional adjustment of a handless veteran by a fine girl; the itchy conscience of a banker by too many drinks.'[51] In the sense that it promotes the ideal of heterosexual romantic love as the basis of social reconstruction, *Best Years* is very much in the tradition of the classical Hollywood narrative: army sergeant Al Stephenson (Fredric March) returns to his patient wife Millie (Myrna Loy), handless sailor Homer Parrish (played by real-life amputee Harold Russell) marries the faithful sweetheart who was waited for him, while air force captain Fred Derry (Dana Andrews), whose wife has carried on affairs in his absence, finds a new love in Al's sensible daughter Peggy (Teresa Wright). *Best Years* is not a radical film – it would take the Vietnam War to radicalize Hollywood's treatment of the maladjusted veteran in films such as *Coming Home* (1978) and *Born on the Fourth of July* (1989) – but that is not to say that its treatment of real problems and anxieties is any less sincere. The solutions it offers, as Robert B. Ray observes, are consensual:

> Despite the divisive quarrels that developed among the three veterans from different services, who return home to their previous, and distinct, social standings, the film's opening sequence (where the three men crowded together in the nose of a B-29 to spot home-town landmarks) clearly implied the superficiality of all subsequent misunderstandings. The concluding wedding scene that united the pilot, the navy groom, and the army sergeant in one deep-focus shot blurred the probability that they were condemned to live in separate, and, to some extent, competing worlds.[52]

In this regard, *The Best Years of Our Lives* exemplifies perfectly Hollywood's ability both to reflect social concerns and to offer consensual solutions to them.

HUAC AND HOLLYWOOD

It is an indication of how quickly political circumstances can change that both the officially mandated propaganda of *Mission to Moscow* and the liberal social conscience of *The Best Years of Our Lives* would, within the space of only a few years, be decried as 'unAmerican' by conservative opinion. The House Committee on UnAmerican Activities (HUAC) had first put

Hollywood under the microscope in 1938 when concerns had arisen that the anti-fascist films of the late 1930s had been inspired by communists. In 1940 the committee's chairman, Martin Dies, named James Cagney, Fredric March and Humphrey Bogart as suspected 'reds', along with writer Philip Dunne, though all four cleared themselves through their testimony to the committee. The anti-communist witch-hunters of HUAC were quiescent during the war while the Soviet Union was an ally, but the cause was taken up again after the war when hysteria about the spread of Communism both at home and abroad reached new heights.

Even before HUAC came to Hollywood, conservative forces in the film industry had been making their voices heard. The Motion Picture Alliance for the Preservation of American Ideals, whose members included such luminaries as Walt Disney, Gary Cooper, John Wayne and Ginger Rogers's mother Lela, had been formed in 1944 with the aim of purging the film industry of 'communists, radicals and crackpots'. And in 1946, the new president of the Motion Picture Producers Association, Eric Johnston, told the Screenwriters' Guild: 'We'll have no more *Grapes of Wrath*, no more *Tobacco Roads*, we'll have no more films that deal with the seamy side of American life. We'll have no more films that treat the banker as a villain.'[53] It is ironic that Johnston should have singled out two films directed by John Ford, whose own politics could hardly be described as radical. Johnston's statement needs to be seen in the context of a mood in which political opinion on the right was reacting against the policies of the pre-war Roosevelt administration. The new chairman of HUAC, Congressman J. Parnell Thomas, was a vocal opponent of Roosevelt and the New Deal.

In 1947 HUAC convened a set of hearings to investigate 'Communist Infiltration in the Motion Picture Industry'. First in closed session, then in public hearings in Washington, the committee interviewed 24 so-called 'friendly' witnesses (including Walt Disney, Gary Cooper, Ronald Reagan and director Sam Wood) who testified to the extent of communist influence in Hollywood, and eleven 'unfriendly' witnesses who refused to co-operate on the grounds that the investigation was a violation of their constitutional rights. Historians agree that there was, in fact, little real evidence of communist influence or sympathy placed before the committee and that HUAC had picked on Hollywood largely for its publicity value.[54] In this sense the committee was successful. There was certainly much publicity arising from the behaviour of the 'Hollywood Ten' who refused to testify as to their political allegiances and who were subsequently held in contempt and briefly imprisoned.[55] While there was some opposition to HUAC within the film industry, exemplified in the formation of the Committee for the First Amendment (whose members included Humphrey Bogart, Lauren Bacall, Danny Kaye, Gregory Peck and John Huston), this did not translate into direct support for the 'Ten'. Indeed, the Hollywood establishment co-operated with the committee through the notorious Waldorf-Astoria decision whereby a group of producers and studio executives (meeting at the New York hotel of that name) pledged not to employ suspected communists and agreed to the institution of a blacklist. Ironically, and much to the embarrassment of the Hollywood establishment, one of the original Ten, Dalton Trumbo, went on to write pseudonymously the Academy Award-winning screenplays for *Roman Holiday* (1953) and *The Brave One* (1956).

The blacklist might be seen as a tactic, rather like the introduction of the Production Code, to safeguard the film industry from external intervention by agreeing to a form of voluntary self-regulation. If so, then its success was short-lived: HUAC returned to Hollywood in 1951, this time against the background of the Korean War and the 'Red Scare' engendered by Senator Joseph McCarthy. Now under the chairmanship of John Wood, the committee proved to be even more inquisitorial than it had in 1947. The distinction between communists, left-wing sympathizers and socially progressive liberals was blurred in the committee's eyes. Over 200 people who refused to testify were blacklisted and there was also an informal 'grey list' for those whose politics were considered even slightly suspect. Careers were destroyed by rumour and hearsay, while blacklisted personnel were forced to leave Hollywood or work under assumed names. The most famous casualty was Charlie Chaplin, whose permit to re-enter the United States was revoked while he was abroad promoting his film *Limelight*; Chaplin did not set foot in America for another 20 years.

Two films, both allegorical, both now regarded as classics, represent Hollywood's different responses to the HUAC hearings. Elia Kazan, who had 'named names' in 1952 – a decision almost certainly prompted not by political conviction but by an understandable desire to save his own career, as Kazan had already established himself as 'the director of choice wherever social issues were central to the production' with films like *Gentleman's Agreement* and *A Streetcar Named Desire*[56] – justified his stance with *On the Waterfront* (1954), written by another 'friendly witness' Budd Schulberg, which revolved around the dilemma faced by a dockyard worker whether to inform on the infiltration of the union by organized crime (a metaphor for the Communist Party of America). It was rewarded by the Hollywood establishment with eight Academy Awards, including Best Film, Best Director, Best Screenplay and Best Actor (Marlon Brando). In contrast, Carl Foreman, who had refused to testify before the committee, wrote the western *High Noon* (1952), in which a town marshal (ironically played by friendly witness Gary Cooper, who won his second Best Actor Oscar) finds himself deserted by the good citizens of Hadleyville (for which read Hollywood) when a gang of outlaws who had terrorized the town several years earlier (for which read HUAC) returns. The subtext of the film was not lost on contemporaries. The liberal periodical *The Nation* commented: 'There must be times these days when Mr Foreman feels that he too, like Marshal Kane, has been deserted by those who should have helped him stand off the bullies and tough guys whose aggressions have so largely destroyed the moral fiber of the Western town that goes by the name of Hollywood.'[57] Foreman, indeed, was forced to spend the rest of his career working in Europe.

John Belton suggests that, with fifty years' hindsight, the HUAC hearings and the blacklist 'emerge as nightmarish aberrations which properly belong to another time, another place, and another generation'.[58] Yet this assessment is at odds with the mixed reception afforded Elia Kazan at the 1999 Academy Awards when he was presented with a Lifetime Achievement Award: the fact that many prominent figures refused to applaud suggests that the fallout from the HUAC hearings remains a point of contention within the Hollywood community. HUAC itself remained in existence until the 1970s, but its influence waned from the mid-1950s as the 'Red Scare' paranoia subsided. The blacklist was gradually broken, though it took the best part of a decade before Hollywood would openly employ blacklisted personnel – Trumbo was hired by producer-star Kirk Douglas to script *Spartacus* (1960) under his own name – and even then some still found it difficult to find work.

THE DECLINE OF THE STUDIO SYSTEM

In the 1950s, however, Hollywood faced a threat even more dangerous than HUAC, namely the debilitating effects of a long-term decline in cinema attendances in America. This decline had become apparent in the late 1940s – following the peak of 1946, attendances fell off to 78 million per week in 1947, 67 million per week in 1948 and 62 million per week in 1949 – though at first the industry tried to kid itself that the decline simply marked a return to normal levels following an artificial boom during the war years. By the 1950s, however, the fallacy of this view could no longer be concealed. The 1950s saw the most severe decline in cinema-going since the Depression – 56 million per week in 1950, down to 50 million by 1955 and 30 million by 1960 – but this time there was to be no reversal of the trend.[59]

The received wisdom is that the decline in attendances was due to the arrival of television – reflected by Hollywood's view of television as an 'enemy' in the early 1950s – though this interpretation has increasingly been challenged in recent years by historians who point out that there is no precise correlation between television ownership and cinema attendances. The decline in cinema-going had begun in the mid-1940s, but it was not until the early 1950s that television had established itself as a mass medium to rival the cinema. While television was undoubtedly a factor, it was not necessarily the only or even the most important one. 'Television was merely a highly visible, superficial symptom of a much more profound change in postwar entertainment patterns rather than the direct cause of the movies' downfall', Belton argues; 'the source of the problem lay elsewhere – in the economic and socio-cultural transformation of blue- and white-collar Americans during the post-war period into the "leisured masses".'[60] Social and demographic changes in America after the war impacted upon the habit of cinema-going: the 'baby boom' saw more people getting married and starting their own families; the increasing affluence of American society made a greater range of leisure opportunities available; and, perhaps most significantly, the acceleration of suburbanization, as people bought cars and houses, reduced the demographic core of the cinema audience, which had always been concentrated in metropolitan areas. It was not only that the size of the audience was diminishing, moreover, but also that it was fragmenting. The family audience which for so long had provided the bread-and-butter for the so-called 'mom and pop' neighbourhood theatres was disappearing, while teens and baby boomers made up the bulk of the theatrical audience.

Hollywood might have responded more quickly to the declining audience if it had not been preoccupied with another concern at the same time. The war had delayed rather than averted the crisis that had been pending since the late 1930s. The Justice Department's anti-trust suit against the majors was reopened in 1946, and on 3 May 1948 the US Supreme Court made its historic ruling that the majors' control of first-run theatres constituted an illegal monopoly and ordered that exhibition should be separated from production and distribution. Referred to as the Paramount Decree, as Paramount had the most extensive theatre holdings and was the first of the studios to be named in the suit, this signalled an end to the system of vertical integration in the film industry. Some historians date the end of the studio system precisely to this date, and, if that might seem somewhat reductive, all are agreed that the Paramount Decree represents a highly significant and symbolic moment for the history of the industry. The eight majors – the Little Three had contested the anti-trust suit alongside the Big Five as they also benefited from the restrictive exhibition practices even though they did not own any theatres – were no longer guaranteed screen time for their films, particularly as the Supreme Court had also outlawed blind and block booking.

The studios fought the decision in the courts to no avail and were soon forced to sign consent decrees divesting themselves of their exhibition interests. Paramount was the first to do so in 1949, followed by RKO in 1950, Warner Bros. and Twentieth Century-Fox in 1952, and MGM, belatedly, in 1959.

Divorcement, coupled with the decline of the cinema audience, dealt a severe blow to the economic base of the film industry. The 1950s witnessed major structural changes in the industry as Hollywood sought to come to terms with these dual problems. Shorn of their movie theatres, the majors now had to concentrate on their role as producer-distributors. There was, once again, a policy of retrenchment and cost-cutting: the majors cut back on their production programmes and made further economies by selling off assets and by releasing stars and other personnel from long-term contracts. The trend during the late 1940s and throughout the 1950s was increasingly towards independent production, with the majors providing studio facilities and distribution for the increasing number of independents. The producer-unit management model that held sway during the 1930s and 1940s was replaced during the 1950s by what has been termed the 'package-unit' model in which individual projects were put together by producers, directors and stars on a film-by-film basis, with agents such as the William Morris Agency, Famous Artists and the Music Corporation of America (MCA) becoming closely involved in the deals.[61] Some studios adapted to the new conditions more easily than others, though the only company to cease production was RKO, which closed down in 1957 when Howard Hughes, who had bought the studio for $9 million in 1948, sold off the last of its assets. Universal, which had one of the more flexible management structures, was probably the main beneficiary of the new conditions. Its production strategy was based on a combination of low-budget formula films made by the studio's own contract staff, particularly comedies (Abbott and Costello, Francis the Talking Mule, the Ma and Pa Kettle series) and horror/science-fiction hybrids (*It Came from Outer Space*, *The Creature from the Black Lagoon*), with more prestigious films made by outside stars and directors. James Stewart, one of the biggest box-office draws of the decade, was tempted to Universal by a profit-sharing deal to star in 'A' class vehicles such as the western *Winchester '73*, the comedy *Harvey* and the musical biopic *The Glenn Miller Story*. Universal's fortunes contrasted sharply with the once-mighty MGM, which of all the majors clung stubbornly to the old ways of doing things. As Schatz observes: 'While its competitors steadily decentralized production, cut back contract personnel to reduce overhead, and made innovative deals with outside independents, Metro reverted to a centralized production setup, with its contract system, regulated output, and star-genre formulations.'[62] Not only was the studio's organization and production strategy out of step with the other majors, but MGM's parent company Loew's insisted on hanging on to its theatre holdings for as long as possible in a vain attempt to fight the Supreme Court's ruling, not relinquishing them until 1959. The company was also beset by bitter corporate power struggles which by the end of the decade had seen the back of Mayer, his replacement Dore Schary and president Nicholas Schenck.

Retrenchment and reorganization within the industry went hand-in-hand with a sustained attempt to lure audiences back into the cinemas. Hollywood adopted a variety of strategies to reclaim its dwindling audiences, but they were all predicated on the assumption that television was the cause of the decline. Thus the film industry sought to differentiate itself from television by offering more extravagant entertainment, with higher production values, than television could provide. Hence the vogue in the 1950s for big, outdoor films such as biblical epics (*The Ten Commandments, Ben-Hur*), westerns (*The Searchers, The Big Country*) and musicals (*South Pacific, Oklahoma!*), reaching its zenith with Mike Todd's production of *Around the World in 80 Days* (1956), a global travelogue with an all-star cast. The increasing use of colour and the industry's adoption of anamorphic widescreen processes (the technology for which had existed since the 1920s) such as CinemaScope, VistaVision, Todd-AO, Technirama and Panavision (which became the industry standard by the 1960s) were part of this strategy to attract audiences away from television. While individual films were enormously successful at the box-office, however, these widescreen-colour extravaganzas did nothing to halt the overall decline of cinema audiences. Had Hollywood been less focused on winning back the general audience, it might have responded more directly to the increasing fragmentation of the audience, especially the greater prominence of teenagers, but it was only small independent producers such as American International Pictures who identified this potentially lucrative market with 'exploitation' films such as *I Was a Teenage Werewolf* and *I Was a Teenage Frankenstein*.

Most historians date the end of the studio system as being some time around the mid to late 1950s. By this time the notion of Hollywood as a 'film factory' turning out movies on a production-line basis had ceased to be an accurate description of the industry. The reality was that Hollywood now concentrated on producing fewer but bigger films. The 'B' movie had all but disappeared by the end of the 1950s, a casualty of television which could produce generic formula entertainment at lower cost. And instead of an annual production of 40–50 films a year that taken together would ensure an overall profit, the studios pinned their hopes on two or three major films a year – a trend, originating in the 1950s, that has been the foundation of Hollywood's production strategy ever since.

SIX

New Hollywood

If, by common consent, the end of the 'old' Hollywood can be identified at *c*. 1960, then the period of the 'new' Hollywood has already surpassed it in historical longevity. In truth, of course, there was no single moment at which the old Hollywood ceased to exist and a new one took its place. The decline of the studio system and the emergence of new industrial structures and practices occurred gradually over a period of years, even decades. At its longest this transitional period could be extended to some two and a half decades, for, while some historians date the decline of the studio system from the Paramount Decree of 1948, the emergence of 'New Hollywood' has generally been identified at some point between the late 1960s and the mid-1970s. In this version of Hollywood's history, the transitional period from the 'old' to the 'new' lasts as long as the 'golden age' itself. That said, however, there is a good case for identifying 1960 as a symbolic turning point due to the congruence of a number of different factors. As David Bordwell elaborates:

> In the film industry, it was widely believed that at the end of the decade Hollywood had reached the end of its mature existence. *This Was Hollywood*, the title of a 1960 book by publicist Beth Day, summarizes many reasons for considering the year as a turning point. Most production firms had converted their energies to television, the dominant mass-entertainment medium by the mid-1950s; many had reduced their holdings in studio real estate; stars had become free agents; most producers had become independent; the B-film was virtually dead. By 1960, a certain technological state of the art had been reached: high-definition color films, wide formats, and high-fidelity magnetic sound had set the standard of

quality that continues to this day. Moreover, other styles began to challenge the dominance of classicism. The international art cinema, spearheaded by Ingmar Bergman, Akira Kurosawa, certain Italian directors, and the French New Wave, offered a more influential and widely disseminated alternative to Hollywood than had ever existed before.[1]

The extent to which post-1960 Hollywood is significantly different from its pre-1960 incarnation has been a matter of much debate. Whereas, in the 1960s and 1970s, journalistic discourse stressed the 'new', the consensus amongst film historians since then has moved towards a perspective that emphasizes continuity rather than change. Thus, Robert B. Ray asserts that 'the majority of American movies of the 1970s were remarkably similar to those of the 1930s'.[2] While Ray is concerned principally with film style, Jim Hillier's study of the industrial context of New Hollywood leads him to suggest that 'Hollywood in the late 1980s and early 1990s does not look that different from the Hollywood of the previous forty years'.[3] There are several issues at stake here, of course, focusing on whether differences between the old and the new are conceptualized in terms of film production, film content or film style. This chapter examines the history of post-1960s Hollywood and considers how the film industry has responded to the changing social, economic and political environment of America and the world in the later twentieth century.

A CHANGING INDUSTRY

On the face of it, the fact that seven of the eight majors that had dominated production during the studio era have remained the leading film companies into the twenty-first century would seem to suggest that the Hollywood oligopoly has remained intact. The casualty was RKO, which ceased operations in 1957; United Artists almost followed suit in the early 1980s but survived through a corporate merger with MGM. The same famous names and emblems – the MGM lion, the Paramount mountain, Columbia's Statue of Liberty and Twentieth Century-Fox's searchlights – remain highly visible, symbolic links with Hollywood's past. Yet those links probably are more symbolic than actual, for the companies that bear their names would be unrecognizable to the moguls who ran them during the studio era. Hollywood in the last four decades of the twentieth century – and in the first decade of the twenty-first – has undergone significant and far-reaching changes in industrial structures and practices.

There were good reasons during the 1960s for the sense of crisis that permeated the industry. The decline in the size of the cinema audience, which had become acute during the 1950s, continued apace. By the late 1960s cinema attendances had fallen to a quarter of their mid-1940s peak, falling below 20 million per week for the first time since records exist, and reaching an all-time low of 16 million in 1971. Thus it was, as John Belton observes, that 'over a span of a mere 20 years, between 1948 and 1968, Hollywood had lost three-quarters of its audience and the nature of moviegoing in America had evolved from the status of ingrained habit to infrequent diversion.'[4] It was not merely that the size of the audience had diminished, furthermore, but that its social composition had altered fundamentally, with a demographic of males between their mid-teens and mid-twenties replacing the family audience that had existed during the 1930s and 1940s. Yet Hollywood responded tardily, and reluctantly, to the changing audience, clinging to the idea that family-oriented entertainment films were the key to its economic health. The fact that such films have continued to be highly successful at the box-office – most dramatically illustrated by the continuing success of Disney's cartoon features from *The Jungle Book* (1967) to the computer-enhanced animations of the 1990s such as *Aladdin* and *The Lion King* – has obscured the more pertinent fact that such films are exceptional rather than typical.

Hollywood's response to crisis, initially, was to carry on much as it had done before. Genre films and star vehicles dominated the studios' production strategies for most of the 1960s. Westerns (*How the West Was Won*, *The Professionals*, *The Sons of Katie Elder*, *True Grit*), sophisticated comedies (*Lover Come Back*, *That Touch of Mink*, *Charade*) and musicals (*Mary Poppins*,

The Sound of Music, *Funny Girl*) dominated the box-office, while the leading stars were mature icons whose popularity had been established in earlier decades (John Wayne, Cary Grant, Rock Hudson, Doris Day, Elizabeth Taylor). It was only towards the end of the decade that relatively new stars such as Paul Newman, Steve McQueen and Clint Eastwood made an impact on the box-office charts – the latter due to the phenomenal international success of a trilogy of 'spaghetti westerns' made in Europe. Roy Pickard suggests that it was the studios' continued reliance on established formulas that was 'their big mistake'. 'In the Sixties,' he elaborates, 'the studios, many of them no longer distinguishable from one another either in style or personnel, began to look like dinosaurs, huge combines that were hopelessly old-fashioned and ill-equipped to meet new and constantly changing situations.'[5] Certainly the distinctive studio 'personalities' that Leo Rosten had identified in 1941 were no longer apparent by the 1960s; stars and directors were now free agents and the studios operated more as production facilities and distributors. For Douglas Gomery, however, the continuation of old formulas was a matter of economic necessity, as 'the economic basis of the Hollywood industry remained the regular production of genre films, those most easily sold on a mass scale around the world'.[6]

The disappearance of a large section of the audience left Hollywood in a precarious state. The uncertainty within the film industry left the studios prime targets for corporate takeovers. The second half of the 1960s witnessed a wave of acquisitions, of which the most significant feature was that giant conglomerates whose primary interest was not actually in the motion picture industry began buying film studios. Thus, Paramount was taken over by the mining and manufacturing giant Gulf + Western in 1966 as part of its expansion into the leisure industry; United Artists was acquired by the Transamerica Corporation, which had its base in insurance and car rental, in 1967; Warner Bros., which had already merged with Canadian Seven Arts in 1967, was taken over in 1969 by Kinney National Services, whose main business was in car rental, parking lots and funeral parlours; and, in the same year, property tycoon Kirk Kerkorian bought a controlling interest in MGM, supposedly because he wanted to use Leo the Lion as a symbol for his hotel chain. David A. Cook explains the interest of these conglomerates in the film industry by pointing out that, despite their financial difficulties, the film studios 'represented good investments, since their shares were temporarily under-valued and they owned huge tracts of real estate in one of the nation's most lucrative markets'.[7] They also owned libraries of old films that could be sold to television, whose potential as a lucrative secondary market was only now being recognized.

It was only towards the end of the 1960s that Hollywood responded, tardily, to the changing social composition of the cinema audience. Some of the biggest box-office hits of the late 1960s were films that focused on young adult protagonists and their problems of social adjustment: *The Graduate*, *Bonnie and Clyde*, *Easy Rider*, *Midnight Cowboy*. Censorship was relaxed when the outdated Production Code was replaced in 1968 by a rating system, with films now being classified 'G' (general audi-ence), 'PG' (parental guidance), 'R' (restricted, meaning that children under sixteen were admitted only if accompanied by an adult) and 'X' (no admittance to the under-sixteens, later changed to under-seventeens). The conventional explanation for the relaxation of censorship is to see it as a response to changing social values and morals during the 1960s. It can also be seen, however, as part of the film industry's strategy of adjust-ing to the changing audience. Just as the introduction of the Production Code in the 1930s had been motivated, in large measure, by Hollywood's desire not to alienate its large family audience, its demise came about when Hollywood recognized that its audience had fragmented and that its main customers were a younger generation who had different expectations of motion picture content. The new climate was not to everyone's liking. Many of Hollywood's old masters retired in the 1960s, with John Ford, for one, declaring that 'Hollywood is now run by Wall St. & Madison Ave., who demand "Sex & Violence". This is against my conscience & my religion.'[8] For others, how-ever, the new climate allowed more serious and 'adult' films, exemplified in the critical and commercial success of John Schlesinger's *Midnight Cowboy*, the sexually frank story of the friendship between a Texan 'stud' (Jon Voight) and a tubercular con artist (Dustin Hoffman), which became the first 'X' film to win the Academy Award for Best Picture.

Most commentators identify the arrival of 'New Hollywood' with the late 1960s and early 1970s when restructuring in the film industry provided an opportunity for a new generation of filmmakers to come to the fore. This historical moment might be compared to the emergence of the *Nouvelle Vague* in France a decade earlier, as it represented both a generational shift within the film industry and the recognition by studio executives that younger directors were more likely to deliver the box-office hits the industry so desperately needed. Hollywood has always depended on new blood, of course, but what was remarkable about the late 1960s and early 1970s was the number of new directors who won both critical and popular acclaim with their early films, including Dennis Hopper (*Easy Rider*, 1969), Paul Mazursky (*Bob & Carol & Ted & Alice*, 1969), Woody Allen (*Take the Money and Run*, 1969), Alan Pakula (*Klute*, 1969), Bob Rafelson (*Five Easy Pieces*, 1970), Hal Ashby (*Harold and Maude*, 1971) and Peter Bogdanovich (*The Last Picture Show*, 1971). There were also several filmmakers who, although having made their directing debuts somewhat earlier, came to prominence at this time, including Robert Altman (*M*A*S*H*, 1970) and John Cassavetes (*Faces*, 1968). The emergence of this 'American new wave' was followed within a few years by the first films from the so-called 'movie brats', a generation of film school graduates born (mostly) during or after the Second World War, including Steven Spielberg (*Duel*, 1971), George Lucas (*American Graffiti*, 1973) and Martin Scorsese (*Mean Streets*, 1973). Francis Ford Coppola, although having made his directing debut some years earlier, is also generally included in this group, as he enjoyed his biggest critical and commercial success in the early 1970s with the two *Godfather* films. Peter Biskind elaborates upon the significance of these filmmakers within the industry:

> Before anyone realized it, there was a movement – instantly dubbed the New Hollywood in the press – led by a new generation of directors. This was to be a directors' decade if ever there was one. Directors as a group enjoyed more power,

prestige and wealth than they ever had before. The great directors of the studio era, like John Ford and Howard Hawks, regarded themselves as nothing more than hired help (over-) paid to manufacture entertainment, storytellers who shunned self-conscious style lest it interfere with the business at hand. New Hollywood directors, on the other hand, were unembarrassed – in many cases rightly so – to assume the mantle of the artist, nor did they shrink from developing personal styles that distinguished their work from that of other directors.[9]

It would be misleading, however, to suggest that these filmmakers represented a homogenous group any more than had the *Nouvelle Vague*. Nor did they all fulfil their early promise. The careers of Coppola and Bogdanovich have been erratic to say the least, Hopper is far better known as an actor and Lucas has concentrated almost exclusively on producing rather than directing since his record-breaking *Star Wars* (1977). Only Spielberg and Scorsese have produced a consistent enough body of work in the subsequent decades to be regarded as genuine *auteurs*, Spielberg enjoying unprecedented commercial success while Scorsese has earned a critical reputation as a director who mixes bold and challenging films (*Taxi Driver*, *Raging Bull*, *The Last Temptation of Christ*, *Kundun*) with more obvious commercial fare (*The Color of Money*, *GoodFellas* and a violent remake of *Cape Fear*).

To what extent, however, was the emergence of new filmmakers accompanied by any significant changes in film style and content? By any standards, films of the late 1960s and early 1970s were markedly different from those of only a decade or so earlier. This period, indeed, witnessed probably the most far-reaching changes in the nature of American movies since the arrival of the talkies. At the start of the 1960s, Hollywood had still predominantly been a consensual cinema that supported the social and political institutions of America. By the end of the decade it had been transformed into, if not quite an anti-establishment cinema, then certainly a cinema that was increasingly critical of the value systems it had for so long implicitly endorsed. The social upheavals of the 1960s – the intensification of the campaign for Civil Rights, the women's movement, the emergence of many strands of sub-cultures and the violent protests against American involvement in the Vietnam War – were bound to leave their mark on Hollywood. The film critic David Thomson, looking back with thirty years' hindsight, felt that the strength of American cinema in the early 1970s was that 'the best films . . . were based on a more rueful and troubled notion of who we were'.[10]

Numerous commentators have pointed to the increasingly loose and open-ended narratives of films in the late 1960s and early 1970s as evidence of New Hollywood's stylistic departure from the classical model. Thomas Elsaesser, for example, argued that in contrast to the tightly structured and goal-oriented narratives of classical Hollywood, New Hollywood was characterized by 'the almost physical sense of inconsequential action, of pointlessness and uselessness, a radical scepticism, in short, about the American virtues of ambition, vision, [and] drive'. He detected, furthermore, 'a kind of malaise already frequently alluded to in relation to the European cinema – the fading confidence in being able to tell a story'.[11] Thomson similarly noted the 'disdain for tidy or cheerful endings' in films such as *McCabe and Mrs Miller* and *The Last Picture Show*, along with 'the absurdity of such notions as villainy or heroism'.[12] Certain established Hollywood genres, such as the western and the musical, were almost to disappear during the 1970s, while others were subject to a form of revisionism that questioned their classical form. In 1970s detective films, for example, such as Robert Altman's *The Long Goodbye* and Roman Polanski's *Chinatown*, the solution of the mystery leaves the protagonists bitter and disillusioned, the implication being that things would have been better left unsolved. The 'fading confidence in being able to tell a story' that Elsaesser detected was most apparent in the emergence of the 'road movie' – literally the most open-ended type of narrative – in films like *Easy Rider* and *Five Easy Pieces*. The success of *Easy Rider*, which took $20 million at the North American box-office against a production cost of only $400,000, suggests that the young audiences at whom it was aimed responded to its theme of social alienation ('A man went looking for America and couldn't find it anywhere', the film's poster declared). It also used unusual techniques (a hand-held camera, squeezed anamorphic images, flash-forwards and a hallucinatory drugs 'trip' sequence) that had more in common with avant-garde and experimental cinema than with the classical Hollywood narrative.

For New Hollywood's critics, the 1970s represent a missed opportunity when a more adventurous and innovative cinema seemed, for a short while, a real possibility, only for that possibility to be denied by conservative interests within the film industry. Cook, for example, believes that 'the vaunted "Hollywood Renaissance" – the European-style auteur cinema that prevailed briefly in America from 1967 to 1975 – was an aberration in the film industry's sixty-year history to date, one that came into being mainly by default at a time of economic and political crisis.'[13] This interpretation, however, is not entirely fair. The film industry was happy to invest in new filmmakers and 'alternative' filmmaking practices as long as they were successful at the box-office. But few of the new directors were to prove any more adept at judging popular taste than the studio executives who backed them, as the commercial failure of Hopper's *The Last Movie* and Rafelson's *The King of Marvin Gardens* demonstrated. Bogdanovich followed the evocative *The Last Picture Show* with a flawed attempt to revive the screwball comedies of the 1930s (*What's Up, Doc?*) and then lost his way with a number of expensive failures (*Daisy Miller*, *At Long Last Love*, *Nickelodeon*). It was left to 'movie brats' Spielberg (*Jaws*) and Lucas (*Star Wars*) to revive Hollywood's economic fortunes in the mid-1970s with a very different style of filmmaking.

BLOCKBUSTERS, SLEEPERS AND INDEPENDENTS

The most prominent production trend in New Hollywood, and that which most differentiates it from the classical period, is the phenomenon of the 'blockbuster' movie. Whereas during the studio period the majors produced an annual programme of 'A' and 'B' features, with the occasional high-profile 'prestige' film, the trend since then has increasingly been towards single movies that it is hoped will bring large profits to the industry.

This trend had its origins in the transitional period between the studio era and New Hollywood, though there is disagreement as to whether the epics of the 1950s and early 1960s are truly the progenitors of the special effects-driven blockbusters and action movies that have been so central to Hollywood's production strategy since the mid-1970s.

Thomas Schatz places the blockbuster in a long-term historical context, arguing that '[the] key to Hollywood's survival and the one abiding aspect of its postwar transformation has been the steady rise of the movie blockbuster'. He identifies three films (*The Ten Commandments* in 1956, *The Sound of Music* in 1965 and *Jaws* in 1975) which 'redefined the nature, scope, and profit potential of the blockbuster movie, and which lay the foundation for the films and filmmaking practices of the New Hollywood'.[14] Screenwriter William Goldman, one of the most astute contemporary observers of the film industry, similarly once remarked that the three most commercially significant Hollywood films were *Gone With the Wind* (in real terms still the most successful film ever made), *The Sound of Music* ('because its phenomenal success paved the way for expensive imitations which almost destroyed Hollywood') and *Jaws* ('because it changed everybody's thinking as to how large an audience there was out there').[15]

The idea of the individual film as a major box-office phenomenon undoubtedly took root in the 1950s. The cycle of biblical/historical sagas (*Quo Vadis?*, *The Robe*, *The Ten Commandments*, *Ben-Hur*) were the first 'epic' films since the silent era. They were costly to produce, but their success lent credence to the view that big, expensive films could return massive profits.[16] 'The beauty of the big picture nowadays', one commentator observed in 1955, 'is, of course, that there seems to be no limit to what the box office return may be.'[17] The corollary of that logic – that big pictures also ran the risk of incurring huge losses – was rudely demonstrated by Fox's *Cleopatra* (1963), which, despite its $62 million gross, still did not return a profit against its $44 million cost (the economics of production and distribution requiring that a film needs to recoup over twice its cost at the box-office in order for the producer to break even). Although Fox recovered its losses (and more) with the success of

The Sound of Music, which earned a staggering $135 million worldwide in its first two years and toppled *Gone With the Wind* as the biggest-grossing movie of all time, the studio's attempts to repeat its success with a string of expensive musicals in the late 1960s (*Doctor Dolittle, Star!, Hello Dolly!*) were dismal failures.

It was during the 1970s, however, that the blockbuster took root in Hollywood as an annual rather than an occasional event, as each of the major studios began investing in films that were deemed to have blockbuster potential. Following the failure of the big-budget musicals of the late 1960s, the success of Universal's *Airport* in 1970 ($45 million domestic rentals against a production cost of $10 million) paved the way for a cycle of disaster movies (*The Poseidon Adventure, Earthquake, The Towering Inferno*) that proved to be the box-office phenomenon of the first half of the 1970s. The disaster movie cycle is significant in so far as its tendency towards special effects and pyrotechnics at the expense of plot and characterization was a portent of future developments. *The Towering Inferno* is especially significant in that for the first time two studios (Fox and Warner Bros.) combined to produce it – a risk-reduction strategy that proved lucrative for both partners (it returned $48 million in domestic rentals against a production cost of $14 million).[18] Although other films in the early 1970s surpassed the disaster movie at the box-office – *The Godfather* ($86 million) and *The Exorcist* ($89 million) – they did not spawn similar cycles. Despite winning another Academy Award for Best Picture, *The Godfather Part II*'s rentals of $30 million were barely a third of the first film, while *Exorcist II: The Heretic* took a disappointing $14 million.[19]

Most commentators agree that *Jaws* was the first 'modern' blockbuster. This verdict is based both on its massive box-office success (it was the first film to take over $100 million in North American rentals alone) and on its promotion as a major 'event' movie (through an extensive publicity campaign in the media and the licensing of product tie-ins). 'If any single film marked the arrival of the New Hollywood', Schatz believes, 'it was *Jaws*, the Spielberg-directed thriller that recalibrated the profit potential of the Hollywood hit, and redefined its status as a marketable commodity and cultural phenomenon as well.'[20] In some respects *Jaws* represents continuity with previous blockbusters, for example in being based on a best-selling novel (*Airport*, *The Godfather*, *The Exorcist*), but in others it set new trends, such as its timing (it was released during the supposedly quiet summer period) and wide opening. While *Jaws* was quickly to be surpassed by *Star Wars* at the box-office, *Star Wars* was, in fact, initially treated by its backer Fox as a 'cult' movie that opened on fewer screens and was granted a wider release when it proved to have 'legs'.

Timothy Corrigan argues that the New Hollywood blockbuster is a phenomenon quite different from the epics of previous decades:

> Far more than traditional epic successes or the occasional predecessor in film history, these contemporary blockbuster movies became the central imperative in an industry that sought the promise of massive profits from large financial investments; the acceptable return on these investments (anywhere from $20 million to $70 million) required, most significantly, that these films would attract not just a large market, but all the markets.[21]

The post-*Jaws*, post-*Star Wars* blockbuster is more than just a film: it is an 'event' in its own right that permeates into the wider culture through saturation advertising and takes on a life of its own through product tie-ins (novelizations, comic books, toys and food products). The expectations of cinema-goers are raised by trailers and magazine promotions weeks, or even months, before the film itself reaches the screen, when it opens on a nationwide basis at thousands of cinemas. The 464-screen opening of *Jaws* in 1975 now seems modest in comparison to the 3,000-plus screen openings afforded to some movies in the 1990s. Since the early 1990s a domestic box-office gross of $100 million has come to represent the industry's benchmark for success, of which up to a third may be taken on the all-important first weekend which is seen as the make-or-break time for a major film.

The massive box-office grosses for blockbusters since the late 1980s – *Batman* (North American grosses of $251 million),

Jurassic Park ($357 million), *Independence Day* ($306 million), *The Phantom Menace* ($430 million) – have certainly been distorted by inflation. In terms of the number of paid admissions their success does not compare with that of *Gone With the Wind*, *Snow White and the Seven Dwarfs* or *The Sound of Music*.[22] Yet, as J. Hoberman points out, when inflation is taken into account, 'seven of the all-time blockbusters were still made between 1975 and 1985'.[23] Furthermore, those seven films (*Jaws*, *Star Wars*, *The Empire Strikes Back*, *Raiders of the Lost Ark*, *E.T.: The Extra-Terrestrial*, *Return of the Jedi* and *Indiana Jones and the Temple of Doom*) were all made, either jointly or separately, by director Steven Spielberg and producer-director George Lucas. The Spielberg-Lucas films are seen as marking a new trend for the blockbuster, away from genres such as the historical epic and the disaster movie and towards the fantasy-adventure film. While, for their admirers, their films embody the sense of wonderment that lies at the heart of the cinema-going experience, for their detractors they represent a juvenilization of cinema in which narrative complexity and psychological depth are sacrificed for size, spectacle and special effects.

How can the enormous popular success of the Spielberg-Lucas films be explained? For all the effort and expense that is thrown into promotion, publicity alone cannot sell a film to a wide audience. Even Spielberg (*1941*) and Lucas (*Howard the Duck*) have experienced occasional failures. Their success arises from the nature of their films as entertainment. These archetypal New Hollywood filmmakers actually embody certain 'old' Hollywood virtues such as uncomplicated storytelling and emotional appeal. Lucas's *Star Wars* films are nothing if not old-fashioned, mythical sagas of good versus evil, while Spielberg's *E.T.* is an unashamedly sentimental story of friendship and loss. If the critics' preferences were for the more innovative, open-ended and ambiguous films of the early 1970s, cinema audiences since the mid-1970s have overwhelmingly favoured the narrative certainties of the adventure film. Whether set 'a long time ago in a galaxy far, far away' (*Star Wars*) or a comic-book past of Nazis and treasure hunts (*Raiders of the Lost Ark*), these films offer moral certainties (good triumphs over evil) and old-fashioned virtues (heroism and chivalry). In this sense they fulfil a deep emotional need.

The success of the Spielberg-Lucas films had a number of significant effects for the film industry. For one thing, *Star Wars* and *Raiders of the Lost Ark* marked the emergence of what William Goldman called the 'comic-book movie' as the most lucrative genre in New Hollywood.[24] It was largely a consequence of the Spielberg-Lucas phenomenon, moreover, that sequels and series films became central to the industry's production strategy. Once the preserve of Hollywood's Poverty Row, sequels and series have been elevated to blockbuster status in New Hollywood. If, on one level, sequels are seen as further evidence of New Hollywood's timidity and lack of imagination, on another level, it might be argued, they have brought a degree of stability to an industry that is at the best of times an inherently risky business. 'After the experimentation of the early seventies', Noël Carroll observed in 1982, 'genres have once again become Hollywood's bread and butter.'[25]

It would be mistaken, however, to suggest that there is nothing more to New Hollywood than the blockbuster. The logic of the blockbuster syndrome, that a small number of films are expected to reap massive profits, is that the majority of films cannot therefore be blockbusters. The major blockbusters are released during the summer and Christmas holiday periods, but exhibitors still need films to show throughout the rest of the year. Schatz suggests that 'we might see New Hollywood as producing three different classes of movie: the calculated blockbuster with the multimedia maketplace and franchise status in mind, the mainstream A-class star vehicle with sleeper-hit potential, and the low-cost independent feature targeted for a specific market and with little chance of anything more than "cult film" status.'[26]

Hollywood has always been alive to the potential of the 'sleeper' – a less expensive film that becomes a box-office success. It is ironic that George Lucas, one of the pre-eminent blockbuster filmmakers, first came to the industry's attention with 'a classic sleeper', *American Graffiti*, which returned $55 million in domestic rentals against a budget of only $775,000.[27] Perhaps the most significant sleeper of New

Hollywood was *Rocky* (1976), an unexpected critical and commercial success ($54 million) that won the Academy Award for Best Picture, spawned four sequels and launched Sylvester Stallone on a career as one of New Hollywood's most highly paid stars. The problem with the sleeper is that success is, almost by definition, impossible to predict. The uncertainty of success is demonstrated by the difference between the major box-office hits of 1989 and 1990. The summer of 1989 is widely regarded as Hollywood's 'blockbuster summer' when the calculated money-spinners (*Indiana Jones and the Last Crusade*, *Batman*, *Ghostbusters II*, *Lethal Weapon 2*) enjoyed saturation releases and between them grossed over $1,000 million at the domestic box-office. In 1990, however, the expected blockbusters (*Dick Tracy*, *Total Recall*, *Die Hard 2*) were outdone by two modestly budgeted romantic comedies (*Pretty Woman* and *Ghost*) and by one family comedy (*Home Alone*).[28]

It is in the third of Schatz's categories, however, 'the low-cost independent feature', that some of the most innovative and interesting of New Hollywood cinema is to be found. One of the distinguishing features of New Hollywood, indeed, is the space that it has opened for independent filmmakers in contrast to the rigid structures of the studio system. A word of caution needs to be exercised over the term 'independent', of course, as there are very few filmmakers who have complete autonomy from studio control. Even so, however, there is ample evidence to suggest that New Hollywood has proved more receptive to the presence of an *auteur* cinema than classical Hollywood ever was. It is difficult to imagine talents such as Woody Allen, John Cassavetes, David Lynch, Jim Jarmusch, Terrence Malick or John Sayles prospering in the 'old' Hollywood. Furthermore, New Hollywood has allowed space for minorities and social groups who have previously been marginalized or excluded from the industry to assert their presence. Black filmmakers (Melvin and Mario Van Peebles, Spike Lee, John Singleton, Ernest Dickerson), homosexual filmmakers (Gus Van Sant, Todd Haynes) and women directors (Susan Seidelman, Amy Heckerling, Penny Marshall, Kathryn Bigelow, Penelope Spheeris) are still in a minority, and their successes have been sporadic, but their

presence is at least an indication that Hollywood has become more receptive to the social groups they represent.

It is simply untrue to claim, as some critics have done, that an American *auteur* cinema did not survive the 1970s. The continued existence of the *auteur* in New Hollywood is both a cultural and an industrial phenomenon. On a cultural level, directors are 'names' familiar to the cinema-going public in a way that they had rarely been during the studio era. The proliferation of both popular and intellectual film and entertainment magazines ensures that directors such as Tim Burton and Quentin Tarantino achieve 'cult' status in a way that studio directors never did. The cult of celebrity, in turn, makes these directors more bankable. In an industrial context, more-over, the looser structures of the film industry since the end of the studio system allow a greater level of freedom for the director on the floor. Although it is fashionable to decry New Hollywood for its reliance on formulaic blockbusters, there has probably been a higher ratio of genuinely original work in the modern period than during the classical era. The difference, however, is in the way the films are marketed, with distinct and separate audiences in mind. During the classical era both *Gone With the Wind* and *Citizen Kane* would have been seen by the industry as prestige pictures made for essentially the same audience, whereas in New Hollywood the *auteur* films are associated with a niche market of cinephiles that is distinct from the general audience for more mainstream fare. Such *auteur* films will usually be handled by specialist distributors (such as Miramax Pictures) and exhibited on the 'art house' circuit. The production of such critically acclaimed films as Steven Soderbergh's *sex, lies and videotape* (1989), Ridley Scott's *Thelma and Louise* (1991), Robert Altman's *Short Cuts* (1993), Steven Spielberg's *Schindler's List* (1993), Martin Scorsese's *The Age of Innocence* (1993), Clint Eastwood's *The Bridges of Madison County* (1995) and Sam Mendes's *American Beauty* (2000) is evidence that there is still a place for serious, intelligent, adult-themed films in New Hollywood.

POLITICS AND NOSTALGIA IN NEW HOLLYWOOD

One of the charges levelled against New Hollywood is that, other than for a brief moment in the early 1970s, it has been politically, culturally and ideologically conservative. This charge does not stand up to close scrutiny. A more accurate description of New Hollywood's politics is that since the late 1960s there have coexisted, on the one hand, a conservative, reactionary tradition and, on the other hand, a liberal, progressive tradition. Neither of these traditions has ever been entirely dominant within the industry, but there have been moments when one or the other has been, albeit temporarily, in the ascendancy. The fact that both these traditions have produced commercially successful films provides yet another warning against reading films in this, or any other era, as straightforward reflections of social conditions.

Robert B. Ray suggests that it was in the late 1960s and early 1970s that American cinema 'divided conspicuously into a Left and a Right'. The symbolic point of divergence, he argues, was the assassination of President Kennedy in 1963:

> For the Left, the assassination signalled that the old assumptions had failed, that there was something deeply wrong with American institutions and culture. The Right, on the other hand, regarded the assassination as an individual act of evil whose source could be located and eliminated.[29]

The 'left' cycle of films, including the likes of *The Graduate*, *Bonnie and Clyde*, *Cool Hand Luke*, *2001: A Space Odyssey*, *Easy Rider*, *Butch Cassidy and the Sundance Kid* and *The Wild Bunch*, gave expression to the voice of the counter-culture by featuring protagonists who were positioned outside society, either fleeing from it or rebelling against it. The 'right' cycle, on the other hand, including such films as *Bullitt*, *Coogan's Bluff*, *Dirty Harry*, *The French Connection*, *Shaft*, *Walking Tall* and *Death Wish*, typically featured authoritarian heroes (often cops or vigilantes) engaged in a war against the disruptive elements in society. The box-office success of both these cycles suggests that audiences were responsive to both visions of American society.

A similar distinction between 'left' and 'right' films can be identified in the filmic representations of the Vietnam War in a cycle of films during the late 1970s and 1980s. With the exception of the patriotic John Wayne vehicle *The Green Berets* (1968), there had been very few films directly about Vietnam during the war itself. Another decade was to pass before the cinema began to come to terms with America's defeat (morally if not necessarily militarily) and Vietnam suddenly became, in the words of one critic, 'Hollywood's favourite war'.[30] Whereas, during the Second World War, the ideological role of the combat movie had been to legitimize war, the Vietnam combat films of the 'left' cycle served the opposite purpose by portraying its futility and confusion. The overriding impression of films such as Francis Ford Coppola's *Apocalypse Now* (1979), Oliver Stone's *Platoon* (1986) and Stanley Kubrick's *Full Metal Jacket* (1987) is that war makes no sense. *Platoon*, for example, dramatizes the ideological division of America over the war through the metaphor of a conflict between two platoon sergeants, the 'good' Sergeant Elias (Willem Dafoe) and the 'bad' Sergeant Barnes (Tom Berenger). The enemies are not the Vietcong but other Americans: Barnes kills Elias, only to be slain himself by new recruit Chris (Charlie Sheen) who has been 'blooded' on his first tour of duty. Yet while the 'left' films of Stone, Coppola and Kubrick won critical acclaim, the biggest commercial success for a Vietnam War film came from the 'right' in the form of *Rambo: First Blood Part II* (1985), in which a former special services veteran (portrayed in barely articulate fashion by Sylvester Stallone) returns to Vietnam to rescue American prisoners still being held there years after the war has ended and single-handedly decimates the North Vietnamese and Russian armies. *Rambo* was part of a cycle of similar films – *Missing in Action* had told much the same story a year earlier – but it was the most successful in capturing a mood in Reaganite America. The ideological agenda of Rambo was to rewrite the 'result' of the Vietnam War, made explicit when Rambo asks his commanding officer 'Do we get to win this time?'

The 1980s have generally been characterized as a decade when the right was in the ascendancy both in Hollywood and in America generally. The films of the 1980s have been seen as responding to the political and social values represented by the presidency of Ronald Reagan, especially through their emphasis on strong leadership and national self-confidence. Robin Wood, for example, has argued that the political upheavals of the 1970s, especially the withdrawal from Vietnam and the Watergate affair that led to the downfall of Richard Nixon, served to undermine confidence in the nation's leaders and that the ideological agenda of 'Reaganite' cinema was to restore that confidence.[31] There is much evidence to support this contention, certainly, not least the fashion for films celebrating the American military (*Top Gun*, *Iron Eagle*) and the revival of Cold War narratives which saw Americans triumphant over Communism (*Red Dawn*, *Rocky IV*, *Rambo III*). Yet, while such films may legitimately be described as 'Reaganite' entertainment, elsewhere in 1980s cinema there is evidence that the social values of Reaganism were being questioned. Oliver Stone's *Wall Street* (1987), ostensibly an endorsement of Reaganite economics (exemplified in the dictum of Michael Douglas's aggressive insider-trader: 'Greed is good!'), is actually critical of the financial institutions and practices that allow a character like Gordon Gekko to reach a position of power. And, albeit more on the fringes of Hollywood than in the mainstream, directors such as David Lynch (*Blue Velvet*) and Tim Hunter (*River's Edge*) offered a distinctly jaundiced view of life in, respectively, small-town and urban America in the 1980s.

Reaganite cinema has been described as 'a cinema of reassurance, optimism, and nostalgia'.[32] One of its recurring themes is that of harking back to a sort of golden age in the 1950s and early 1960s before Vietnam and Watergate had dented Americans' confidence and self-belief. This nostalgia takes various different forms, ranging from a romanticized pæan to childhood (*Stand By Me*) to a salutatory hymn to the pioneers of the US space programme (*The Right Stuff*). It also explains a vogue for time-travel films (both *Back to the Future* and *Peggy Sue Got Married* contain the obligatory joke about people from the 1980s finding themselves in the 1950s and being ridiculed when they say that Ronald Reagan is the president) and the popularity of sentimental fantasies which, if not necessarily set in the past, nevertheless reflect 'old-fashioned' values (*Cocoon*, *Field of Dreams*). The Marxist critic Fredric Jameson has coined the term 'nostalgia film' to describe films either set in the past or invoking the values of the past. The nostalgia film, he argues, arose from a situation in which 'we were unable today to focus on our own present, as though we have become incapable of achieving aesthetic representations of our own current experience'. The nostalgia film, therefore, is somewhat removed from the films addressing present day social problems that critics had so admired in the early 1970s. For Jameson, predictably, the nostalgia film is 'a terrible indictment of consumer capitalism itself – or, at the very least, an alarming and pathological symptom of a society that has become incapable of dealing with time and history'.[33]

While Jameson provided a critique of contemporary American cinema from the perspective of the intellectual left, Michael Medved's book *Hollywood vs. America*, which caused a stir upon its publication in 1992, represented an all-out attack on Hollywood from the voice of the moral right. Medved, film critic of the *New York Post*, argued that America was in a period of moral and cultural decay and that Hollywood was largely to blame for this state of affairs. In language that recalled the Motion Picture Research Council of the 1930s, Medved damned Hollywood as 'an alien force that assaults our most cherished values and corrupts our children. The dream factory has become the poison factory.'[34] Medved's targets ranged from the 'irresponsible' violence of the action movies of stars such as Arnold Schwarzenegger to the sexually explicit content of films such as *Fatal Attraction* and *Basic Instinct* (both big box-office successes) and even took in the supposed debunking of Jesus Christ in Scorsese's controversial *The Last Temptation of Christ* for good measure.

Although there is no evidence of a direct causal relationship, it has often been the case that books about the cinema are linked to trends in film production. In the 1970s, for example, the publication of Marjorie Rosen's *Popcorn Venus* and Molly Haskell's *From Reverence to Rape*, both of which were widely reviewed and debated, seemed to anticipate a number of films dealing with women's issues in the sort of terms the authors had discussed (examples of such films in the mid- and late 1970s included Scorsese's *Alice Doesn't Live Here Anymore*, Paul Mazursky's *An Unmarried Woman*, Richard Brooks's *Looking for Mr Goodbar* and Claudia Weill's *Girlfriends*). Whether by chance or design, in the aftermath of Medved's book there was a trend towards what became known as 'feel-good' movies that affirmed the sort of traditional values and morality that Medved believed had disappeared from Hollywood. The romantic comedy *Sleepless in Seattle* (1993), for example, affirmed faith in romantic love rather than sexual gratification, while *Dave* (1993) was nothing less than a modern reworking of Capra's fables of the 1930s in which basic American decency overcomes political self-interest. The film that most caught the mood of America during the early years of the Clinton presidency, however, was Robert

Zemeckis's *Forrest Gump* (1994), which painted a nostalgic picture of recent American history through the eyes and adventures of a small-town simpleton (Tom Hanks) with a nice line in home-spun philosophy ('Life is like a box of chocolates – you never know what you're going to get'). *Forrest Gump* was a multiple Academy Award-winner (Best Picture, Best Director, Best Screenplay, Best Actor) and a huge box-office success (domestic grosses of $329 million and worldwide of $635 million made it the fourth biggest film of the 1990s behind *Titanic, The Phantom Menace* and *Jurassic Park*). *Forrest Gump* came to be seen, like *The Best Years of Our Lives* half a century earlier, as paradigmatic of social concerns in America at the time. Yet, depending upon one's perspective, the film can be seen as either liberal or conservative in its ideology. On the one hand, it demonstrates progressive credentials in that it is critical of war and social prejudice and features a single mother (Mrs Gump, played by Sally Field) as a positive role model. Its success at the Oscars could be explained in terms of its being 'the sort of mushy, faintly liberal stuff the Academy likes'.[35] On the other hand, however, it can be seen as a critique of the counter-cultural values of the 1960s (it is implied that Forrest's girlfriend Jenny contracts AIDS due to promiscuity and drug-taking) and an endorsement of social conservatism. It won the approval, for instance, of the right-wing presidential candidate Pat Buchanan who echoed Medved when he described the film as 'a morality play, where decency, honesty, and fidelity triumph over the values of Hollywood'.[36] What these different responses would seem to indicate is that *Forrest Gump* appealed simultaneously to both left/liberal opinion and conservatives. Its tremendous popular success suggests that it appealed to a wide section of the American public – or at least the cinema-going public – and that it became, like *The Best Years of Our Lives*, one of those 'state-of-the-nation' films that attracts wider commentary in society at large.

THE GLOBAL ECONOMY OF NEW HOLLYWOOD

Hollywood has always been a global institution. Even during the studio period it was a rule of thumb in the film industry that while an 'A' feature would typically recoup its production costs in the North American market, the bulk of its profits would come from its foreign revenues. In New Hollywood the balance between domestic and foreign revenues has shifted towards a ratio of approximately 40:60 and even up to 30:70 for some blockbusters. Europe and Japan are the major overseas markets for Hollywood movies which, increasingly, are produced with the international market in mind. The increasing importance of the overseas market has brought about significant changes both in New Hollywood's business practices and in the style and content of its films. In the last two decades of the twentieth century, especially, the forces of global capitalism, a renewed faith in the economics of the free market and technological advances have combined to put film at the forefront of what critics of globalization have variously dubbed the 'Hollywoodization', 'Coca-Colonization' or 'MacDonaldization' of world culture.[37]

Hollywood has rarely, if at all, been stable for long periods. The majors, which had been forced to respond to the Depression in the 1930s, to divorcement in the 1940s, to the rise of television in the 1950s, to the wave of corporate mergers and acquisitions in the 1960s and to the emergence of the 'movie brats' as a force to be reckoned with in the 1970s, had to adapt yet again in the 1980s and 1990s in response to changing economic environments and industrial structures. This time it was the expansion of the media and leisure industries that necessitated change and restructuring at the corporate level. Entertainment has become the second largest American export category (after military hardware) and the major film studios have now become part of supra-national entertainment and media empires. The key concept in the latest round of corporate mergers and acquisitions has been that of 'synergy' – the recognition that different entertainment media can do better collectively than separately. The majors now came within the orbit of multi-billion dollar media corporations with interests in other entertainment and leisure industries. This process was signalled in 1985 when the Australian media tycoon Rupert Murdoch acquired the ailing Twentieth Century-Fox (which had been in the red for three successive years) and brought it within the orbit of his News International Corporation which also has interests in press and television. Fox's profitability was restored through supplying film and television products for Murdoch's television outlets, including Fox Television in the USA and the satellite station British Sky Broadcasting which broadcasts throughout Europe. Murdoch's acquisition of Fox was followed in 1989 by a merger between Warner Communications and Time, Inc., to create Time Warner. This move aligned Time's magazine and cable television channels with Warner's film studios, recording interests and worldwide distribution network, thus creating 'the largest communications and media enterprise in the world'.[38] It also resulted in one of the most lucrative franchises of the 1990s, as Time owned DC Comics, whose Batman comic strip was turned by Warners (with the aid of the dark vision of director Tim Burton) into the box-office mega-hit of 1989, spawning three sequels and a blitz of spin-off merchandising that, for the first film alone, was worth over $1 billion – four times its domestic box-office earnings.[39] Time Warner has itself since merged with the Internet giant AOL (America OnLine) to create an even more powerful corporate megalith.

It was not the interests of corporate synergy alone, however, which motivated all of this new round of acquisitions. In 1989 and 1990 the Japanese electronics giants Sony and Matsushita took over Columbia Pictures and MCA/Universal respectively, for the sums of $3.4 billion and $6.5 billion, the latter acquisition representing 'the largest single take-over of an American company by a foreign concern'.[40] These acquisitions were part of an on-going battle between the Japanese companies focusing on competing technologies for home entertainment. In the 1970s Sony had lost out when its Betamax home video system had lost out to the cheaper VHS system of its rival; the corporation's acquisition of Columbia was, to some degree at least, an attempt to steal a march on its rivals over digital formats for film and music. Although it was widely rumoured in the early 1990s that Sony intended to switch to a new video format (Columbia's library of nearly 3,000 film titles and 23,000 television episodes being pawns in the battle), legal challenges ensured this did not in fact transpire. Thereafter, the new Sony Pictures devoted its energies to trying to establish a film franchise that would ensure a steady income from movie releases and licensed merchandising. There were persistent rumours in the late 1990s that Sony intended to produce its own series of James Bond films to rival the long-running, highly lucrative franchise of MGM/UA, though again this was forestalled in the courts. The abortive rival Bond series was described as 'just one of several franchises now being developed by Sony to provide an annuity in sequels; others include *Men in Black*, *Jumanji*, *Bad Boys*, *Godzilla*, *Starship Troopers*, *Charlie's Angels* and *Ghostbusters*'.[41] At the time of writing the success of *Spiderman* (2002), which became the first film to pass a $100 million gross on its opening weekend, suggests that Sony has found the franchise it had been looking for.

The takeover of Hollywood studios by foreign interests (an attempt by Giancarlo Parretti of Pathé Communications to gain control of MGM/UA in the early 1990s failed when Parretti's financial chicanery was exposed) was made possible by the *laissez-faire* policies of the Reagan government, which had deregulated the marketplace. The Supreme Court decision that had forced the studios to relinquish their exhibition interests in 1949 was reversed in 1985, whereupon the majors immediately began buying into cinema chains again. This decision, which effectively gave rise to a new period of vertical integration for the film industry, also coincided with the rise of the multiplex cinema – the multiple-screen, usually out-of-town cinemas that have become the face of modern exhibition. Their re-entry into the exhibition sector has resulted in the majors increasing their control over which films could be shown and where, to the detriment of independent producers and distributors. Moreover, the majors have expanded their exhibition interests into overseas markets, establishing their own chains of multiplexes in other territories. Paramount and Universal, for example, combined forces in order to be able to control the overseas distribution and exhibition of their films through the distributor United International Pictures (UIP) and the multiplex chain United Cinema International (UCI). MGM/UA and Warner also own their own multiplex chains. The multiplex revolution was both a response to and in large measure a contributory factor in a general increase in cinema-going during the 1980s and 1990s.

The majors' re-entry into the exhibition sector exemplifies contradictory impulses within the political economy of New Hollywood. On the one hand, since the late 1980s theatrical exhibition has ceased to account for the majority of film revenues. By the mid-1990s only 35 per cent of earnings came from theatrical release (including both domestic and overseas markets); the remainder came from the so-called 'ancillary' markets (television, video – rental and sell-through – and, from the late 1990s, the new technology of DVD).[42] It is important to recognize the importance of these markets to the film industry as they provide an extremely valuable source of extra income at a time of ever-escalating production costs. It is estimated that worldwide video/DVD revenue may return up to eight times the negative cost. Television networks now pay in the region of $20 million for terrestrial broadcast rights of major blockbusters. Even some films that have been deemed box-office failures on their theatrical release (such as *Waterworld*, the 'waterlogged' 1995 fantasy adventure that cost a reported $150 million) have eventually turned a profit through ancillary sales. Yet on the other hand, despite the existence of these other markets, Hollywood's perverse economic logic still judges a film on the basis of its domestic theatrical revenues. The North American market remains the focus of attention for the industry because it provides an indicator of how well a film will perform in other markets. As *Variety* put it, the domestic theatrical release is 'the engine that drives performance in the ancillary and foreign markets'.[43] While this is not always necessarily the case – *Waterworld*, for example, grossed almost twice as much overseas ($166 million) as it did in North America ($88 million) – it does illustrate that the film industry's economic strategies have not changed fundamentally since the 1950s. Hollywood is an exemplary model of a business that privileges visible 'up-front' profitability: it requires fast returns to pay off investors and bank loans, so in this respect 'quick bucks' at the domestic box-office are more important to the industry than revenue from video and television sales that will trickle in over a period of several years.

It is the global economy of New Hollywood, nevertheless, that to some extent helps to explain the nature of much

American cinema. If the corporate blockbuster has been criticized for its simplistic plots, risible dialogue and over-reliance on special effects, this is partly a consequence of the need to sell these big-budget movies on an international scale. It has been suggested that in the cinema of Lucas and Spielberg, and of their acolytes such as Robert Zemeckis (*Back to the Future*, *Who Framed Roger Rabbit*), Joe Johnston (*Honey I Shrunk the Kids*, *Jumanji*) and Chris Columbus (*Home Alone*, *Harry Potter and the Philosopher's Stone*), there has been a return to the 'cinema of attractions' in so far as stunts and spectacle are privileged over narrative and characterization. As Tom Gunning observes: 'Clearly in some recent spectacle cinema has reaffirmed its roots in stimulus and carnival rides, in what might be called the Spielberg-Lucas-Coppola cinema of effects.'[44] A cinema of spectacle and visual effects crosses boundaries of language and culture in the way that silent cinema once had done: the comic-strip adventures of Luke Skywalker or Indiana Jones can be easily understood in any language. It is significant that the genre which consistently performs better in foreign markets than domestically is the action movie featuring stars such as Schwarzenegger, Stallone and Bruce Willis. The Willis vehicle *Die Hard with a Vengeance*, for example, grossed $100 million in the North American market but another $253 million in overseas markets.

The economics of New Hollywood are such that a basic rule of thumb is the bigger the budget, the more important the overseas market. This is amply demonstrated by the case of James Cameron's *Titanic* (1997), which at the time of writing holds the record as the most expensive and the biggest-grossing film in cinema history. *Titanic*, produced by Paramount and Fox, was plagued by escalating costs (it eventually came in at an estimated $200 million) and poor word-of-mouth (there were many rumours of it being a troubled production) so that some industry insiders predicted a box-office disaster of *Heaven's Gate* proportions. That the film became the highest-grossing of all time – the first to take over $1 billion at the box-office – took most commentators by surprise, though pundits were then quick to explain its success by pointing out that epic romantic sagas set against the background of tumultuous historical events

(*Gone With the Wind, Doctor Zhivago*) were amongst the most popular films ever made. Even so, *Titanic's* domestic gross of $600 million would have represented a relatively small profit margin were it not for the fact that the film took another $900 million worldwide. The unusual decision to hold the world première in Tokyo on 1 November 1997, some seven weeks ahead of its US release (19 December), needs to be seen not only as an indication of the importance attached to the international market for this most expensive of productions, but also as a deliberate attempt to ensure the film had the chance to earn back some of its cost before American reviewers had the chance to savage it and possibly kill its box-office chances. As it happened the reviews of *Titanic* were mixed, though the trade press was generally enthusiastic. When the film finally opened in North America, however, it bucked the trend of most blockbusters (a big opening weekend followed by diminishing returns in the following weeks) and actually increased its revenues in the second and third weeks of release. 'By this time', as Peter Krämer observes, 'it was perfectly clear that *Titanic* had managed to combine the performance characteristics of two different production trends in contemporary Hollywood: the big splash of the action-adventure film aimed primarily at young males rushing to see the film on the opening weekend and the ability to make waves of the "sleeper" hit, usually a romantic comedy, serious drama or "weepie" aimed primarily at women who tend to wait for recommendations from their girlfriends and whose attendance several weeks into the release give the film what the industry calls "legs".'[45] But it also proved to be an exceptional, one-off success, what William Goldman calls a 'non-recurring phenomenon'.[46] It did not offer the scope for sequels, nor was it indicative of new trends in production. Significantly, *Pearl Harbor* (2001), clearly an attempt to replicate the *Titanic* formula of a love story against a real historical background, was rather less successful than expected despite worldwide grosses of $450 million.[47]

Titanic drew criticism from the British press who objected to Cameron's distortion of the historical record for dramatic ends. If, in terms of its box-office performance, *Titanic* was an exceptional film, on another level it exemplified perfectly what might be termed 'the world according to Hollywood'. *Titanic's* extravagant success in the international market locates it firmly within the global economy of *fin-de-siècle* corporate Hollywood. While, in European eyes, Hollywood had been associated with American cultural imperialism since the 1920s, at the end of the century these concerns were more acutely felt than they had ever been. Hollywood's share of the world market doubled between 1990 and 2001, partly the result of the Asian economic crisis of the late 1990s, but partly the result of the consolidation of worldwide production, distribution and exhibition interests by the US film industry.[48]

A crude version of Marxist political economy would see the entertainment industries as vehicles of capitalist ideology. Yet the assumption that all American popular culture is propaganda for the American Dream is misleading. Some of the most successful US exports are in fact highly critical of traditional American values. Stephen Price argues that Tim Burton, one of the most commercially successful New Hollywood directors (*Beetlejuice*, *Batman*, *Edward Scissorhands*, *Sleepy Hollow*), rather than becoming more cautious as he enjoyed increasing box-office success, 'only grew bolder until he succeeded at subverting the parameters of blockbuster filmmaking with *Batman Returns*, a picture that is the antithesis of commercially conservative filmmaking'.[49] Fox's most successful commodity in the Murdoch era has been not a film franchise but the television cartoon series *The Simpsons*, a satire of Americana that has an international cult following. As Arthur Marwick observes: 'This show makes a lot of money for its owners; [but] it is certainly no agent of bourgeois hegemony.'[50] Cultural production in the age of New Hollywood, in conclusion, offers a greater diversity of thematic and ideological positions than its detractors would allow, in large measure because Hollywood is now responding to the demands and needs of a global marketplace rather than manufacturing entertainment primarily for American audiences.

SEVEN

American Genres, American Society

Genres have been the lifeblood of American cinema since the early 1900s when different types of story film became the dominant form of motion pictures. As the genre critic Barry Keith Grant puts it: 'Stated simply, genre movies are those commercial feature films which, through repetition and variation, tell familiar stories with familiar characters in familiar situations'.[1] The genres most commonly associated with American cinema include the western, the musical, the gangster film, the melodrama, the comedy, the horror film and the science-fiction film. While distinctions between genres are sometimes blurred – *Alien* (1979), for example, could legitimately be described as both a horror and a science-fiction film – it is more usual for genre criticism to focus on the unique characteristics of particular genres.

   Genres can be conceptualized in different ways. For the film industry, they represent a form of product standardization and differentiation: each genre film is similar in some way to others of the same type (every western shares common characteristics with other westerns), whereas each film genre is different from others (westerns are distinct from science-fiction films, which are distinct from musicals, and so on). Genres help to regulate film production and to minimize the economic risks inherent in the industry. The prominence of the western in Hollywood production, for example, was due essentially to the fact that for a period of sixty years or so westerns were reliable box-office earners. One of the most noticeable production trends of New Hollywood is how a major box-office success breeds more films of the same type, such as the cycle of disaster movies in the early 1970s following the success of *Airport*, or the science-fiction boom of the late 1970s in the wake of *Star Wars*.

Although genres have been part of the film industry since it first began to organize on mass-production lines, it was only in the late 1960s and early 1970s that the notion of genre was adopted in a thoroughgoing way by film critics and theorists. Until then the films that attracted most attention tended to be those, such as *Citizen Kane* or *The Grapes of Wrath* or *The Best Years of Our Lives*, that stood out from the norms of Hollywood production. Genre criticism emerged from an intellectual dissatisfaction with the *auteur* theory that held sway in film studies throughout the 1960s as the focus of theoretical interest shifted from the idea of the filmmaker as artist towards the ideological processes at work in popular cinema. The idea of genre became central to this project because, as the American critic Robert Warshow – one of the early pioneers of genre criticism – had put it: 'For a type to be successful means that its conventions have imposed themselves upon the general consciousness and become the accepted vehicles of a particular set of attitudes and a particular aesthetic effect.'[2]

As the advent of genre criticism coincided with the heyday of 'high theory' in film studies, it is no surprise that it was informed by the methods of structuralism and semiotics. The principal weakness of most theoretical approaches to genre, however, is that in seeing genres as 'structures' they detach the films from their industrial and cultural contexts. Genres become reduced to purely theoretical constructs that remain fixed and immutable. Historical approaches to genre, however, see genres as flexible structures that change and mutate over time in response to various industrial, social and political determinants. Film historians see genres as means of examining the ideological dilemmas and cultural values prevalent in society. Thomas Schatz, for example, argues that 'genre can be seen as a form of social ritual' and, employing Gramscian terminology, suggests that American film genres are 'formal strategies for renegotiating and reinforcing American ideology'.[3] Similarly, John Belton asserts that 'by looking at the large body of individual films within individual genres, we can see how those genres help to shape and are shaped by our understanding of American culture, character, and identity'.[4] This chapter considers the relationship between American genres and American society through case studies of five genres (western, gangster film, *film noir*, musical and melodrama), each representing a different ideological and aesthetic response to the concerns and anxieties that have informed American society. These particular examples have been chosen because they also provide illuminating insights into why certain genres have been prominent in different historical periods.

THE AMERICAN FILM PAR EXCELLENCE

It was André Bazin who described the western as 'the American film *par excellence*'.[5] The western is unarguably the most uniquely American of all film genres, for, while westerns have been made elsewhere in the world (Italian 'spaghetti westerns', for example), the subject matter of the western is American and its thematic concerns revolve around issues of American nationhood and identity. The western dramatizes and mythologizes the founding of the American nation. It is intimately connected with the American past, chronicling the exploration and settlement of the frontier. To quote one recent historian of the genre: 'From Jamestown in 1607 to statehood for New Mexico and Arizona in 1912, three hundred years of the nation's history chronicled westward movement, settlement and development; and, as the journey to a new homeland was part of Americans' own or ancestral experience, Westerns appealed both to national identity and to individual heritage.'[6]

Just as 'the West' was not a fixed geographical space, but a constantly shifting and expanding frontier, so too the western is not a fixed pattern but rather, as Jim Kitses put it in his pioneering study of the genre, 'a varied and flexible structure, a thematically fertile and ambiguous world of historical material shot through with archetypal elements which are themselves ever in flux'.[7] Kitses drew upon Henry Nash Smith's seminal work of cultural history, *The Virgin Land*, seeing the western as revolving around 'a series of antinomies' – wilderness/civilization, individual/community, nature/culture, West/East – which shift continuously across the genre. Kitses's model allows a more flexible narrative pattern for the western than

Will Wright's structuralist analysis of the genre, which concludes that most, if not all, westerns are variations on the same 'classical' plot. The classical plot, in Wright's assessment, 'is the story of the lone stranger who rides into a troubled town and cleans it up, winning the respect of the townsfolk and the love of the schoolmarm'. 'The classical plot defines the genre', Wright adds, '. . . the other plots – vengeance, transition, professional – are all built upon the symbolic foundation and depend upon this foundation for their meaning.'[8]

Alan Lovell, concerned with the cultural history of the genre rather than its structural form, identified the origins of the western narrative in nineteenth-century melodramatic literature, especially the tripartite characterizations of virtuous hero, virginal heroine and menacing 'heavy' villain.[9] As a genre, the western predates the cinema; the film western drew upon a number of established traditions and cultural forms. The visual iconography of the genre, especially the prominence of landscape (mountains, prairies, deserts), owed much to the 'western' paintings of Frederic S. Remington and Theodor R. Davis and to the work of pioneering photographers such as William H. Jackson and Timothy O'Sullivan. Many early westerns, especially, were adapted from the work of western novelists, of whom the most influential were Owen Wister (whose famous novel *The Virginian* was turned into one of the first sound westerns in 1929, the film which brought Gary Cooper to stardom) and Zane Grey (whose pulp novels provided titles and plots for dozens of 'B' westerns between the 1910s and the 1940s). Another influence on the western film can be identified in the 'Wild West' shows popularized in the late nineteenth century by Buffalo Bill Cody, which combined speciality acts (such as sharpshooter Annie Oakley and rodeo rider Buck Taylor) with dramatic reconstructions of events such as Custer's Last Stand and an attack by outlaws on the Deadwood Stage – the sort of incidents that would feature in countless western films.

Although the western was a staple of Hollywood film production from the 1910s, the genre is, by general consent, agreed to have reached its maturity on the eve of the Second World War. There were a number of 'big' silent westerns during the 1920s that dramatized the settlement of the West (*The Covered*

Wagon, *The Iron Horse*, *Tumbleweeds*), but for most of the 1930s the genre was mainly the province of Poverty Row studios that turned out series films and serials to fill the lower half of double bills. The western was afforded scant critical regard until the production season of 1939–40 saw a cycle of 'A' westerns from the major studios, including *Jesse James*, *Stagecoach*, *Dodge City*, *Union Pacific*, *Drums Along the Mohawk*, *Northwest Passage*, *Virginia City*, *The Return of Frank James*, *Brigham Young* and *The Westerner*.[10] The most celebrated of these films, undoubtedly, is John Ford's *Stagecoach*, which Bazin described as 'the ideal example of the maturity of a style brought to classical perfection . . . the ideal balance between social myth, historical reconstruction, psychological truth, and the traditional theme of the western *mise-en-scène*'.[11] While the essence of a genre can never be reduced to a single film, *Stagecoach* has come to be seen as paradigmatic of the western due to its deployment of most of the genre's principal themes and motifs: the honourable hero who has become an outlaw in order to avenge the death of his father (the Ringo Kid was to be John Wayne's star-making performance after a decade spent in the doldrums of 'B' westerns), the journey through hazardous territory of a diverse group of passengers (a narrative device frequently said to be modelled on Maupassant's short story *Boule-de-suif*, though the accredited source of the screenplay, by Dudley Nichols, is a story by Ernest Haycox entitled *Stage to Lordsburg*), the Indian attack, the timely arrival of the US Cavalry, the climactic showdown on Main Street and the final union of hero and heroine. It dramatizes both the conflict between the supposedly civilized community and the savage wilderness of the West – a theme that occurs throughout the oeuvre of its director – and the conflicts within civilization (outwardly respectable characters turn out to be morally compromised, whereas the hero and heroine are social outcasts, an outlaw and a prostitute).[12] However, the fact that this most archetypal of all westerns does not fit the schemata of the 'classical' plot as outlined by Will Wright serves as a warning against seeing the western, or any other genre for that matter, as reducible to a rigid structuralist paradigm.

The western was quiescent during the Second World War, when contemporary war films were naturally the dominant action genre, but it enjoyed a revival after the war that was to bring the genre to the forefront of American popular cinema where it remained for the next 30 years. From 1946 until 1976 westerns were regularly among the leading box-office attractions, while many of the leading male stars of the period (John Wayne, James Stewart, Gary Cooper, Henry Fonda, Gregory Peck, Burt Lancaster, Kirk Douglas, Clint Eastwood) were closely associated with the genre. The prominence in the western of icons of mature masculinity, and the relative marginalization of women from most western narratives, has inevitably led to the western being characterized as a 'male' or 'masculine' genre (in much the same way that the melodrama is sometimes labelled 'the woman's film'). This charge against the western is undoubtedly correct; it is also misplaced. The ideology of the western, so often caricatured in the apocryphal phrase 'a man's gotta do what a man's gotta do', attempts to resolve the contradictory impulses between individualism and socialization. In this schemata women invariably represent the domesticating influences of civilization – a lifestyle that the western hero has to reject if he is to maintain his sense of individual identity. Thus it is that one of the most familiar images of the genre is the solitary hero riding off alone into the sunset.

It was in the decade following the Second World War that the western underwent its most far-reaching transformation. Two westerns of 1946 represent the past and future trajectories of the genre. John Ford's *My Darling Clementine*, even more than *Stagecoach*, deserves to be regarded as the apotheosis of the classical western. A highly romanticized retelling of the Wyatt Earp myth, *My Darling Clementine* is a lyrical metaphor for the civilizing of the West. The film's characterizations balance the virtues and vices of both 'Western' and 'Eastern' influences: the heroic, morally unimpeachable Earp (Henry Fonda) represents the positive values of the westerner with his virtues of self-reliance, stoicism and quiet dignity, whereas the villainous Clantons stand for the savagery of the untamed, lawless frontier; the different faces of the East are represented by the consumptive, alcoholic, doomed gunfighter Doc Holliday (Victor Mature) and the loyal, virtuous Clementine (Cathy Downs) who follows Doc to Tombstone and stays to become its new

schoolmarm. While the arrival of civilization in Tombstone is symbolized in the celebrated church dance sequence (the church is only half-built and has no roof, so that the distinctive landscape of Ford's beloved Monument Valley is visible in the background), the climactic gunfight at the OK Corral (in which all the Clantons are killed and Doc Holliday dies a heroic redemptive death) represents the taming of the West and the imposition of legal authority. It is hard to define the special visual quality of *My Darling Clementine* – a quality described by Lindsay Anderson as 'some kind of moral poetry'[13] – but its *mise-en-scène* is more elaborate than *Stagecoach*, its compositions of people and landscape more studied. *Clementine* has been described variously as a 'utopian western' and a film 'that celebrates the West and America as a perfectible society'.[14] Its lyrical romanticism and emotional restraint is a stark contrast to the other significant western of 1946, *Duel in the Sun*, which *Time* magazine called 'the costliest, the most lushly Technicolored, the most lavishly cast, the loudest ballyhooed, and the sexiest horse opera ever made'.[15] There is nothing at all restrained about *Duel in the Sun*, which has an operatic quality in its representation of a passionate, ultimately doomed love affair between a cowboy (Gregory Peck) and his half-breed lover (Jennifer Jones) against the background of a range war between homesteaders and cattlemen.

Duel in the Sun represented a trend in the post-war western away from the classical form and towards what Bazin termed the 'superwestern'. Bazin's 'superwestern' should not be confused with the epic western (that was to follow in the 1960s); he described it, rather, as 'a western that would be ashamed to be just itself, and looks for some additional interest to justify its existence – an aesthetic, sociological, moral, psychological, political, or erotic interest, in short some quality extrinsic to the genre and which is supposed to enrich it.'[16] Examples of the post-war superwestern included *Duel in the Sun* (the western as erotic spectacle), *Pursued* (the western as Greek tragedy with Freudian overtones), *High Noon* (the western as political allegory) and *Shane* (the western as self-conscious, aestheticized myth). A more familiar label is that of 'psychological western', a trend which originates with *The Ox-Bow Incident* (1943) but which reaches its fullest extent in the 1950s with films exploring the anxieties and neuroses of the western hero. Psychological westerns of the 1950s explored the 'crisis of masculinity' associated with post-war social problems: generational conflict (*The Proud Ones*), juvenile delinquency (*The Left-Handed Gun*), racism (*The Searchers*) and even the suggestion of homosexuality (*Warlock*). Perhaps in response to contemporary domestication, as the generation of men who had fought in the war settled down with wives and families, a clutch of westerns in the mid-1950s featured heroes who found themselves emasculated by strong, independent women (*Rancho Notorious*, *Johnny Guitar*, *Forty Guns*). The alternative to domestication for the western hero was an ever more solitary existence at the periphery of civilization. The character of the obsessive loner reached its apogee in a series of westerns directed by Anthony Mann (*Winchester '73*, *Bend of the River/Where the River Bends*, *The Naked Spur*, *The Far Country*, *The Man from Laramie*) which recast the star persona of James Stewart into a complex, flawed anti-hero, disillusioned with society and often seeking vengeance.

John Ford's mature westerns between the late 1940s and the early 1960s illustrate the transitions taking place within the genre. His 'cavalry trilogy' of 1948–50 (*Fort Apache*, *She Wore a Yellow Ribbon*, *Rio Grande*) are hymns of praise to the US military in the pacification of the West, while *Wagon Master* (1950), one of his most underrated films, is a small-scale epic of westward expansion in the classical tradition. Ford then took a sabbatical from the western until *The Searchers* (1956), thought by many critics to be his masterpiece, the story of an ex-Confederate soldier (superbly played by John Wayne) who undertakes an obsessive five-year quest to avenge the death of his brother and sister-in-law, killed by a Comanche raiding party, and to find his abducted niece. Ethan Edwards's intention, however, is not to rescue the girl but to kill her because he considers her racially and sexually tainted through having been forced to live as a squaw to the Comanche leader. Although, ultimately, Ethan is unable to bring himself to kill her, the ending of the film leaves him as a social outsider: the famous closing shot is from inside the home as the door closes on Ethan, who turns his back on domestication and walks off into the desert. *The Searchers* is one of the most beautifully photographed of all westerns (the Technicolor cinematography by Winton C. Hoch captures the changing hues of the passing seasons in Monument Valley), but it also has a psychological depth that was absent from Ford's earlier westerns.[17] His last great film was to be *The Man Who Shot Liberty Valance* (1962), both an elegy on the passing of the Old West and a meditation on the relationship between history and myth. It is in *Liberty Valance* that the mantra central to Ford's westerns, indeed to the genre as a whole, is best expressed: 'This is the West, sir. When the legend becomes fact, print the legend.'

Genres tend to be cyclical in nature, and the western is no exception. Almost as if in response to the psychological westerns of the 1950s with their complex, angst-ridden heroes, the major westerns of the 1960s restored an uncomplicated, confident type of masculinity that was thoroughly at ease with itself. This was the decade of the 'professional western': a type of western in which heroes ply their trade either as lawmen or as hired guns, protecting society against external threats but standing apart from it and maintaining a degree of emotional detachment. The trend towards the professional western began in the late 1950s with John Sturges's *Gunfight at the OK Corral* and Howard Hawks's *Rio Bravo*. Despite the presence of a nominal romantic interest in each, these two films are essentially about the relationships between men, to which end they also reflected a growing tendency of the genre to team major male stars (Burt Lancaster and Kirk Douglas in *Gunfight at the OK Corral*, John Wayne and Dean Martin in *Rio Bravo*). In his analysis of the films of Howard Hawks, Robin Wood argues that *Rio Bravo* is the perfect combination of Hawks's male-centred world-view and the traditional masculine ethos of the western:

> The action of *Rio Bravo* is played out against a background hard and bare, with nothing to distract the individual from working out his essential relationship to life. The virtual removal of a social framework – the relegating of society to the function of a *pretext* – throws all the emphasis on the characters' sense of *self*, on their need to find a sense of purpose and meaning not through allegiance to any developing order, but within themselves, in their own instinctual needs.[18]

Similar themes of professional group loyalty and the virtual removal of any social framework occur throughout the professional westerns of the 1960s, including *The Magnificent Seven*, *The Professionals*, *El Dorado* (Hawks's virtual remake of *Rio Bravo*), *The War Wagon*, *True Grit* and *The Wild Bunch*. These films also exemplified another theme that was becoming increasingly prominent: the closure of the frontier and the sense that the time of the traditional western hero had passed. It is significant in this context that the professional gunfighters of *The Magnificent Seven*, *The Professionals* and *The Wild Bunch* have to travel to Mexico to ply their trade; the latter two films are set, moreover, around the time of the First World War, over two decades after the frontier had officially been declared closed.

The theme that most occupied westerns during the 1960s and afterwards, however, was the inevitability of social progress. This is best illustrated at the beginning of Sam Peckinpah's elegiac *Ride the High Country* in 1962 (released in Britain with the more evocative title of *Guns in the Afternoon*). Buscombe explains how the iconography of the film uses visual indicators of modernization to disrupt the audience's expectations:

> Knowing the period and location, we expect at the beginning to find a familiar Western town. In fact, the first few minutes of the film brilliantly disturb our expectations. As the camera roves around the town we discover a policeman in uniform, a car, a camel, and Randolph Scott dressed up as Buffalo Bill. Each of these images performs a function. The figure of the policeman conveys that the law has become institutionalized; the rough and ready frontier days are over. The car suggests, as in *The Wild Bunch*, that the West is no longer isolated from modern technology and its implications. Significantly, the camel is racing against a horse; such a grotesque juxtaposition is painful. A horse in a Western is not just an animal, but a symbol of dignity, grace and power. These qualities are mocked by it competing with a camel; and to add insult to injury, the camel wins.[19]

A similar sequence takes place at the beginning of *The Shootist* (1976), John Wayne's final film, as ageing gunfighter J. B. Brooks arrives in a town that has telephone poles, tramlines and motor cars. The arrival of the railroad, a symbol of progress in pre-war westerns such as *Union Pacific*, symbolizes the closing of the frontier in Sergio Leone's masterful *Once Upon a Time in the West* (1968). And in *Butch Cassidy and the Sundance Kid* (1969), technology helps put paid to the protagonists' career as bankrobbers. Butch (Paul Newman) is dismayed to find a bank protected by a variety of security measures. 'What was the matter with the old bank this town used to have? It was beautiful', Butch asks a guard. 'People kept robbing it', he is told. 'That's a small price to pay for beauty', Butch laments.

Since the mid-1970s the western has ceased to be the staple genre that it had been for so long. There are a number of likely reasons for its demise. There is a strong case to argue that the western went into decline when it ceased to 'print the legend' and became more concerned with exploring the historical reality of the West. The early 1970s witnessed a trend for westerns offering revisionist accounts of the legendary figures of the West (*Doc*,

The Life and Times of Judge Roy Bean, *Pat Garrett and Billy the Kid*, *Buffalo Bill and the Indians*). Such revisionist westerns, however, were no more successful than sporadic attempts to make 'realistic' westerns (*Will Penny*, *Junior Bonner*, *McCabe and Mrs Miller*, *Tom Horn*, *Heaven's Gate*). Although none of these films is entirely without merit, they lack the mythic potency and emotional appeal of earlier generations of westerns. The Vietnam War, which severely dented Americans' national pride and which revealed the US military as perpetrators of atrocities against civilians, destroyed the confidence in the armed forces displayed in films such as Ford's cavalry trilogy. The cavalry westerns of the early 1970s (*Soldier Blue*, *Little Big Man*, *Ulzana's Raid*) are brutal and bloody affairs in which the US Cavalry is shown to be responsible for genocide against the native population. The retirement and/or death of the major western stars of the post-war era is another important factor in the genre's decline. It is as if the western could not outlive its leading iconic figures: Gary Cooper (died 1961), Randolph Scott (retired in the early 1960s), James Stewart (retired in the 1970s) and, most especially, John Wayne (died 1979). The only star legitimately to assume the mantle – and, moreover, to actually look comfortable in the saddle – is Clint Eastwood, whose forays into the genre have resulted in some interesting if flawed films (*High Plains Drifter*, *Pale Rider*) and one self-consciously mythical exploration of violence and masculinity (*Unforgiven*). All of these are specific reasons for the decline of the western. A more general explanation for its demise, as Belton suggests, is related to social change. 'The popularity of the Western endures just so long as it continues to address the basic concerns of a technophobic American populace', he argues. 'It begins to fade just at the point that America attempts to reconcile itself with certain realities that underlie its status as a highly industrialized, mass society.'[20] The western represents the founding myth of American national identity based on the pioneering spirit. In the 1960s, this pioneering spirit found a different expression in the 'new frontier' proclaimed by Kennedy – a metaphor taken up in the 'final frontier' of the television series *Star Trek*. It is surely no accident that the virtual disappearance of the western in the late 1970s coincided with the emergence of science-fiction as a major genre. In this interpretation, the genre has not so much died as it has mutated into a different form, for the ideologies, themes and motifs that inform the science-fiction films of the last three decades are very similar to those that once found expression in the western.

THE TRAGIC HERO

The gangster film is often seen as a companion to the western. It is, after the western, the genre that is most identifiable by its iconography. Both genres feature recognizable physical environments, distinctive character types and particular objects (clothes, guns, different types of transport) that identify them. And certain stars are indelibly associated with each genre: Cooper, Wayne and Stewart with the western, Edward G. Robinson, James Cagney and Humphrey Bogart with the gangster film. It is not only in the prominence of a set of visual conventions, however, that the gangster film bears comparison with the western. Similarities exist on a thematic level too. Colin McArthur, in his pioneering study of the gangster film, argued that 'the western and the gangster film have a special relationship with American society'. 'It could be said,' he adds, 'that they represent America talking to itself about, in the case of the western, its agrarian past, and in the case of the gangster film/thriller, its urban technological present.'[21]

In the case of the gangster film, indeed, as Andrew Tudor puts it, 'the construction of the genre was almost contemporaneous with the construction of the events themselves'.[22] The origins of the classical gangster film can be identified in the historical experience of 1920s America, especially Prohibition and the high profile of criminals running organized protection rackets and prostitution. Al Capone had only recently been jailed (for tax evasion) and the notorious St Valentine's Day massacre (1929) was a recent memory when the first recognizable gangster film, *Little Caesar* (1930), went into production at Warner Bros. It was followed by *The Public Enemy* (1931) and *Scarface* (1932) – the latter produced by Howard Hughes – and between them these three films established the codes and conventions of the gangster film. This triptych of films had much in common:

they were allegedly based on real criminals (*Little Caesar* and *Scarface* on Al Capone, *The Public Enemy* on Hymie Weiss), they were violent (thus attracting the attention of censors and moral watchdogs) and they presented their protagonists as highly individualistic, greedy, acquisitive men who transgressed legal and moral boundaries in their desire to find wealth and power. It is commonplace to interpret the 'heroes' of gangster films as representing the dark side of the American Dream of material wealth secured through private enterprise. Robert Warshow, in a seminal essay, claimed that 'the gangster is the "no" to that great American "yes" which is stamped so big over our official culture'.[23] Warshow developed the idea of the gangster film as a modern tragedy and of the figure of the gangster as a tragic hero. He argued that the narrative structure of the classical gangster film resembles the tragedy because it 'presents a steady upward progress followed by a very precipitate fall'.[24] The gangster protagonist exhibits certain admirable character traits (individualism, confidence, self-belief), but his tragedy arises from the fact that he steps outside acceptable social and moral frameworks to express them. Schatz takes this interpretation further, suggesting that society itself is at least partly responsible for the gangster's fall because 'it denies individual expression and provides minimal options to the struggling, aggressive male from an inner-city, working-class background. The only options to a life of crime – or so these films would seem to assert – are the police force, the priesthood, or the city transit company.'[25] In the gangster films of the early 1930s, especially, set against the background of social and economic hardship caused by the Depression, there is much substance to this assessment.

For a genre that has been the locus of so much interest, the gangster film had probably the shortest classical period of any major genre. By the mid-1930s there were already signs of a substantial ideological realignment within the genre. Richard Maltby even suggests that the gangster film as such is better understood as a cycle than as a genre on the grounds that it 'was the product of a single season (1930–3) and, at least within the industry's operating definitions, comprised no more than 23 pictures'.[26] The conventional wisdom is that the introduction of the Production Code led to the 'cleaning up' of the gangster film. The Code specifically declared that '[no] film shall be produced which will lower the moral standards of those who see it' and that 'the sympathy of the audience shall never be thrown on the side of crime, wrongdoing, evil, or sin'.[27] This is demonstrated in the shift from films focusing on the gangster as central protagonist to films that focused on the activities of law enforcement agencies in fighting crime. Thus the wrong-doers of *Little Caesar* and *The Public Enemy* became the heroes of *Bullets or Ballots* (Robinson) and *G-Men* (Cagney). There were further modifications in the late 1930s when gangster protagonists were either presented as cowards (*Angels with Dirty Faces*) or were shown dying a redemptive death (*The Roaring Twenties*). While these changes were certainly, in some measure, a response to censorship regulations and concerns over the screen representation of violence, that is not the only explanation. Schatz, for example, relates the changing screen face of the gangster to the 'considerable cultural confusion' caused by 'America's shift from a primarily rural-agricultural to an urban-industrial nation, compounded by the Depression, Prohibition, and other vagaries of city life'.[28]

Unlike the western, however, the gangster film, in its various forms, became indelibly associated with one studio. Most of the 'classic' gangster films of the 1930s and 1940s were produced by Warner Bros. (*Little Caesar*, *The Public Enemy*, *Angels with Dirty Faces*, *The Roaring Twenties*, *High Sierra*, *White Heat*). Nick Roddick argues that the gangster film fit Warners' 'social conscience' in that it represented 'a hero whose antisocial individualism could speak to the contradictions of capitalist ideology'.[29] The prominence of the gangster film in Warners' production strategy, especially during the 1930s, was the outcome of both industrial and aesthetic determinants. Gangster films, Roddick asserts, were 'ideally suited to Warners' streamlined production methods' because they were relatively inexpensive to make and could be filmed in the studio, using contemporary sets, with a minimum of exteriors. The visual style of 1930s gangster films is dominated by spare sets and low-key lighting, creating a world of dark alleys and seedy rooms that is characteristic of the genre. The fact that the major stars of gangster films also happened to be contracted to Warners (Robinson, Cagney, Bogart) is a happy accident – with their proletarian 'tough-guy' image these actors were ideally suited to the genre in the way that Wayne and others were ideally suited to westerns. Warners, interestingly, made relatively few westerns during the 1930s: indeed, the sight of Cagney and Bogart facing off in western garb (in *The Oklahoma Kid*) is quite unsettling.

The gangster film is, arguably, a less stable genre than the western, in that it has been subject to more flux and variation in short periods of time as cycles within the genre come and go. Thus the classical gangster film of the early 1930s was supplanted first by the law-enforcement variation (*G-Men*, *Racket Busters*, *I Am the Law*) and then by the 'social problem' gangster film that attempted to explain the circumstances that gave rise to the gangster (*Angels with Dirty Faces*, *Dead End*). The emergence in the 1940s of *film noir*, which overlaps with the gangster film to a considerable degree, made the genre even more malleable. The post-war years saw a trend towards documentary-style crime thrillers utilizing real locations (*The House on 92nd Street*, *The Naked City*, *The Asphalt Jungle*), though the traditional gangster film made a triumphant return in the late 1940s when Robinson (*Key Largo*) and Cagney (*White Heat*) essayed two of their greatest performances as psychotic villains. *White Heat*, an uncompromisingly brutal film with strongly oedipal overtones in the persona of Cagney's mother-fixated Cody Jarrett, was the last of the great Warner Bros. gangster pictures, symbolically killing off its protagonist in a fiery inferno. From the 1950s the gangster film followed several different trajectories: the return of the law-enforcement film (*The Enforcer*, *The Big Heat*, *The FBI Story*), the crime syndicate film (*The Big Combo*, *New York Confidential*, *Underworld USA*) and biopics of actual gangsters now named for the first time in films (*Al Capone*, *Baby Face Nelson*, *Machine-Gun Kelly*, *The Rise and Fall of Legs Diamond*). In contrast to the classic gangster films of the 1930s, which were mostly the work of unpretentious studio directors such as Mervyn Le Roy, William Wellman and Raoul Walsh, the gangster films of the 1950s and 1960s were a fertile ground for budding *auteurs* such as Don Siegel, Sam Fuller and Roger Corman who revelled in the low-budget, violent, 'exploitation' style of filmmaking.

The relaxation of censorship was constantly tested by the gangster film, which, along with *film noir*, was the most violent of the 'realistic' genres (the violence in 'non-realistic' genres such as the horror film is different due to their obviously fantastical content). Arthur Penn's *Bonnie and Clyde* (1967) was the first major gangster film to appear after the Production Code was rewritten in 1966 to allow films 'suggested for mature audiences' (this system was replaced by an age-classification system two years later). *Bonnie and Clyde* is a landmark film for several reasons: it was the first to glamorize its gangster protagonists as romantic heroes (in the attractive personae of its young stars Warren Beatty and Faye Dunaway) and it set new standards for the representation of screen violence. It is also, quite possibly, the first occasion on which a gangster film displayed the sort of allegorical overtones that were relatively commonplace for the western. The bloody climax of the film, in which Bonnie and Clyde drive into an ambush and are ruthlessly gunned down, seems a direct reference to the Kennedy assassination. Clyde's slow-motion death, in which part of his head is blown off, resembles the morbid fascination with the cine-footage of Kennedy's death captured by amateur filmmaker Abraham Zapuder.

The high point of the gangster film in New Hollywood, both commercially and artistically, came in the 1970s with Francis Ford Coppola's two *Godfather* films (a third, less successful, film followed in 1990). *The Godfather* was the first truly epic gangster film, a tale of family honour as an ageing Mafia don (Marlon Brando) passed the mantle to his son (Al Pacino). *The Godfather* draws explicit parallels between organized crime and big business, presenting the son Michael as much as a businessman as a gangster, albeit that he is capable of extreme ruthlessness in dealing with his enemies. More controversially, it also suggests comparisons between the social role of the Mafia and that of the Church, as Don Corleone is seen *in loco parentis* to the Italian immigrant community in New York. *The Godfather Part II* was both a prequel and a sequel to the first film, chronicling the life of the young Don Corleone (Robert De Niro) in Sicily and Michael Corleone's consolidation of his power after his father's death. The main difference between the *Godfather* saga and earlier gangster films is that the gangster is no longer a social outsider; he has become socially respectable and, in a perverse sort of way, has his own code of honour that upholds traditional social institutions such as the family. Whereas in the 1930s the gangster had been society's rotten apple, now it is society itself that is rotten. One commentator, for instance, writes that the *Godfather* films 'portrayed a normative culture so lethally inimical to human needs that the only way to survive and find meaning within it was to create an alternative criminal society'.[30] In this sense the gangster film becomes a vehicle for expressing dissatisfaction with societal norms. *The Godfather* and *The Godfather Part II* both won an Academy Award for Best Film – the latter becoming the first sequel ever to do so – and thus suggesting that the gangster film, once the scourge of moral watchdogs, had finally won critical legitimacy.

The post-*Godfather* history of the gangster film once again reveals the genre's ability to adapt to changes in the film industry and in society at large. The two outstanding gangster films of the 1980s, both directed by Brian De Palma, were an updated remake of a genre classic (*Scarface*) and a mythic reworking of the law-enforcement film (*The Untouchables*). The early 1990s saw a cycle of 'gangsta' films (*Boyz N the Hood, Juice*) focusing on black protagonists but essentially exploring the same issue as the classic gangster film, namely the choice between crime or poverty for modern urban youth. A sign of the continuing vitality of the genre, in contrast to the western, is that it attracted both established filmmakers such as Martin Scorsese (*GoodFellas, Casino*) and Michael Mann (*Heat*) and emergent new talents such as the Coen brothers (*Miller's Crossing*) and Quentin Tarantino (*Reservoir Dogs*), whose films were characterized by their knowing, ironic references to the genre's past and by their self-conscious experimentation with its narrative and stylistic conventions.

Gangster films may not have been produced in the same quantities as certain other genre films (though there is a degree of slippage between the gangster film and related genres such as the police procedural and the detective story), but they have maintained their place in the generic profile of American cinema when others, such as westerns and musicals, have all but disappeared. Jack Shadoian's astute commentary on the genre, written in the 1970s, still rings true: 'The genre has survived because the issues it addresses have always been central to the American experience, because its formal properties have given them a clarity of outline and lucidity of exposition, and because it has been infinitely flexible in adapting itself to shifting social and cultural conditions.'[31]

A DARK MIRROR TO POSTWAR AMERICA

In 1947 *Life* magazine noted, with some distaste, 'Hollywood's profound postwar affection for morbid drama'. The films of the time, it contended, presented 'a panting display of psychoneuroses, unsublimated sex and murder most foul'.[32] In the same year John Houseman, writing in the *Hollywood Quarterly*, characterized post-war America as being in 'a period of general anxiety and low cultural energy'. He complained that the nation's screens were populated by 'a whining herd of petty chiselers, perverts, halfwits, and nymphomaniacs' – albeit basing his analysis on just the one film, *The Big Sleep* (1946) – and deplored the 'violent and deplorable retrogression' this entailed for American cinema.[33]

Houseman called this new phenomenon simply 'the tough movie'. It was the French who coined the term '*film noir*' to describe this trend in American cinema when, following the end of the Second World War, a glut of Hollywood films that had been unavailable due to the Occupation flooded onto French screens. Nino Frank seems to have been the first to use the term in 1946 when he described a batch of American movies made earlier in the 1940s (*The Maltese Falcon, Double Indemnity, Laura* and *Murder My Sweet*) as '*films "noirs"*'. The term was soon picked up by others and within a few years had passed into critical discourse, exemplified by the publication of Raymond Borde and Etienne Chaumenton's book *Panorama du Film Noir Américain* in 1955. It was here that the term '*film noir*' was linked, in a preface by Marcel Duhamel, to the crime and detective novels published in France by the Gallimard Press under the generic title of '*Série Noire*' (the 'Black Series'), which included French translations of the 'hard-boiled' school of American crime fiction such as Dashiell Hammett, Raymond Chandler, James M. Cain and Cornell Woolrich.[34]

Thus it is that *film noir* was a term first used by film critics rather than by the film industry itself, and, furthermore, that it is a term that originated outside America. American critics, indeed, did not share the enthusiasm of the French for this type of film and it was not until the 1970s that *film noir* began to receive sustained attention in American film studies. Paul Schrader, a film critic later to become a screenwriter and director, suggested that the neglect of *film noir* was due to it being seen as unwholesome and unAmerican. 'For a long time *film noir*, with its emphasis on corruption and despair, was considered an aberration of the American character', he wrote. 'The western, with its moral primitivism, and the gangster film, with its Horatio Alger values, were considered more American than the *film noir*.'[35] It was, ironically, during another period of perceived social malaise in the early 1970s that the *film noir* cycle of the 1940s and 1950s came under close critical scrutiny.

The fact that *film noir* is a critical construction rather than an industry category raises obvious theoretical problems around its status as a genre. So, too, do the historical specificity of *film noir* and the differences between the generic codes of films that are categorized as *noir*. Most commentators, indeed, prefer to see *film noir* as a movement, a cycle or a mode than as a genre in the purest sense. Belton sees the 'essentially schizophrenic nature' of *film noir* as the root of the problem of classification, asserting that '*film noir* is not a genre, but every *film noir* is *also* a genre film'.[36] The canon of films that are identified as belonging to the *noir* movement – which has grown from the 22 identified by Borde and Chaumenton to over 300 listed by Alain Silver and Elizabeth Ward in their *Film Noir: An Encyclopedic Reference to the American Style* – includes films that could be located in a range of generic categories.[37] Many of the canonical *noir* films belonged to the lineage of the detective or private-eye thriller (*The Maltese Falcon, Laura, Murder My Sweet, The Big Sleep, The Lady in the Lake, Kiss Me Deadly*), others crossed over into the territory of the gangster film (*The Killers, The Set-Up, Brute Force, Gun Crazy, They Live by Night, Thieves' Highway*), others

focused on returning servicemen who find themselves unwittingly involved in crime (*The Blue Dahlia, Cornered, Somewhere
in the Night*), while others still can probably best be described as
femme fatale thrillers (*Double Indemnity, The Postman Always
Rings Twice, Gilda, Out of the Past, The Lady from Shanghai*).
While most *noir* films are typically crime thrillers of one sort or
another, *noir* characteristics have also been identified in other
genres such as the social problem film (*The Lost Weekend*), the
melodrama (*Mildred Pierce*), the costume film (*Gaslight*) and the
western (*Pursued*). The distinguishing characteristics of *film
noir* are to be found less in its narrative patterns and structures
than in its thematic concerns (disillusionment, alienation, loneliness, amnesia, paranoia) and in its formal and stylistic elements (fragmentary *mise-en-scène*, disorienting camerawork,
shadowy chiaroscuro lighting and non-linear narration, especially the extensive use of flashbacks).

The particular historical moment of *film noir*, which most
historians identify as being between the early/mid-1940s and
the mid/late 1950s, has inevitably resulted in the movement
being interpreted as a response to social problems, particularly
in the aftermath of war. It has long been the tendency of critics
to see *noir* films as a reflection of social malaise. 'Is this not an
outcrop of the national masochism induced by a quite aimless
and heavily industrialized society proceeding rapidly on its way
to nowhere?' asked British critic Richard Winnington, rhetori-
cally, in response to *Out of the Past* (released in Britain with the
morbid title *Build My Gallows High*).[38] This view has been
endorsed by some film historians, Schatz, for instance, asserting
that *film noir* 'documented the growing disillusionment with
certain traditional American values in the face of complex and
often contradictory social, political, scientific, and economic
developments'.[39] And David A. Cook adheres to an old
metaphor in stating that '*film noir* held up a dark mirror to post-
war America and reflected its moral anarchy'.[40]

The notion of *film noir* as a reflection of social reality is
nuanced, however, by film theorists who instead emphasize its
status as an aesthetic construct. Rather than holding up a mirror
to society, they argue, *film noir* creates its own image of the
world through its formal properties and visual style. It is a filmic

world, not necessarily an image of the real world. Schrader, for example, argues that '*film noir* attacked and interpreted its sociological conditions, and, by the close of the *noir* period, created a new artistic world that went beyond a simply sociological reflection, a nightmarish world of American mannerism which was by far more a creation than a reflection.'[41] Schrader's view is echoed by Robert B. Ray, who also sees *film noir* as creating its own highly stylized world. In *film noir*, he argues, it is less the story that matters than the style: thus *noir* differs from the classical norm with its emphasis on unobtrusive, invisible narration. The film that Ray cites as the best example of this tendency is Orson Welles's *Touch of Evil* (1958), which is often seen as marking the end of the main period of *noir* filmmaking. Welles, argues Ray, 'used a tawdry melodrama . . . as an occasion to create a stylistic universe whose deep shadows, looming close-ups, oblique camera angles, prowling camera, and crowded compositions intimated a sense of entrapment and loss that went far beyond the mere events of the plot'.[42] *Touch of Evil* is famous for the long, continuously mobile tracking shot that opens the film, but it is also marked by extreme camera angles and highly expressionist, fragmented *mise-en-scène*.

Film noir, therefore, can – and has – been seen as both a reflection of the mood of the times and as a stylistic creation in its own right. Can these two positions be reconciled? In the sense that the reflectionist metaphor assumes some relationship to social reality, whereas the textualist reading detaches *film noir* from its immediate social context, there would seem to be little common ground between the two interpretations. Indeed, the visual style of *film noir*, with its disorienting devices and expressionist camera angles, is defiantly non-realist. But if the physical world represented in *film noir* is not strictly a reflecting mirror of social reality, its aesthetic and emotional effects do undoubtedly create a sense of unease and ambiguity. Another way of conceptualizing *film noir* is to see it as a mode that is intended to create a particular emotional reaction on the part of the audience. Textualist critics have argued that the *mise-en-scène* of *film noir* is 'designed to unsettle, jar, and disorient the viewer in correlation with the disorientation felt by *noir* heroes'.[43] The visual style of *film noir* should be seen as stylized means of representing social dislocation – in a manner similar to the German Expressionist cinema of the 1920s – rather than as a reflection of social reality.

That said, however, *film noir* cannot be detached from its historical context. A purely textualist interpretation does not explain how and why this style of filmmaking emerged and flourished at a particular historical juncture. As so often, a number of interrelated factors can be advanced to explain the historical moment of *film noir*. Paul Kerr, for example, has argued that *film noir* arose from 'the conjunction of a primarily economically determined mode of production, known as B filmmaking, with what were primarily ideologically defined modes of "difference"'.[44] Most *noir* films, Kerr argues, were B-pictures in that they were relatively cheap to produce, their minimalist sets and low-key black-and-white photography perfectly suited (like the 1930s gangster film) to the demands of economical production. The 'modes of difference' he cites were related to the increasing acceptance of colour films: still a relative novelty at the beginning of the *noir* period in the 1940s, colour had become the industry's norm by the late 1950s when the *noir* cycle came to an end. Although Kerr's argument is flawed in that by no means all *noir* films were in fact B-movies – some, such as *The Big Sleep* (starring Humphrey Bogart and Lauren Bacall) and *Gilda* (with Rita Hayworth and Glenn Ford) were A-class star vehicles – there is some substance to his interpretation of *noir* aesthetics in so far as by the late 1950s black-and-white was no longer regarded as a cinematic shorthand for realism (as it had been, say, during the 1930s and 1940s) and was now seen as a more stylized, non-realistic mode of representation. Another interpretation is to explain the visual style of *film noir* through the influence of *émigré* filmmakers who had begun their careers in Europe, specifically in Germany, and who were thus highly influenced by the cinema of German Expressionism. It is certainly correct that many of the key creative figures involved in the production of *film noir* were European *émigrés*, such as directors Fritz Lang, Robert Siodmark, Billy Wilder and Otto Preminger, and cinematographers Karl Freund and Rudolph Maté. It would be mistaken, however, to see *film noir* as an entirely 'European' practice, for other key practitioners, such as directors John Huston and Howard Hawks and cinematographer James Wong Howe, had been schooled in Hollywood's studio system.

Most American films, even if they are critical of society and its values, ultimately offer solutions to social problems. This rarely happens, however, in *film noir*. There is rarely the opportunity for redemption offered by the gangster film or the western; institutions such as the law are shown to be at the worst corrupt and at the best merely ineffectual; and even the nominal heroes are often presented as flawed and unattractive characters. It has been argued that as *film noir* is characterized by a 'pessimistic vision . . . implying a universal corruptibility', it therefore 'does not lend itself readily to social criticism or comment'.[45] It has also been argued, moreover, that due to its essential pessimism and moral squalor, *film noir* is a subversive mode of filmmaking that kicks against the social optimism and moral certainties of most American movies during the classical era. Thus *film noir* undermines the audience's expectations and denies them the happy endings to which they have become accustomed. *Film noir* is therefore a vehicle through which 'the disquieting forces of fear and paranoia creep into what used to be, for most American audiences at least, the stabilizing and reassuring experience of going to the movies'.[46]

One of the most subversive aspects of *film noir*, or so it has been claimed, is to be found in its representation of gender. The preponderance of strong-willed, manipulative and sexually predatory female characters in *film noir* has attracted the attention of feminist critics who have seen these films as a site for questioning the patriarchal order that underlies Hollywood cinema. The *femme fatale* film, for example, undermines the sanctity of the family through its narrative of women who plot to murder their husbands and dupe their unwitting lovers into helping them (*Double Indemnity*, *The Postman Always Rings Twice*). Even though the *femmes fatales* of *film noir* ultimately suffer for their transgressive behaviour, they often emerge as stronger and more assertive characters than the angst-ridden, uncertain male protagonists. To the extent that they are shown to be in control of their own sexuality, figures such as Barbara Stanwyck's Phyllis Dietrichson (*Double Indemnity*) and Rita

Hayworth's eponymous Gilda might be claimed as images of female empowerment. But to what extent is *film noir* genuinely subversive in its representation of gender? On this question, even feminists disagree. On the one hand, Janey Place argues that *film noir* is 'hardly "progressive" in these terms – it does not present us with role models who defy their fate and triumph over it'.[47] On the other hand, however, Sylvia Harvey contends that *film noir* 'allows for the production of the seeds of counter-ideologies' and that it exhibits a 'subversive significance' which 'cannot finally be contained'.[48] A fair assessment would probably be to say that while *film noir* was hardly subversive in the radical way that feminist critics of the 1970s would prefer, it was about as subversive as Hollywood could be in the 1940s given the restrictions of the Production Code and the social conventions of the time.

Film noir has attracted much critical attention largely on account of its difference from the norms of classical Hollywood cinema. Steve Neale suggests, however, that 'as a concept *film noir* seeks to homogenize a set of distinct and heterogeneous phenomena; it thus inevitably generates contradictions, exceptions and anomalies and is doomed, in the end, to incoherence'.[49] The parameters of *film noir* are more flexible than other generic categories and are defined by critics rather than by the discourses of film production or film reviewing. Quite apart from its imprecise generic status, moreover, *film noir* highlights another anomaly of film history, namely the difference between the level of critical interest in a cycle of films and the cultural significance of those films. It is invariably the case that pessimistic, gloomy films that seem to be responding to some kind of social malaise attract more attention than positive, upbeat films that offer optimistic images of social harmony and integration. This is not to say that *film noir* is unimportant, but it has certainly been privileged in film history at the expense of other films from the same period. Taken collectively, the *film noir* movement was a significant production trend in post-war Hollywood, but individual *noir* films rarely featured amongst the box-office top ten at a time when the major attractions were sentimental dramas (*The Bells of St Mary's*), comedies (the *Road* movies), westerns (*Duel in the Sun*) and musicals (*The Jolson*

Story). As Belton observes: '*Film noir* ... does not entirely dis-
mantle American myth and American identity in the 1940s; it
provided one major current within (and clearly beneath) a flood
of films that reaffirm traditional American values and identity'.[50]

UTOPIAN FANTASIES

At the opposite end of the generic spectrum to *film noir* is the
Hollywood musical. There is no more optimistic genre than the
musical, which offers utopian images of social harmony, individual fulfilment and personal well-being. The musical creates
its own fantasy world in which characters express themselves
through song and dance and in which the main problem, such as
it is, is simply the course of true love. While musicals are not
unique to Hollywood, the genre is widely held to have reached
its most perfect form in the American cinema and to have a
particular resonance with American culture. 'The essence of the
American musical is the spirit it evokes – the mystique of the
American way of life,' British critic Roger Manvell wrote in
1955, towards the end of the period considered the musical's
'golden age'. 'The best musicals', he contended, 'have the vitality of a nation which has no inhibitions when it comes to singing
about the heartaches and happiness of contemporary life, or
laughing at its own absurdities or glamourising the sheer love of
sex and material success.'[51]

Although it was long recognized as a popular and prolific
genre, the musical made a relatively late entry onto the agenda
of film studies. It did not immediately suggest itself as a vehicle
for the exploration of national identity (unlike the western and
the gangster film), it was not obviously ripe for psychoanalytical
interpretation (unlike the melodrama and the horror film) and
it did not seem to offer the subversive potential that some critics
detected in *film noir*. The musical's apparent lack of psychological depth and its detachment from any serious engagement with
social reality made it appear trivial in comparison to the thematic concerns of other genres. As Jane Feuer put it in 1982:
'Westerns might now be seen as a conflict between chaos and
civilization, but Fred Astaire remained ineffable.'[52] Whereas

other genres could be seen as being 'about' something, all the musical was about was entertainment – pure and simple.

Yet entertainment is rarely pure and never simple. The deceptively simple popular appeal of the musical disguises a complex set of formal, aesthetic and ideological strategies. Indeed, the musical is theoretically one of the most complex of all genres, and is certainly, as Schatz observes, one of the 'least understood'.⁵³ With its foregrounding of performance and spectacle, the musical challenges the conventional model of the classical narrative feature film built on straightforward and unobtrusive narration. It is, paradoxically, one of the most ritualistic and conventionalized of all genres, yet also one of the most spontaneous. And, for all that the boy-meets-girl plots of musicals might seem trivial in the extreme, the genre is an ideological vehicle that not only promotes but positively validates a definite set of values. It reinforces traditional social practices (courtship) and values (heterosexual romantic love) to a fuller extent than any other genre. Oddly, given that some musical stars have attracted their own gay fan cultures (Judy Garland being the most prominent example), the musical is the most avowedly heterosexist, and possibly even homophobic, of film genres.⁵⁴

Even the utopian myth at the heart of the musical is not the straightforward matter that it might at first appear. Utopia – the idea of a perfect society – is a profoundly political and ideological notion. The utopia promised by the Hollywood musical is a specifically American utopia of affluence and material well-being. In so far as the musical was also one of the most expensive types of films to produce, this seems entirely apt. It is through the musical that American cinema offers visions of social optimism during the Depression (*Gold Diggers of 1933*) and promotes the attractions of capitalism to a Soviet lady commissar (*Silk Stockings*, a musical remake of *Ninotchka*). The social vision of the musical is of a stable and harmonious society: it resolves generational conflict (*The Jazz Singer*), reconciles separated couples (*The Barkleys of Broadway*), overcomes racial differences (*South Pacific*) and brings an end to factional strife (*West Side Story*).

As a genre, the film musical was born with the advent of sound, though its origins can be identified in non-filmic musical forms such as vaudeville and Broadway. The first 'talkie' is also often regarded as the first musical, though *The Jazz Singer* is probably best understood as a part-talking picture and as a film with musical moments (Al Jolson's songs) rather than as a pure musical (a film structured around musical numbers). There were over 200 musical films of one sort or another over the next three years (1928–30) – thus making the musical far more prominent in the generic profile of American cinema than the gangster film or even the western – and, although the number of musicals declined in the early 1930s, the genre had re-established itself as a staple of Hollywood production by 1933–4.[55]

The formal history of the musical has been written both in terms of a generic typology (identifying different types such as the revue film, the operetta, the college musical, the backstage musical, the rock musical, and so forth) and in terms of a studio-based history that privileges the role of certain producers (Busby Berkeley, Arthur Freed) and to a lesser extent directors (Vincente Minnelli, Stanley Donen) in the artistic development of the genre. Neale asserts that the musical 'has always been a mongrel genre' and 'has been marked by numerous traditions, forms and styles'.[56] Like other genres, the musical is not a static entity, but is subject to continuous flux and transition, often in quite rapid ways. In the late 1920s, for example, there was a short-lived vogue for the all-star revue musical as each of the major studios seized the opportunity of the new sound technology to showcase its contract artistes (MGM's *Hollywood Revue of 1929*, Warners' *The Show of Shows*, *Paramount on Parade* and Fox's *Movietone Follies*). This cycle quickly gave way to the backstage musical (MGM's *Broadway Melody* and *It's A Great Life*, Paramount's *Glorifying the American Girl*, RKO's *Rio Rita*, Warners' *On with the Show*) and the operetta (Warners' *The Desert Song*, MGM's *The Rogue Song*, Paramount's *The Vagabond King*). The operetta, with its fairy-tale settings and traditional arias, reached the zenith of its popularity in the cycle of films starring Jeanette MacDonald and Nelson Eddy between 1935 and 1942 (*Naughty Marietta, Rose Marie, Maytime, Sweethearts, I Married an Angel*), all produced at MGM by Hunt Stromberg.

It is universally agreed that the most significant developments in the musical during the 1930s occurred at Warners and

RKO. Two cycles of films in particular represented significant advances in the genre's formal history due to the strategies they developed for incorporating the performance of musical numbers into the classical narrative feature film. Warners recruited Broadway producer Busby Berkeley, who, in three films all released in 1933 (*42nd Street*, *Gold Diggers of 1933*, *Footlight Parade*), brought a new level of visual spectacle to the traditional backstage musical. The Berkeley films culminated in elaborate production numbers in which the camera, instead of filming from the front of the proscenium (the imaginary 'arch' that separates the stage from the spectator), was involved in the actual numbers through its new-found mobility. The Berkeley production numbers have been described both as political – 'It takes only a little imagination to see Berkeley's stars and flowers and circles (photographed from above) as symbols of an harmonious nation' – and as a form of erotic spectacle: 'And of course we are treated to the typical Berkeley "crotch shot" in which the camera travels down a row of girls spread-eagled on the floor as one by one their legs "go down" for the phallic lens.'[57] These elements are perhaps best combined in *Gold Diggers of 1933*, in which the three main production numbers are in turn satirical ('We're in the Money'), blatantly sexual ('Pettin' in the Park' bizarrely features a precocious child looking up girls' skirts) and a political commentary ('My Forgotten Man').

At RKO, in the meantime, a very different style of musical was emerging through the celebrated cycle of films teaming Fred Astaire and Ginger Rogers. The famous duo had in fact first danced together as a supporting act in *Flying Down to Rio* (1933), which had more in common with Berkeley-type spectacle (lines of chorus girls on aeroplane wings), but it was in the eight films they made as a star team (*The Gay Divorcée*, *Roberta*, *Top Hat*, *Follow the Fleet*, *Swing Time*, *Shall We Dance*, *Carefree*, *The Story of Vernon and Irene Castle*) that the essence of the Astaire-Rogers musical emerged. With their shining Art Deco sets, the Astaire-Rogers films created fantasy spaces that were far removed from the realistic backstage locations of the Warner musicals. Astaire, moreover, along with producer Pandro S. Berman and dance choreographer Hermes Pan, pioneered what has come to be termed the 'integrated musical' in which song-and-dance routines were used to advance the plot rather than being pre-sented as staged numbers before the footlights. The Astaire-Rogers dance routines become elaborate rituals of courtship and seduction ('Night and Day' in *The Gay Divorcée*, 'Cheek to Cheek' in *Top Hat*, 'Never Gonna Dance' in *Swing Time*) in which Fred gradually woos Ginger and breaks down her initial resistance.[58]

The aesthetic and formal differences between the 'inte-grated' and 'unintegrated' musical are intimately connected with the internal logic (or verisimilitude) of the genre. In the integrated musical it is natural for characters to burst into song or to start dancing, usually at moments of heightened emotion, and no narrative explanation for their action is required. In the unintegrated musical, however, there has to be a narrative reason for the song-and-dance routines (hence the frequency of the 'putting on a show' plot). While the uninte-grated musical continued to proliferate, the dominant trend in the genre throughout the 1940s and into the 1950s was towards the perfection of the integrated musical. If the Astaire-Rogers films remain the most fondly remembered musicals in Hollywood's history, it is the great MGM musicals of the late 1940s and early 1950s that are generally deemed by film critics to represent the artistic peak of the genre. A prestigious produc-tion unit under Arthur Freed specialized in the production of Technicolor musical extravaganzas (*The Pirate*, *Easter Parade*, *On the Town*, *An American in Paris*, *Singin' in the Rain*) that have come to occupy a privileged place in the genre's history.[59] While the popular favourites among this group are probably the exu-berant *On the Town* and the ingeniously self-referential *Singin' in the Rain*, it was the more ambitious *An American in Paris*, directed by Vincente Minnelli and choreographed by star Gene Kelly, that was intended to legitimize the Hollywood musical as a serious as well as a popular art form. The artistic ambitions of the film (some critics would say its artistic pretensions) are evi-dent in the 'American in Paris' ballet that takes up the last twenty minutes of the film and which is presented as a fantasy sequence (itself a frequent device in the Freed-Kelly films) that is imagined by Kelly's character.

During the early 1950s the musical became self-referential,

exemplified in films such as *Singin' in the Rain* (Hollywood telling its own history through a nostalgic and satirical account of the arrival of talking pictures) and *The Band Wagon* (Fred Astaire playing a thinly disguised version of himself as an ageing Hollywood song-and-dance star). Feuer, pointing out that such self-reflexivity tends to be associated with *auteur* films, argues that it serves an entirely different purpose in the musical. Whereas, usually, 'we tend to associate reflexivity with the notion of deconstruction within film-making practice', in the musical it is used 'to perpetuate rather than to deconstruct the codes of the genre. Self-reflective musicals are conservative texts in every sense.'[60]

From the mid-1950s the musical split into several lineages, none of which ever became entirely dominant. The traditional musical persisted in the form of big-budget, widescreen adaptations of Broadway shows, especially those of Richard Rodgers and Oscar Hammerstein (*Oklahoma!*, *The King and I*, *South Pacific*) which were the major box-office successes of the mid- and late 1950s, but a new direction was signalled by the emergence of the rock musical foregrounding rock'n'roll performers such as Elvis Presley (*Jailhouse Rock*) and Bill Haley (*Rock Around the Clock*) and aimed principally at the teenage audience. The phenomenal success of the Rodgers-Hammerstein adaptation *The Sound of Music* in 1965 seems something of an aberration, for the trend was away from the saccharine-sweet family musical and towards more adult-oriented films such as Bob Fosse's *Sweet Charity* (1968) and *Cabaret* (1972). In the 1970s the genre fragmented even further: the so-called 'anti-musicals' which attempted to deconstruct the genre, such as Robert Altman's *Nashville* and Martin Scorsese's *New York, New York*, were far less successful at the box-office, however, than the disco musical (*Saturday Night Fever*) and the teen-nostalgia musical (*Grease*). However, as a genre the musical was now a spent force, demonstrated by the commercial failure of attempts to revive the 1930s romantic musical (Peter Bogdanovich's *At Long Last Love*) and the Broadway show musical (Richard Attenborough's *A Chorus Line*). Rick Altman suggests that 'the musical' (as a genre) has now given way to 'the musical film' (a film including musical sequences).[61] The musical film has been a sporadic feature of

American cinema in the 1980s and 1990s, often exploiting the latest trend in pop music (*Breakdance*, *Flashdance*, *Dirty Dancing*) and rarely amounting to anything more than an elongated pop video. The classic American musical, it seems safe to conclude, was very much a product of the studio system and has not out-lasted the mode of production that created it.

FAMILY VALUES

The melodrama is another genre that presents problems of def-inition. In the film industry the term 'melodrama' was originally used to describe thrillers, action films and serials. In film criti-cism, the adjective 'melodramatic' was often employed in a derogatory sense to indicate a highly theatrical film that privi-leged heightened emotion over psychological realism. It was film theorists who appropriated the term 'melodrama' in the 1970s and used it to refer, rather imprecisely, to the female-centred narratives that proliferated in American cinema, espe-cially during the 1940s and 1950s. Thus 'melodrama' became elided with what the film industry had traditionally described as 'the woman's film'. Although more recent theoretical work has tended to conceptualize melodrama (rather like *film noir*) as a style or a mode that ranges across different genres, the notion of melodrama as a genre in its own right persists in much film writing. It is typically used to describe films centering either on female protagonists or on the family. In essence, melodrama, whether it is seen as a genre or as a mode, focuses on the private, domestic sphere (so often gendered as feminine) rather than on the public sphere that is the focus of narrative interest in genres such as the western and the gangster film.[62]

It is one of the paradoxes of classical Hollywood that, although women were all too often cast in stereotyped gender roles (shopgirl, secretary, dutiful wife, seductive temptress), there were also more genuinely female-centred narratives during the classical period than since. The conventional explanation for this is the prominence of women, particularly mature women, in the cinema-going audience between the 1930s and the 1950s in contrast to the predominantly young, male audience that has become increasingly dominant since the 1960s. While this may be an over-simplification, it is important to take into account Hollywood's own view of whom its audience is in accounting for production trends. The female-centred melodrama became especially prominent during the late 1930s (*Stella Dallas, Jezebel, Gone With the Wind*) and early/mid-1940s (*Rebecca, Now, Voyager, Since You Went Away, Mr Skeffington, Mildred Pierce*). Evidence that films such as these were made primarily with the female audience in mind is provided by *Variety*'s review of the 1937 Barbara Stanwyck vehicle *Stella Dallas* which described it as '[a] tear jerker of A ranking. There are things about the story that will not appeal to some men, but . . . the wallop is inescapably there for femmes'.[63]

Film critic Molly Haskell has argued that the melodramas of the 1930s and 1940s tend to revolve around one of two female archetypes. The first is the 'superfemale' – 'a woman who, while exceedingly "feminine" and flirtatious, is too ambitious and intelligent for the docile role society has decreed she play'.[64] Bette Davis is the archetypal superfemale, and *Now, Voyager* (1942), a glossily romantic fairy-tale of an 'ugly ducking' who turns into a swan, is probably the most famous Davis vehicle. Maria LaPlace suggests a parallel between the film's narrative trajectory and the construction of Davis's own star persona as that of 'a plucky, resourceful, "self-made" woman, whose success is due not to beauty, but to personal qualities of talent, determination, and down-to-earth self-awareness'.[65] The second archetype is the 'superwoman' – a woman who 'has a high degree of intelligence or imagination, but instead of exploiting her femininity, adopts male characteristics in order to enjoy male prerogatives, or merely to survive'.[66] This archetype is best exemplified by Joan Crawford in *Mildred Pierce* (1945), a sort of proto-feminist melodrama in which a dowdy housewife breaks with social convention by leaving her husband and, through hard work and enterprise, builds her own career as a successful businesswoman. It is significant that this type of film was made at a time of social change for women when, due to the war, more older, married women were being recruited into the labour force; it is equally significant that the female-centred melodrama became less prolific in the late 1940s when there was a drive 'to get women out of the office and back into the home'.[67]

The 1940s witnessed the peak of the 'woman's film' in Hollywood. A different type of melodrama arose during the 1950s in which male as well as female domestic problems were expressed (leading some commentators to dub such films 'male weepies'). The entry point of film theorists into these films, as it had been with the western, arose from the work of certain directors. What John Ford, Anthony Mann and Budd Boetticher were to the western, Douglas Sirk, Nicholas Ray and Vincente Minnelli were to the melodrama. Sirk (*Magnificent Obsession, All that Heaven Allows, Written on the Wind, Imitation of Life*), Ray (*Rebel without a Cause, Bigger Than Life*) and Minnelli (*The Bad and the Beautiful, Tea and Sympathy, Some Came Running, Home from the Hill*) initially attracted attention for their use of *mise-en-scène*, through which, it was argued, they transformed banal scripts into powerful statements of authorial vision. Thomas Elsaesser has suggested that technical developments including colour, widescreen, deep-focus cinematography and wide-angle lenses 'encouraged a new form of sophisticated melodrama' and that directors such as Sirk, Minnelli and Ray 'began showing a similar degree of visual culture as the masters of silent film-drama'.[68] Sirk's films in particular are notable for the way in which the colour-coding of characters' dress is invested with thematic significance: cold colours such as blue, green and grey to express loneliness and repression, warm colours such as red and orange to express emotional and sexual satisfaction.

The same directors were also at the forefront of attention when critics began to see the melodrama as a vehicle for exploring social values and institutions. The themes of the melodrama – family, gender, class, race, sexuality – make it a ripe subject for ideological analysis. Like *film noir*, melodrama, and in particular the family melodrama, was seized upon for the subversive possibilities it offered within classical Hollywood cinema. Elsaesser, for example, asserted that 'the best American melodramas of the fifties [were] not only critical social documents but genuine tragedies, despite or rather because of the happy ending: they record some of the agonies that have accompanied the demise of the "affirmative culture".[69] Schatz even goes so far as to claim that 'the 50s melodramas are actually among the most socially self-conscious and covertly "anti-American" films ever produced by the Hollywood studios'.[70] The melodrama offers a distinctly jaundiced view of that most sacred of American social institutions, the family. The melodramas of the 1950s present the family as torn apart by generational conflict – between father and son (*Rebel without a Cause*), between mother and daughter (*Imitation of Life*) – and as a seething hotbed of material and sexual jealousy (*Written on the Wind*).

The content and themes of the melodrama have made it a particularly ripe subject for feminist and psychoanalytic criticism. For feminist critics, the melodrama provides a type of narrative 'motivated by female desire and processes of spectator identification governed by female point-of-view'.[71] Laura Mulvey, typically combining feminist and psychoanalytical perspectives, argues that there are in fact two trends within melodrama. She distinguishes between, on the one hand, the woman's melodrama 'coloured by a female protagonist's dominating point-of-view' and, on the other hand, the male oedipal melodrama which is concerned with 'tensions in the family, and between sex and generations'.[72] Sirk emerges as the key director here in that his films straddle both the female melodrama (*All that Heaven Allows*) and the male oedipal melodrama (*Written on the Wind*). In Mulvey's analysis, the male oedipal melodrama is the more easily resolved (there is usually some form of narrative reconciliation between generations and sexes), but the female melodrama is problematic in that it leaves unresolved the wider questions of women's place in a patriarchial society.

The melodramas of the 1950s can also be seen as part of Hollywood's response to the rise of television. In 1956 *Variety* noted the trend for 'unusual, off-beat films with adult themes that television could not handle'.[73] The melodrama was frankly sensationalist in its use of 'adult' subject matter such as marital infidelity (*From Here to Eternity*), drug addiction (*The Man with the Golden Arm*), sexual awakening (*Baby Doll*) and rape (*Peyton Place*). In the early 1960s taboos such as lesbianism (*The Children's Hour*) and paedophilia (*Lolita*) were also breached.

The sensational best-sellers of Harold Robbins, with their trashy tales of greed and sex (*Never Love a Stranger*, *The Carpetbaggers*, *Where Love Has Gone*, *Stiletto*), provided a ready source of story material between the late 1950s and the early 1970s. By this time, however, the film melodrama was already being displaced, its place in American popular culture being assumed by the television mini-series (*Rich Man, Poor Man*) and the soap opera (*Dallas*, *Dynasty*).

How can the decline of the melodrama be explained? Unlike the decline of the western, for which a range of cultural factors have been advanced, the disappearance of the melodrama seems to hinge mainly on the changes in the relationship between Hollywood and its audiences. Although films continue to be made that privilege the woman's point-of-view (*Steel Magnolias*, *Fried Green Tomatoes at the Whistle Stop Cafe*, *Thelma and Louise*), they tend to be non-mainstream films produced for the 'art house' circuit. This suggests that the film industry no longer believes in the existence of a large female audience for traditional 'women's pictures'. The most successful attempt to revive the melodrama in recent times was *Titanic*, widely seen as a modern equivalent of *Gone With the Wind* in that it uses real historical events as the epic background to a fictional love story. Peter Krämer has argued that, for all its state-of-the-art special effects, *Titanic* was 'an evocation of Hollywood's past . . . a neglected tradition of filmmaking which clearly put women first'.[74] The film's phenomenal success is explained through its 'rediscovery' of the female audience – audience research revealed that 60 per cent of ticket sales for *Titanic* were to women – and its placing of a female protagonist at the centre of the narrative. Yet *Titanic* also proved to be a 'non-recurring phenomenon': a one-off success that did not offer the potential for sequels or imitations. As a mainstream genre, the melodrama has not survived in New Hollywood. The fact that certain genres have endured, whereas others have not, provides strong evidence that film genres are intimately connected with their particular social and historical contexts.

EIGHT

European Cinemas in Peace and War

The 1930s and 1940s were the most tumultuous decades in modern European history, the events of those years determining the geopolitical and cultural map of the continent for the rest of the century. The Depression, the horrors of the Second World War and the Holocaust, post-war reconstruction and the onset of the Cold War were events of far-reaching historical consequence. It was against this background that the cinema reached the zenith of its appeal as both a popular art form and as an instrument of propaganda and social control. In these years Europe was a 'contested continent' in which competing political systems (totalitarianism and liberal democracy) and ideologies (Communism and Fascism) were in conflict. The cinema, by dint of both its popular appeal and its ability to present ideas and values in dramatic terms, became an important weapon in the propagandist's arsenal. It was adopted as an instrument of state propaganda in regimes such as Soviet Russia, Fascist Italy and Nazi Germany; and even in democracies where the practice of propaganda was officially frowned upon, its potential for winning the hearts and minds of publics at home and abroad was recognized and exploited. This appropriation of cinema for political purposes coincided with the height of cinema-going as a social practice: in most countries attendances reached their highest ever levels during and immediately after the Second World War. While the 1930s and 1940s saw the consolidation of the national cinemas that had emerged in Europe after the First World War – a trend accelerated by the institutionalization of talking pictures from *c.* 1930 – there are nevertheless some striking similarities in the characteristics of European cinemas during this period. Two particular themes are worth highlighting. On the one hand, following the avant-garde

195

experiments of the 1920s, there was a shift in many national cinemas towards realism. There were different styles of realism – Poetic Realism in France, Socialist Realism in the USSR, documentary film in Britain and Neo-Realism in Italy – but all these nationally specific movements shared certain common characteristics, not least of which was a political as well as an aesthetic commitment to portraying the lives and experiences of 'ordinary' people in contrast to the glossy star vehicles of Hollywood. On the other hand, popular film preferences were strongly oriented in favour of entertainment and escape, with genres such as the musical, the comedy and the romantic drama prominent in the production strategies of all national cinemas. This division – sometimes characterized as between 'realism' and 'tinsel', or as between a critically respectable cinema and a low-brow popular cinema – reached its most polarized form during the Second World War.

Although critics and commentators often speak of 'European cinema', the nature of research into the national cinemas of Europe, especially during the 1930s and 1940s, is such that while certain countries have been quite thoroughly explored (especially France, Britain, Germany and Italy, which between them accounted for some three quarters of all European film production), other important film-producing nations have been relatively neglected (the Scandinavian countries especially). The eminent French scholar Pierre Sorlin contends that while the smaller film-producing nations 'have made excellent movies which deserve close attention for the part they have played in the evolution of cinematic language', nevertheless 'these films are isolated works which are not merged into a wider, less artistic, production' and that consequently 'there is little that the social historian can gain from an analysis of these movies'.[1] My own account, like so many others, is inevitably biased in favour of those national cinemas where the films are known outside their own borders and where other scholars have already undertaken substantive research into the nature of cinema as a social institution and a cultural practice. But while this chapter focuses, therefore, on the 'big four' of France, Britain, Germany and Italy, I have also tried to extend my discussion to other national cinemas wherever this has been possible.

A comparative approach to film history reveals that the spread of cinema was uneven across Europe. Demographic factors such as population size and the extent of urbanization obviously impacted upon patterns of cinema-going. The Soviet Union had the largest number of cinemas of any country in the world – estimated at some 30,000 in 1939 – but produced only around three dozen films annually for most of the 1930s. Following the Soviet Union the countries with the greatest number of cinemas at the end of the 1930s were Germany (6,500, including Austria), Britain (5,300), France (4,600), Italy (4,000) and Spain (3,500).[2] As one would expect, the number of cinemas broadly reflects the most populous countries, though there are some anomalies. Poland, the fifth most populous nation (34.6 million people in 1940), had only 769 cinemas, while less populous countries such as Sweden (6.4 million) and Belgium (8.3 million) had a disproportionately large number of cinemas (1,900 and 1,100 respectively). With no precise correlation between the number of cinemas and population size, there were evidently national and cultural differences in the extent to which cinema was established as a social institution.

For those countries where reliable statistics exist, however, there is evidence of some general patterns in cinema-going habits. There seems to have been an increase in cinema attendances in the late 1920s, coinciding with the advent of talking pictures, followed by a decline in the early 1930s, attributable to the effects of the Depression. Then, from approximately the mid-1930s, there is an overall increase in cinema attendances, maintained throughout the Second World War and (except for Britain) into the 1950s. In Britain there were 903 million paid cinema admissions in 1934 (the first year for which statistics exist), rising to 990 million in 1939. Annual attendances passed 1,000 million for the first time in 1940 and did not fall below that level until 1957, reaching a peak of 1,635 million in 1946.[3] There is good reason to concur with A.J.P. Taylor's assessment that cinema-going was 'the essential social habit of the age'.[4] The most dramatic increase in cinema-going, however, took place in Germany during the Third Reich where the number of annual ticket sales almost quadrupled over ten years from 238 million in 1933 to 1,117 million in 1943.[5] The wartime increase in the popularity of cinema in both Britain and Germany can be explained in part by the public's appetite for escapism and by the fact that, at a time of shortages and rationing, the cinema was a cheap and easily available form of entertainment.

The anomaly amongst the major nations was France. Although the 1930s are often described as 'the golden age of French cinema', Susan Hayward contends that 'the cultural myth of the cinephilic French is just that – a myth. The French are not and, with the exception of one period in history, have never been avid film-goers.'[6] Cinema attendances remained fairly constant during the 1930s at between 200 and 230 million per year, and, while there was, as elsewhere, a wartime increase, it did not reach the levels of Britain and Germany, reaching a peak of just over 300 million in 1943.[7] The average number of cinema visits per head of population was between five and six a year, half that of Germany and only a fifth that of Britain. There are various possible reasons for the failure of the cinema in France to reach a wider audience. The effects of the Depression, for one thing, lasted longer in France than else-where, reducing the amount of income available for leisure activities. The stagnation of the French population – which remained static at just under 42 million between the early 1910s and late 1930s – meant there was no increase in the overall potential audience. Another possible explanation, although one that is impossible to quantify, is that there may have been more cultural resistance on the part of French audiences to the American movies that dominated the screen in those countries open to Hollywood imports.

It has long been the received wisdom that Hollywood movies were more popular with European cinema-goers than the indigenous product. On one level, this would seem to be borne out by statistics: in the 1930s American movies accounted for 50 per cent of all films exhibited in France, 65 per cent of those exhibited in Italy and over 70 per cent of those exhibited in Britain.[8] And, on another level, anecdotal evidence that audi-ences preferred Hollywood movies is provided by contempo-raries who feared the pernicious effects of Americanization.

Such fears were most acute in Britain, where there were no linguistic barriers in the way of American films and where some organizations were concerned about the adoption of American slang phrases by British children. 'We don't want our children to go about saying "Oh, yeah" and "O.K. kid" and there is no doubt a tendency to Americanize the English language throughout the film that is, I think, deplorable', declared an advocate speaking on behalf of the Birmingham Cinema Enquiry Committee in 1931.[9]

More recent research, however, has qualified the assumption that home-grown films were not popular with cinema-goers. While not denying the popularity of American movies, there is evidence to suggest that national cinemas provided strong competition for Hollywood in their domestic markets. In some of the smaller countries, American films, whilst being the most numerous, came second at the box-office to the home-grown products. In Denmark in 1938, for example, nine Danish films earned half of the domestic box-office revenues.[10] Popularity polls, furthermore, indicate that stars such as Arletty and Jean Gabin in France, Hans Albers and Heinz Rühmann in Germany and Vittorio De Sica in Italy were just as popular with home audiences as American stars. The complex nature of audience tastes, including regional differences, is amply illustrated by John Sedgwick's research into popular film preferences in Britain. Sedgwick's findings, based on empirical statistical data, affirms 'the dominant collective position occupied by the principal Hollywood studios' but also shows that 'British films were of interest to indigenous audiences', calculating that a third of the top fifty films for the years 1932–7 'were made by home-based production companies'.[11]

Americanization – which was synonymous with Hollywood at this time – was one of the concerns expressed by those who wished to regulate the content of films. Other concerns, which applied equally to Hollywood movies and home-made products, were those perennial issues of crime, morality and sexuality voiced by reformers, politicians and churchmen. Most European cinemas were heavily regulated through mechanisms of censorship and control that had some degree of official or semi-official status. The most illiberal censorship regimes, outside the totalitarian states, were to be found in those countries where the Roman Catholic Church exerted the strongest influence. Probably the most restrictive, socially, was the Irish Free State, where the 1923 Censorship of Films Act had 'put in the hands of state censors ill-defined and subjective criteria for issuing certificates for the public exhibition of films'.[12] The first Irish film censor, James Montgomery, adopted the Ten Commandments as the basis of his code and over the next forty years he and his successors, Richard Hayes and Martin Brennan, banned some 3,000 films including *The Outlaw*, *Mildred Pierce*, *The Big Sleep*, *Brief Encounter* (for the sympathetic depiction of an extra-marital love affair) and *Outrage* (Ida Lupino's film dealing with the consequences of rape). In Spain state censorship was in place long before the Franco regime; one of its early victims was Luis Buñuel, whose documentary about poverty (*Las Hurdes*, 1932) was banned for many years. Following the Spanish Civil War, the forces of Fascism and Catholicism effectively colluded in promoting an officially endorsed, ideologically acceptable morality that included not only politics (loyalty to the regime) but also religion (any form of anticlericalism was banned) and the representation of social life (women were expected to be loyal wives and servants). A similar collusion between church and state occurred in Mussolini's Italy – 'the only country', in the words of director Alberto Lattuada, 'where the religious power, the monarchical power and a dictatorship existed as a unique triumvirate'.[13] Oddly, however, Luchino Visconti's *Ossessione* (*Obsession*, 1942), an intense drama of illicit sexual passion which outraged both church and government, was initially passed by the censor (it was later withdrawn).

For all the moral imperatives of censorship, however, there is a case to argue that European films were, to some extent at least, freer to deal with 'adult' subjects than was allowed in Hollywood under the Production Code. The reputation of some European cinemas for their sexiness, even in the 1930s, is well deserved. There is no consensus as to which was the first 'sex film', or even what the term means, though the most famous (or notorious) was undoubtedly the Czech film *Extase* (*Ecstasy*, 1932), which, while not the first to depict full female nudity (as is sometimes claimed), was probably the first to depict sexual intercourse. Its story of a frustrated young married woman (Hedy Lamarr) who meets and makes love to another man – and whose facial expressions during the act clearly indicate she is enjoying the experience – led to the film being condemned by the Vatican and banned both in the USA and in Britain. The early sound era in Germany, coinciding with the last years of the Weimar Republic, was a period of relative permissiveness in film censorship which 'opened up new opportunities for provocative subject matter'.[14] In the early 1930s, for example, there were melodramas exploring themes such as sexual obsession (Josef von Sternberg's *Der Blaue Engel/The Blue Angel*) and lesbianism (Leontine Sagan's *Mädchen in Uniform/Girls in Uniform*). This brief window of opportunity for controversial themes ended abruptly with the Nazi accession to power in 1933, though it could be argued that German cinema under the Third Reich was rather more permissive in allowing erotic imagery than most other cinemas of the time. Even in France, for instance, a brief nude appearance by Arletty in Marcel Carné's *Le Jour se lève* (*Daybreak*, 1939) was removed by the censor.

It would be mistaken to assume that it was only in the totalitarian states that political censorship was exercised. Even in the western liberal democracies, censorship boards were concerned to prevent the circulation of films that might inflame 'revolutionary' sentiments, especially during a time of socio-economic hardship. We have already seen how Soviet films such as *Battleship Potemkin* were banned in France and Britain. The British Board of Film Censors, which exercised an effective policy of pre-censorship by vetting scripts before films went into production, maintained a ban on a film of Walter Greenwood's novel *Love on the Dole* throughout the 1930s, even though it had been produced for the stage.[15] The BBFC, while not in itself a state body, was unequivocally part of the establishment which promoted political and social consensus in cinema and prohibited any form of political extremism. In France, where censorship was exercised through a *commission de contrôle* under the Ministry of the Interior, political conservatism was very much the order of the day regardless of which party was in government.

The existence of this censorship apparatus in the liberal democracies, no less than in the totalitarian states, indicates the extent to which the cinema was regarded as a means of social control. This is not to say, however, that a crude Marxist view that sees the cinema as a form of establishment conspiracy is necessarily appropriate. A more useful interpretation is to understand the cinema as a means of promoting consensus based on a set of shared values and ideologies. Jeffrey Richards has advanced this argument in respect of British cinema in the 1930s:

> The actual films were used either to distract or to direct the audience's views into approved channels, by validating key institutions of hegemony, such as monarchy and Empire, the police and the Law, and the armed forces, and promoting those qualities useful to society as presently constituted: hard work, monogamy, cheerfulness, deference, patriotism.[16]

British films of the 1930s offered images of a stable social hierarchy at home (*Hindle Wakes*, *South Riding*) and just colonial government abroad (*Sanders of the River*, *Rhodes of Africa*); they presented patriotic images of the monarchy (*Victoria the Great*, *Sixty Glorious Years*), the armed services (*Brown on Resolution*, *OHMS*) and the British Empire (*The Drum*, *The Four Feathers*). Crucially, however, Richards adds that '[the] public seem on the whole to have been happy with the films they were given during the 1930s, and those films for the most part played their role in maintaining consensus and the *status quo*.'[17] For, while the governing classes and the political establishment could determine the nature and content of films, they could not influence audience taste – a factor that was recognized by propagandists in the totalitarian states as well as in the democracies.

CINEMA AND STATE

The extent of state involvement in the cinema varied enormously from one nation to another. It ranged from, at one end, nationalization (such as in the Soviet Union and Nazi Germany), through various forms of protectionism (France, Britain) to virtual *laissez faire* (Ireland). Yet, for all the different levels of state intervention, there was a common view of the cultural and economic significance of national cinemas. The First World War had demonstrated the potential of cinema as a vehicle of propaganda; the Second World War would see that potential fulfilled. Yet it was not only during times of national emergency and total war that cinema had a propagandist role. The interwar years saw a heightened appreciation of the value of film as a medium of national projection and a vehicle for promoting ideals and values to publics at home and abroad. The international climate of the 1930s, especially, was such that competing ideologies and systems of government vied for influence and prestige. As this coincided with the institutionalization of talking pictures, which made the promotion of political ideologies and cultural values more accessible to the mass public, film acquired a greater than ever importance as an instrument of state.

While it was in the totalitarian states that film was used most directly and overtly for propaganda purposes, democratic governments were also anxious that it should be used to project positive images of national life and culture. Lacking the powers of coercion available to the dictators, the governing classes in the democracies appealed to the patriotism of their national film industries. In 1932, for example, a French civil servant told representatives of the film industry: 'It is your duty to collaborate with the French government in such a manner that the French cinema industry may be directed towards the highest and noblest aims and that productions of France may hold their premier place in all the world.'[18] In Britain the President of the Board of Trade, Oliver Stanley, similarly declared in 1937 that 'I want the world to be able to see British films true to British life, accepting British standards and spreading British ideals'.[19] Even in smaller film-producing nations there was interest in the use of the medium for national projection. In 1922 the *Irish Times* expressed the view that 'we must produce features in which the country and the people can take national pride'.[20]

The rhetoric of politicians focused on the cultural value of film; the policies adopted, however, betray that the prime motivation was economic. Most governments stopped short of direct state subsidy to support their domestic film industries and instead opted for forms of economic protectionism that were designed to provide a more even playing field against the competition from Hollywood. The most common strategy was the introduction of a 'quota' system, which took various forms. On the one hand, some governments imposed a limit on the import of foreign films – a policy followed by Germany from 1925 and by France from 1931. In France, the restriction of imports resulted in French films increasing their share of the domestic market, from around ten per cent in the late 1920s to a steady 30 per cent by the mid-1930s. On the other hand, the policy adopted in Britain with the Cinematograph Films Act of 1927 was to impose a minimum quota of British films on exhibitors and distributors. The outcome of this Act was not, however, entirely as legislators had intended, for while it gave a much-needed boost to the British production sector, some producers took advantage of the situation by turning out cheaply made films known as 'quota quickies' that harmed the reputation of the industry until further legislation laid down requirements of cost and quality for films that could be counted towards the quota.

The smaller nations, even more vulnerable to American competition, also took steps to protect their domestic film industries. The Danish Cinema Law of 1933, intended to promote the educational and cultural value of film, was a barrier against both vertical and horizontal integration: distributors were prohibited from owning cinemas and nobody could control more than one film company at a time. In Finland home production was encouraged by exempting Finnish films from the tax levied on film exhibition. Throughout Scandinavia, indeed, the promotion of an indigenous film culture was part of Social Democratic politics during the 1930s.

In the totalitarian regimes, meanwhile, the state took a more direct role in the control of the film industry. Even so there were different models of state intervention and the extent of official control varied. The most complete example of state intervention was in the Soviet Union, where the controls already introduced in the 1920s were extended. In 1930, as part of the first Five-Year Plan, the Soviet film industry was centralized under one organization, Soyuzkino, whose director, Boris Shumyatsky, was appointed personally by Stalin. Soyuzkino was set up with the intention of making the Soviet cinema self-sufficient, but while it managed to negotiate the adaptation to sound it was hampered by inefficiencies, and production during the 1930s averaged only around 35 films a year. Hollywood movies, which had been widely shown during the 1920s, were now prohibited in the Soviet Union. The great Soviet filmmakers of the 1920s, especially Sergei Eisenstein, were now out of favour due to their supposed 'artistic errors'. Compliance with the doctrine of Socialist Realism was essential for filmmakers under the Stalinist regime.

In the Fascist states, Italy and Spain, the nature of state control was rather different. The Fascists had no axe to grind with capitalist film industries provided that the filmmakers were prepared to support the regime. In both Italy and Spain, it can be argued, economically weak film industries benefited from generous levels of state support and subsidy. In Italy, for example, the Fascist regime supported the film industry by taxing non-Italian language films, subsidizing production and investing in a brand new studio complex, Cinecittà outside Rome, personally opened by Mussolini in 1937. It also set up the film school Centro Sperimentale di Cinematografia and promoted the Venice Film Festival as a showcase for Italian cinema. The domestic production industry was not large enough to supply the Italian market alone, but the importation of films was controlled by a regulation which ingeniously required that foreign films had to be dubbed locally into Italian, rather than shown in their original language or subtitled, thus making it possible to substitute dialogue to render films politically acceptable. This practice was also adopted by Spain which, like Italy, did not want to ban foreign films outright due to their popularity with audiences. Through the Noticiario Cinematografico Español, established in 1942, the government assumed control of newsreel and documentary production. The mechanisms of state control established in Spain in the early 1940s were to last until the 1970s. The long-serving Minister of Culture, Admiral Luis Carrero Blanco, personally supervised Spanish film production until his assassination by Basque separatists in 1973.

The example of Germany exemplifies how the interests of both the state and the film industry could be managed to their mutual benefit. It used to be assumed that when the Nazis came to power in 1933 they took over the mass media, including the film industry, in order to control all cultural production. In fact, however, the Nazis did not immediately set out to nationalize the film industry. They had no need to: a majority share holding in the largest company, Ufa, was held by Nazi supporter Alfred Hugenberg. Julian Petley has argued that the interests of both the party and the industry were to maintain a capitalist oligarchy rather than to follow the Soviet model of openly taking over private firms. Thus, he suggests, 'the reorganisation of the German film industry during the Third Reich was undertaken by government and the most powerful sectors of the industry (namely Ufa and Tobis) working in closest co-operation and very much to the latter's advantage.'[21] Indeed, he even contends that 'many in the industry welcomed the new regime, for various different reasons, and that the most powerful interests were able to shape government policy to their own ends, namely the establishment of a monopolistic market situation'.[22] The *Reichslichtspielgesetz* (Reich Cinema Law) of 1934 extended the state's powers of censorship to scripts and treatments and instituted a system of distinction marks (*prädikate*) to encourage the production of approved films; in return the new regime set up a *Filmkreditbank* to subsidize production. The film industry was compliant with the Nazi regime because it benefited from the rapid increase in cinema-going during the 1930s and, after 1940, from a virtual closed market situation as imports were banned and the occupied territories came under German control. There is a sense in which the German cinema was a victim of its own success, as it was during the war that nationalization of the film industry was effected. This was a matter of economic necessity, as the German film industry now had to supply an enlarged domestic market at a time when most imports had been lost. Since the late 1930s the Nazis had secretly been buying controlling interests in the main production companies (Ufa, Tobis, Bavaria). In early 1942 a giant holding company Ufa-Film GmbH (known as Ufi to distinguish it from Ufa) assumed control of the entire German film industry on behalf of the government. Thus a *de facto* nationalization, that had not been intended when the Nazis came to power, arose as a consequence of war.

The advent of talking pictures was the occasion of both industrial and stylistic change in all the major film-producing countries. The expense of sound conversion and the increased costs of film production brought about a process of consolidation that saw the emergence of large vertically integrated combines on the model of the American film industry. Yet no European industry, at least in the liberal democracies, ever achieved the same level of oligopoly as the American industry. In Britain the two major companies, British International Pictures and the Gaumont British Picture Corporation, expanded during the 1930s but were still unable to fill the quota for British films themselves, which was supplemented by independent producers such as Alexander Korda's London Films and Herbert Wilcox's British and Dominions Film Corporation as well as the notorious 'quota quickies'. In France the era of vertical integration was short lived, as the two giants that emerged in the 1920s – Gaumont-Franco-Film-Aubert and Pathé-Natan – were beset by difficulties: the former nearly went bankrupt, the latter was broken up following revelations of financial irregularities. The increase in French production during the 1930s was sustained mainly by small companies, many of them set up to make just one film. In the smaller film-producing nations there tended to be one major company that enjoyed varying degrees of state support: Nordisk Tonefilm in Denmark, Svensk Filmindustri in Sweden, the Compañia Industrial del Film Español in Spain.

The early 1930s are often characterized as a period of stagnation, even regression, in terms of film style as filmmakers sought to come to terms with the technical limitations of early sound recording technology. Many films of this period did indeed succumb to dialogue at the expense of camera mobility and editing, though even so the early 1930s should not be dismissed out of hand. The input of theatrical people into the film world, such as Marcel Pagnol in France and Bertolt Brecht in Germany, can be seen as part of the on-going process to bring greater cultural and intellectual respectability to the cinema. Pagnol, whose plays of southern French life had been successful in the 1920s, adapted them for the cinema in the 1930s. His 'Marius' trilogy of 1931–6 (*Marius*, directed by Alexander Korda; *Fanny*, directed by Marc Allégret; and *César*, directed by Pagnol himself) are more than just filmed theatre. Ginette Vincendeau contends that the trilogy combines both cinematic and theatrical techniques through which 'an effect of realism emerges'.[23] Indeed, with their mixture of melodrama and tragedy and their artful blend of studio interiors and real locations (Provence, Marseilles) the Pagnol films to some degree anticipated the more celebrated cinema of Poetic Realism. Brecht was an entirely different case. He had collaborated with G. W. Pabst on the adaptation of his play *Die Dreigroschenoper* (*The Threepenny Opera*, 1931), with music by Kurt Weill, before writing *Kuhle Wampe* (1932), a politically and artistically powerful critique of world capitalism. Whereas *Die Dreigroschenoper* was a lavish production utilizing large studio sets of London's Docklands, *Kuhle Wampe* (the title refers to a camp for the dispossessed) was a spare, austere, semi-documentary shot mostly on location. Its stark portrayal of how the Depression affects a young German family and its avowedly procommunist solution to social deprivation unsurprisingly resulted in its banning when the Nazis came to power in 1933. Germany, indeed, was the one major film-producing nation where a type of realism did not become the dominant aesthetic of the 1930s.

There is no straightforward definition of realism in relation to the cinema. Realism is more than just true-to-life stories; it is also an aesthetic, a style, a mode of expression. The 1930s gave rise to an array of different kinds of realism, all imbued with nationally specific characteristics and used to various artistic and political ends. Yet these realist cinemas also shared some common features: they demonstrated a commitment to representing the lives of 'ordinary' people; their formal, aesthetic and ideological strategies were significantly different from the classical cinema of Hollywood (to an extent that they could legitimately be described as 'alternatives'); they were (for the most part) critically acclaimed; and they have been accorded a prominence in aesthetic film history in the same way as the avant-garde practices of the 1920s have dominated critical discussion of silent cinema.

The identification of the 1930s as the 'golden age' of French cinema, for example, is based on a style of filmmaking that came to be known as 'Poetic Realism'. It was a style characterized by narratives of despair and disillusionment, featuring fatalistic and doomed protagonists who are victims of social conditions and circumstances. The focus on social outsiders and the anti-Fascist politics of the cinema of Poetic Realism has led to it being associated with the Popular Front, the short-lived coalition of socialists and communists that formed a government under Léon Blum in 1936–7. The co-operative spirit of the Popular Front was allegorized in *La Belle équipe* (*They Were Five*, 1937), in which a group of unemployed workers win a lottery and decide to invest the money by setting up a riverside café ('Chez Nous') which is run as a collective venture. Although the film is not without tragedy (one of the men dies in an accident), its resolution is optimistic as the protagonists resolve their differences and the café is a success. The director Julien Duvivier had originally wanted the film to have an unhappy ending with one of the men being killed in a jealous feud over a woman – just as the Popular Front itself had been riven by internal tensions that soon tore it apart – but the film's producers insisted on a happy ending for commercial reasons.

Most film historians identify Poetic Realism as emerging in French cinema during the mid-1930s, in the films of directors such as Julien Duvivier, Marcel Carné and Jean Renoir, though there is a reasonable case to make that the features of Poetic Realism were already apparent in earlier films by other hands. Jean Vigo, whose career was cut short by his death in 1934 at the age of only 29, provides a stylistic link between the avant-gardes of the 1920s and the Poetic Realists. Vigo's films are anarchist fables in the truest sense: they celebrate a life of freedom from legal and social authority. His short feature *Zéro de Conduite* (1933), a tale of student rebellion in a boarding school for boys replete with Surrealist touches, was banned by the French censors until 1945. His last film, *L'Atalante* (1934), anticipates the cinema of Poetic Realism with its account of life on a canal barge, free from the restrictions of society, and its atmospheric use of real locations. Vigo died of cancer before *L'Atalante* was released, and the film was shown in a drastically mutilated form by distributors who feared that its unconventional alternative to bourgeois morality would offend audiences.

Whereas for film historians the cinema of Poetic Realism is associated with the work of a small number of key directors, for contemporary audiences it was embodied in the persona of actor Jean Gabin. Gabin, a large-featured though handsome leading man, was the leading French star of the 1930s whose ability to project a sense of brooding romantic intensity made him the ideal tragic hero. Gabin was usually cast as a social outsider, a loner who is independent, courageous, romantic but ultimately doomed. His defining performance was in the title role of Duvivier's *Pépé le Moko* (1937) as a notorious gangster, hiding out in the Casbah of Algiers but longing to return to France, whose love for a visiting Parisian socialite leads ultimately to his death. Vincendeau describes Gabin as 'the emblem of a pervasive sense of doom and [a] pessimistic vision of society' and his Pépé as 'the perfect expression of a blocked French society turned towards its past'.[24] Gabin played similar roles in two films directed by Marcel Carné: in *Quai des brumes* (*Port of Shadows*, 1938) he is a Foreign Legion deserter who falls in love with a gangster's mistress, while in *Le Jour se lève* he is a fugitive hunted for the murder of a man who has seduced the girl he loves.

Unarguably the most significant French filmmaker of the 1930s, however, was Jean Renoir. Even in the wake of the denial of the *auteur* theory and the role of individual agency in the production process, it is impossible to deny Renoir the epithet of 'great': judged by any standards his films of the 1930s stand as one of the most impressive bodies of work in the history of cinema.[25] The second son of the famed Impressionist painter Auguste Renoir, Jean Renoir directed his first films in the 1920s, but it was the films he made during the 1930s on which his reputation rests. Renoir's films are characterized by their expression of humanistic values and by their multifaceted examination of relationships between classes and genders. Historians have seen Renoir's films of the 1930s as documents that embody the mood of the times. 'No one understood better than he the underlying themes of this decade, or explored more widely the range of conventions available to it', writes Eric Rhode.[26] His films are characterized by their social consciousness and by their dissection of the hypocrisy of conventional bourgeois morality. This is apparent even in the least ostensibly political of his films such as *Boudu sauvé des Eaux* (*Boudu Saved from Drowning*, 1932) and *Une Partie de Campagne* (*A Day in the Country*, 1936). In the former a tramp (Michel Simon), pulled from the river by a bookseller, not only resists the efforts of his benefactor to reform him but even seduces the mistress of the house in which he becomes a guest; in the latter the wife and daughter of a Parisian family, picnicking at a country inn, are seduced by two young men, under the apparently approving eye of the innkeeper (played by Renoir himself). His films became increasingly political as the decade went on, though Renoir himself never belonged to a political party. His politicization was signalled by *Le Crime de Monsieur Lange* (1935), made 'under a very special set of circumstances which were indicative of significant changes that had occurred both in the French film industry and in French society as a whole'.[27] The film's narrative of a publishing house which collapses following financial mismanagement by its owner, but which is successfully turned around as a co-operative by its workers, might be seen as an allegory not only of the Popular Front but also of the French film industry itself following the collapse of Pathé-Natan and the rise of smaller production companies which allowed greater freedom for filmmakers. It was following *Le Crime de Monsieur Lange* that Renoir was invited to make a film sponsored by the Communist Party of France, *La Vie est à nous* (*The People of France*, 1936) – banned by the censors until 1969 – and *La Marseillaise* (1937), a chronicle of the French Revolution on behalf of the Popular Front.

Renoir's greatest international success came with *La Grande Illusion* (1937), a bold pacifist drama made at a time of increasing international tension. *La Grande Illusion* uses a First World War prisoner-of-war narrative to explore themes of patriotism and social change. The friendship and common outlook between aristocratic French officer Captain de Bœldieu (Pierre Fresnay) and his German captor Colonel von Rauffenstein (Erich von Stroheim) suggests that class affinities are greater than national loyalties for the old order which these characters represent. The film symbolizes the passing of the *ancien régime* ('I do not know who will win this war, but the result will be the end of the Rauffensteins and the Boeldieus', the German officer remarks ruefully) and the emergence of a new meritocratic social order. Boeldieu sacrifices his life in order that the working-class Captain Maréchel (Jean Gabin) and the Jewish Rosenthal (Marcel Dalio) can escape from the prison. While the friendship between Boeldieu and Rauffenstein represents an aristocratic bond that overcomes national differences, the love affair that develops between the escaped Maréchel and a German widow suggests the possibility of *rapprochement* between the two nations.

Renoir followed *La Grande Illusion* with an adaptation of Emile Zola's *La Bête Humaine* (*The Human Beast*, 1938), starring Gabin and Simone Simon, and then ended the decade with the highly controversial *La Règle du Jeu* (*The Rules of the Game*, 1939) which caused howls of protest from critics and public and was savagely cut by its distributors after its Paris premiere resulted in a near-riot. The film is commonly interpreted as a critique of French society on the eve of war – Renoir's expressed intention was to present 'an exact description of the bourgeoisie of our time'[28] – and it is easy to understand how its narrative of extra-marital dalliances during a weekend at a country château so outraged contemporaries at a time when the threat of war made urgent the need for social and national unity. Peter Wollen argues that *La Règle du Jeu* 'was an unalloyed auteur film, conceived and produced outside the film industry'.[29] A commercial disaster, even when re-released after the Second World War, the critical reputation of *La Règle du Jeu* was rehabilitated by André Bazin and François Truffaut who compared it to *Citizen Kane* for its use of deep-focus cinematography and its complex, multi-layered narrative.

The era of Poetic Realism came to an end with the Second World War, when the new Vichy regime banned most of the Poetic Realist films and several leading directors, including Renoir and Duvivier, left to work abroad. As Hayward reminds us, however, 'whilst in each age there are great directors, just as with other aesthetic modalities, they are not the dominant tendency and their work must be examined alongside that of other contemporaries'.[30] The cinema of Poetic Realism was just one strand of a national cinema that also included a large proportion of now-forgotten popular genre films (colonial adventures, comedies and thrillers) and star vehicles. It did not in itself represent French national cinema in its totality any more than the *Nouvelle Vague* would do a quarter of a century later.

Socialist Realism, in contrast, provides a rare example of an aesthetic that came to dominate the production of an entire national cinema over a long period of time. The idea of Socialist Realism was formulated by Maxim Gorky at the first All-Union Congress of Soviet Writers in 1934: he contrasted it with the 'critical realism' of nineteenth-century literature which exposed the imperfections of society but did not suggest how to improve it. It soon became the official doctrine for all artistic production in the Soviet Union and remained the dominant aesthetic until Stalin's death in 1953. Soviet artists were required to adhere to a set of official tenets that were, nevertheless, rather vaguely defined as the principles of *partiinost* ('party-mindedness') and *narodnost* ('people-centredness'). Socialist Realism was, therefore, both a political and an aesthetic doctrine. Filmmakers were expected to follow the Communist Party line and not to criticise any aspects of Soviet politics or society. There was a shift away from the idea of the masses as a historical force that had characterized the films of the 1920s and towards heroic portraits of individuals who were presented as role models for what a good Soviet citizen should be. There was, in fact, nothing very 'realistic' at all about Socialist Realism, which projected an idealized image of life in Stalinist Russia. Formal experimentation was discouraged and film narratives had to be made in a style that was easily understood and accessible to the masses.

While most of the narrative and stylistic traits associated with Socialist Realism have been identified in Soviet cinema from the early 1930s, the film widely recognized as the first complete model of the doctrine was *Chapayev* (1934). This was a heavily fictionalized story of a Bolshevik hero during the Russian Civil War which won Stalin's personal approval and became the model for the cinema of Socialist Realism. Made by the brothers Sergei and Georgi Vasiliev, *Chapayev* was closer in formal and stylistic terms to classical cinema than the montage films of the 1920s, using individual characters for easy identification, including a romantic subplot (machine-gunner Petka falls in love with second-gunner Anna) and simple narrational devices (in one scene Chapayev explains battle tactics by laying out potatoes on a table). The ideological import of the film arises from the way in which Chapayev himself, at first characterized as an individualist who is resentful of his superior officer, subordinates his personal ambitions to the greater good of the people and the party. *Pravda* saw *Chapayev* as the first of a new style of film that would 'mobilise for the fulfilment of new tasks and explain about the achievements, as about the difficulties, of socialist construction'.[31]

Socialist Realism pervaded all film genres from the historical epic (*Peter the First*) and the biographical film (*Childhood of Maxim Gorky*) to musicals (*Volga-Volga*). A genre peculiar to Soviet cinema is the 'tractor musical' (*The Rich Bride*, *Tractor Drivers*), in which farmers sing cheerfully about their efforts to surpass their work quotas. While this may seem absurd to modern eyes, the association of work with personal fulfilment was in fact one of the main features of Socialist Realism. It is pointless to speak of critical success in a state such as the Soviet Union where artistic criticism was determined by party doctrine; it is equally pointless to discuss notions of popular success as these were the only films that people could see. In due course most of the Formalist filmmakers of the 1920s adapted to the new doctrine, even Eisenstein. Eisenstein's first completed sound film was the patriotic epic *Alexander Nevsky* (1938) about the thirteenth-century Russian prince (characterized as a proto-socialist) who routed an invasion by Teutonic Knights. Made at a time when the Soviet Union was arming in response to the threat of Nazi Germany, the film ends with a clear message for the present: 'Those who come to us with sword in hand will perish by the sword.' Eisenstein's aesthetic rehabilitation was illustrated by the award of the Order of Lenin in February 1939 and, although *Alexander Nevsky* was withdrawn following the Nazi-Soviet pact of August 1939, it was triumphantly re-released following the German attack on the Soviet Union in June 1941. Eisenstein, appointed head of the Mosfilm studio complex in 1940, spent the next four years working on an epic film of *Ivan the Terrible*, one of the rulers acceptable to Stalin due to his strong leadership and 'progressive' reforms. Two parts of the film were completed, the first released in 1945, the second banned on Stalin's orders in 1946 when he found that it did not accord with his idea of the historical Ivan. Eisenstein, who suffered a heart attack in 1946, died in 1948 at the age of fifty.

In Britain, meanwhile, a very different type of realism was emerging. The rise of the British documentary movement is generally attributed to the efforts of the Scottish-born John Grierson, widely acknowledged by his contemporaries as the 'father' of documentary film. It was on the strength of Grierson's *Drifters* (1929), a short feature about herring fishermen that was influenced by the aesthetics of Soviet montage cinema, that the British government was persuaded to establish its own documentary unit. Thereafter Grierson's importance was not as a filmmaker *per se* but as head of the Empire Marketing Board Film Unit and its successor the General Post Office Film Unit, through which he brought together a group of young, mostly left/liberal filmmakers including Paul Rotha, Basil Wright, Edgar Anstey, Arthur Elton and Harry Watt. Grierson provided the intellectual and aesthetic leadership, writing extensively about 'the creative interpretation of actuality' and playing a prominent role in progressive film culture as represented by magazines such as *Cinema Quarterly*, *World Film News* and *Documentary News Letter*. Grierson believed in documentary as a vehicle for the education of the public and for promoting the principles of liberal democracy. 'This sense of social responsibility makes our realist documentary a troubled and difficult art, particularly in a time like ours,' he wrote, adding that documentary film was qualitatively different from both the newsreels ('a speedy snip-snap of some utterly unimportant ceremony') and the commercial feature film ('acted stories against artificial backgrounds').[32]

The documentary movement has often attracted such hubristic labels as 'Britain's outstanding contribution to the film'.[33] It would be fair to say, however, that its influence has been exaggerated. There is evidence to suggest, for example, that documentary films were considerably less successful with cinema audiences, and were thus less attractive to exhibitors, than they were in the eyes of progressive film critics. They received, at best, a limited theatrical distribution, and were more often than not seen in non-theatrical venues, especially schools. The most acclaimed documentary of the 1930s, the GPO Film Unit's *Night Mail*, was less a film of social import than a lyrical and self-consciously aestheticized promotional film for the Royal Mail, employing the talents of poet W. H. Auden and composer Benjamin Britten. In achieving critical respect for a tradition of indigenous British filmmaking, the documentary movement enjoyed a degree of cultural kudos that was otherwise lacking for British cinema in comparison with countries such as France, Germany and the Soviet Union. At the same time, however, the critical success of documentary meant that 'documentary realism' became the major criterion by which British feature films would be judged, thus contributing to the critical disdain and historical neglect of popular genre films (comedies, thrillers, melodramas, musicals) during the 1930s and beyond.

But what of the films themselves? In a recent reappraisal of the documentary movement, Brian Winston suggests that Grierson's achievement was that he 'brilliantly squared the documentary circle – right-wing money, left-wing kudos and films of dubious social worth in the middle'.[34] Yet this assessment, whilst a useful corrective to some of the more extravagant claims made by the first generation of British film historians (including several of the documentarists themselves), is more than a little unfair. Films such as Elton and Anstey's *Housing Problems* and *Enough to Eat*, both made with industrial sponsorship, remain powerful social documents that are implicitly critical of the government for not taking sufficient steps to address the problems of slum housing and malnutrition. There was, arguably, greater scope for social criticism in the films made with industrial sponsorship than in those made for the GPO Film Unit, especially following Grierson's departure in 1937 when the civil service and Treasury paymasters were quick to reassert their control over the independent-minded documentarists.[35] Grierson was succeeded as Supervising Producer of the GPO Film Unit by the Brazilian filmmaker Alberto Cavalcanti, under whose direction the unit moved away from the educational emphasis of his successor and instead embraced the techniques of narrative filmmaking in films such as *North Sea* and *The Saving of Bill Blewitt*. These were story films that used scripted dialogue and studio reconstructions of events, but they remained true to the documentary tradition in their use of non-professional actors. The short films of the late 1930s paved the way for the celebrated narrative-documentary features of the Second World War, including *Target for Tonight*, *Coastal Command* and *Western Approaches*. While the ideological and formal characteristics of documentary had by now shifted quite radically from the mantra of 'the creative interpretation of actuality', the Griersonian tradition of intellectual independence and social conscience would emerge again in the Free Cinema movement of the 1950s and in the socially and politically committed television 'docu-dramas' by the likes of Ken Loach and Tony Garnett in the 1960s.

IDEOLOGY AND ENTERTAINMENT

It was the use of film as a medium of state propaganda, especially in Nazi Germany and the Soviet Union, that first attracted historians to the study of cinema.[36] Following the pioneering studies of the 1970s, historians of film propaganda have since widened the net to include not only other dictatorships (Fascist Italy) but also liberal democracies (especially Britain during the Second World War) where film was used to promote national unity and social cohesion. Recent research has challenged numerous received wisdoms about film propaganda: it is now recognized, for example, that propaganda was not exclusively the preserve of the totalitarian states, while long-held assumptions about the effectiveness of film propaganda (specifically the notion that German propaganda was very successful in indoctrinating the public with Nazi ideology, whereas British propaganda was highly shambolic and largely ineffective) have been qualified. There has still, however, been relatively little comparative study of film propaganda, as most historians have focused on national case studies. Yet, for all the political and ideological differences between the dictatorships and the democracies, there are certain common factors that affected the role and nature of film propaganda in those states and societies where they were most fully exploited. A comparative analysis of film propaganda in Nazi Germany and wartime Britain demonstrates the limitations as well as the possibilities of film propaganda.

The extent to which received wisdoms have been challenged by empiricist research is no better exemplified than in the case of Germany. There is still a tendency amongst some commentators to equate German cinema under the Third Reich with the sort of aggressively nationalistic and virulently racist propaganda exemplified in its two most notorious films, *Triumph des Willens* (*Triumph of the Will*, 1935) and *Der Ewige Jude* (*The Eternal Jew*, 1940). Geoffrey Nowell-Smith, for example, describes the cinema of the Third Reich as 'a programme of stage management of reality, linking entertainment to the most noxious forms of nationalistic propaganda'.[37] However, such judgements are based on a narrow section of German film production. In truth, as David Welch points out, only about one-sixth of the 1,097 feature films produced in Germany between 1933 and 1945 could be considered as overtly propagandistic.[38] The difficulties in regarding all German cinema as Nazi propaganda are explained by Sabine Hake:

> Labels such as 'Nazi cinema' or 'Nazi film' suggest a complete convergence of narrative cinema, cultural politics, and Nazi ideology that was never achieved, given the continuing popularity of foreign films and the ubiquity of American products; the conflicting ideas about film-making among members of the industry and the Propaganda Ministry; the changing attitudes towards propaganda and entertainment before and during the Second World War; and the difficulties of controlling the actual conditions of film exhibition in the Reich and its occupied territories.[39]

The cinema of the Third Reich, indeed, was far from the monolithic institution that has often been assumed and was subject to all manner of internal and external pressures that make it impossible to regard all films as direct or even indirect propaganda.

While it would be an exaggeration to describe the organization of German film propaganda as chaotic, there is ample evidence to suggest that when the Nazis came to power their propaganda policy was unco-ordinated and not always well conceived. This became apparent in the regime's first efforts at political propaganda, a triptych of films in 1933–4 (*SA-Mann Brand*, *Hitlerjunge Quex* and *Hans Westmar*) eulogizing the *Kampfzeit* ('time of struggle'). These films of Nazi martyrs (*Hans Westmar* and *Hitlerjunge Quex* were inspired by Horst Wessel and Herbert Norkus) were heavy-handed attempts at propaganda that portrayed the struggle between National Socialists and Communists as a righteous crusade and showed their protagonists dying heroically for the movement. None of these films was especially successful and they met with a mixed reception even from senior party members. Goebbels, who disliked this type of propaganda which he regarded as too crude, told the film industry that 'I do not want to see films that begin and end with National Socialist parades'.[40] He was privately dismayed when Hitler personally commissioned Leni Riefenstahl to direct *Triumph des Willens*, a film record of the 1934 Nazi Party Rally in Nuremberg that was released with great fanfare in March 1935. *Triumph des Willens* quickly came to be seen as the definitive filmic statement of National Socialist ideology in general and 'the Führer myth' in particular. Riefenstahl brings an almost Wagnerian quality to the staging of spectacle (mass rallies, torchlight processions) and the representation of Hitler as a mythic, godlike figure (in the famous opening sequence he arrives by plane, as if descending from a great height, before making his triumphant procession through the crowds). Goebbels swallowed his jealousy of Riefenstahl and awarded her film the *Nationaler Filmpreis* (National Film Prize) in recognition of its 'magnificent cinematic vision of the Führer' and its 'passionate artistry' in support of the movement.[41] It also enjoyed international prestige, winning the Gold Medal at the 1935 Venice Film Festival and, more surprisingly, the Grand Prix at the 1937 Paris Film Festival.

Triumph des Willens represented the high point of Nazi propaganda: it enshrined the 'Hitler myth' so completely that no further films of the sort ever needed to be commissioned. Goebbels, for his part, was firmly of the opinion that feature films should provide escapist entertainment for the masses and that direct propaganda should be confined to the newsreels. Only 96 films were commissioned directly by the Ministry of Popular Enlightenment and Propaganda during the Third Reich, though these *Staatsauftragsfilme* (state-commissioned films) received greater funding and more publicity. The role of the *Staatsauftragsfilme* in disseminating official doctrine is exemplified by the production of a number of anti-Semitic films in 1940 at a time when the regime wished to prepare the ground for the escalation of its racial policies. These films – *Die Rothschilds* (*The Rothschilds*), *Jud Süss* (*Jew Süss*) and *Der Ewige Jude* (*The Eternal Jew*) – also illustrate the limitations of film propaganda in promoting Nazi ideology to the public. *Die Rothschilds* and *Jud Süss* were both historical costume pictures, while *Der Ewige Jude* purported to be a documentary about the 'Jewish problem'. *Jud Süss* was a fictionalized drama about Joseph Süss-Oppenheimer, financial adviser to the Duke of Württemberg in the 1730s. He is characterized both as rapacious (he imposes exorbitant taxes on the citizens) and sexually threatening (raping the innocent heroine whilst having her husband tortured). Steve Neale argues that *Jud Süss* is 'a classic realist text' in which 'the anti-semitic component of Nazi ideology is inscribed within that text in a similar manner to the inscription of Populism within Hollywood texts [of the 1930s]'.[42] In contrast, he argues, *Der Ewige Jude* uses an entirely different mode of address that marks it as 'propaganda' because 'propaganda documentaries are a mode in which the spectator is constituted as a social subject in a struggle'.[43] *Der Ewige Jude* uses the techniques of associative montage (shots of Jewish people/shots of rats) to create the idea of the Jewish race as a disease that is spreading across the world. The Allied Commission of Control for Germany later described *Der Ewige Jude* as 'probably the vilest and subtlest of its kind ever made for popular consumption by the masses'.[44] Yet there is evidence to suggest that it was not well received by German audiences, particularly as it followed so soon on the heels of *Jud Süss*.

The failure of *Der Ewige Jude* reinforced Goebbels's belief that the most effective propaganda was subtle and indirect. The majority of *Staatsauftragsfilme* were to be feature films in which the propaganda content was incorporated, as in *Jud Süss*, in a classical narrative framework. The main themes of German propaganda during the war were, on the one hand, the heroic representation of 'great men' from Germany's past (*Bismarck, Friedrich Schiller, Carl Peters, Der Grosse König*) and, on the other hand, the demonization of her enemies, for example through narratives of British atrocities against the Boers (*Ohm Krüger*)

and the Irish (*Mein Leben für Irland*). Yet there were inconsistencies within propaganda policy and by no means all German films were necessarily as Goebbels had intended. An interesting example is *Titanic* (1942), which, whilst attributing the sinking of the liner to the corruption of a Jewish-capitalist plutocracy, was rather more sympathetic in its representation of British stiff-upper-lipped heroism than would have been expected given the contemporary context. For reasons that are not entirely clear, *Titanic* was not released in Germany, though it was shown in the occupied territories, while its director, Herbert Selpin, was arrested and died in a Gestapo prison.[45]

For all the interest of film historians in propaganda, however, the popular film culture of Nazi Germany was essentially one of stars and genres. This 'unknown' popular realm of German cinema under the Third Reich has recently been the subject of investigation by revisionist scholars who have reclaimed genres such as the musical and the romantic comedy from the historical neglect into which they had long fallen.[46] Germany had its own star system, with several of its leading actresses modelled on Hollywood examples: the Swedish-born Zarah Leander, for example, was promoted as the 'German Garbo', while exotic dancer Marika Rökk was frequently compared to Ginger Rogers and Eleanor Powell. The regime recognized the ideological and cultural value of stars as role models, and Goebbels frequently intervened in casting decisions. The most popular genres were comedy and romantic drama; the *Heimatfilme* (homeland film) and the Viennese operetta also featured prominently in the generic profile of popular cinema. The most successful films at the box-office during the war included musicals such as *Die Grosse Liebe* (*The Great Love*, 1942) and *Wunschkonzert* (*Request Concert*, 1940) and romantic costume dramas such as *Das Herz der Königin* (*The Heart of the Queen*, 1940).

German cinema throughout the Nazi period was a 'classical' cinema in which the motifs of pleasure, spectacle and entertainment were prominent. Goebbels was keen that the production values of German films should be on a par with those of Hollywood, especially after the ban on American films (which the Propaganda Minister personally opposed) in 1939. Thus, German musicals such as *Es Leuchten die Sterne* (*The Stars Are*

Shining, 1939) and *Stern von Rio* (*Star of Rio*, 1940) contained elaborately choreographed dance routines in the style of Busby Berkeley. Goebbels, who admired films such as *Snow White and the Seven Dwarfs* and *Gone With the Wind*, promoted German films that would match the colour and spectacle of Hollywood. The film that came closest to fulfilling his ambition was Josef von Baky's *Münchhausen* (1943), produced to celebrate the twenty-fifth anniversary of Ufa, that has been described as 'the Third Reich's consummate cinematic achievement'.[47] Starring the popular Hans Albers as the 'liar baron', *Münchhausen* is, on one level, a thoroughly escapist fantasy that uses Agfacolor and special effects to create a fantastic world far removed from the harsh realities of the Second World War (the film was released shortly after Goebbels, in the wake of Stalingrad, had made his famous 'total war' speech). On another level, however, the film might be interpreted as a form of allegorical propaganda, a testament of faith in the triumph of German technical ingenuity and inspirational leadership. Eric Rentschler sees the film's use of illusion and fantasy as symbolic of the illusionary nature of the Nazi regime: 'A rare Nazi film of the fantastic, *Münchhausen* is also a Nazi fantasy.'[48]

British cinema of the Second World War has been subject to almost as many myths and misconceptions as German cinema. It was long held, for example, that the Ministry of Information (MOI), the government department responsible for official propaganda policy, was largely ineffective, crippled by a bureaucratic inertia that meant, in the words of Paul Rotha, that 'a film tended too often to become a file and not a film'.[49] The documentarists, who were well versed in the dissemination of information, considered themselves to have been excluded from the official propaganda machinery at the outbreak of war because, as Edgar Anstey put it, 'the Chamberlain government was very much opposed to everything we stood for'.[50] Yet these accounts are partial. While, at the outset, the MOI was affected by institutional and political problems that led to several ministers leaving in fast succession, these had mostly been overcome by mid-1940 so that it was working efficiently with cultural producers, including filmmakers from all sectors of the industry. Unlike in Germany, where the film industry came under increased state control, the British film industry retained its independence. Rather than sponsoring individual films – a policy that was abandoned after one feature film, *49th Parallel* (1941) – the MOI preferred instead to let filmmakers work within the guidelines it suggested, in return for which it helped in the provision of facilities and the release of actors and production personnel from military service. The exclusion of the documentarists is very much a myth, as shortly after the outbreak of war the GPO Film Unit was put at the disposal of the MOI and in 1940 was fully incorporated into the official film propaganda machinery where, renamed the Crown Film Unit, it came to specialize in the production of narrative-documentaries about aspects of the armed services.[51]

If the common critical perception of German cinema rests upon *Triumph des Willens* and *Der Ewige Jude*, the common perception of British cinema during the Second World War rests on a body of realist films that exemplify what came to be known as the 'wartime wedding' between the fictional feature film and the documentary style. British films such as *In Which We Serve*, *Millions Like Us*, *Fires Were Started*, *San Demetrio, London* and *The Way Ahead* were notable for their unsensational narratives, restrained heroics and sober visual style – a type of national cinema that met with warm approval from the critics and won moderate box-office success. Roger Manvell, a contemporary critic who later became a film historian, identified 1942 as the year in which British cinema reached its maturity:

> 1942 was to be one of the richest periods for the war film in Britain. It was the year in which human considerations began to overcome the jingoistic nationalism with which most countries blinkered themselves at the beginning of the war. Similarly, the 'war story' with a patriotic slant began to give place to the 'war documentary', which derived the action and to a greater extent the characterization from real events and real people.[52]

As so often, however, the official history (Manvell had been a Regional Films Officer for the MOI during the war) tells only part of the story. While the canonical realist films were successful enough, they were rather less successful than the early-war patriotic films that mixed melodrama and heroics, such as *Convoy* (1940) and *Ships With Wings* (1941). Michael Balcon, the Head of Production at Ealing Studios, later disparaged these films on the grounds that the stories betrayed 'a certain lack of authenticity' and claimed that 'I was personally convinced that the approach must be realistic'.[53] Balcon's own preference was for later films such as *San Demetrio, London* (1943), which Ealing historian Charles Barr describes as 'the culmination of Ealing's war programme, the ideal fulfilment of Balcon's policy'.[54] Yet, by the time the 'wartime wedding' had been consummated, the war film as such was already in decline at the British box-office. It was supplanted, from 1943, by melodrama, specifically by the flamboyant costume pictures forthcoming from the Gainsborough studio such as *The Man in Grey* and *The Wicked Lady*. In contrast to the restrained narratives and sober visuals of the realist films, the Gainsborough melodramas offered sensation, sexuality and spectacle in their narratives of sadistic, whip-wielding aristocrats and bosom-heaving heroines.[55]

Relations between filmmakers and policy-makers remained quite harmonious during the war: the MOI kept the industry informed of the sort of subjects it felt would make good propaganda, while the industry, for the most part, was happy to follow official guidelines. There were, however, occasional points of tension, most notoriously in the row over *The Life and Death of Colonel Blimp* (1943). In making a film based on David Low's famous cartoon character – a symbol of military incompetence and political reaction – filmmakers Michael Powell and Emeric Pressburger were deliberately courting controversy. Indeed, they attracted the combined wrath of the War Office, the MOI and even the Prime Minister himself, who called it a 'foolish production' that was 'detrimental to the morale of the Army'.[56] What the episode illustrates, however, are the limitations on the British government's control over the film industry. That the MOI decided it had no powers to prevent the film from being made, even in the face of Churchill's determined opposition, was due to the intervention of the minister, Brendan Bracken, who realized that such a move would be politically insensitive in a democracy at war when so much British propaganda was based around the notions of freedom of speech and opinion. In the event, *The Life and Death of Colonel Blimp* was far from being the virulent satire that the authorities had feared; it was, in fact, quite sympathetic to the ideals of the old aristocratic officer class, who, it nevertheless makes clear, have been displaced by a younger, meritocratic generation who have risen through the ranks.

If British and German film propaganda served different ideological ends, there were, nevertheless, many similarities in the methods and techniques they employed. This is amply demonstrated by a comparison of two major feature films produced towards the end of the war that both deployed inspirational episodes from national history to mobilize support for the war effort. Britain's *Henry V* (1944), directed by and starring Laurence Olivier, is a triumphalist, patriotic epic that makes explicit its propagandist intent through a title caption dedicated 'to the Commandos and Airborne Troops of Great Britain – the spirit of whose ancestors it has been humbly attempted to recapture in some ensuing scenes'. *Henry V* asserts the moral righteousness of the English cause, downplays social divisions, emphasizes national unity, and depicts the triumph of the English army, against overwhelming odds, in vanquishing a mighty continental foe. While *Henry V* is a film about the British at last taking the offensive (after so many years of defensive propaganda exemplified in the title of the famous short documentary of the Blitz, *Britain Can Take It!*), its German equivalent, *Kolberg* (1945), directed by Veit Harlan, is about a nation on the defensive, though equally defiant in tone. Goebbels intended that this film, the most expensive production during the Third Reich, would be his personal testament to the resistance of the German people against their enemies. A sign of the prestige and significance attached to the film was that entire regiments were withdrawn from the line to enact the battle scenes. The heroic defence of the city of Kolberg against the Napoleonic armies in 1807 is a clear allegory for the defence of Germany in 1945, using the metaphor of 'rising from the ashes' to assert the inevitability of final victory. More subtly, the film's depiction of differences between the Prussian leaders hints at divisions within the Nazi leadership as the resolute Gneisenau persuades the wavering King Friedrich Wilhelm III to continue the struggle. Goebbels, indeed, remained one of the more resolute senior

Nazis right to the end. In April 1945, as the Red Army closed in on Berlin, he is reported to have told his staff at the Propaganda Ministry: 'Gentlemen, in a hundred years' time they will be showing a fine colour film of the terrible days we are living through. Wouldn't you like to play a part in that film? Hold out now, so that a hundred years hence the audience will not hoot and whistle when you appear on the screen.'[57] Although the German cinema would rise again, it would not, however, be in the form that Goebbels had intended.

LIBERATION AND RECONSTRUCTION

The extent to which 1945 represents a 'rebirth' or 'new beginning' for the film industries of Europe is open to debate. There was much talk amongst communists and socialists of a 'Year Zero' when social and political reconstruction could start from scratch – a notion enshrined in the title of Roberto Rossellini's film *Germania, Anno Zero* (*Germany, Year Zero*, 1947). Governments and filmmakers both recognized the role that cinema could play in the process of reconstruction, which affected victors and vanquished alike. Yet, as Ulrike Sieglohr remarks: 'To argue that the years immediately following the Second World War were a period of reconstruction and cultural renewal suggests both the continuities of old structures as well as new beginnings.'[58] While some restructuring of national film industries inevitably took place, many of the personnel of wartime and pre-war cinema continued their careers into the post-war period and the popular genres and styles of filmmaking remained much as before. The balance was very much in favour of continuity rather than change.

As far as Hollywood's relations with European cinemas were concerned, for example, the war had been a temporary aberration from the normal patterns. The war had closed off most European markets (with the exception of Britain) to American films, but the end of the war would see the US film industry energetically seeking to re-establish itself in territories that had been lost. In 1945 the MPPDA set up its overseas branch the Motion Picture Export Association (MPEA) and, with the collusion of the us State Department, set up distribution networks in the liberated and occupied countries. The five-year backlog of Hollywood films, combined with a shortage of indigenous European product in 1945, meant that American movies quickly reasserted their dominance of European screens. The Americans were able to dump hundreds of films into the French, Italian and (West) German markets, dressing up their economic opportunism with the rhetoric of political and cultural liberation. Hollywood argued that its escapist entertainments provided ideal propaganda to counter the combined threats of the old enemy of Fascism (which many feared would once again raise its head even after the defeat of the Axis powers) and the new enemy of Communism (represented by the Soviet control over most of Eastern Europe which saw the onset of the Cold War). 'Whether one calls it propaganda or information', wrote the editor of *Film Daily*, 'it is evident that as a result of World War II, the motion picture from this day must be regarded as an instrument of public policy as well as a great popular medium of entertainment.'[59] This argument carried most weight in Germany, where the MPEA was able to establish a monopoly of distribution throughout the American Zone of Control. European governments, for their part, were aware of the popular appeal of American movies and of the need to provide affordable entertainment during a time of austerity caused by food shortages and continued rationing. And they had no desire to upset the Americans, who were providing economic assistance for reconstruction through Marshall Aid. At the same time, however, they could ill afford the outflow of dollars to American distributors at a time when the home production industries were in such a perilous state.

Various strategies were adopted in an attempt to counter Hollywood's economic and cultural encroachment into postwar Europe, with mixed results. In France the Blum-Byrnes Agreement of 1946 removed all restrictions on the import of American films as part of a deal that saw the us government cancel millions of dollars' worth of debts. This agreement infuriated the French production sector, resulting in the formation of the Committee for the Defence of the French Cinema and a concerted political campaign to revise the terms of the agreement. The result was a typically French solution: the government bowed to domestic pressure by a unilateral revision of the agreement, reintroducing a quota for foreign films, but appeased the Americans by not actually enforcing the quota.[60] In Italy the Andreotti Law of 1949 required that exhibitors had to set aside eighty days a year for Italian films and charged a flat rate fee of 2.5 million lire for the distribution of each foreign film. Following the Anglo-American propaganda efforts of the war, relations between Hollywood and Britain hit rock bottom in the late 1940s. In 1946 the MP Robert Boothby had linked film imports with food shortages, declaring that the nation faced a choice between 'Bogart or bacon'.[61] In 1947 the Labour Chancellor of the Exchequer Hugh Dalton imposed an *ad valorem* tax of 75 per cent on every imported film. This brought about a retaliatory boycott of the British market by the MPEA and, when British producers were unable to supply enough films to meet demand in their home market, the British government was forced to back down. The Anglo-American Film Agreement of 1948 provided an acceptable compromise by limiting the dollar remittances allowed to American companies but placed no limit on the number of films that could be imported. It was an inevitable outcome given Hollywood's position of economic strength in relation to the weakened European film industries.

It was the need for economic rebuilding that, to a large extent, militated against any wholesale changes in the structures and personnel of the film industries of Europe. In the countries most severely affected by the war, revival of production after 1945 was achieved through employing tried and trusted personnel and practices. There is a strong argument, for example, that 1940 represents more of a turning point for the French film industry than 1945. With 'golden age' directors like Renoir, Clair and Duvivier having left for Hollywood, cinema during the Vichy regime provided opportunities for new directors to come to the fore, such as Henri-Georges Clouzot, Yves Allégret and Jacques Becker. These men continued working in the post-Vichy cinema alongside the returned exiles. The Vichy regime, detested for its co-operation with the occupying German authorities, had, however, introduced new economic controls which helped to establish a more secure base for the film industry after the acute instability of the 1930s. Most of these were maintained after the war, along with the film school set up under Vichy, the Institut des Hautes Etudes Cinématographiques (IDHEC). Although French production almost ground to a halt in 1944–5, it quickly revived so that in 1946 there were 96 films produced and by the early 1950s production had returned to its pre-war level of 100–120 films per year.[62] In Germany, which was divided into four separate zones of control, film production resumed again in 1946. Thomas Elsaesser has demonstrated conclusively that 1945 was far from being a 'zero hour' for German cinema.[63] Over half the filmmakers active in the German film industry after 1945 had begun their careers during or even before the Third Reich, including Veit Harlan, Helmut Käutner and Wolfgang Staudte. The major changes that occurred in post-war German cinema were not at the level of personnel but rather at the level of institutional structure with the dismantling of the nationalized film industry. Ufa's main facilities, including the Babelsberg Studios and the Agfa film laboratories, happened to fall within the Soviet Zone of Occupation and would, in time, become the basis of the East German state organization DEFA (Deutsches Film Aktiengesellschaft). Even following the institution of the two Germanies in 1949, however, there were still, according to Sabine Hake, 'correspondences between filmic practices in East and West Germany'.[64]

Developments in Eastern Europe were more uniform than in the West, due principally to the Soviet Union strengthening its hold on the satellite states. The model was one of nationalization along the model already instituted in the Soviet Union during the 1930s. The Polish film industry was nationalized in 1945, with Alexander Ford becoming head of the new state body Film Polski. The Czechoslovak film industry, which had been in German hands since 1939, was nationalized in 1945; Hungary, Romania and Bulgaria followed suit in 1948. The Hungarian film theorist Béla Balász returned from exile to teach at the new Academy of Dramatic and Film Art, but within a few years was removed from his post as the doctrinaire adoption of Socialist Realism made his brand of formative theory unacceptable. Yugoslavia, the only Communist state with sufficient independence from Stalinism, was also the only one without an established film industry of its own at the end of the war.

The conventional interpretation of the nature of European cinema in the post-war period is what has been termed 'the return of modernism'.[65] Thompson and Bordwell identify three distinguishing formal and stylistic features: a greater sense of objective reality (episodic slice-of-life narratives in contrast to the tight plotting of classical Hollywood, the use of long takes and filming on location); a greater sense of subjective reality (exploring the psychological motivation of characters); and authorial commentary (reflexive narration, in contrast to the invisible narration of classical Hollywood). Such characteristics were not unique to the post-war period and can be identified, in different forms, in the avant-garde movements of the 1920s and the work of experimental film-makers such as Luis Buñuel and Jean Cocteau, but the difference now was that 'they were absorbed by directors working in commercial feature production'.[66]

While the cinema of Vichy France has been passed over in most histories, it did create one indisputable masterpiece in Marcel Carné's *Les Enfants du Paradis* (*The Children of Paradise*, 1945), which has been called 'one of the most aesthetically satisfying films of all time'.[67] Such is the uncomfortable place of Vichy in French history that *Les Enfants du Paradis* is often cited as marking the beginning of post-Vichy cinema, but production began in 1943 and the film was made during the Occupation, though its release coincided with the Liberation. Stylistically *Les Enfants du Paradis* represents continuity with the main trends of pre-war French cinema: it combines the romantic fatalism of Poetic Realism with the theatricality of Pagnol in its story of the lives and loves of a group of actors in the Parisian theatre of the 1840s. Carné intended the film, at the time the most expensive ever made in France, as a tribute to the theatre, but the timing of its release made it something more, being seen as a testament to the survival of French artistry and elegance during the Occupation. Acclaimed as one of the greatest achievements of French cinema, *Les Enfants du Paradis* would, however, later be seen as representative of the *tradition de qualité* that the young turks of the *Nouvelle Vague* so disliked.

The most influential filmmaking trend of the period emerged in Italy between the mid-1940s and the early 1950s. In the context of aesthetic film history, Italian Neo-Realism is one of the modernist film movements that distinguishes European cinemas from Hollywood and can be placed in a tradition that also includes German Expressionism and Poetic Realism. It shares with those movements a distinctive formal and aesthetic character of its own (in this instance one characterized by location shooting, naturalistic lighting, long takes, true-to-life stories, unscripted dialogue and the use of non-professional performers) and is centred on the work of a group of key practitioners (Roberto Rossellini, Vittorio De Sica, Cesare Zavattini, Luchino Visconti and Giuseppe De Santis). For all its aesthetic significance to critics such as André Bazin, however, Neo-Realism needs to be understood in relation to its social and political contexts. The Allied invasion of Italy in 1943 and the fall of Mussolini created the conditions in which different filmmaking practices could emerge: the Italian film industry was severely disrupted by the fighting, Cinecittà was abandoned and nationwide distribution ceased as the Allies advanced. Film production became localized, while the lack of studio facilities encouraged the practice of filming on location. Rossellini's *Roma, Città aperta* (*Rome, Open City*, 1945), generally regarded as the first true Neo-Realist film, was shot mostly on location in the war-ravaged streets and tenements of Rome and was made on a tiny budget, using whatever equipment and film stock was available. The film has a raw, rough-edged quality that critics were quick to dub 'realist' when it was shown abroad. The British critic Dilys Powell believed that 'its impact was partly accidental, the result, not of the director's art and imagination alone, but also of the accident of poor physical material which gave the story the air of fact'.[68] While this is undoubtedly true to a degree, the success of Rosellini's film with audiences as well as critics was such that others in the same style soon followed suit.

For Rossellini, moreover, Neo-Realism was primarily a social rather than an aesthetic movement. He claimed that

Neo-Realism gave expression to 'a need that is proper to modern man, to tell things as they are, to understand reality, I would say, in a pitilessly concrete way, conforming to that typically contemporary interest, for statistical and scientific results.'[69] The early Neo-Realist films were intimately connected with the politics of resistance: *Rome, Open City* used the story of a partisan and a priest killed during the liberation of Rome to urge the need for unity between Communists and Catholics in the struggle against Fascism (in reality a fragile unity that would very soon disintegrate in the face of intractable political and social differences after the war), while Rossellini's next film, *Paisà* (1946), used an episodic narrative to explore social relations between the Italian populace and their American liberators.

The social commitment of the Neo-Realists to examining 'life as it is' meant that the thematic concerns of their films soon shifted from the resistance narratives exemplified in Rossellini's early films to the examination of the social problems of reconstruction. The most celebrated Neo-Realist film, De Sica's *Ladri di Biciclette* (*Bicycle Thieves*, 1948), though not without its moments of humour (such as the protagonist Ricci struggling to come to terms with using a knife and fork), exposes the problems of post-war unemployment and poverty through the simple story of a worker whose livelihood depends upon his bicycle. In a manner not dissimilar to Ford's *The Grapes of Wrath*, *Bicycle Thieves* (one of those films whose title is usually rendered in English due to its international success) contains a strong element of social criticism whereby institutions such as the Church, the police and the worker's union are shown as indifferent and unhelpful. While *Bicycle Thieves* examined urban problems, Visconti's *La Terra Trema* (*The Earth Trembles*, 1948) focused on the problems affecting the countryside, specifically the plight of Sicilian fishermen. Within a few years, therefore, the euphoria of the Liberation had given way to a jaundiced and critical view of social and political reconstruction.

Like so many other critically privileged film movements, Neo-Realism was relatively short-lived and represented a small corpus of key texts. The last of the accepted Neo-Realist classics was De Sica's *Umberto D* (1951), which Bazin felt was 'one of the most revolutionary and courageous films of the last two years – not only of the Italian cinema, but of European cinema as a whole'. It was, Bazin declared, an example of 'total neo-realism', even more so than *Bicycle Thieves*, in which film, he now felt, there 'was still a concession to classical dramaturgy'. *Umberto D*, in contrast, 'rejects any relationship to traditional film spectacle'.[70] What Bazin meant, in effect, was that *Umberto D* was a film without a story in the conventional sense: it depicts the dying days of an old man and his dog, the man being driven to attempt suicide due to the poverty of his existence. The film is notable for containing long sequences where nothing much happens in dramatic terms, such as Umberto preparing for bed and the landlady's maid waking and making coffee. Whereas, for Bazin, *Umberto D* represented the 'culmination' of Neo-Realism, for writer Cesare Zavattini the film was 'not a conclusion but a point of departure'. In his *A Thesis on Neo-Realism*, published in three parts in 1952–3, Zavattini envisaged even more bold and ambitious films, achieving an even closer representation of everyday life. 'The time has come to tell each member of the audience that he is the true protagonist of life', Zavattini declared, suggesting that the Neo-Realist project still had a long way to go: '[The] men of the Italian cinema, in order to continue to search for and to conserve their own style and inspiration, having once courageously set ajar the doors of reality and truth, must now open them wide.'[71]

Zavattini's vision was not to be fulfilled; by the time he was writing Neo-Realism had already run its course. *Umberto D* was a commercial failure that prompted De Sica to turn his back (albeit temporarily) on directing and return to acting, mostly in light comedy fare, for the rest of the 1950s. In truth, however, the decline of Neo-Realism had been signalled long before the failure of *Umberto D*. Few Neo-Realist films had been popular with Italian audiences, who preferred the Hollywood movies that flooded Italy after the war. They were also unpopular with the Catholic Church and with politicians, who attacked them for presenting negative images of Italian society. Giulio Andreotti, the under-secretary with responsibility for the cinema, declared that De Sica had 'rendered a wretched service to his country' with *Umberto D*.[72] There were also signs of stylistic divergence within the movement itself. Even some of the canonical Neo-Realist films, including *Bicycle Thieves*, had departed from the pure model of Neo-Realism by including scenes shot in studios with scripted dialogue and professional actors. In the late 1940s Neo-Realist directors moved even further away from the theoretical ideal by turning to melodramatic storylines and using stars to bring glamour: De Santis's *Riso Amaro* (*Bitter Rice*, 1949) brought eroticism and sensuality to the rice fields of the Po Valley in the form of its star Silvana Mangano, while Ingrid Bergman starred in Rossellini's *Stromboli* (1949) and began a torrid affair with the director that damaged both their careers in a furore of negative publicity. The overriding reason for the decline of Neo-Realism, however, was that it had outlived its brief historical moment. Neo-Realism emerged at the end of the war and was intricately connected with the politics of liberation and recon-struction. By the early 1950s, with the first indications of recovery that would lead to the post-war 'economic miracle', the social problems of the late 1940s became less acute and the public's appetite for films of social criticism, never very strong to begin with, disappeared almost completely.

That said, however, Neo-Realism was to have a profound effect on the aesthetic history of film as practitioners in other countries adopted some of the techniques of the Neo-Realists, without ever achieving the same international critical recogni-tion. Perhaps the nearest thing to Neo-Realism was the emer-gence in post-war Germany of the so-called *Trümmerfilme* ('rubble films') which dealt with life amongst the ruins of German cities in the aftermath of war. Films such as *Die Mörder sund unter uns* (*The Murderers Are Among Us*, 1946) and *Ehe im Schatten* (*Marriage in the Shadows*, 1947) dealt with the prob-lems of social dislocation and war guilt.[73] Ironically, given that the main aim of the *Trümmerfilme* was to overcome the 'Nazi aesthetic' of cinema under Goebbels, they were far less suc-cessful at the box-office than those Nazi 'entertainment' films which the Allies deemed suitable for exhibition. A form of 'Spanish Neo-Realism' flourished briefly in the 1950s when the films of Luis Garcia Berlanga (*Welcome, Mr Marshall*, 1951) and Juan Antonio Bardem (*Death of a Cyclist*, 1955) attracted attention on the international festival circuit, though social criticism was not approved by the Franco regime and the movement was short-lived.

The international critical success of Neo-Realism was an indication of the degree of cultural respectability that was now being attached to the cinema. This was apparent on a number of different levels: the growth in the number of intellectual film magazines in the late 1940s and early 1950s (such as *Cahiers du Cinéma* in France and *Sequence* in Britain); the emergence of the international film festival circuit (the Cannes Film Festival was founded in 1946) which brought more non-European and non-American films to the attention of European audiences; the burgeoning film society movement (1947 saw the foundation of the International Federation of Ciné-Clubs); and the origins of the international 'art cinema' movement focused around individualistic directors admired by cinephiles, including France's Robert Bresson, Italy's Federico Fellini and Sweden's Ingmar Bergman. The growth of an international film culture gave impetus to the archiving of films and the membership of the International Federation of Film Archives (founded in 1938 but suspended during the war) increased from four to 33 in the decade after 1945.

For all its newfound cultural respectability, however, film remained essentially a popular medium. European cinema-goers still habitually favoured the sort of escapist fare represented on the one hand by Hollywood and on the other hand by the indigenous generic traditions of domestic national cinemas. In most territories the post-war decade marked the peak of cinema-going as a social practice. With the exception of Britain, where attendances declined steadily after the peak of 1946, cinema-going was on the increase. In France, for example, annual attendances between 1947 and 1956 were around the 400 million mark, almost twice their pre-war level.[74] In Italy attendances rose to a peak of 819 million in 1955; in the German Federal Republic (GFR) the peak was reached one year later at a similar figure of 817 million.[75] Sorlin estimates that 1955 marked the high point of cinema admissions across Western Europe with over 3,000 million tickets sold, and, even allowing for his caveat that this does not take account of differences between countries, there is every reason to agree with his observation that '[the] decade which followed the Second World War was a Golden Age for film exhibitors'.[76]

How are we to explain this increase in cinema-going in the decade after the war? While the continued popularity of American movies suggests that the cinema was still fulfilling the role of a provider of entertainment and escapism, this alone is insufficient as an explanation for the increase in cinema attendances in most countries. The reasons are due to a peculiar set of historical conditions that are unique to the post-war decade. Following the economic crises of the late 1940s, the countries of Western Europe entered, in the early 1950s, into a period of sustained economic growth and recovery that lasted until the oil crisis of 1973–4. The 'economic miracle' in Italy, France and the GFR had a profound impact upon all forms of leisure and popular culture. Increasing levels of affluence meant that people had more disposable income to spend on leisure activities, while in societies such as Italy, France and Spain, which had large rural populations, increasing urbanization saw large numbers of people moving to the towns and cities where most cinemas were located. It is useful here to make a comparison between these European countries and the United States, where the shift away from city centres to the suburbs had occurred at the same time as a decline in cinema admissions. To relate cinema-going to urbanization, moreover, helps to explain why Britain was an anomaly amongst the major countries in the post-war period. Another factor that differentiated Britain from other Western European nations is television. Although it would be misleading to assume a direct correlation between cinema attendances and television ownership, the fact cannot be ignored that television became more widespread in Britain than it did in other European countries. Thus, in Britain in 1955 there were some 4,500,000 television sets, whereas in France in the same year there were only 260,500 sets and in Italy only 190,000.[77] It was a combination, therefore, of demographic, economic and cultural factors that created the conditions and circumstances in which cinema-going in Europe could enjoy its 'golden age' in the decade following the Second World War.

NINE

New Waves, New Cinemas

In most histories of cinema in Europe the 1950s are typically characterized as a stagnant and mediocre decade that saw little in the way of innovation or artistic prestige. In contrast, the 1960s are seen as a time of experimentation in film form and technique that represented the most exciting period of innovation since the avant-gardes of the 1920s. While the view of the 1950s as a 'doldrums era' – a phrase originally coined by critic Raymond Durgnat in respect of British cinema[1] – has increasingly been called into question by film historians who have looked anew at the popular genres that proved so successful and durable at the box-office, it is, nevertheless, impossible to deny both the aesthetic and the social significance of the 'new wave' cinemas that emerged across Europe at the turn of the decade. These 'new waves' or 'new cinemas' coincided with the 'cultural revolution' of the 1960s that saw fundamental and far-reaching changes in popular attitudes, values, customs, morals and behaviour.[2] On one level the new cinemas (henceforth I will render these without the inverted commas) may be seen as reflecting the social and cultural changes of the 1960s: they examine such themes as the place of young people in society, changing social and sexual mores, permissiveness and anti-authoritarianism. On another level they can also be seen as artefacts of the cultural revolution themselves, for, while most new cinemas were stylistically quite diverse, what they exemplified collectively was a break with the classical tradition of narrative filmmaking and the foregrounding of style over narrative rather than the conventional subordination of style to narrative. The new cinemas were also identified, to a greater extent than any previous movement in cinema history, with filmmakers who styled themselves as *auteurs* and who regarded film as a personal expression of individual artistry. Each country's new cinema exhibited its own peculiar traits and characteristics, but there were nevertheless certain structural factors common to the major film industries that created the conditions in which these movements could emerge simultaneously in different countries.

NEW WAVE CINEMAS IN CONTEXT

The emergence of new filmmaking practices was made possible by a congruence of various industrial, economic and social factors that affected all the major film-producing nations of Europe in the late 1950s and early 1960s. Foremost amongst these was the sudden decline in cinema-going that occurred almost simultaneously in most countries in the late 1950s. After the peak year of 1955, cinema attendances across Europe began to fall away at an alarming rate as far as the film industry was concerned. The decline was most sudden and precipitous in France, where attendances fell sharply between 1957 (when there were 411 million ticket sales) and 1963 (290 million) and thereafter continued to decline steadily throughout the 1960s. In the German Federal Republic over two thirds of the cinema-going audience disappeared between 1956 (817 million admissions) and 1966 (257 million). In Britain, where cinema attendances had been declining since the mid-1940s, the decline accelerated in the late 1950s and over half the audience disappeared between 1955 (1,181 million) and 1960 (500 million). In Italy the erosion was less precipitous and came later, though there was still a downward trend: 819 million in 1955, 745 million in 1960, 680 million in 1965.[3]

How can this decline in cinema-going be explained? As in the United States, it would seem that the conventional explanation of the rise of television is unsatisfactory in itself to account for the decline in the popularity of cinema. There is, in fact, no direct correlation between television ownership and cinema-going. In France, where the drop in audiences was most dramatic, television ownership was less extensive than in either Italy or Britain: even by 1965 there were only 133 television sets per thousand inhabitants in France, compared with 193 in Italy and 214 in Britain.[4] It was not television alone, therefore, that accounted for the decline in cinema-going. Historians have tended to offer more complex arguments, relating the declining popularity of cinema to the rise in living standards and the greater number of leisure opportunities that were available to consumers by the late 1950s/early 1960s. In Italy, for example, spending on sport (football especially became more popular due to television coverage) increased at the same time as spending on cinema decreased. Pierre Sorlin argues that, in Italy at least, increased consumer spending was a major factor:

> Much more than television, it was the spread of labour-saving devices and electrical appliances which led people to save on entertainment. Oddly enough, films helped to legit-imize the diminution in spending which would subsequently devalue them. They taught people how to live, how to occupy their empty hours. Cinema-goers tasted the life of the rich; they were introduced to an equality of consumption, which was not equality of status, but they were lured into believing that rich and poor could aspire to the same level of comfort and life-style.[5]

Increasing car ownership, especially, opened up new patterns of leisure behaviour, as people had the opportunity to travel at their own convenience. The increase in the number of private motor vehicles was, indeed, a recurring feature of European art films in the 1960s: Federico Fellini's *8½* and Jean-Luc Godard's *Weekend*, for example, both include sequences where their pro-tagonists are caught in massive traffic jams.

While the decline in cinema-going came later in Europe than it had in America, one of its consequences was the same. Those who still went to the cinema were increasingly held to be young people under thirty. The late 1950s saw the emergence of a participatory youth culture centred on rock music, new trends in fashion and an increased awareness of sexuality and personal appearance. The 'economic miracle' of the 1950s had created a new class of young, affluent, leisure-oriented consumers with-out familial responsibilities. Film producers in Europe were quicker than their American counterparts in responding to this demographic change in their core audience. In France the great commercial success of 28–year-old Roger Vadim's *Et Dieu . . . créa la femme* (*And God Created Woman*, 1956), the film that turned Brigitte Bardot into an international sex symbol, suggested to producers that the way forward lay with younger directors who were assumed to be more in tune with the youth audience. Positive moves were made to encourage young directors. The Groupe des Recherches et d'Essais Cinématographiques (GREC) was set up to provide grants for new filmmakers; an *avances sur recettes* scheme that provided interest-free loans repayable from profits was also intro-duced. Other countries followed the French example. In 1965 the GFR established the Kuratorium Junger Deutscher Film (Board of Curators of Young German Film) which financed the production of some twenty films between 1966 and 1968. New film schools were set up in the GFR, the Netherlands and Sweden to encourage young filmmakers into the industry, and film festi-vals in Hyères (France) and Pesaro (Italy) were launched as showcases for new talent.

It would be misleading to suggest that all new wave move-ments consisted entirely of brand-new directors. In Italy, for example, the acclaimed films of the 1960s were made by a mix-ture of experienced hands (Luchino Visconti, Vittorio De Sica, Federico Fellini) and newcomers (Bernardo Bertolucci, Marco Bellocchio, Pier Paolo Pasolini). It was in France that the high-est proportion of new directors came to the fore: 67 directors made their first features in 1959–60. This represented the high-est number of new directors since the early 1930s, when the arrival of sound was the occasion for a similar upheaval in the film industry, and was made possible, to some extent, by the retirement or death of an unusually large number of established French directors in the 1950s. Writing in 1961, the French film critic Jacques Siclier observed: 'The cinema has become the preferred means of expression for those tagged by Georges Sadoul as "the 1960 generation"; and, at any rate during the last two years, this generation has been able to find favourable con-ditions in the film industry.'[6]

New talent inevitably brings with it new ideas and new work-ing practices. A common feature of the new wave filmmakers was their rejection of established traditions and genres, a break with what they regarded as the stultifying traditions of the past. In France, for example, young filmmakers reacted against what they termed *le cinéma de papa*; '*Papas kino ist tot!*' ('Daddy's cinema is dead') was the rallying cry of the young West German filmmakers who signed the Oberhausen Manifesto in 1962. In Britain the reaction was less polemical, though in 1957 Lindsay Anderson had criticized 'the rather tepid humanism of our cinema' which he considered to be 'snobbish, anti-intelligent, wilfully blind to the conditions and problems of the present, [and] dedicated to an out-of-date, exhausted national ideal'.[7] Another shared characteristic of the new waves was the notion of the film director as an artist whose films expressed his (or her) personal vision. Whether expressed as *la politique des auteurs* (France) or as *Autorenfilm* (Germany) there was a commitment to the concept of an artistic cinema of personal expression. It was in the pages of the polemical film magazine *Cahiers du Cinéma* that François Truffaut made the distinction between directors who were *auteurs* and those who were mere *metteurs-en-scène*. A *metteur-en-scène* was a director who simply translated a film script written by others into visual terms, whereas *auteurs* 'often write their dialogue and some of them themselves invent the stories they direct'.[8]

What were the formal and stylistic characteristics of the new wave cinemas? 'The main movement of the period', Roger Manvell wrote in 1966, 'has been towards greater naturalism in subjects, characterization and technique, and following this towards a more imaginative understanding of what realism can mean when it is taken beyond mere superficial "likeness" in the portrayal of people and places.'[9] The realist impulse is evident in the influence on the new cinemas of new modes of documentary filmmaking that emerged at around the same time, such as Free Cinema in Britain, Direct Cinema in the United States and *Cinéma Vérité* in France, which made use of lightweight, hand-held cameras and portable sound equipment that allowed greater flexibility for outdoor filming. Naturalism also took the form of looser, more open-ended and ambiguous narratives that were similar to the films of directors such as Bergman and Buñuel. One of the principal characteristics of art cinema,

according to Bordwell, is 'the ambiguous interaction of objective and subjective realism' which 'reached its apogee' in the
work of European filmmakers in the late 1950s and 1960s: 'The
fullest flower of the art-cinema paradigm occurred at the
moment that the combination of novelty and nationalism
became the marketing device it has been ever since: the French
New Wave, New Polish Cinema, New Hungarian Cinema,
New German Cinema, New Australian Cinema . . .'[10] For
Bordwell, therefore, the international new cinemas collectively
are part of the broader category of art cinema. The association
of new wave filmmakers with art cinema was strengthened by
their success on the international festival circuit.

What all the new wave cinemas shared, besides their stylistic
innovation and critical success, was a more frank examination of
social issues and human behaviour than had been possible
before. One of the characteristics of the cultural revolution of
the 1960s, as Arthur Marwick would have it, was 'a new frankness, openness, and indeed honesty in personal relations and
modes of expression'.[11] In the cinema this was made possible by
a relaxation of censorship, at least in most Western European
countries. In 1966 Manvell observed 'that the operation of film
censorship has changed so radically since the late 1950s'.[12] It is a
statement that needs to be qualified somewhat: censorship in
Ireland and Spain, for example, remained much as it had since
the 1930s. At the other extreme, Denmark abolished film censorship in 1960 (except for children's films) and legalized
pornography in 1969. In many societies, however, this was a
period in which attitudes to the moral censorship of films were
in a state of transition. French films dealing with marital infidelity – Louis Malle's *Les Amants* (*The Lovers*, 1958) and Roger
Vadim's *Les Liaisons Dangereuses* (*Dangerous Liaisons*, 1960) –
were often banned by local mayors. Similar fates befell
Visconti's *Rocco e i suoi fratelli* (*Rocco and His Brothers*, 1960) and
Michelangelo Antonioni's *L'avventura* (1960) in Italy. In Britain
the liberalization of censorship, while far from being radical,
nevertheless made great strides in the early 1960s, mainly due to
the more relaxed policy of the bbfc which, under its new secretary, John Trevelyan (appointed in 1958), actively sought to
encourage filmmakers dealing with 'adult' subject matter in a

'responsible' manner. Thus it was that Trevelyan approved of films made in the style of British social realism and was prepared to negotiate with filmmakers over the amount of sex and swearing (what the BBFC coyly referred to as 'language') that was permissible. It was largely a consequence of Trevelyan's wish to make the 'X' certificate (introduced in 1951 as an 'adults only' category and hitherto associated mainly with horror and exploitation films) respectable that films were able to address previously taboo subjects such as homosexuality (Basil Dearden's *Victim*, Joseph Losey's *The Servant* in the early 1960s) and abortion (Lewis Gilbert's *Alfie* in 1966).[13]

In Britain the political censorship of films had largely ceased after the Second World War, but elsewhere in Europe state censorship continued to be the norm, usually exercised by official bodies that were politically aligned with the governments of the day. The examples of Italy and France provide an interesting comparison in this respect. Film censorship in Italy was as stringent throughout the 1950s as it had been under Mussolini; the Cinema Laws of 1949 and 1956 were designed to uphold moral standards and to ensure that films did not reflect badly upon Italian society. A change was signalled, however, by a new Cinema Law in 1962 which lessened the state's powers of pre-production censorship. This was partly a response to pressure from the film industry and partly due to the election of a new centre-left government with a more liberal outlook. While Italy was relaxing the political censorship of films, however, France was tightening hers through a decree of 1961 that required all scripts to be approved by the Centre National de la Cinématographie (CNC). Political censorship was more stringent than at any time since the Vichy regime, demonstrated by the banning of two films dealing with the Algerian War: Godard's *Le Petit Soldat* (*The Little Soldier*, 1960) and Gillo Pontecorvo's *La Battaglia di Algeri* (*The Battle of Algiers*, 1965). It was not until the violent protests of 1968–9 brought home to the authorities the extent of popular unrest that a relaxation of film censorship in France was effected.

The extent of political censorship in the countries of the Soviet bloc was variable and far from uniform in its application during the 1950s and 1960s. All countries experienced a degree of liberalization following Stalin's death in 1953, though this 'thaw' was short-lived in most countries. Poland, Hungary and Yugoslavia probably allowed the greatest degree of artistic freedom to filmmakers, while the German Democratic Republic and the Soviet Union were among the more tightly regulated regimes. The vagaries of censorship in the Soviet bloc are best exemplified by the case of Czechoslovakia. In the 1960s, as the doctrine of Socialist Realism waned, more adventurous directors (politically and artistically) came to the fore. The Czech New Wave, centred on directors such as Miloš Forman, Evald Schorm and Jiří Menzel, flourished in the mid 1960s. Oddly, perhaps, while their films were sometimes banned in Czechoslovakia itself, they were shown widely abroad, winning prizes on the festival circuit and briefly placing Czech filmmakers at the vanguard of international cinema. Menzel's *Closely Observed Trains* (1966) was the biggest international success, winning an Academy Award as Best Foreign Film and the Grand Prix at the Mannheim Festival. The relative freedom allowed to Czech filmmakers was abruptly curtailed, however, by the Soviet invasion of 1968. Menzel's next film, *Larks on a String* (1969), an anti-communist satire, was not shown until 1990, while other directors left to work abroad, Forman enjoying the greatest success when he moved to America.

NEW WAVE CINEMAS IN WESTERN EUROPE

If the new wave in cinema can be said to have begun anywhere, then it was in France. This is not to deny the place of other national cinemas in the movement; one of the most distinctive features of the new wave, indeed, was the extent to which stylistic developments were shared between countries due to the circulation of these films on the international art house circuit. It was in France, however, that the new wave had the greatest impact and where it was, albeit briefly, a genuinely popular phenomenon rather than just another artistic movement. This, at least, is one aspect in which the *Nouvelle Vague* differs from previous film movements such as German Expressionism or Italian Neo-Realism. Originally, of course, '*la nouvelle vague*' did not refer specifically to the cinema at all. The phrase was coined in 1958 by Françoise Giroud, editor of *L'Express*, to refer to what she perceived as the new youthful spirit that was abroad in the country as a whole. Seized upon by journalists and, especially, film critics, the term came to be associated in particular with the array of (mostly young) directors who were at the forefront of French cinema. It was in France that the romantic notion of the young filmmaker-artist making highly personal films in defiance of conventional practices reached its apogee.

Just who were the *Nouvelle Vague*? This is a question to which there is no definitive answer. At the time, any new director making their first film tended to be included. Thus it was that the *Nouvelle Vague* extended beyond the well-known figures such as Truffaut and Godard and also encompassed many directors who remain relatively unknown (Jacques Baratier, Louis Félix, Robert Hossein, Jean-Daniel Pollet and Edmond Séchan are likely to be names familiar to only the most assiduous French cinephiles). It would be wrong to assume that the *Nouvelle Vague* was a unified movement with a coherent set of thematic concerns or stylistic practices. 'Like the British Angry Young Man Movement it was less a movement than a useful journalistic catchphrase', a British critic remarked ten years later; 'under it, a very heterogeneous bunch of film-makers were lumped together, some of them readily, but most of them willy-nilly.'[14] Film historians, however, have tended to focus on a small nucleus of directors, principally François Truffaut, Jean-Luc Godard, Eric Rohmer, Claude Chabrol and Jacques Rivette. All these had been film critics before they became filmmakers. Rohmer and Chabrol had published a book on Alfred Hitchcock in 1957 and all wrote for *Cahiers du Cinéma*, where, under the auspices of André Bazin (who died in 1958 at the age of 40), they contributed to the polemical *politique des auteurs*. For some commentators, such as James Monaco, this group *is* the *Nouvelle Vague* and their films represent an attempt to put into practice 'a new theory of film' worked out in the pages of *Cahiers du Cinéma*.[15]

Arthur Marwick suggests that the best way of historicizing the *Nouvelle Vague* is 'to break the wave into three distinctive wavelets'.[16] The first of these consisted of what might be termed proto-*Nouvelle Vague* films in so far as they came before the term had gained any wide currency but which anticipated some of the thematic concerns of the movement. Films such as Vadim's *Et Dieu . . . créa la femme* and Malle's *Les Amants* were stylistically quite conventional; their importance lay in their sexual frankness and their focus on female sexuality. Both these films were controversial and aroused the wrath of religious groups; both were also enormously successful at the box-office and demonstrated to French producers that young directors could make money. Malle, who like Vadim never became a central figure in the movement, asserted the commercial imperative that lay behind the *Nouvelle Vague*:

> It just happened that I was the first of my generation to make feature films. Just before Chabrol, a year before Truffaut, and I think two years before Godard – but we followed in rapid succession. When I made *Ascenseur* at the end of 1957, there was no such thing as the New Wave, it was all the old structures of the French film industry, and it was very difficult for a young filmmaker to break through. Then suddenly there were four, five, six first-time directors. The one thing people always forget to mention about the New Wave – the reason the New Wave was taken so seriously – is that our first films (or even first two films) were very successful commercially. Suddenly producers discovered that these young men were making films for a quarter the price of Clément and Becker, and that they were very successful at the box office. So overnight we became very fashionable, and every producer in Paris wanted to make films with us.[17]

The second wavelet comprised a small group of former documentary filmmakers – Alain Resnais, Agnès Varda, Georges Franju – who entered features at the same time as the *Nouvelle Vague*. Marwick labels these the 'structuralists' due to their links with writers such as Marguerite Duras and Alain Robbe-Grillet – leading proponents of the *Nouveau Roman* (New Novel) – and to the highly verbal, closely scripted nature of their films. Thompson and Bordwell describe the same filmmakers as the 'Left Bank group'.[18] In contrast to the cinephiles of *Cahiers*, these filmmakers were more interested in the relationship between film and other arts, especially literature. Resnais collaborated with Duras (*Hiroshima, mon amour*) and Robbe-Grillet (*L'Année dernière à Marienbad*) to create two highly complex, deeply textured films exploring the ambiguities of memory. Both films employ non-linear narratives and experiment with narrative time by interweaving past and present. Writing in *Cahiers du Cinéma*, Godard remarked that 'seeing *Hiroshima* gave one the impression of watching a film that would have been quite inconceivable in terms of what one was already familiar with in the cinema'.[19] Franju's first feature was a Surrealist horror film, *Les Yeux sans visage* (*Eyes without a Face*, 1959), while Varda, who had already made one feature in the mid-1950s, came to prominence with *Cléo de 5 à 7* (*Cléo from 5 to 7*, 1962), a film set in 'real time' focusing on an actress awaiting the results of medical tests.

The third wavelet comprises the *Cahiers* group, whose breakthrough came in four films released in 1959–60: Chabrol's *Le Beau Serge* (*Handsome Serge*) and *Les Cousins*, Truffaut's *Les Quatre cents coups* (*The 400 Blows*) and Godard's *A bout de souffle* (*Breathless*). Even in this group there is such a diversity of technique that it is impossible to define a *Nouvelle Vague* style as such. Chabrol was probably the most technically proficient; he was also more conventional (or less adventurous) than his colleagues and his career faded during the 1960s. It was the early films of Truffaut and Godard, however, that came to define the spirit of the *Nouvelle Vague*. Initially collaborators – Truffaut wrote the script of *A bout de souffle* – their subsequent careers followed divergent paths that are paradigmatic of the stylistic trajectories of the *Nouvelle Vague*, for, while Truffaut moved comfortably into the commercial mainstream, Godard was to become an increasingly isolated figure whose desire to break the rules of filmmaking pushed him further towards the margins of film culture.

Les Quatre cents coups is the *auteur* film *par excellence*: its narrative of a juvenile delinquent who gets involved in petty crime and is finally sent to reform school reflects Truffaut's own adolescence, while much of the film was shot on location around the Rue des Martyrs in Montmartre where the director grew up.

In the words of one critic, *Les Quatre cents coups* 'is a film which above all questions what it is to create a personal history in film. Antoine Doinel as protagonist becomes a means for Truffaut to test the potential of cinema to create a first person subject, and to make of his life a case history in images'.[20] Truffaut followed it with *Tirez sur le pianiste* (*Shoot the Piano Player*, 1960), an homage to American *film noir* based on a pulp thriller by David Goodis, and *Jules et Jim* (1962), a *ménage à trois* period drama adapted from a novel by Henri-Pierre Roche and probably his best-known work. Stylistically, Truffaut's films are characterized by their freewheeling camera movements and by abrupt changes of mood from humour to tragedy. They also privilege style over narration, using devices such as irises that had not been seen since the silent cinema.

Godard was undoubtedly the most radical of the *Nouvelle Vague* directors in his refusal to adhere to accepted norms of film form and narration. '*A bout de souffle* was the sort of film where anything goes: that was what it was all about', he explained. 'What I wanted was to take a conventional story and remake, but differently, everything the cinema had done.'[21] To this end he employs all manner of jarring discontinuity devices, especially jump-cuts, which in conventional film grammar would be regarded as mistakes. The result of this breaking of the rules of classical narration is a kinetic style of cinema that quite literally seems 'out of breath'. Godard's output during the 1960s was prolific, encompassing playful deconstructions of genres such as romantic comedy (*Une femme est une femme*), the gangster film (*Bande à Part*) and science-fiction (*Alphaville*), and sociological studies of modern life (*Vivra sa vie*, *Une femme mariée*, *Masculin-Féminin*, *Deux ou trois choses que je sais d'elle*). *Le Mépris* (*Contempt*, 1963), a Franco-Italian co-production made at the Cinecittà studios in Rome, represented a break from the low-budget origins of the *Nouvelle Vague*; a film about filmmaking in which Godard cast himself as assistant to Fritz Lang (playing himself), it was a satire of the film industry that was replete with cinematic references. Always idiosyncratic in his use of form and technique, Godard veered towards the avant-garde in the later 1960s in films such as *Pierrot le fou* and *Weekend*, breaking down narrative into a more fragmentary structure and using inserts such as inter-titles, advertisements and comic strips that did not bear an obvious relation to the story.

Most commentators agree that by this time the *Nouvelle Vague* had run its course. Truffaut intimated that its life was very short indeed: 'The New Wave was born in 1959, and by the end of 1960 it was already an object of contempt. For a year it had some prestige in public opinion.'[22] Film critics and audiences soon tired of the publicity surrounding the new directors, and once the *Nouvelle Vague* had suffered their first commercial failures – Truffaut with *La Peau douce* (*The Soft Skin*, 1963), Chabrol with *Les Godelureaux* (1961) – producers were less keen to invest in their films. The most successful French film of the 1960s was the glossy romantic drama *Un homme et une femme* (*A Man and a Woman*, 1966), admittedly made by a new director (Claude Lelouch), but far removed from the rough-edged and cynical style of the *Nouvelle Vague*. However, while the *Nouvelle Vague* itself flowered only briefly, its impact and influence on filmmakers elsewhere was enormous.

In 1960, for example, the Italian film critic Morando Morandini observed that Italian filmmakers 'began, timidly enough, to embark on a slightly bolder policy largely as a result of the French example. This year films are being made in Italy which two or three years ago could not have been attempted.'[23] The year 1960 is widely regarded as 'the *annus mirabilis* for Italian cinema'.[24] Three films in particular – Fellini's *La Dolce Vita*, Visconti's *Rocco e i suoi fratelli* and Antonioni's *L'avventura* – won critical acclaim at home and abroad (though they also attracted controversy) and were successful enough at the home box-office for 1960 to be the first occasion since the end of the Second World War when Italian films were more popular with domestic audiences than Hollywood imports. These three films heralded the beginning of the New Italian Cinema that was to emerge during the 1960s. Yet, like their French counterparts, the three films were very different in tone. *Rocco e i suoi fratelli* is the closest of the films to the Neo-Realist tradition – unsurprising, perhaps, given that Visconti had been at the forefront of Neo-Realism and that *Rocco* marked his return to the 'southern problem' that he had previously examined in *La Terra Trema* – though its narrative has an epic (some commentators have even described it as 'operatic') quality due to its heightened sense of tragedy. Penelope Houston described it as 'a kind of souped-up neo-realism, owing part at least of its tension to the obvious clash between the lure of the decadent and the counter-impulse to construct a sweeping social panorama of our times'.[25] In a sense *Rocco* is two films in one: a realist drama about the problems facing an Italian family from the south who move to Milan, exploring themes such as social prejudice, economic exploitation and the loss of traditional family values, and a sensational melodrama involving two of the five brothers who become infatuated with the same woman, a prostitute. While the style of *Rocco* is realist, the other two films are modernist, exhibiting the episodic and ambiguous narratives that were also characteristic of the French films. *La Dolce Vita* both embodies the spirit of the permissive society and provides a critique of the social values of the time. Its depiction of the hedonistic lifestyle of the Roman aristocracy is deceptively seductive – scenes of Marcello Mastroianni and Anita Ekberg frolicking in the Trevi Fountain did nothing to harm its popularity – but its protagonist (also called Marcello) finds himself increasingly disillusioned and alienated from the decadence in which he is both a participant and an observer. A sense of disillusionment is also manifest in *L'avventura* – a mood for which critics coined the term 'Antoniennui' – which is certainly the most ambiguous of the three films. Antonioni is less interested in telling a story – the film involves the disappearance of a young woman on a yachting holiday and the attempts of her friends to find her – than he is in exploring his favourite themes of social alienation and the difficulty of communication. The film offers no sense of narrative closure: the missing girl is never found, while the outcome of the affair between her friend Claudia (Monica Vitti) and lover Sandro (Gabriele Ferzetti) remains unclear following the wordless ending in which neither says anything. (The scene was later parodied in De Sica's comedy *After the Fox* in which Peter Sellers, masquerading as a film director, has his stars Victor Mature and Britt Ekland saying nothing to each other in order to demonstrate 'the lack of communication in society'.)

Mira Liehm identifies several features that the New Italian Cinema shared with other new waves: a denial of objective

realism in favour of subjectivity; the rejection of closed plots; a 'ferocious contempt for film grammar'; and the rejection of the social and political status quo.[26] With the exception of Pontecorvo's *La Battaglia di Algeri* – a film that in any case is perhaps more suitably placed within the paradigm of Third Cinema as it was financed almost entirely by the newly independent Algerian government – Italian cinema of the 1960s was not overtly political. It was, however, critical of social conventions and mores, probably to a greater extent than the French *Nouvelle Vague*. Marco Bellocchio's debut feature *I pugni in tasca* (*Fists in the Pocket*, 1965) uses the story of a dysfunctional epileptic family as a metaphor for society at large. 'Film sometimes needs symbols, and to me epilepsy meant all the frustration, all the troubles and weaknesses often found in the young,' Bellocchio said.[27] The most successful Italian film of the decade was the satirical comedy *Divorzio all'italiana* (*Divorce, Italian Style*, 1961), more conventional in style than the more critically acclaimed films, though nevertheless socially progressive in so far as it anticipated the campaign for reform of the divorce laws by half a decade.

Arguably the most consistent of the new waves, stylistically and thematically, was the British. The impulse here came from two directions. Most of the British New Wave films took as their source material either the novels of the 'northern realists' (John Braine, Alan Sillitoe, Stan Barstow, David Storey) or the drama of the so-called 'Angry Young Men' (John Osborne, Keith Waterhouse and – to include an angry young woman – Shelagh Delaney). These sources were turned into films by directors whose first experience of filmmaking had been in documentaries through their association with the Free Cinema movement of the mid-1950s (Tony Richardson, Lindsay Anderson, Karel Reisz and cameraman Walter Lassally). There is some debate, however, over the extent to which these directors should be seen, like their French counterparts, as men of the cinema, or whether they represented the continuation of the theatrical influence that commentators have so often seen in British cinema. 'It wasn't *Momma Don't Allow* that brought Tony Richardson into the directorial chair of *Look Back in Anger*, it was the fact that he had directed the play on the London stage', Durgnat avers. 'The films are based on proven successes in other media, their production stimulated by the influence of new talents on commercial producers.'[28]

The film generally seen as marking the beginning of the British New Wave was Jack Clayton's film of John Braine's novel *Room at the Top* (1959). Dilys Powell, for example, admired the 'creative courage' and 'consummate authority' of a film which had 'an emotional directness not often found in a British film' and concluded her review by declaring that '[it] gives one faith all over again in a renaissance of British cinema.'[29] *Room at the Top*, advertised as 'a savage story of lust and ambition', is a powerful critique of class and money in post-war Britain told through the story of the abrasive Joe Lampton (Laurence Harvey) who pursues his employer's daughter in order to further his own social and financial status. The film was undoubtedly groundbreaking in its frank examination of bitter class divisions and the highly sexual nature of Lampton's affair with an older woman (Simone Signoret). 'The love scenes are quite unlike the usual dormitory charade', Powell remarked; 'a quarrel has the savageness of people who are still in love.' *Room at the Top* was a commercial as well as a critical success; it opened, albeit briefly, a window in the early 1960s for a cycle of films dealing with contemporary British society in a similarly frank and realistic manner.

Room at the Top had been produced by brothers John and James Woolf, experienced hands of the British film industry who had been active as independent producers for over a decade. Most of the key British New Wave films that followed, however, were brought to the screen by Woodfall Films, set up by director Tony Richardson, playwright John Osborne and Canadian producer Harry Saltzman, initially with a view to adapting Osborne's plays for the screen. Richardson did indeed direct film adaptations of Osborne's *Look Back in Anger* (1959) and *The Entertainer* (1960), while Woodfall also produced films of Alan Sillitoe's *Saturday Night and Sunday Morning* (1960, directed by Karel Reisz) and *The Loneliness of the Long Distance Runner* (1962, directed by Richardson) and Shelagh Delaney's *A Taste of Honey* (1961, directed by Richardson). These films – and others such as John Schlesinger's films of Stan Barstow's *A Kind of Loving* (1961) and Keith Waterhouse's *Billy Liar* (1963) and Anderson's film of David Storey's *This Sporting Life* (1963) – were notable for their stark black-and-white cinematography and for their use of natural lighting and real locations, often utilizing the back streets, canals and workshops of grim northern industrial towns. They also showcased the talents of a new generation of younger, naturalistic actors (Albert Finney, Tom Courtenay, Alan Bates, Richard Harris) who portrayed frustrated, rebellious working-class protagonists. The films' representation of a rather sordid image of everyday life in the provinces quickly earned them the label of 'kitchen sink' drama.

Some commentators have since been less than sympathetic

to the representation of working-class life in the films of the British New Wave. Roy Armes, for instance, takes a distinctly jaundiced view, patronizing the major directors associated with Free Cinema (Richardson, Reisz, Anderson) as 'the university-educated bourgeois making "sympathetic" films about proletarian life, not analysing the ambiguities of their own privileged position'.[30] John Hill, however, rejects this interpretation and argues instead that the filmmakers deliberately set out to distance themselves from the subject matter:

> It has been a common enough criticism of the 'new wave' films that, although about the working class, they nonetheless represent an outsider's view . . . The importance of the point, however, is less the actual social background of the film-makers, none of whom ever lay claim to be just 'one of the lads', than the way this 'outsider's view' is inscribed in the films themselves, the way the 'poetry', the 'marks of enunciation' themselves articulate a clear distance between observer and observed.[31]

Arthur Marwick, characteristically, has no truck with talk of 'marks of enunciation' and argues that the historical significance of films like *Room at the Top* and *Saturday Night and Sunday Morning* lay not in the textual features of the films themselves but rather in their status as cultural artefacts which 'showed that critical change was actually taking place during the particular few years in which they were made'.[32] The point worth stressing here is that the British New Wave did last only a few years, most commentators agreeing that *This Sporting Life* (a commercial disappointment) marked the end of the movement. Richardson and Woodfall enjoyed their greatest popular success with the saucy costume romp *Tom Jones* (1963), while Saltzman hit the jackpot when he left Woodfall and teamed up with American producer 'Cubby' Broccoli to make a film series based on Ian Fleming's James Bond novels.

The last of the Western European new waves to emerge, somewhat belatedly, was in the GFR. It has long been the accepted wisdom to date the origins of what came to be known as the New German Cinema precisely to February 1962 when a group of young filmmakers attending the 8th West German Short Film Festival at Oberhausen issued a manifesto declaring their intention 'to create the new German feature film' and asserting their 'freedom from the conventions of the industry . . . from the influence of commercial partners . . . from the tutelage of other groups with vested interests'.[33] Yet in fact, of the 26 signatories of the Oberhausen Manifesto, only Alexander Kluge, Volker Schlöndorff and Edgar Reitz went on to sustain long careers as feature film directors; and, moreover, none of the directors central to the New German Cinema when it made its international breakthrough in the 1970s (Rainer Werner Fassbinder, Werner Herzog and Wim Wenders) had been amongst the Oberhausen signatories. Thomas Elsaesser suggests that 'a distinction needs to be made between the Young German Film and the New German Cinema in terms of the politics of film-making, as well as in terms of style and subject-matter'.[34] The Young German Film of the 1960s arose from the initiative taken at Oberhausen and included directors such as Roger Fritz, Hansjürgen Pohland, Jean-Marie Straub and Will Tremper, whereas the New German Cinema succeeded it in the 1970s and achieved a greater level of international prominence, principally through the efforts of the 'big three' of Fassbinder, Herzog and Wenders.

The most notable feature of the New German Cinema was its diversity. Anton Kaes describes it as 'a loose alliance of autonomous *auteurs* who had little in common except their status as outsiders'.[35] Thompson and Bordwell agree that it was 'an even more amorphous group than most New Cinemas of recent decades'.[36] This is apparent from a comparison of the work of its three major exponents. Wenders, arguably the most accessible, made films about male anxiety and alienation that mirrored the early films of New Hollywood but within a German context. Films such as *Im Lauf der Zeit* (*Kings of the Road*, 1976) and *Alice in den Städten* (*Alice in the City*, 1978) are open-ended 'road' movies notable for their use of long takes and elaborate camera movements. Herzog, in contrast, was the *enfant terrible* of New German Cinema, exploring the themes of obsession and madness in films whose protagonists exist beyond the edge of civilization: a Spanish conquistador intent upon discovering the fabled city of Eldorado (*Aguirre der Zorn Gottes/Aguirre, Wrath of God*, 1972), the true tale of a man who spends his life confined to one room (*Jeder für sich und Gott gegen Alle/The Enigma of Kasper Hauser*, 1975) and an eccentric Irishman intent on hauling his ship overland through the Amazon (*Fitzcarraldo*, 1982). However, it is Fassbinder who to most people symbolizes New German Cinema in the way that Truffaut and Godard have come to symbolize the *Nouvelle Vague*. Until his premature death from a drugs overdose in 1982 at the age of 36, Fassbinder was a remarkably prolific filmmaker who worked mostly with the Antiteater, a closely knit troupe of actors and technicians. Fassbinder moved from domestic melodrama early in his career (influenced especially by the films of Douglas Sirk) to political melodrama in his later films. Three films in particular – *Die Ehe der Maria Braun* (*The Marriage of Maria Braun*, 1978), *Lola* (1981) and *Veronika Voss* (1982) – constitute an unofficial trilogy covering the founding years of the GFR. These films can be seen as a critique of the social and political decisions taken under the leadership of the first post-war German Chancellor, Konrad Adenauer. The films are allegorical: Maria Braun rebuilds her life after the war (the 'economic miracle' of the 1950s) but dies in a gas explosion that may or may not be suicide (illustrating Fassbinder's deep personal scepticism about Germany's recovery); Lola is a prostitute in a small town where ex-Nazis still occupy positions of power (inability to break with the past); and Veronika Voss, modelled on the real-life Sybille Schmitz, is a fading actress down on her luck in post-war Germany (Fassbinder uses Art Deco set designs and glossy black-and-white cinematography to imitate the visual style of the films of the 1930s in which Veronika would have appeared). Fassbinder described them as 'very political films' and explained why he was attracted to films about the past: 'In order to understand the present, what has and will become of a country, one has to understand its whole history or at least have worked on it.'[37]

The symbolic end of New German Cinema came in 1982 with the death of Fassbinder and the political change from the Socialist Chancellor Helmut Schmidt to the conservative Christian Democrat Helmuth Kohl whose government withdrew much of the state funding for cinema. The government had been willing to subsidize New German Cinema when the movement was perceived as an 'official' German film that would bring cultural and artistic prestige – the height of its international recognition came with the award of the Best Foreign Film Oscar to Volker Schlöndorff's film version of Günter Grass's labyrinthine novel *Die Blechtrommel* (*The Tin Drum*, 1979) – but it is hardly surprising that state subsidy dried up as the filmmakers became increasingly critical of the state itself. Films such as Margarethe von Trotta's *Die Verlorene Ehre der Katherina Blum* (*The Lost Honour of Katherina Blum*, 1975) and the episodic portmanteau piece *Deutschland im Herbst* (*Germany in Autumn*, 1978), including segments by Fassbinder, Kluge, Reitz and Schlöndorff, were political tracts attacking what they perceived as the state's oppression of civil liberties in response to the rise of international terrorism in the 1970s. Moreover, New German Cinema had never been a popular cinema in the way that, albeit briefly, its French, Italian and British counterparts had. New German Cinema had always been what Elsaesser terms 'a cultural mode of production' rather than an economic mode of production and its demise came about when, for political and economic reasons, that cultural mode of production was no longer sustainable.[38]

NEW WAVE CINEMAS IN EASTERN EUROPE

The new wave in cinema was not confined to Western Europe. In the early 1960s new waves emerged in several Eastern bloc countries, including Czechoslovakia, Poland, Yugoslavia and Hungary. As in the West, a congruence of factors – political, economic and cultural – created the conditions in which a more personal, artistic cinema could briefly flourish. With the doctrine of Socialist Realism waning, filmmakers had greater scope for experimentation in form and style. This liberalization was more apparent in the satellite states than in the Soviet Union itself. Several Eastern European states, including Poland,

Czechoslovakia and Hungary, reorganized their film industries in an attempt to counter the rising popularity of television. Those film industries moved away from the centralized system adopted by the Soviet Union and towards a more decentralized model, in which filmmakers worked in smaller self-contained units. As the satellite states had always been more open to imported films than the Soviet Union, filmmakers were also aware of developments elsewhere in Europe.

The most favourable conditions for the existence of a new wave cinema were found in Czechoslovakia. Peter Hames argues that the Czech New Wave should be seen as part of a wider process of liberalization in politics and culture generally: 'The development of creative ideas in the film industry should be seen as one aspect of a wider phenomenon – the growth of ideas in economics, politics, literature and the arts that made up the Czechoslovak Reform Movement.'[39] This reform movement coincided with the presidency of Antonín Novotný (1957–68), though Novotný himself was hardly a liberal and was indeed trying to reimpose a greater level of state control before the 'Prague Spring' of 1968 brought Russian tanks in to crush the reform movement. Until then, and between 1963 and 1968 in particular, Czech (and Slovak) filmmakers experienced conditions that were as favourable as many of their counterparts in the West. Indeed, the combination of state sponsorship for film production and artistic licence enjoyed by filmmakers was such that Lindsay Anderson was prompted to declare that Czech cinema 'had every chance of becoming the best in the world'.[40]

Like other new wave movements, the Czech New Wave was stylistically diverse and is best understood as a group of highly individualistic filmmakers who all just happened to be working in the same industrial and cultural conditions. The main stylistic influences were Neo-Realism and the *Nouvelle Vague*. The two best known films of the Czech New Wave, Ján Kadár and Elmar Klos's *A Shop on the High Street* (1965) and Jiří Menzel's *Closely Observed Trains* (1966), both mix humour and tragedy in a manner not dissimilar to Truffaut's early films whilst exhibiting the social awareness of Neo-Realism. Both films are satirical allegories of authority and dissent, which, whilst set during the Nazi occupation of Czechoslovakia, contained clear messages for the present. *A Shop on the High Street*, which told the story of an impoverished carpenter (shades of *Bicycle Thieves*) who accepts a job as an 'Aryan controller' of a Jewish business and finds himself accepted by the Jewish community, explores a moral dilemma that had obvious contemporary overtones. It was, as Basil Wright points out, as much an 'anti-totalitarian film' as it was an 'anti-Nazi film'.[41] *Closely Observed Trains* is the story of a shy young railway clerk who is more concerned with losing his virginity than in the horrors of the war around him. The representation of the German regime as petty and officious draws clear parallels with Communist bureaucracy. The film is also notable for its sexual permissiveness – it is replete with sexual jokes such as the station master who uses a rubber stamp on the bare bottom of his girlfriend – indicating that the sexual revolution of the 1960s extended behind the Iron Curtain.

The historical significance of the Czech New Wave, Hames suggests, was that it marked 'a collective attempt to create a more satisfying culture that interacted with the other arts and the political, economic, and social changes of the sixties'.[42] While the authorities may have been uncomfortable with the political messages contained in some of the films, they were keen to support the cinema as a cultural medium, especially when the films began winning prizes on the international festival circuit. To an extent, therefore, the Czech New Wave became part of a state-sponsored cultural agenda that its proponents probably never intended. The Soviet invasion of 1968 and the subsequent tightening of restrictions signalled the end of the Czech New Wave. Controversial films were banned, the autonomous film units were disbanded and the industry was purged. Cinema, and the other arts, moved back towards the more repressive structures of the 1950s.

The Czech New Wave was the most prominent of the new cinemas of Eastern Europe in terms of its international recognition, but it was not an isolated case. A similar pattern of liberalization and artistic innovation followed by political reaction occurred in Poland. The Polish School, as it is generally known, can be divided into two periods. The first of these, in the 1950s, emerged in the context of the post-Stalinist thaw and was centred around directors such as Jerzy Kawalerowicz and Andrzej Wajda. Wajda achieved international recognition for his 'resistance trilogy' of 1954–8 (*A Generation, Kanal, Ashes and Diamonds*) which were acclaimed for their combination of 'gritty realism' and 'poetic vision'. It is tempting, given the political situation in Poland after 1945, to interpret these films of Polish resistance to the Nazis as allegories of resistance to Soviet Communism, though, as Thompson and Bordwell point out, the politics of the trilogy shifts and only the last film, which examines divisions within the resistance movement, can be considered anti-Communist. 'In the course of the trilogy', they write, 'his [Wajda's] representation of the underground evolves from ideologically correct criticism of the army (*A Generation*) through a grim celebration of its stubborn heroism (*Kanal*) to an ambiguous affirmation of the non-Communist Resistance.'[43]

Wajda had served in the Home Army (the non-Communist Polish Resistance) during the war and his films were undoubtedly influenced by his own experiences. He was young enough (born 1926) to be considered a 'new' director in the 1950s. Wajda's outlook, though, was vastly different from the only slightly younger directors who emerged in the 1960s such as Roman Polanski and Jerzy Skolimowski. To the extent that their films concentrated on contemporary youthful subjects these directors are more directly comparable to the likes of the French *Nouvelle Vague*. In the words of one historian of Polish cinema:

> The young generation was also united in its attitude to film-making. It considered it as something entirely personal, not simply a profession but a method by which they could express their own concerns, the concerns of their country and their generation, a form of dialogue with society, as it were. This attitude is reflected in their style, which is that of a personal record, subject less to the strict canons of dramatic form than to the logic of thought, of a confession, an essay, a dialogue. This attitude and aesthetic approach is after all shared by the young generation of film-makers in various countries.[44]

Polanski, a film school graduate who had made several acclaimed shorts, in fact made only one feature film in his native country, the psychological thriller *Knife in the Water* (1962), an intense drama that combines deep-focus photography with some of the narrational techniques of art cinema.

Polanski went into exile after *Knife in the Water* and became a peripatetic filmmaker working in Britain, America and France. Wajda also went for several years without making a film in Poland and moved instead into international co-productions. That the Polish School never achieved quite the same recognition as the Czech New Wave was due in large measure to the more restrictive conditions for filmmaking in Poland. While films were rarely banned outright, political pressure and critical rejection retarded the careers of Polish filmmakers. In the aftermath of the student demonstrations of 1968 there was a purge of the film industry that forced many personnel into exile, including both newcomers such as Skolimowski and old hands such as Aleksander Ford.

Other new cinemas in Eastern Europe remain rather less well known outside their own countries. The *Novi Film* movement in Yugoslavia coincided with the peak of the Czech New Wave (1963–8) though only the films of Alexander Petrovic (*I Even Met Happy Gypsies*) and Dušan Makavejev (*Innocence Unprotected*) achieved any degree of critical recognition in the West. Miklós Jancsó (*The Round-Up*, *The Red and the White*) is the best-known proponent of the New Hungarian Cinema of the 1960s. In common with other new cinemas in Eastern Europe, these movements combined a critical examination of their nation's past (especially the legacy of the Second World War) with an awareness of the aspirations of contemporary youth. Whether the freedom that these filmmakers had enjoyed, albeit temporarily, was a factor in the longer term historical process that saw the Communist stranglehold on Eastern Europe weakened, remains a matter of much conjecture.

AFTER THE NEW WAVES

Most of the new waves were short-lived, but collectively their significance is greater than the sum of their parts. The 1960s was the first occasion on which distinctive 'national schools' emerged in many European cinemas, extending beyond the usual film cultures with a tradition of artistic production (principally France, Germany and Italy) and embracing other film-producing nations which had not hitherto been associated with the art film. Unlike earlier movements, such as German Expressionism or Italian Neo-Realism, the new waves indicated that an artistic cinema could also be a popular cinema. European films challenged American movies at the box-office and their stylistic innovations influenced the new generation of Hollywood *auteurs* who came to the fore in the late 1960s. But to what extent did the new cinemas, as some of their more ardent proponents would claim, change the face of cinema in any significant or even radical ways?

The new waves had been born, in part, from the industry's response to the decline in cinema-going. That they did nothing to halt the decline is evident from statistical evidence. Audiences continued to decline throughout the 1960s and 1970s. In Britain annual attendance fell from 500 million in 1960 to 326 million in 1965, 193 million in 1970 and 103 million by 1976. In Italy the cinema audience halved during the 1970s, from 524 million at the start of the decade to 270 million by its end, while in Spain two thirds of the audience disappeared between 1971 (331 million) and 1985 (101 million).[45] In France and West Germany, where there had been a precipitous decline in the early 1960s, the rate of attrition eased somewhat but the overall trend was still downwards. In most Western European countries the nadir was reached in the late 1970s and early 1980s, since when there has been a slight upward trend in cinema-going, generally attributed to the rise of the multiplex. Even so, however, attendances are only a fraction of what they had been in the 1950s. Cinema is no longer the mass medium that it had been in the 'golden age' between the 1920s and the 1950s. One of the consequences of the decline in cinema-going has been a decline in film production since the late 1970s when, following an artificial boom in the first half of the decade due to an explosion in the number of pornographic films, the effects of the oil crisis of 1973–4 were belatedly felt. Severe inflationary pressure in the 1970s made film production more expensive. The economics of the industry were now such that even a modestly budgeted film stood little chance of recouping its costs in the domestic market. Thus it was that the 1970s saw the virtual disappearance of the genre films made for domestic consumption that had been the staple products of most national cinemas since the advent of sound.

Film production, always an inherently risky undertaking, has become even more risky now that the mass market for films has disappeared. European filmmakers since the 1970s have increasingly had to rely on state support (not always financial), funding from television and international co-productions in order to get films made. Those countries which saw the election of right-of-centre governments (Margaret Thatcher in Britain, Helmuth Kohl in the GFR) found politicians less inclined to assist the film industry, believing that it should stand on its own feet in the marketplace. The Thatcher government, for example, abolished the quota system and the Eady Levy. A more enlightened policy was followed in France, where politicians attached a cultural as well as an economic significance to the cinema. Jack Lang, Minister of Culture during the presidency of François Mitterand in the 1980s, encouraged private investment through a system of tax exemptions. The French film industry maintained its position as the leading producer in Western Europe and one where American penetration of its domestic market, whilst high at 50 per cent, was significantly lower than countries such as Italy (70 per cent), the Netherlands (80 per cent) and Britain (90 per cent).[46]

A sign of the changing times was that the major new source for film finance came from the cinema's old enemy – television. As most European countries operated state-owned television broadcasting until the 1980s, investment in 'artistic' films was seen as a means of fulfilling their cultural remit as national broadcasters, as well as providing 'product' to fill the schedules. It was the GFR which led the way, where the two public television stations WDR (Westdeutsche Rundfunk) and ZDF (Zweites Deutsches Fernsehen) invested in the New German Cinema during the 1970s. Some German filmmakers adapted to these conditions by making episodic films that could also be screened as television series, notably Fassbinder's *Berlin Alexanderplatz* (1980) and Edgar Reitz's *Heimat* (1983). The German example was followed elsewhere. The deregulation of broadcasting in France and Italy during the 1980s created private firms which began investing in film production and by the end of the decade a third of all films were being financed entirely by television. Britain's Channel 4, which began broadcasting in 1982, backed a number of low-budget films that achieved critical success, including Peter Greenaway's *The Draughtsman's Contract* (1982) and Hanif Kureishi's *My Beautiful Laundrette* (1984).[47] The French cable television company Canal + has been the leading producer of French films since the late 1980s and has even invested in non-French projects, including Hollywood films such as *Terminator 2* and *JFK*.

Another strategy that European filmmakers have increasingly adopted has been that of international co-production where finance is shared between investors in several countries. For 'big' films, especially, this strategy has now become more or less an economic necessity, though even smaller productions have often had to seek funding through this means. It would probably be fair to say, however, that the strategy has met with, at best, limited success. Only Bertolucci's *The Last Emperor* (1987), a visually sumptuous biopic of Pu Yi, the last Emperor of China, could be considered a major international success (nine Oscars, including Best Film). Since the late 1980s the European Community/European Union has supported co-productions through its MEDIA initiatives and by offering an *avance sur recettes* through its Eurimages commission. The investment in 'European' films is both a political and a cultural issue: the dream that the single European market might in turn lead to a pan-European film industry that would rival Hollywood in the global marketplace. In a sense it can be seen as a late twentieth century revival of the 'Film Europe' movement, this time with a greater level of co-ordination and state support. However, many co-productions have been accused of being bland 'Europuddings' that lack any defining national characteristics and are indistinguishable from one another.

Perhaps the most significant trend in European filmmaking during recent decades has been the emergence of a style of 'Eurofilm' that represents a return to the sort of 'quality' cinema once so despised by the young turks of the *Nouvelle*

Vague. Many of the successful European films of recent decades have been a sort of middle-brow, prestige cinema that falls somewhere between mainsteam genres and art cinema. Examples of this cinema would include the likes of British 'heritage' films of the 1980s and 1990s (*A Room with a View*, *Howards End*, *The Remains of the Day*, *Elizabeth*), the revival of interest in the work of Marcel Pagnol in French cinema (*Jean de Florette*, *Manon des Sources*, *Le Château de ma mère*, *La Gloire de mon père*) and the nostalgic Italian comedy-dramas that have been so successful on the international 'art house' circuit (*Nuovo Cinema Paradiso*, *Il Postino*). On the one hand, these films exhibit both the literacy and the pictorialism that has often been seen as one of the characteristics of European cinema in contrast to the kinetic and visceral pleasures of the effects-driven Hollywood blockbuster. On the other hand, however, they are more accessible than the art cinema tradition with its ambiguous narratives and lack of closure; they tell their stories in relatively straightforward and conventional terms without resort to alienating modernist devices.

This is not to say that contemporary European cinemas lack their *auteurs* and stylists. Perhaps the most lasting legacy of the new waves has been the privileging of the director as the artistic force in filmmaking. As in New Hollywood, contemporary European directors are 'names' who cultivate their own reputations as stylists. Nowhere has this been more evident than in France, where critics coined the term '*le cinéma du look*' to describe the films of a new group of young directors who came to prominence in the 1980s and 1990s. The films of Jean-Jacques Beineix (*Diva*, *Betty Blue*, *Roselyne et les lions*), Luc Besson (*Subway*, *Nikita*, *Léon*) and Léos Carax (*Mauvais Sang*, *Les Amants du Pont-Neuf*) are characterized by their glossy visual styles and their *mise-en-scène* of consumerist fantasy (chic fashion accessories, high-tech gadgetry) that resemble television commercials and pop videos. Critics allege that the films are shallow, that everything is about surface appearances – in this sense they have rightly been described as 'postmodern'.[48] Yet their combination of generic playfulness and stylistic excess make these filmmakers legitimate claimants to the mantle of heirs of the *Nouvelle Vague*.

What of the new wave filmmakers themselves in the post-new wave cinema? Truffaut died in 1984; his last films, such as *Le Dernier Métro* (*The Last Metro*, 1980), a star vehicle for Gérard Depardieu and Catherine Deneuve, indicate that he had become fully absorbed into the commercial mainstream. Godard, for his part, turned his back on mainstream cinema following the commercial failure of his *Tout va bien* (1972) and retreated into the alternative world of experimental filmmaking. Chabrol proved to be the most durable of the *Nouvelle Vague* directors, making over forty films, the most successful of which, such as *Le Boucher* (1970) and *L'Enfer* (1993), are taut psychological thrillers in the Hitchcockian tradition. Rohmer, who had won critical acclaim in the early 1970s with his closely observed character studies of emotion and desire such as *Ma nuit chez Maud* (*My Night with Maud*) and *Le Genou de Claire* (*Claire's Knee*), continued into the 1990s with beautifully crafted morality tales such as *Conte de Printemps* (*A Tale of Springtime*) and *Un Conte d'hiver* (*A Winter's Tale*). Rivette remained the most committed of the *Nouvelle Vague* directors to an artistic cinema of personal expression, creating in *La Belle Noiseuse* (1991) a parable of the creative process through the story of the relationship between a troubled painter (Michel Piccoli) and his temperamental muse (Emmanuelle Béart). Antonioni (*Identification of a Woman*) and Fellini (*Fred and Ginger*) continued directing films into the 1980s. The most successful of the filmmakers of the New German Cinema has been Wenders, whose career has alternated between Europe and Hollywood, achieving his greatest success with the wistful fantasy *Wings of Desire* (1987).

For all the uncertainty and instability of production, however, European cinemas have still continued to provide space for innovative and individualistic filmmakers who defy the accepted conventions of film. This is largely a consequence of the compartmentalization of the cinema-going audience, institutionalized at the level of exhibition by the expansion of multiplex cinemas catering mainly for Hollywood movies on the one hand and the continued existence of an 'art house' audience interested in more adventurous films on the other. The tradition of narratively ambiguous art cinema with complex structures and humanistic values was maintained in the films of the

Polish filmmaker Krzysztof Kieslowski, particularly the haunting *La Double Vie de Véronique* (*The Double Life of Véronique*,
1991) and the highly acclaimed 'Three Colours' trilogy (*Trois
Couleurs: Bleu, Trois Couleurs: Blanc* and *Trois Couleurs: Rouge*)
which garnered most of the major festival prizes in the early
1990s.[49] Arguably the most idiosyncratic of modern *auteurs* has
been Spain's Pedro Almódovar, who first came to international
prominence with the sexually explicit melodrama *Matador*
(1986) and has since specialized in bizarre, farcical comedy-
dramas such as *Mujeres al Borde de un Ataque de Nervios* (*Women
on the Verge of a Nervous Breakdown*, 1988) and *Atame!* (*Tie Me
Up! Tie Me Down!*, 1990).

Peter Wollen has suggested, somewhat controversially, that
the 'last new wave' of European cinema was to be found in
perhaps the most unlikely of national cinemas: Britain. Wollen
is dismissive of the claims of the British New Wave of 1959–63
to be the equivalent of the *Nouvelle Vague*; instead he identifies
British directors of the 1980s, specifically Derek Jarman and
Peter Greenaway, as the rightful heirs of Godard and Resnais.
Both Jarman and Greenaway were art school graduates of the
1960s who became filmmakers in the late 1970s. Their films
combined a strong sense of visual style with a distinctively
political tone that was in opposition to the socially divisive
Thatcherite ideology of the 1980s. Greenaway (*The
Draughtsman's Contract, A Zed and Two Noughts, The Belly of an
Architect, Drowning by Numbers, The Cook, The Thief, His Wife
and Her Lover, Prospero's Books*) is an art cinema director highly
influenced by structuralism and formalism whose films recall
Alain Resnais, especially through their rigid formal organization in camera movement and *mise-en-scène*. His most overt
political allegory is *The Cook, The Thief, His Wife and Her Lover*,
recognized by all commentators as a stinging attack on
Thatcherite greed and consumption. Jarman, who died of AIDS
in 1994, was an avant-garde filmmaker whose films (*Jubilee, The
Tempest, The Last of England, War Requiem, Caravaggio,
Wittgenstein*) are complex meditations on national identity
bringing together a range of familiar and unfamiliar motifs. His
experiments with narrative structure and technology (often
using video and non-standard film gauges such as Super 8) are

comparable to Godard, while his use of intellectual montage recalls the 'poet' of the British documentary movement, Humphrey Jennings. It was through the work of these filmmakers, Wollen claims, that 'Britain finally produced the "Last New Wave", a series of uncompromising films made by original, oppositional, visually oriented modernist auteurs'.[50] Yet these films remained on the margins of film culture – Jarman's in particular had very limited distribution – and were often regarded as incomprehensible even to those who admired their bold imagery and formal experimentation. British (and European) audiences preferred the less challenging, more accessible 'heritage' films of Merchant-Ivory and their counterparts to the radical, visionary works of Greenaway and Jarman.

One of the criticisms levelled against much contemporary European cinema, indeed, is that is lacks the political edge that directors in the 1960s were supposed to have brought to their work. It is an unfair charge. For one thing, as we have seen, most of the new cinemas were not avowedly political. Godard's political 'awakening', following the popular protests of 1968, signalled the end of his career as a commercial filmmaker. And, for another thing, many contemporary filmmakers are motivated by political concerns. The films of Britain's Ken Loach (*Fatherland, Hidden Agenda, Riff-Raff, Raining Stones, Land and Freedom, Carla's Song*), for example, demonstrate that there is a niche for avowedly left-wing films that do not couch themselves in an impenetrable modernist aesthetic. That Loach has been dependent upon European funding for most of his films is both an indictment of the timidity of the British film industry and an example of the benefits to be reaped from co-production arrangements. It also demonstrates the weaknesses of national cinemas – both as historical entities and as theoretical constructs – in *fin de siècle* Europe. At the turn of the century, indeed, it would seem that the way forward for European cinema is through pan-European co-operation rather than relying on narrow concepts of the national. This might represent the new European ideal, but it possibly also signals the end of the sort of distinctive national schools exemplified by the new wave cinemas of the 1960s.

TEN

Popular Genres, Popular Pleasures

In orthodox film histories there has long been a tendency to differentiate between Hollywood (which is equated with 'entertainment') and Europe (equated with 'art'). The two preceding chapters have explored various movements and cycles of European cinema that belong to this tradition of serious, socially committed, aesthetically challenging filmmaking that is typically associated with the Old World. Yet, just as there is more to Hollywood than Fred Astaire, so too there is much more to European cinemas than avant-garde movements and new waves. The bulk of production in European countries consists of less acclaimed, indeed quite often critically despised, traditions of popular cinema. Yet it is a popular cinema that has largely been written out of film history. As Richard Dyer and Ginette Vincendeau observe: 'The popular cinema of any given European country is not always acknowledged even in the general national histories of film in that country. When it is, it is generally marginalized in favour of the often little-seen but critically-acclaimed art film traditions.'[1]

Until the decline in film production in the late 1970s, most European film industries were organized around the regular production of genre films. Only recently, however, have these indigenous genres begun to receive the same scholarly attention as American genres. There are two general reasons for this neglect: industrial and cultural. The industrial reason is that in Europe most genre films were made primarily for the domestic market. With rare exceptions (such as the British Hammer horror films and Italian 'spaghetti westerns'), European genre films have not been widely exported. One reason why these genres have been written out of film history is simply that they remain unseen outside their countries of origin. The cultural reason is that, for many years, European genres were regarded – quite unfairly – as lacklustre imitations of Hollywood. This attitude is best summed up by Jacques Rivette's dismissal of British cinema in the pages of *Cahiers du Cinéma*: 'British cinema is a genre cinema, but one where the genres have no genuine roots . . . There are just false, in the sense of imitative, genres.'[2] Only very recently has there been evidence of what the editors of the first issue of the *Journal of Popular British Cinema* saw as a 'welcome trend to treat British film genres in relation to their cultural and historical conditions, as well as dealing with them as particular stylistic and thematic configurations'.[3]

As with my discussion of American film genres and their social contexts, limitations of space preclude a comprehensive overview of genre production in all European national cinemas. I have focused, therefore, on five areas (some of them, as will become evident, entailing a degree of slippage between several genres) that are common to most of the popular cinemas of Western Europe. The war film has been a major genre, particularly in the decades after 1945 when the experience of war was a recent memory for all Europeans and national cinemas adopted various strategies for either commemorating the conflict or coming to terms with uncomfortable aspects of the past. The comedy has been a staple of all national cinemas and has proved remarkably durable over a long period of time; it is also one of the few genres that continues to thrive. The spy thriller is associated predominantly with Britain and France, revolving as it does around ideologies of nation and empire, and covering a wide range of stylistic possibilities from the colourful visual spectacle of James Bond to the existentialism of Cold War thrillers such as *The Third Man* and *The Spy Who Came in from the Cold*. Italian peplums and spaghetti westerns provide a culturally significant (if artistically despised) example of how European filmmakers achieved international success with films that both imitated and parodied the conventions of American cinema. Finally, the amorphous category that I have labelled 'horror, exploitation and sex' includes films that deal, in different ways, with violence and sexuality, as well as illustrating how the relaxation of censorship brought about significant changes in the content of popular cinema.

In most European cinemas the 'war film' as a genre is virtually synonymous with films about the Second World War. Filmic representations of the First World War, which peaked around 1928–32 and again in the 1960s at the time of the fiftieth anniversary, have been significantly fewer in number. They also tend to represent the war in a similar fashion regardless of their national origin. The overriding impression of films such as the French *Verdun*, the British *Journey's End* and the German *Kameradschaft*, all produced a decade or so following the Armistice, is of the futility of war, focusing on life and death in the trenches. None of these films, despite their sincere anti-war messages, quite made the impact of Universal Pictures' *All Quiet on the Western Front* (1930), based on the novel by German author Erich Maria Remarque (*Im Westen nichts Neues*) and generally regarded as the definitive film about the First World War. The Second World War has given rise to more myth-making and narrative differences, partly because national experiences of the war were so different (a 'good war' for Britain, a more uncomfortable war for France and Germany) and partly because the war against National Socialism could be presented as a morally justifiable crusade that allowed greater scope for the sort of tales of heroism and daring deeds that make entertaining films.

It was in Britain that films about the Second World War first became a staple genre. War films had been produced for propaganda purposes during the war (*In Which We Serve*, *The First of the Few*, *The Way Ahead*) but had declined in popularity during the mid- and late 1940s when British audiences preferred more escapist fare such as the Gainsborough costume melodramas. The genre was revived in 1950 with the success of two factually based war films – a biopic of a Special Operations Executive heroine (*Odette*) and a prisoner-of-war escape story (*The Wooden Horse*) – and for the rest of the decade war films were regularly among the top box-office attractions. *The Cruel Sea* (1953), *The Dam Busters* (1955), *Reach for the Sky* (1956) and *Sink the Bismarck!* (1960) were all the biggest attractions of their year. The war films of the 1950s were different from the propaganda films of the war in several crucial respects. Whereas wartime films had downplayed social differences in promoting the ideology of 'the people's war', the films of the 1950s tended mostly to refocus narrative interest on the officer class, especially in the cycle of prisoner-of-war films which portrayed escaping as a gentlemanly sport (others in this vein included *The Colditz Story*, *Albert RN* and *Danger Within*). And, whereas wartime propaganda films had made deliberate efforts to include the presence of Americans and even Russians in the war, the films of the 1950s focused almost exclusively on the British war effort at the expense of other nations. There is an emphasis on events and theatres in which the British had been involved (*Dunkirk*, *The Battle of the River Plate*) and even when the French Resistance is involved (as in *Carve Her Name with Pride*) it is a peripheral presence in a narrative about a British heroine.[4]

As so often with films that are successful at the box-office, the popular success of war films was not matched by their critical reception. The genre was regarded by most critics as dull and insipid. It was backward-looking and obsessed with past glories rather than present realities. 'It is both tedious and disquieting, our addiction to war films', wrote William Whitebait, film critic of the *New Statesman*, upon the occasion of the royal premiere of *Dunkirk* in 1958. 'A dozen years after World War II we find ourselves in the really quite desperate situation of being, not sick of war, but hideously in love with it.' Whitebait went on to suggest that the popularity of war films arose from uncertainties over the present as Britain's decline as a great power became apparent:

> So while we 'adventure' at Suez, in the cinemas we are still
> thrashing Rommel – and discovering that he was a gentle-
> man! – sweeping the Atlantic of submarines, sending the Few
> to scatter Goering's many. The more we lose face in the
> world's counsels, the grander, in our excessively modest way,
> we swell in this illusionary mirror held up by the screen. It is
> less a spur to morale than a salve to wounded pride; and as art
> or entertainment dreadfully dull.[5]

For British audiences in the 1950s the war film provided a

degree of certainty and comfort (knowledge of what the outcome will be). Reliving the Second World War, and privileging
Britain's role in winning it, was a means of reasserting national
pride in the face of decline. The war film, Whitebait acknowledged, 'creates an imaginary present in which we can go on
enjoying our finest hours.' It is an assessment that has been
endorsed by film historians. Roy Armes, while acknowledging
that most war films represent 'positive statements of a belief in
man's abilities and innate decency', concludes that 'with the
passing of the years they seem increasingly archaic memories of
a self-deluding era's retreat into a cosy never-never land'.[6]

The British style of war film – characterized by its sober
narratives, restrained heroics, undemonstrative emotions and
austere black-and-white photography – has made it somewhat
unfashionable in film studies circles that privilege films of visual
spectacle and melodramatic excess. Andy Medhurst points out
that the war film has fallen into 'the realms of the formally conservative and the ideologically irredeemable', but argues instead
that films such as *The Cruel Sea* and *The Dam Busters* should
rightly be seen 'as films about repression, rather than hopelessly
repressed films'.[7] For their critics, British war films are populated with male protagonists who have difficulty in expressing
their emotions, exemplified by a scene in *The Dam Busters*
where Wing Commander Gibson (Richard Todd) is seen chok-
ing back his grief at the death of his dog, Nigger. Yet this charge
is more than a little unfair. British war films are certainly not
devoid of melodrama: films such as *The Cruel Sea* and *Ice Cold in
Alex* examine how men at war make mistakes and have to cope
with emotional stress. In this sense the 'stiff-upper-lipped'
behaviour of the protagonists is a necessary narrative device of
the genre. As Christine Geraghty points out of *The Dam Busters*:
'Gibson's suppression of feelings is presented as appropriate
rather than problematic, and the use of the dog as his most
explicit emotional attachment is in keeping with the way in
which class and masculinity are brought together in this isolated
but self-sufficient figure.'[8]

British war films of the 1950s are predominantly examina-
tions of masculinity and national identity. That they propagate
myths about the war is undeniable; yet, as John Ramsden has

shown, British producers and directors were at great pains to make the films as authentic as possible.⁹ It is significant in this regard that British war films were better received by British audiences than American war movies, including those made in Britain by American producers, such as *The Red Beret* and *Cockleshell Heroes*.¹⁰ During the 1960s, however, the popularity of war films declined. Those which were most successful at the box-office were now in the style of *Boys' Own* adventure stories (*The Guns of Navarone, Where Eagles Dare*). The success of Darryl F. Zanuck's production of *The Longest Day* (1962) ushered in a cycle of international films reconstructing major campaigns of the war (*Battle of the Bulge, Battle of Britain, A Bridge Too Far*) that depended on American studios for financial support. The day of the modest, documentary-style British war film was over.

The legacy of National Socialism and the question of German guilt made the German experience of war very different from the British. Obviously post-war German cinema was unlikely to propagate a heroic myth of the war in the same manner as the British celebrated their 'finest hour', though stories of individual heroism, such as that of Luftwaffe ace Hans-Joachim Marseille in *Der Stern von Afrika* (*The Star of Africa*, 1957) were made in the Federal Republic. A more usual narrative strategy for West German war films of the 1950s, however, was to dramatize stories of German resistance to Nazism in films such as *Canaris, Des Teufels General* (*The Devil's General*) and *Der Arzt von Stalingrad* (*The Doctor from Stalingrad*). Pierre Sorlin suggests the political motive behind these films at a time when the GFR was becoming a member of NATO and the Common Market:

Defeated Germany was being progressively reintegrated into the concert of western nations in the 1950s . . . During this period the Germans were anxious to prove they had not been entirely infected by Nazism, and in this respect films celebrating the persistence of a strong individual opposition to Hitler were apt to please dominant opinion as well as those foreigners who did not conceive of a European future without Germany. The films made in 1954–57 were not blatant propaganda but were merely adapted to the circumstances. Once Germany was rehabilitated the producers abandoned the field.[11]

In focusing on the German resistance to Hitler (such opposition did exist, historians have suggested, though through the efforts of individuals and small groups rather than as a general movement), West German cinema was simply creating its own myths of the war in a manner not entirely dissimilar to British films of the same period. Indeed, there are some similarities between British and German films. British films also made the distinction between Nazis (characterized as cruel, ruthless and fanatical) and 'good Germans' (characterized as basically decent, honourable soldiers who disliked the excesses of Hitler).

The political desirability of distinguishing between Nazis and other Germans was no longer such an issue by the time of *Das Boot* (*The Boat*, 1981). Directed by Wolfgang Petersen, this was a major box-office success both in Germany and abroad; an expanded version of the film was shown as a television mini-series. Like *All Quiet on the Western Front*, to which it bears a number of similarities, *Das Boot* presents the experience of war through the eyes of a young newcomer (a war correspondent) who joins a German U-boat crew and experiences the dangers of submarine life at first hand. The film is notable for its claustrophobic atmosphere and for its tragic ending, in which most of the crew are killed. For all the film's supposedly anti-war theme, however, the British *Monthly Film Bulletin* felt that commercial considerations had mediated against a serious examination of Germany's past:

> [The] Germans have produced, out of their side of the last conflict, a film acceptable to their ex-foes by playing into the values and stereotypes of something like the 1950s British model ... What all this suggests is that Wolfgang Petersen and his collaborators are so busy looking over their own shoulders – 'dealing' with the problem of German guilt by luxuriating in a sense of doom about the enterprise of U-96 and its crew – while looking towards those ex-Allied markets, that they can't begin to investigate the subject in a more honest way.[12]

Yet this reaction to the film is somewhat unfair. *Das Boot* explores the psychological effects of war rather than making a case for or against its conduct. To criticise the film for avoiding 'the problem of German guilt' misses the point. The fact that the protagonists of the film are German is almost irrelevant: they could equally have been British or American and much the same incidents and experiences could have been portrayed. The narrative incidents (the depth-charge attack, the crash-dive, the Christmas celebration) and the character types (the experienced captain, the naive newcomer, the crew member who panics and deserts his post) are standard conventions of the war film in most national cinemas.

The issue of guilt arising from the Second World War has been no less problematic in French cinema. Just as the German resistance films of the 1950s can be seen as a response to broader political issues of the time, so filmmakers in France have used the Occupation period for political ends. The peak years of the resistance narrative in French cinema were 1958–62, when some thirty films about the Occupation were produced. That this cycle coincided with the early years of the Fifth Republic under the presidency of the wartime leader of the Free French, Charles de Gaulle, is surely no accident. Susan Hayward argues that 'the resurrection of the Resistance "as a good thing" was once again not without its political expediency' and suggests that 'producers had seen a winner in cashing in on de Gaulle's iconographic prestige and milked it for what it was worth'.[13] French cinema promoted a national myth of the Resistance – exaggerating the extent of active participation and marginalizing the internal dissent within the movement – in much the same way as British cinema promoted the myths of Dunkirk and 'the Few'.

It was not until the 1970s that French filmmakers dared to question these myths. The election of Giscard d'Estaing to the presidency in 1974 was seen by leftist intellectuals as marking the end of Gaullism and allowing a more detached look at the past. Louis Malle's *Lacombe, Lucien* (1973) anticipated this 'new history' through its controversial examination of collaboration. The film follows a naive youth who attempts to join the Maquis in 1944 but is turned away because he is seeking adventure rather than politically committed; frustrated, he is recruited by the Gestapo instead and works as an informer. *Lacombe, Lucien* is morally ambiguous: it does not condemn its protagonist for becoming a collaborator and it shows him falling for a Jewish girl whilst at the same time betraying his schoolmaster, a Maquis leader, to the Germans. The film provoked mixed reactions: it was a box-office success, but caused such a storm of controversy that Malle was forced to leave France and work in America for the next decade. Malle believed that the controversy surrounding the film was 'a series of misunderstandings' and that 'in its description of characters and events the film exposes all the ambiguities and contradictions in behaviour that belonged to that period'.[14] Perhaps the controversy was due less to the suggestion that some French people worked voluntarily for the Gestapo (this is a matter of historical record) and more to its presentation of Fascism as an attractive alternative (Lucien joins the Gestapo not through ideological commitment but is lured by the promise of money, a gun and women).

Later Resistance films have not courted so much controversy. Malle returned to French cinema and to the subject of the Occupation with *Au revoir les enfants* (1987), a major commercial and critical success (winning seven Césars, the French equivalent of the Oscars) which suggested that his reputation had been rehabilitated. *Au revoir les enfants* explores the friendship between two French boys, one of them Jewish, and was based to some extent on Malle's own memories of the war. Guy Austin considers that, in contrast to *Lacombe, Lucien*, 'this is a positive portrayal of the French during the Occupation, especially the priests who – in contrast with the complicity of the Catholic Church in the Vichy regime – shelter Jewish boys in their school'.[15] And *Lucie Aubrac* (1997) is based on the true story of the wife of a resistance fighter who organizes his rescue from a Gestapo prison and escapes with him to Britain. Thus the national experience is represented through a personal narrative, focusing on a romantic couple played by leading French stars Carole Bouquet and Daniel Auteuil. The effect of the film, as one critic put it, is 'to generate the oceanic feeling of the French as one big anti-Nazi family'.[16]

COMEDIANS AND COMEDIES

Comedy is among the oldest of film genres: the Lumieres' *L'Arroseur arrosé* (*Watering the Gardener*, 1895) is the first known example of a 'joke' or 'gag' film, a type that proliferated during the early days of the medium. The relationship between cinema and music hall led to the filming of entertainers and novelty acts that were included in early cinema programmes, and by the time of the First World War comic performers were prominent attractions in all the major film-producing nations. Many early film comedians were better known by their character names: thus France had Romeo and Calino, Italy had Coco and Frico, Britain had Pimple and Winky and Russia had Mitjukha and Arkasha. The French comedian Max Linder, whose screen persona as a dandified man-about-town caught the mood of the Edwardian era, was the most famous early film comedian and was acknowledged as an influence by Charlie Chaplin and Mack Sennett. The emphasis on physical, slapstick comedy meant that comedies could easily be exported from one country to another. When the French comic André Deed was lured away from Pathé by the Italia Company of Turin, his hapless character of Cretinetti was easily translated into other nations by the simple expedient of renaming him: thus he became Foolshead in Britain, Müller in Germany, Toribio in Spain and Glupishkin in Russia. There was a short-lived 'golden age' of European silent comedy before the First World War, though many performers were either killed or wounded in the trenches (Linder, for example, was gassed and never fully recovered) and American performers emerged to fill the void.[17]

The advent of talking pictures made comedy a much more specifically national genre. A staple of most national cinemas was the low-budget comedy film made exclusively for the domestic market. These films tended to feature performers who, due to the culturally specific nature of indigenous humour and comic traditions, could not easily be translated into other languages. Raimu and Fernandel in France, Totò in Italy, Heinz Rühmann in Germany, and Will Hay and George Formby in Britain were all among the most popular stars in their own countries during the 1930s but were little known abroad. For all that comedy is not ostensibly a serious genre, the popularity of certain performers has led to them being seen as role models for social behaviour and cultural values. Sabine Hake, for example, argues that the star persona of Heinz Rühmann resolves tensions in German society arising from 'the petit-bourgeois desire for social acceptance . . . As the personification of the little man – oppressed, repressed, but always in a good mood – Rühmann comically re-enacted the crises of masculinity in numerous comedies about the difficulties of everyday life.'[18] The emphasis on good humour in the face of social adversity was also a feature of British music hall comedians such as Gracie Fields and George Formby who moved into films during the 1930s. Jeffrey Richards sees these performers as agents of consensus whose films found solutions to social problems, overcoming adversity with song and a cheery disposition.[19]

For all their popularity with domestic audiences, the comedian-centred comedies of the 1930s were accorded scant regard by critics who typically regarded them as frivolous and unrealistic. It was not until after the Second World War that European cinemas produced comedy that was acclaimed by critics in a way that hitherto had been reserved for Chaplin. It was also the first occasion since before the First World War in which European comedy films were seen and admired outside their country of origin. Although very different in style, the Ealing comedies from Britain and the films of Jacques Tati from France were both successful with overseas audiences. 'Continental spectators were delighted by the freshness of the Ealing comedies', Sorlin remarks; 'the film buffs enjoyed a funny, critical but unpatronising self-portrait of British life, while the "popular" public liked the absence of sophistication and the humorous dialogue.'[20] Tati, a meticulous and painstaking actor/filmmaker who made only six completed feature films over a quarter of a century, won even greater international recognition and came to be regarded as an *auteur* of comic genius on a par with Chaplin.

Ealing comedy is very much part of the respectable face of British cinema; its critical reception at the time was probably in part a reaction against the despised Gainsborough melodramas that had been top attractions at the British box-office in the mid-1940s. Dilys Powell, writing in 1961, six years after the last of the recognized canonical Ealing comedies, mused: 'I fancy that when the next batch of histories comes to be written we find that Ealing comedy is suddenly being regarded as the intellectual's treat'.[21] 'Ealing comedy' is a descriptive label that refers to a cycle of films made at the studio between the late 1940s and the mid-1950s. The canon is relatively small, usually held to consist of *Whisky Galore!*, *Passport to Pimlico*, *Kind Hearts and Coronets*, *The Lavender Hill Mob*, *The Man in the White Suit*, *The Titfield Thunderbolt*, *The Maggie* and *The Ladykillers*, sometimes extended to include *Hue and Cry*, *The Magnet*, *The Love Lottery* and *Barnacle Bill*. Most of these films have certain common characteristics which distinguish them as a group, though there are also some important differences between individual films. While Ealing comedy is typically regarded as quaint, nostalgic, sentimental and populated by amiable, tea-drinking eccentrics, the canonical films include two black comedies (*Kind Hearts and Coronets*, *The Ladykillers*) and a satire of corporate capitalism (*The Man in the White Suit*).[22]

Celebrated by many for their qualities of timeless Englishness, the Ealing comedies are nevertheless very much products of their historical contexts. The early films in the cycle (*Whisky Galore!*, *Passport to Pimlico*) illustrate a sense of post-war frustration with continued bureaucratic controls, represented through the Scottish islanders who conceal a shipment of whisky from Customs and Excise and the inhabitants of a London borough who declare their independence when they unearth an ancient charter. Ealing's Head of Production, Michael Balcon, believed that 'the comedies reflected the country's mood, social conditions and aspirations. The country was tired of regulations and regimentation, and there was a mild anarchy in the air.'[23] John Ellis, however, writing from the perspective of the film theorist, argues that 'Ealing's comedy style was new in that it dealt with the utopian desires of the lower middle class rather than its resentments'.[24] In his interpretation the films express aspirations for social mobility, exemplified by the timid bank clerk who pulls off a bullion robbery (*The Lavender Hill Mob*) and the poor relation of an aristocratic family who murders his way to a dukedom (*Kind Hearts and*

Coronets). In contrast to these 'progressive' comedies, later films in the cycle are typically seen as conservative reactions to change, expressed through nostalgic affection for old steam trains (*The Titfield Thunderbolt*) and steamboats (*The Maggie*).

Tati's films are to some extent comparable to the Ealing comedies in so far as they also explore bourgeois aspirations and are characterized by a satirical look at modern life. The key difference, however, is that whereas the Ealing films tend to be focused on communities and do not unduly privilege individuals (comic actors tend to be cast in supporting rather than starring roles), Tati's own comic performances are central to his films. Tati, a former music hall artiste, came to prominence with *Jour de Fête* (*Day of the Fair*, 1949), which won the Grand Prix at Cannes and is widely regarded as 'a milestone in French screen comedy'.[25] Tati's genius was that he was able to combine both character comedy and visual comedy, combining the techniques seamlessly in the tale of a village postman who adopts modern American delivery methods and unwittingly disrupts everyone's routine. Tati's films recall the pantomime tradition of Keaton and Chaplin (there is very little dialogue; speech tends to be mumbled and incoherent) and make innovative use of both naturalistic and non-naturalistic sound for comic effect.

Tati's most famous character, the amiable, maladroit Monsieur Hulot, first appeared in the delightful *Les Vacances de Monsieur Hulot* (*Mr Hulot's Holiday*, 1953) which, among other things, is notable for its authentic background (the seaside resort of St Marc-sur-Mer in Brittany) and episodic narrative. Hulot unwittingly disrupts the peace and quiet of the resort with his breakdown-prone car, his fishing rod and his unconventional way of playing tennis; he is the well-intentioned misfit whose attempts to ingratiate himself into polite society result in comic disaster. Tati revived Hulot in later films that, rather like Chaplin's *Modern Times*, explore the plight of the individual in the increasingly regimented, automated modern world. In *Mon Oncle* (*My Uncle*, 1958) Hulot makes a trip to Paris and finds himself completely at sea in an unfriendly urban environment; *Playtime* (1968) is another satire of urban routine and leisure habits; and *Traffic* (1970) satirizes the culture of the motor car in what effectively amounts to a comic equivalent of the nightmarish traffic jam of Godard's *Weekend*. In the course of his films, argues Susan Hayward, Tati 'creates an observant satire on contemporary France as it moves into becoming a society of consumption'.[26]

The Ealing comedies and the Tati/Hulot films are rare examples of comedy that was successful internationally whilst still being seen to represent peculiar national characteristics. Most comedy, however, remains rooted in specific cultural contexts. The British *Carry On* films – a series of some 29 low-budget films released between 1958 and 1978, the best of which were either in the tradition of institutional comedy (army, hospitals, police) or genre spoofs (westerns, horror films, costume films, British Empire films) – represent the vulgar, low-brow vein of British film comedy in contrast to the genteel respectability of Ealing. The appeal of the *Carry On* films, suggests Andy Medhurst, is that 'they really aren't recuperable for proper culture . . . they display a commitment to bodily functions and base desires that will always render them irreducibly vulgar, inescapably Not Art'.[27] The 'Monty Python' films of 1975–83 (*Monty Python and the Holy Grail, Monty Python's Life of Brian, Monty Python's Meaning of Life*) exemplified the zany, absurdist tradition of British comedy; they also tested the boundaries of good taste (the hilarious *Life of Brian* courted controversy as a spoof of the life of Jesus Christ) and remain very much an acquired taste.

European film comedy remains something of a paradox: most comedies remain indigenous films that do not translate into other cultures, but some of the biggest international successes for European cinemas have been comedies. What most of these films have in common is that, like the Ealing and Tati films, they can be understood as responses to social and cultural concerns. Italian cinema has been especially rich in this regard. Franco Brusati's *Pane e cioccolata* (*Bread and Chocolate*, 1973), for example, uses the tale of an Italian immigrant (Nino Manfredi) seeking work in Switzerland to explore questions of social and racial prejudice. Roberto Benigni's *La vita è bella* (*Life is Beautiful*, 1998) sharply divided opinion: praised by some critics as an inspired comedy, attacked by others for its alleged trivialization of the Holocaust. Benigni is a clown in the best tradition of European comedy whose humour arises from a combination of physical dexterity and pathos. He plays Guido, an Italian-Jewish bookseller, who, incarcerated in a concentration camp with his son, attempts to shield the youngster from the horrors around them by pretending that it is all a game. It was this element of the film that outraged some critics, but, as Arthur Marwick explains, they missed the point: 'That this defies all reality should have alerted critics to the obvious fact that we are watching a fable.'[28]

In contemporary European cinema, moreover, comedy is 'the genre most capable of resisting the onslaught of American blockbusters'.[29] The biggest British successes of the 1990s, for instance, were all comedies: *Four Weddings and a Funeral*, *The Full Monty*, *Shakespeare in Love* and *Notting Hill*. A caveat needs to be lodged in so far as all these films were backed by American money and three of them featured Hollywood leading ladies with an eye on the US box-office. Nevertheless, the writers are British (Richard Curtis, Simon Beaufoy, Tom Stoppard) and the subjects and themes are British. *Four Weddings* and *Notting Hill* demonstrate the continuing British obsession with class and the comedy of social embarassment; *The Full Monty* is tinged with social realism, focusing on the efforts of unemployed steelworkers to earn a living by becoming male strippers; *Shakespeare in Love* is a postmodernist comedy full of deliberate anachronisms that pleased the *literati*. It is in France, however, that comedy has most effectively served as a bulwark against Hollywood. It was accidental that the release of *Les Visiteurs* (1993) coincided with the GATT (General Agreement on Tariffs and Trade) negotiations which brought to a head French resistance to the import of American culture, but the fact that it took twice as much at the French box-office as *Jurassic Park* was seen by many commentators as a triumph of indigenous French culture over Americanization. *Les Visiteurs* is an example of the comedy of displacement in which outsiders (in this case a twelfth-century knight and his manservant) find themselves in an unfamiliar environment (they are transported into the modern world). One commentator claims that '*Les Visiteurs* was transformed into a veritable cult film which clearly struck a chord with the national audience across social divisions'.[30] For conservatives it

exemplified the values of chivalry and honour as the knight
(Jean Reno) defends traditional values against modernization,
while for left/liberal progressives it represented egalitarianiasm
through the servant (Christian Clavier) who is able to free himself from serfdom. In this sense the film demonstrates superbly
the ability of comedy to cross class barriers and to appeal to
audiences of different social, regional – and, in this case,
national – backgrounds.

THE SPY THRILLER

In European national cinemas the spy thriller is associated primarily with Britain and France. This is unsurprising given the
origins of the spy story in popular fiction, for, as Sorlin reminds
us, 'it must not be forgotten that spy novels were an old tradition
ushered in by Le Queux in the 1890s and highly popular on both
sides of the Channel'.[31] If the Anglo-French writer William Le
Queux has as much claim as anyone to be regarded as the 'father'
of the spy story, writing numerous tales of intrigue in the courts
and governments of Europe, the main practitioners of the genre
in the early twentieth century were mostly British: E. Phillips
Oppenheim, Erskine Childers and George Chesney all penned
stories of continental threats to Britain and the British Empire.
'The spy thriller has been, for much of its history, a British
genre, indeed a major cultural export', writes literary critic
Michael Denning.[32] It is for this reason that the spy thriller has
been seen to have specific resonances with British culture and
politics in a way that the western does for America: the narrative
ideologies of the spy story revolve around patriotism, nationhood, imperialism, class and masculinity.

Most academic work on the spy thriller has focused on its literary form. Denning, for example, identifies two distinct lineages within the genre. On the one hand there are 'those that we
might call magical thrillers where there is a clear contest
between Good and Evil with a virtuous hero defeating an alien
and evil villain', while on the other hand there are 'those that we
might call existential thrillers which play on a dialectic of good
and evil overdetermined by moral dilemmas, by moves from

innocence to experience, and by identity crises'.[33] This difference might also be categorized as that between the 'sensational'
and the 'realist' spy thriller. The 'magical' or 'sensational' thriller
is based around narratives of flight and pursuit, requiring physical courage on the part of the hero to overcome the conspiracy of
the villainous foe who represents a threat to the social and political order of the state. It is exemplified by the novels of John
Buchan, 'Sapper' (H. C. McNeile) and Ian Fleming with their
fast-moving plots and larger-than-life villains. The 'existential'
or 'realist' thriller, in contrast, explores the moral ambiguities
and uncertainties of espionage and exposes the seedy side of the
profession. It is represented by the novels of Graham Greene,
Eric Ambler, John le Carré and Len Deighton.

The same lineages are apparent in the history of the spy film.
Alfred Hitchcock's British films of the 1930s are paradigmatic
of the genre, including both sensational adventure thrillers (*The
Man Who Knew Too Much*, *The 39 Steps*, *The Lady Vanishes*) and
more ambiguous realist thrillers (*Secret Agent*, *Sabotage*).[34] It is
easy to understand the prominence of spy narratives in the
1930s during a time of increasing international tensions. While
the spy thriller dramatizes threats to the state from enemy
powers, however, censorship codes meant that the identity of
those powers was never revealed in films of the 1930s, except for
those in a historical setting such as the First World War (*Secret
Agent*, based on W. Somerset Maugham's Ashenden stories,
being a case in point). The same was true of French cinema, as
Hayward observes: 'Spy films were another favourite (including
attempts at rehabilitating the myth of Mata Hari), but all the
while glossed over the reality of Nazi Germany.'[35] Even the film
that most explicitly raises the question of French national security, *Double crime sur la ligne Maginot* (*Double Crime on the
Maginot Line*, 1937), does not identify the enemy, though audiences can have been left in little doubt given the political context of the time. In Hitchcock's *The 39 Steps* a character is shot
dead just as he is about to reveal that the enemy spy ring is
smuggling secrets 'on behalf of the Foreign Office of —',
though the iconography of the film (the villains wear Gestapo-
style leather overcoats) leaves viewers in no doubt who the
unnamed enemy is. Sorlin argues that the spy films of the 1930s

provided a substitute for war films: 'Spy stories were a possible makeshift; the war was in the background, but its depiction was vague enough to allay the censors' fears.' He also points out that spy narratives were a genre exclusively of the western democracies: 'Espionage, which was ignored by the Germans and Italians, fascinated the democracies; it was the theme of nearly half of the English movies [that featured war subjects] and of one third of the French ones.'[36]

During the Second World War the spy story merged with the secret mission narrative in Britain; understandably it was not a prominent genre of Vichy cinema. The post-war thriller tended more towards the existential type than the sensational lineage. Dilys Powell, like other British critics, felt that 'when Hitchcock went to Hollywood we let an irreplaceable gift slip through our fingers', but still thought that British cinema was capable of producing a 'decent thriller – sometimes, as in the work of Carol Reed, rising to the level of creative imagination'.[37] It would be fair to say that Reed's *auteur* status is disputed even in Britain: his reputation rests mainly on three films made in the late 1940s (*Odd Man Out, The Fallen Idol, The Third Man*), none of which was strictly speaking a spy thriller in the sense that their protagonists were not spies or secret agents. *The Third Man* (1949), which is set against the political background of the four-power occupation of Vienna after the war, is a close relation of the spy thriller. It is also universally recognized as one of the classics of British cinema. It stands out from the run-of-the-mill thriller for many reasons: it is international rather than parochially British (Joseph Cotten, Orson Welles, Valli and Trevor Howard were the stars); it is a tale of moral confusion and duplicity without a conventional happy ending (the story and screenplay were by Graham Greene); and above all, it creates a superbly atmospheric picture of post-war Vienna, achieved through Robert Krasker's expressionist black-and-white cinematography and the memorable zither music of Anton Karas. Like American *film noir* of the same period, *The Third Man* creates its own stylized representation of the physical world – 'the creation of a nightmare atmosphere in which the most commonplace things seem unreal and menacing'[38] – that is one of the key ingredients of the film thriller.

The spy films of the 1950s are humdrum affairs, usually set against the background of the Cold War and limited, ideologically, by the anti-communist political agenda of the time.[39] The genre was revitalized, however, in the early 1960s by the extraordinary success of a series of British secret agent adventures that would become the most enduring franchise in the history of cinema. James Bond, the fictional Agent 007 of the British Secret Service, was the protagonist of a series of snobbery-with-violence thrillers by English author Ian Fleming published between 1953 and 1966. The increasing popularity of the novels in the late 1950s and early 1960s, coupled with relaxations in censorship as regards permissible levels of sex and violence, persuaded United Artists to back producers Albert R. Broccoli (American) and Harry Saltzman (Canadian) who had acquired the film rights from Fleming and believed that Bond could make the transition to the screen. Although backed by American money, the production base of the Bond films is in Britain (usually at Pinewood Studios) and the generic lineage to which they belong is British (the imperialist spy thriller). Through the adroit casting of Sean Connery, Broccoli and Saltzman successfully detached the screen Bond from the somewhat snobbish character of the books and remade him as a modern, classless hero in tune with the changing social climate of the 1960s. The first two Bond films (*Dr No*, *From Russia With Love*) were hugely popular in Britain and Europe; the third and fourth films (*Goldfinger*, *Thunderball*) were also major box-office successes in America and turned 'Bondmania' into an international cultural phenomenon.[40]

The massive success of the Bond films requires explanation. Terence Young, director of *Dr No*, believed that it made the impact it did because it arrived towards the tail end of the British New Wave: 'It fitted the mood of the people, anyway in Britain. I think people were getting tired of the realistic school, the kitchen sink and all those abortions.'[41] Yet while this might explain the success of the early Bond films in Britain, it does not explain the on-going popularity of the franchise or the global extent of their appeal. Why have these films about a British secret agent been so successful around the world and for such a long period of time? Richards attributes their success to 'an unbeatable blend of conspicuous consumption, brand-name snobbery, technological gadgetry, colour supplement chic, exotic locations and comic-strip sex and violence'.[42] The Bond films are stylish and visually exciting; Bond himself is the essence of 'cool', the 'gentleman agent with a licence to kill' (in the words of the early trailers) who rarely breaks into a sweat while saving the world from the diabolical schemes of criminal masterminds in between enjoying a hedonistic lifestyle of brand-name consumer products and casual sexual encounters with an array of pulchritudinous female starlets. The globe-trotting nature of Bond's adventures detaches him from the parochial Britishness that had characterized so many previous thrillers and associates him with the defence of western civiliza-tion rather than just the remnants of the British Empire.

Critical reaction to the early Bond films was sharply divided. For one critic *Dr No* was 'vicious hokum skilfully designed to appeal to the filmgoer's basest feelings'; but for another 'the film is full of submerged self-parody, and I think it would be as wrong to take it solemnly as it would be to worry that Sherlock Holmes's beastliness to Doctor Watson encourages intellectual arrogance or the taking of cocaine'.[43] The Bond films were slow to attract scholarly attention, their formulaic plots and stereo-typed, two-dimensional characters regarded as a sort of film-making by numbers. 'If I fail to be entertained by *Goldfinger*, it is because there is nothing there to engage or retain the attention; the result is a nonentity, consequently tedious', Robin Wood wrote. In contrast to Hitchcock's American spy thrillers such as *North by Northwest*, Wood felt that *Goldfinger* was nothing more than 'a collection of bits, carefully calculated with both eyes on the box office, put end to end with no deeper necessity for what happens next than mere plot'.[44]

Whatever their qualities as films, there is no question that the Bond series represents 'a remarkable production achieve-ment' in the context of a British cinema that has rarely been able to turn out internationally successful genre films.[45] The longevity of the series can be explained through the strategies the producers have adopted to reinvigorate the franchise when it has looked in danger of becoming stale (as critics have alleged continuously since the late 1960s). The Bond series is in a

process of constant renewal. This is most evident in the periodic changes of star (George Lazenby succeeded Connery for one film only, since when Roger Moore, Timothy Dalton and Pierce Brosnan have all taken on the role) which ensure that the character of Bond remains a contemporary figure. Furthermore, the films have responded to technological progress (the US Space Shuttle first flew in 1981, but Bond had got there two years earlier in *Moonraker*) and to geopolitical change (embracing the ideology of détente in the 1970s, responding to the renewal of Cold War tensions in the 1980s, and negotiating the break-up of the Soviet empire in the 1990s). Having long since abandoned even a notional resemblance to their original source materials, the Bond films exemplify pre-eminently the tendency of the contemporary blockbuster towards spectacle and special effects above narrative and characterization. They also provide an exception to the law of diminishing returns that affects other franchises: the Bond series is still going strong after forty years and twenty films. The films' popularity shows no sign of diminishing.

A sign of the impact which the Bond films made was the vogue for gimmicky spy thrillers that arose both in Europe and in Hollywood in the mid-1960s. From Hollywood there came James Coburn as Derek Flint (*Our Man Flint, In Like Flint*) and Dean Martin as Matt Helm (*The Silencers, Murderer's Row, The Ambushers, The Wrecking Crew*). British cinema revived Bulldog Drummond as a Bond-style secret agent (*Deadlier Than the Male, Some Girls Do*) and also adapted John Gardner's Boysie Oakes (*The Liquidator*) and James Leasor's Dr Jason Love (*Where the Spies Are*). The array of European Bond imitations is bewildering: France produced the 'Coplan' series, Italy the 'Agent 077' series, while other spy films of indeterminate origin include *From the Orient With Fury*, *Agent OS14: Operation Poker* and *Kiss the Girls and Make Them Die*. One French commentator was moved to remark that 'the cloak and dagger film is to France what the western is to America'.[46] Only one or two of the '*de cape et d'épée*' films, however, attracted much notice: Chabrol's *An Orchid for the Tiger* and Philippe de Broca's *That Man from Rio* are probably the best of the crop.

More successful, in the eyes of critics and audiences, were a handful of films which sought to differentiate themselves from Bond by portraying espionage in a more ambiguous, realistic way that emphasized the moral uncertainties of the spying game. These 'anti-Bond' films were mostly British in origin and, with their tales of defectors and moles in the secret services, they can be seen as a response to the spy scandals that had rocked the British establishment in the early 1960s (the Portland Down affair, the Profumo scandal and the defection of Kim Philby). Harry Saltzman produced a trilogy starring Michael Caine as bespectacled Cockney spy Harry Palmer based on the novels of Len Deighton (*The Ipcress File, Funeral in Berlin, Billion Dollar Brain*); there were also three adaptations of John le Carré (*The Spy Who Came in from the Cold, The Deadly Affair, The Looking Glass War*) from different producers. These films were rooted firmly in the political context of the Cold War (in contrast to the Bond movies, which had replaced Fleming's Russian villains with the apolitical international terrorist organization SPECTRE). Martin Rubin argues that these films are closer to the paranoia and sense of danger that is an essential characteristic of the thriller than the fantastic adventures of 007 and his imitators:

> In contrast to the free-floating, fantasy-oriented world of Bond & Co., the anti-Bond films develop a more thrilleresque sense of a solidly ordinary world transformed by paranoia and danger. There is greater attention given to the routine, less glamorous aspects of the spy's profession – paperwork, leg work, office politics, bureaucratic squabbling. . . . The color-ful vacation spots that dominate the Bond movies are avoided in their anti-Bond counterparts. The twin capitals of these films are London and Berlin: two gray, history-shrouded cities reflecting and blurring into each other.[47]

The visual style of films such as *The Spy Who Came in from the Cold* is dominated by bleak, austere landscapes that are the very antithesis of the tourist playgrounds of Bond, while their nar-ratives are located emphatically in the existential lineage of the genre. They represent a gloomy, downbeat alternative to the glossy, consumerist fantasy of the Bond films and thus demonstrate the versatility of the spy thriller in both aesthetic and ideological terms.

PEPLUMS AND SPAGHETTI WESTERNS

No discussion of European genres would be complete without some mention of the unique style of Italian popular cinema. 'The history of Italian cinema,' remarks Morando Morandini, 'is littered with the corpses of new genres which were born, flour-ished briefly, and were then destroyed by the repetition *ad nau-seum* of formulas which had brought their initial success.'[48] Italian popular cinema is often derided for seeming to consist of nothing more than derivative genre films (cop films, spy films, macabre mysteries, erotic/pornographic films) turned out by the dozen in order to cash in on the latest fad. Two of these genres deserve attention, however, in so far as they were also successful outside Italy. Both the 'peplum' (derived from the Greek *peplos*) and the 'spaghetti western' enjoyed periods of international popularity that require explanation. Dubbed (often hilariously) into English, they were especially successful in America where they were shown in drive-in cinemas catering to predominantly youth audiences. Their representation of sexuality (in the case of the peplum) and violence (in the spaghetti western) differentiated them from the standard Hollywood fare of the time.

The peplum refers to a particularly Italian style of mythical-historical epic that had been a feature of Italian silent cinema and experienced a revival between the end of the 1950s and the mid-1960s. The film that revived the genre was Pietro Francisci's *Le fatiche di Ercole* (*The Labours of Hercules*, 1958) which starred former Mr Universe Steve Reeves as the legendary hero; unremarkable in itself, its success came about when US entrepeneneur Joseph E. Levine acquired the international distribution rights and spent more on promotion than the film had cost to make. While critics had much fun at the film's expense (the most over-used cliché being that acting honours were divided equally between Reeves's torso and co-star Sylva Koscina's bosom), its elements of mythological adventure and erotic spectacle turned it into a major hit. Reeves was launched onto a successful career playing Hercules and other mythical superheroes (*Hercules Unchained*, *The Giant of Marathon*, *Goliath and the Barbarians*, *The Trojan Horse*). Other Hollywood musclemen followed, including ex-Tarzan star Gordon Scott (*Samson and the Seven Miracles of the World*, *Goliath and the Vampires*, *Gladiator of Rome*) and Mark Forest (*Goliath and the Dragon*, *Maciste the Mighty*, *The Lion of Thebes*). A coup of sorts was achieved when Reeves and Scott played Romulus and Remus in Sergio Corbucci's *Duel of the Titans* – the equivalent of contemporary musclemen such as Schwarzenegger and Stallone appearing together in the same film.

There has been little scholarly interest in the peplum. As one commentator observes, 'the peplum is a minor genre which caters for rather uneducated audiences and does not appeal to "sophisticated" filmgoers (with the exception of a few wayward enthusiasts); and film critics tend either to dismiss the genre with mild sarcasm or to lambast it for being ideologically unsound'.[49] Yet the genre is deserving of attention for two particular reasons. First, it represents a rare point of convergence between popular culture and the academy (the classical humanities). Criticisms that peplums are historically inaccurate miss the point; their tales of heroism and mythical quests are popularized versions of the epic poems of Homer and Virgil. And second, in so far as the genre exemplifies the foregrounding of spectacle over narrative, it can be seen both as an alternative to classical Hollywood cinema and as a precursor of the New Hollywood blockbuster with its emphasis on violent action and muscular display. Ridley Scott's *Gladiator* (2000), for example, arguably owes as much to the visual style of the peplum as it does to Hollywood gladiatorial epics such as *Spartacus*. In this regard it is important to note that while their production values may seem lamentable by Hollywood standards, peplums were quite expensive productions for Italian cinema due to their use of colour and widescreen (usually the Dyaliscope process) and so were dependent upon co-productions and international distribution to ensure their profitability.

The stylized violence of the peplum was taken to even greater extremes in the vogue for so-called 'spaghetti westerns' between the mid-1960s and mid-1970s. 'Spaghetti western' was a term of abuse used by US critics to deride Italian attempts at this sacrosanct American genre; the native term was '*western all'italiana*'. Yet, as Christopher Frayling has shown, Europeans have long been fascinated with tales of the American West, exemplified by the western stories of German writer Karl May and French author Blaise Cendrars (who wrote the novel translated into English as *Sutter's Gold* and filmed both in Hollywood and, as *Der Kaiser von Kalifornien*, in Germany during the 1930s).[50] It was the success in Europe of *The Magnificent Seven* (1960) – a film that had been only moderately successful in America – that alerted European producers to the appeal of the western for European audiences; indeed, it is significant that many European westerns were to borrow that film's motifs of professional gunfighters and a Mexican setting. The first Euro-western of the 1960s was made in West Germany: *Der Schatz im Silbersee* (*The Treasure of Silver Lake*, 1962) followed the strategy of the peplum by importing a second-division American star (Lex Barker, another former Tarzan) for the first of a series of films based on Karl May's Winnetou stories. But it was Sergio Leone's *Per un Pugno di Dollari* (*Fistful of Dollars*, 1964) that turned the Euro-western into an international phenomenon.

Leone's film was in fact an Italian-Spanish-West German co-production (a 'spaghetti-paella-bratwürst western'). It was an uncredited reworking of Akira Kurosawa's samurai film *Yojimbo* (just as *The Magnificent Seven* had been derived from the same director's *Seven Samurai*) starring Clint Eastwood (at the time a television rather than a film star) as a laconic stranger (known as 'El Cigarillo' in Europe and as 'The Man With No Name' in the English-speaking markets) who rides into a border town and provokes a power struggle between two rival gangs, hiring his deadly services out to both sides. *Fistful of Dollars* (the English prints lost both preposition and indefinite article from the title) introduced an entirely amoral 'hero' to the western and brought unprecedented new levels of violence to the genre (at one point the hero is savagely beaten by one of the gangs; he survives to kill them all in a gunfight). Two sequels followed: *Per Qualche Dollari in Piu* (*For A Few Dollars More*, 1965) teamed Eastwood's character with Lee Van Cleef as a pair of bounty hunters tracking down a sadistic bandit; *Il Buono, Il Brutto, Il Cattivo* (*The Good, the Bad and the Ugly*, 1966) had Eastwood, Van Cleef and Eli Wallach (the 'heavy' of *The Magnificent Seven*) searching for a shipment of Confederate gold during the Civil War.

The 'Dollars trilogy' is remarkable in several respects. Leone's films are far from the pale imitations of Hollywood westerns that some critics allege. Rather, they parody and even critique the conventions of the genre. The social framework of Garden and Desert is entirely absent; Leone's characters are driven either by greed or by revenge. The visual style is kinetic and vibrant, making extensive use of close-ups and zooms; the gunfights are ritualistic, elongated set pieces that achieve a level of operatic intensity through Ennio Morricone's bravura music. Frayling argues that while the visual codes and conventions are borrowed from the Hollywood western, the thematic concerns of Leone's films are specifically Italian, particularly his heavy religious symbolism (monasteries, churches and cemeteries all feature prominently) and the representation of villains as a sort of western Mafia with their own codes of honour and loyalty; he concludes that 'the resulting fusion of a *rhetoric* gleaned from the Western with Italian cultural values, seems a world away from the traditional, "historically-based" image of the frontier'.[51]

The 'Dollars' films were released in America by United Artists in 1967; their success was such that another studio, Paramount, backed Leone's next project, the epic *C'era una Volta il West* (*Once Upon a Time in the West*, 1968) which many commentators, Frayling included, regard as his masterpiece. Based on an original story by Bernardo Bertolucci, *Once Upon a Time in the West* reintroduces the social framework missing from the 'Dollars' films through the theme of the end of the frontier and the coming of civilization (represented by the building of the railroad). Leone demonstrates his affinity with the genre through many visual references to other westerns (*The Iron Horse*, *Shane*, *The Searchers*); at the same time he disrupts conventions, for example in the casting of Henry Fonda (the upright Wyatt Earp of *My Darling Clementine*) as a vicious hired killer. In *Once Upon a Time in the West* Leone develops his extreme stylization and formalism to its fullest extent; he even rehearsed actors' movements on set to Morricone's music which, unusually, was composed before the film was shot. However, it was less successful than his previous films and was released in a severely edited version that made the narrative incomprehensible.

Most spaghetti westerns – approximately 400 were made between 1964 and 1975 – were far less adventurous than Leone's, preferring violence and gimmicks to thematic depth. 'The aims of the makers of spaghetti westerns were comparable more with the aims of those who made Hollywood "B" westerns in the 1930s than with the makers of big-budget Hollywood westerns in the 1940s and 1950s,' Christopher Wagstaff observes. 'The product was to be suited to a market.'[52] Like the westerns of Hollywood's Poverty Row, spaghetti westerns were extremely formulaic; they operate according to their own narrative codes and conventions (the device of betrayal and swapping sides, for example, is frequently employed to justify the bloody showdowns that are an essential feature of the genre); and a core group of writer-directors (Sergio Corbucci, Sergio Sollima, Duccio Tessari, Luigi Vanzi) and actors (Lee Van Cleef, Fernando Sancho, Klaus Kinski) figure prominently in the genre's history. Also in common with Hollywood B-westerns, series were built around recurring characters: Sabata, Sartana, Ringo and Django (the latter character appeared in some 30 films played by several different actors, of whom Franco Nero was the first). The genre survived until the mid-1970s, when ticket price inflation brought about the closure of many of the provincial cinemas where spaghetti westerns were most popular and so removed the audience that had sustained their production for a decade.[53]

HORROR, EXPLOITATION AND SEX

The violence that characterized the spaghetti western was representative of a trend across much popular cinema during the 1960s and 1970s. Nowhere is this better exemplified than in the emergence of the horror film as one of the most prolific of film genres. The horror film had been a relatively minor genre in European cinemas before the late 1950s. German films of the 1920s are usually categorized in terms of an aesthetic movement (Expressionism) than a genre; while *Das Kabinett des Dr Caligari* and *Nosferatu* are undeniably early landmarks of the horror film, they do not in themselves constitute a genre or even a cycle. In the 1930s the horror film was most associated with Universal Pictures which produced classic versions of *Dracula* and *Frankenstein* and many sequels that lasted into the 1940s. These Hollywood horrors were characterized by their expressionist trappings, cobwebby castles and futuristic laboratories; they were usually set either in a vaguely defined 'middle Europe' or in a foggy studio recreation of Victorian England. For all that most horror stories are based on European myths, there were relatively few indigenous European attempts at the genre. British films of the 1930s (*The Ghoul, Dark Eyes of London*) were influenced by the visual style of Universal horror and even imported stars associated with the genre (Boris Karloff, Bela Lugosi). French filmmakers were more inclined towards what critics termed the *fantastique*, which had links with Surrealism, than horror. The *fantastique* is exemplified pre-eminently by Jean Cocteau's haunting fairy-tale *La Belle et la Bête* (*Beauty and the Beast*, 1946), though it can hardly be claimed as a major genre.

The emergence of the horror film as a major genre of European film production was marked in the late 1950s by the success of a small British studio, Hammer, which became so indelibly associated with the genre that 'Hammer horror' became a descriptive label in the same way as 'Ealing comedy'. Hitherto a specialist in low-budget crime films, Hammer was persuaded by the success of *The Quatermass Experiment* (1955) – a film adaptation of a BBC science-fiction serial with horrific elements – to turn its hand to 'a classical horror picture'.[54] The success of *The Curse of Frankenstein* (1957) – it cost only £80,000 but earned $8 million worldwide – spurred the studio to profitable remakes of other horror classics, including *Dracula*, *The Mummy*, *The Two Faces of Dr Jekyll* and *Curse of the Werewolf*. As a small company, Hammer was more able to respond quickly to market trends than the big combines such as Rank and ABPC and was therefore able to specialize in genre production of this kind.

It has become the received wisdom that the early Hammer horror films were greeted with howls of protest from critics. C. A. Lejeune ranked *The Curse of Frankenstein* 'among the half-dozen most repulsive films I have encountered', while the *Daily Telegraph* critic Campbell Dixon suggested it should give rise to a new certificate 'for Sadists Only'.[55] In common with the reception of the early James Bond films, however, other critics dismissed the films as formulaic hokum of no artistic merit. Most film historians have concurred with this. Armes, for instance, dismissed the whole Hammer horror cycle as 'essentially a new manipulation of the old clichés with a little more visual and verbal explicitness'.[56] The first commentator to take Hammer seriously was David Pirie who, writing towards the end of the horror cycle in the early 1970s, suggested that the films should be placed within the Gothic tradition that could be traced back to the late eighteenth- and early nineteenth-century English novel. In contrast to Rivette's assertion that British genres 'have no genuine roots', Pirie claimed the Gothic horror film, exemplified by Hammer, as 'the only staple cinematic myth which Britain can properly claim as its own, and which relates to it in the same way as the western relates to America'.[57]

Hammer horror is sensational, but at its best it is also highly literate. This is most apparent in the *oeuvre* of Terence Fisher, who directed most of the early films and in whose work there is a clear Manichean framework that presents Good and Evil as co-eternal forces in perpetual conflict. Fisher, dismissed by many critics as a commercial hack, claimed by others as a genuine *auteur*, employs an unobtrusive style of direction that does not detract attention from the narrative or the *mise-en-scène*.[58] The Hammer horrors are notable for their highly expressive visual style and for their garish use of colour, differentiating them from the black-and-white expressionist style of the Universal films. The relaxation of censorship allowed the films to afford greater prominence to visceral excess than the more restrained style of Universal horror. The hostile reaction of some critics was due to the transgressive nature of the films, especially the cycles featuring Frankenstein (who defies the laws of God and man in his relentless pursuit of scientific knowledge) and Dracula (who initiates a succession of nubile and mostly willing young women into the world of darkness through his highly unconventional style of coitus). Yet these films were less problematic for the censors than the modern, psychological horror film exemplified by Michael Powell's notorious shocker *Peeping Tom* (1960). As Vivian Sobchack observes: 'The containment provided by literary tradition, generic convention, and period costume allowed Hammer's Gothic horror films to exploit eroticism and sadism beyond what was generally acceptable in more realistic genres.'[59]

It would be fair to say that, following the early films in the cycle, the later Hammer horrors became increasingly derivative. 'Instead of deepening their impact by exploring other aspects of the Gothic tradition', Armes complains, 'Hammer (and Fisher) are content to return over and over again to the same tired old themes, each time spicing the rehash a little more strongly to meet the public appetite for more explicit violence or nudity.'[60] The most popular Hammer franchises, Frankenstein and

Dracula, were milked for all they were worth, though Fisher also made what many aficionados regard as his best film, *The Devil Rides Out*, during the period of Hammer's supposed atrophy. By the early 1970s, however, the Hammer style of horror, once condemned as repulsive, seemed rather tame in comparison to the increasingly explicit horror films that were being produced in Italy, Spain and France.

It had been the success of *The Curse of Frankenstein* that prompted other European film industries to turn to horror film production. As was the case with Fisher and Hammer, certain directors stand out amidst the dross of genre production (the horror film is probably the easiest type of film to make badly). Unlike the restrained and economical style of Fisher's direction, however, European horror specialists such as Mario Bava and Jess Franco seize every opportunity to draw attention to their narration through flamboyant camera movement and visual trickery. Their mastery of *mise-en-scène* compensated for the technical shoddiness of some of their films; in France, especially, these directors were claimed as *auteurs* by genre magazines such as *Cinefantastique*. Bava, who, like Fisher, had worked his way up through the film industry, came to prominence with his first film as solo director, *La Maschera del Demonio* (*The Mask of the Devil*, 1960). The film combined 'visually poetic black and white photography, thus linking it to the classical horror film' with 'overt images of sadism and bodily corruption, which almost overwhelmed narrative drive and coherence'.[61] The intent to shock is evident in the opening sequence in which a woman (Barbara Steele) is executed for adultery by having a spiked mask fitted to her face. Italian horror films were soon to surpass Hammer in their levels of visceral gore. The Spanish-born Franco was a prolific director who made over 160 films under various pseudonyms, switching between genres such as the spy film, spaghetti westerns and horror. His first serious horror film was *Gritos en la Noche* (*The Awful Dr Orloff*, 1962), an expressionist black-and-white shocker which initiated 'an entire subgenre mixing horror and medical science fiction motifs in a gory way which borders on the pornographic'.[62] Franco was influenced by many sources, including the Universal horror films of the 1930s (especially *Murders in the Rue Morgue*) and the novels of Edgar Wallace (which, intriguingly, were also the basis of a popular cycle of thrillers, some with horrific elements, in West Germany during the 1950s and 1960s). In his later films, he abandoned the expressionist trappings of *The Awful Dr Orloff* in favour of glossy colour photography and zoom-happy camerawork. Jointly, Bava and Franco represent the trend in European horror of the 1960s towards ever more explicit tales of madness, delirium and torture. One of the recurring motifs of Italian horror films, especially, is of hapless heroines being victimized and tortured (both physically and psychologically) by sadistic madmen. The titles alone give an indication of their salacious content: *The Whip and the Flesh*, *The Orgies of Dr Orloff*, *The Castle of Unholy Desires*, *The Torture Chamber of Dr Sadism*. It is little wonder that the horror film has attracted criticism from feminists on account of its misogyny.

Violence has always been a prominent feature of the horror film, but the relaxation of censorship in the late 1960s and early 1970s allowed filmmakers to show explicitly what had only ever been alluded to in the classical horror films of directors like James Whale. There was a trend for historically based horror films which used witchcraft trials as a pretence for scenes of the torture of (usually female) victims. The cycle began with British director Michael Reeves's much-admired *Witchfinder General* (1968), which has been claimed as an existential exploration of human cruelty; it quickly degenerated into crass exploitation with the likes of Adrian Hoven's *Mark of the Devil* and Franco's *The Bloody Judge*. For all their sadistic content, however, a serious undercurrent has been detected in these films in so far as they can be seen as a response to 'the difficulties involved in the maintenance of a male authority that is largely dependent upon female submission in the face of an increased female resistance to this submissive role'.[63]

The other essential ingredient of the horror film is sex. The early 1970s witnessed the emergence of the female (often lesbian) variant of the vampire film. If the witchcraft films represented a reactionary backlash against feminism as male authority figures adopted extreme measures in their attempts to assert control over the female body, then the female vampire films of the early 1970s can be seen as giving expression to women who are in control of their own bodies and their own sexuality. This, at least, would be the academic interpretation; film producers were undoubtedly motivated by the exploitation potential of female nudity in the newly permissive climate of the times. Hammer's attempts to jump on the bandwagon (*Countess Dracula*, *The Vampire Lovers*, *Lust for a Vampire*, *Twins of Evil*) soon seemed tame in comparison to the acres of naked female flesh displayed in the likes of Franco's *Vampyros Lesbos* and *La Comtesse Perverse* (*The Bare-Breasted Countess*). The French director Jean Rollin, meanwhile, was inexplicably acclaimed by some cineastes for his surrealist sex-and-horror films character-ized by their bizarre imagery and largely wordless plots (*The Naked Vampire*, *Thrill of the Vampire*, *Requiem for a Vampire*). One critic absurdly applauds Rollin's films 'as a fantasy chronicling some of the (at times) misogynist erotic motifs underpinning French surrealism' and defends an extended scene of a dungeon orgy-cum-rape in *Requiem for a Vampire* on the grounds that 'the stylized sadean sex scenes add their own dimension of obsessive intensity'.[64]

The trend in the early 1970s towards more explicit sexual content in the horror film anticipated the emergence of pornography as a major genre of European cinema. 'Sex films' had comprised a minor, if prolific, genre in many national cine-mas for several decades, usually in the form of pseudo-socio-logical studies that were ostensibly made for education but were in fact intended for titillation. The nudist film that emerged in the 1950s (the first British 'nudie', *Nudist Paradise*, was made in 1957) gave way in the 1960s to the urban 'sex doc-umentary' such as the Italian 'Mondo' films and the West German 'Housewife Report' (*Hausfrauen-Report*) and 'Helga' series. These films, which invariably promised more than they delivered, were in turn superseded towards the end of the decade by more sexually explicit films from Scandinavia (*I Am Curious – Yellow*, *Sexual Freedom in Denmark*) following the lib-eralization of pornography laws there. It was in the 1970s, however, that the soft-core pornographic film (one involving the simulation of sexual acts) became a staple of French, Italian and West German cinemas. Former horror directors such as

Franco and Rollin turned their talents to pornography, and porn starlets such as Sybill Danning and Lina Romay acquired cult followings.

The critical reaction to sex films has tended, on the whole, to be even more disdainful than the reception of horror films. Most films in the genre tend towards the same plot devices (schoolgirls, prostitution, wife-swapping) and narrative conventions (sex in various locations and positions). In the early and mid-1970s, however, there were a few attempts at making 'artistic' sex films that would bring some measure of critical respectability to the genre. Bernardo Bertolucci's *Ultimo Tango a Parigi* (*Last Tango in Paris*, 1973) was a commercial success on account of its scenes of a naked Marlon Brando and Maria Schneider engaging in simulated sex in an empty apartment. In contrast to most sex films it depicts the act itself as a mechanical and unrewarding experience. However, its explicit content caused it to be banned in Italy where it was condemned by the courts as 'obscene, indecent, and catering to the lowest instincts of the libido'.[65] Less controversial, and even more successful, was Just Jaeckin's *Emmanuelle* (1974), an international hit that did as much as any film to turn soft-core pornography into a mainstream genre. *Emmanuelle*, which starred Dutch actress Sylvia Kristel as the bored wife of a diplomat who embarks on a journey of sexual discovery in Thailand, is really little more than a glossy travelogue that contains some sex scenes. Its success spawned several sequels and countless imitations: for the next five years (1974–9) pornographic films accounted for 50 per cent of all French film production. As Hayward observes: 'Pornography had not just come of age: for that year at least [1974] it was France's leading national cinema product – a curious state of affairs if ever there was one.'[66] Jaeckin followed *Emmanuelle* with another glossy piece of erotica, *Histoire d'O* (*The Story of O*, 1975), in which the heroine (Corinne Clery) submits willingly to a regime of bondage and sado-masochism at the hands of various lovers.

It is difficult to draw any firm conclusions about the popularity of sex films in the 1970s. For its supporters, pornography is a sociological phenomenon that is seen as a sign of liberalism and sexual freedom. In this regard the wave of sex films in the 1970s can be seen as a belated consequence of the cultural revolution of the 1960s. For its detractors, however, pornography is a symptom of a sick society that is ill at ease with itself. Probably both positions have something to recommend them. The fact that most sex films are made by men (just as most films are) would tend to lend weight to the feminist argument that pornography provides a means whereby men can control and position women, literally 'putting them in their place'. In this sense it is a conservative, even reactionary genre. There is another sense, however, in which the sex film is transgressive. The genre provides a guilty pleasure for its spectators in transgressing the normative moral codes that govern sexual behaviour. That it emerged as a major force when it did was due largely to the congruence of two factors: the relaxation of censorship and an increasingly permissive attitude towards sexuality in western society at large.

The 1970s were to be the heyday of exploitation cinema. With occasional exceptions, horror and sex films have been absent from cinemas since the end of the 1970s. Hayward dates the end of the French porn film at 1979 when new taxes were levied on porn films and the cinemas that showed them; David McGillivray identifies *Emmanuelle in Soho* (1981) as marking the end of the British sex film.[67] The legalization of hard-core pornography in some countries, shown in specially licensed cinemas, was one nail in the coffin of the soft-core sex film; the widespread availability of home video recorders from the early 1980s was another. While low-budget sex films and horror films continue to be made (there are, thankfully, far fewer sex-and-horror films than there were in the 1960s and 1970s), they are produced for the home video market and are only rarely afforded a cinema release (as in the case of Clive Barker's *Hellraiser* in 1987). The video film industry is a highly lucrative market, especially for pornography, though such straight-to-video fare has not yet attracted the attention of film critics and historians. It is video that now provides the equivalent of those bread-and-butter genre films on which European national cinemas had depended for over half a century.

ELEVEN

The Challenge of Third Cinema

The cinema of the Third World provides a number of historical and theoretical challenges for the film historian. There is, most obviously, a problem of definition. The term 'Third World' entered into international political discourse during the 1950s, generally being credited to the French demographer Alfred Sauvy who used the analogy of the 'third estate' of France before the Revolution (the 'third estate' were the unrepresented commoners in contrast to the 'first estate' of the nobility and the 'second estate' of the clergy). 'Third World' was used to refer to the 'non-aligned' nations of Africa, Asia and Latin America in contrast to the 'first world' of capitalist democracies in Europe, North America and the Pacific and the 'second world' of the Communist bloc. The decline of European colonialism in the 1950s and 1960s led to the emergence of new, often highly politicized states that were anxious to distance themselves from their colonial pasts. It should not be assumed that all Third World countries were newly independent ex-colonies (most Latin American nations had been politically independent since the nineteenth century), however, nor that all former colonies were necessarily Third World (the 'tiger economies' of Asia had more in common with the capitalist West than with the economically impoverished African nations). It is also important to realize that cinema was already well established in some Third World countries long before the term 'Third World' itself was in common usage: there were healthy, if relatively small, indigenous production industries in Egypt, Mexico, Brazil and Argentina, for example, from the 1930s.

To complicate the issue further, the term 'Third Cinema', as it is used in film studies, is not synonymous with the cinema of the Third World. It tends to be used to refer to the radical filmmaking practices that emerged during the 1960s, principally in Latin America, to a lesser extent in Africa. It does not usually incorporate the popular cinemas of Asia, which tend to be seen as modes of film practice that are distinct from Third Cinema. 'Third Cinema' was a term first used by Latin American filmmakers and then adopted by 'first world' film theorists to describe a particular mode of film practice that was politically, culturally and aesthetically different both from classical Hollywood and its imitators and from European art cinema. This perspective is exemplified by Robert Stam, who, while acknowledging that 'although the cinematic traditions of many countries later recognised as belonging to the Third World go back to the first decades of this century', avers nevertheless that 'it was in the 1960s that Third World cinema as a self-aware movement emerged on the First World film scene by winning prizes and garnering critical praise'.[1] It is easy to understand why film theorists in Europe and America were attracted to the Third Worldist political films of the 1960s: they challenged traditional assumptions about film form and ideology that allowed them to be claimed, like avant-garde practices elsewhere, as 'alternatives' to the dominant Hollywood model. The British theorist Paul Willemen has even gone so far as to argue that Third Cinema extends beyond the Third World, including also the work of minority groups in other countries. He called for 'the re-actualisation of the Third Cinema debates in the UK in the 80s', asserting that independent black filmmakers 'now constitute the most intellectually and cinematically innovative edge of British cultural politics'.[2] These comments were made in the context of debates around 'otherness' and social exclusion in Thatcherite Britain, exemplified by the films of Isaac Julien (*Territories*) and John Akomfrah (*Handsworth Songs*), though this attempt to extend the Third Cinema paradigm has not found much favour with other commentators or with the filmmakers themselves. My own discussion of Third Cinema, therefore, will focus on the filmmaking practices of Latin America and Africa (Asia and the Middle East are discussed in later chapters) and does not extend to minority filmmaking in western countries.

The origins of cinema in Latin America and Africa came, as in so many parts of the world, with the arrival of the Cinématographe Lumière in the 1890s. The spread of indigenous film production, however, proceeded unevenly throughout the continents. In Latin America the first feature films were made in Brazil (1913), Cuba (1913), Venezuela (1913), Argentina (1915), Mexico (1916), Chile (1916), Colombia (1922), Bolivia (1923) and Peru (1927). Latin American film production was dominated by the largest countries (Argentina, Mexico, Brazil) which had domestic markets of a sufficient size to sustain indigenous production. It was several decades, however, until there was any significant level of production elsewhere in the continent, while in the smaller countries such as Ecuador, Paraguay and Uruguay there has never been a production sector of any size. African production was even slower to become established, with only Egypt boasting a production sector before the Second World War. The first Egyptian feature film was released in 1927 and by the mid-1930s Egypt was producing around a dozen films a year that were exported throughout the Arab world. It was not until much later, however, that the first indigenous features were made in the countries of sub-Saharan Africa, including Ghana (1951), the Ivory Coast (1964), Nigeria (1966), Senegal (1967), Gabon (1967), Mali (1968), Angola (1968), Cameroon (1972), Madagascar (1973), Upper Volta (1973) and Benin (1974). While Latin America accounts for approximately six per cent of world film production, and while its films are known on the international 'art house' circuit, Africa is the smallest continental producer and its films remain among the least known outside their countries of origin.

Teshome Gabriel, a leading theorist of Third Cinema, has argued that the history of film production in the Third World consists of three identifiable phases. The first phase – 'the unqualified assimilation' – involves a close identification with Hollywood. This association was often deliberate on the part of producers: Egypt's Misr studio that opened in the 1930s was dubbed 'Hollywood-on-the-Nile'. The style of films is described thus by Gabriel:

Hollywood thematic concerns of 'entertainment' predomi-
nate. Most of the feature films of the Third World in this
phase sensationalise adventure for its own sake and concern
themselves with escapist themes of romance, musicals, comedies etc. The sole purpose of such industries is to turn out
entertainment products which will generate profits.[3]

The arrival of sound in the early 1930s gave a boost to established production industries due to the demand for films in the
vernacular language. The musical became a staple genre of
Third World cinemas: the *chanchada* in Brazil, the *ranchera* in
Mexico and the *tanguenera* in Argentina all adapted the conventions of the Hollywood musical to the local idiom.

The political economy of Third World cinema is significant
in so far as, while Latin America and Africa were clearly dependent upon, respectively, the US and European film industries,
the relationship was not quite as entirely one-sided as has often
been assumed. Although American films were the dominant
screen presence throughout Latin America, this market was less
significant for Hollywood than Europe, accounting for only ten
per cent of foreign earnings in the 1930s.[4] There was a short-
lived trend for Spanish-language films made specifically for the
Latin American market, though they were hardly successful
enough to warrant the expense of making them. When
Hollywood lost its lucrative European markets during the
Second World War, however, Latin America became more
important. There was a wartime vogue for films with Latin
American subjects (*Down Argentine Way*, *That Night in Rio*, *They
Met in Rio*, *Rio Rita*) and the Brazilian-born Carmen Miranda
enjoyed a brief period of popularity as an exotic Hollywood star.
Ironically, however, such films were more successful in the US
market than in Latin America, where they were often found
'distasteful' by audiences offended by their stereotyped representations.[5] There is some evidence, therefore, of cultural resistance to American movies, suggesting that the 'assimilation' of
Hollywood into Latin American film culture, at any rate, was
not entirely 'unqualified'. The situation in Africa was rather different, however, for, while Latin America was politically independent, most of Africa was ruled by European nations until the

1950s. Accordingly it was European (principally French and British) films that dominated exhibition in most of the continent. Some colonial administrators, interestingly, believed that showing films to native audiences could be counter-productive. 'The success of our government of subject races depends almost entirely on the degree of respect which we can inspire,' one British Colonial Office mandarin observed. 'Incalculable is the damage that has already been done to the prestige of Europeans in India and the Far East through the wide-spread exhibition of ultrasensational and disreputable pictures.'[6]

The second phase of Third World cinema identified by Gabriel is 'the remembrance phase' which involves 'indigenisation and control of talents, production, exhibition and distribution' and a 'movement for a social institution of cinema in the Third World'.[7] At an industrial level this development typically involved an increased level of state support for national cinemas. The Argentinian president Juan Perón, elected in 1946, sponsored various measures to support the film industry, including quotas and subsidies, though these were largely without effect as Perón also struck a deal with the Motion Picture Export Association of America which gave favourable terms to US distributors. When Perón was overthrown by a military coup in 1955 the new *junta* abolished the import restrictions but also increased the level of state subsidy to encourage domestic production. A similar pattern emerged in Brazil a decade later. The modernizing regime of liberal president João Goulart supported the film industry through quotas, tax exemptions and the establishment of the Grupo Executivo da Indústria Cinematográfica (GEICINE) to co-ordinate national film policy. When Goulart was overthrown by a military coup in 1964, the new regime maintained continuity in film policy, absorbing GEICINE into the Instituto Nacional do Cinema (INC) which encouraged film production through loans and prizes.

The interest in cinema as a national institution was also evident in the emergence of an intellectual film culture in the postwar period, exemplified by the appearance of film societies and ciné-clubs. Italian Neo-Realist films were particularly influential in Latin America. The Brazilian documentarist Nelson Pereira dos Santos, whose *Rio 40°* (1955) showed the life of boys selling peanuts in the city's slums, remarked 'that we could film using average people rather than known actors; that the technique could be imperfect, as long as the film was truly linked to its national culture and expressed that culture.'[8] It was at this time that Latin American cinema also began to win international recognition. Luis Buñuel, the Spanish director who had worked with Salvador Dali making experimental Surrealist films in France in the 1920s, resumed his directing career in Mexico in the late 1940s and won a prize at the 1951 Cannes Film Festival for his third Mexican film *Los Olvidados* (*The Young and Lost*, 1950), a vivid portrait of street life and vagrancy in Mexico City.

Gabriel avers that films of 'the remembrance phrase' are characterized by a 'growing insistence on spatial representation' that 'arises out of the experience of an "endless" world of the large Third World mass'.[9] This style is exemplified by the *Cinema Nôvo* movement in Brazil during the 1960s, led by filmmakers such as Glauber Rocha, Ruy Guerra and Nelson Pereira dos Santos, whose films combined social themes with aesthetic innovation. *Cinema Nôvo* dramatized the lives and struggles of labourers and peasants, focusing on the rural rather than the urban. Films such as Rocha's *Barravento* (*The Turning Wind*, 1962), Guerra's *Os Fuzis* (*The Guns*, 1963) and Santos's *Vidas secas* (*Barren Lives*, 1963) portrayed the social deprivation of fishing and agrarian communities. Gabriel's analysis of the style of Third World cinema during this phase is particularly applicable to *Cinema Nôvo*, wherein 'the landscape depicted ceases to be mere land or soil and acquires a phenomenal quality which integrates humans with the general drama of existence itself'.[10]

Cinema Nôvo is historically important because it represents 'a link between the western New Cinemas of the early 1960s and later Third World movements'.[11] On the one hand *Cinema Nôvo* was influenced by the stylistic and technical features of the *Nouvelle Vague*, especially the use of hand-held cameras. On the other hand, however, *Cinema Nôvo* was more politically and socially committed than most of the European new waves. *Cinema Nôvo*, in the words of filmmaker Carlos Diegues, was 'making political films when the New Wave was still talking about unrequited love'.[12] It is instructive to note that *Cinema*

Nôvo did not disappear following the military coup of 1964, but continued to attract sponsorship from Embrasfilme, the centralized state agency set up in 1969 to control film production. It is an indication of the cultural prestige attached to *Cinema Nôvo* by the authorities that Rocha could make a film like *Antonio des Mortes* (1969), which allegorized the new regime in the form of a cold-blooded killer. What ultimately killed the movement was not censorship but the indifference of home audiences to the films, for, while they were critically successful when shown abroad, Brazilian cinema-goers remained stubbornly disposed towards light entertainment such as carnival musicals.

The third phase in Gabriel's history of Third World cinema is 'the combative phase'. This phase is characterized by 'film-making as a public service institution' in which the film industry 'is not only owned by the nation and/or the government, it is also managed, operated and run for and by the people'. Its theme is the 'lives and struggles of Third World peoples'. In this phase cinema has become 'an ideological tool'. Gabriel elaborates thus:

> A Phase III film-maker is one who is perceptive of and knowledgeable about the pulse of the Third World masses. Such a film-maker is truly in search of a Third World cinema – a cinema that has respect for the Third World peoples. One element of the style in this phase is an ideological point-of-view instead of that of a character as in dominant Western conventions.[13]

This describes 'Third Cinema' as it was to become known: the radical, politicized, militant cinema that emerged in the later 1960s. This type of filmmaking was most closely associated with countries that had recently experienced revolution such as Cuba and Algeria. It was nurtured by the new revolutionary governments and was supported by a state-sponsored film culture including festivals and film journals. Film industries were nationalized in Cuba (1959) and Algeria (1964). The political cinema of the Third World varied in style from fairly crude agitprop style newsreels and documentaries to highly complex, symbolic feature films that won the admiration of critics in the

West as much for their formal innovation and boldness as for the revolutionary import of their ideology. In the eyes of the film-makers, however, politics and aesthetics were inseparable.

The exemplar of a revolutionary Third World cinema in the 1960s was Cuba. One of the first acts of Fidel Castro's government after overthrowing the Batistá regime in 1959 had been to set up the Instituto Cubano del Arte e Industria Cinematograficos (ICAIC), under Che Guevara's brother Alfredo, to co-ordinate national film policy. The ICAIC published its own film journal (*Cine Cubano*) to encourage discussion of films, trained filmmakers and, by the mid-1960s, controlled all film production, distribution and exhibition in the country. It had produced some 500 newsreels, 300 short documentaries and over 50 feature films by the early 1970s; these films were also exported to Europe and the Soviet Union. The success of Cuban cinema, in the eyes of Thompson and Bordwell, was that it 'could blend modernist conventions with narrative forms to which mass audiences had become accustomed'.[14] Its most successful films were probably Tomás Gutiérrez Alea's *Memorias del subdesarrollo* (*Memories of Underdevelopment*, 1968) and Humberto Solas's *Lucia* (1968) which 'became paradigms of political filmmaking within Latin America'.[15] *Memorias del subdesarrollo* used unusual narrative techniques including unmotivated flashbacks, intellectual montage (there are allusions to *Battleship Potemkin*) and a voice-over interior monologue to tell the story of an intellectual uncertain about his commitment to the revolution, while *Lucia* retold the history of revolutionary struggle through three episodes from Cuban history, each focused on a woman called Lucia, each episode using different styles and techniques.

Political cinema in Africa followed different paths, depending upon the historical experiences of the nations involved. The closest parallel to the Cuban model was Algeria, where the war of liberation against France provided the impetus for a revolutionary political cinema. The newly independent Algerian production company Casbah Films part-financed Gillo Pontecorvo's *La Battaglia di Algeri* (*The Battle of Algiers*, 1965). There is some debate whether *The Battle of Algiers* can properly be placed within the Third Cinema paradigm on account of its having been made by Italians. One commentator suggests that it is more accurately described as 'a European film about the Third World'.[16] Pontecorvo is, arguably, more objective about the war than some critics would have preferred, though his sympathies are clearly with the Algerian National Liberation Front; the part-fictional, part-documentary style of the film is very much in the tradition of Third Cinema. In any event, it was only the first step for Algerian cinema. In 1969 the government took control of production and distribution through the Office National pour le Commerce et l'Industrie Cinématographique and sponsored both fictional feature films and documentaries about the war of liberation.

Black African cinema in the 1960s and 1970s explored the theme of the suppression of indigenous cultures by white European colonialism, though it was more sporadic than its Latin American counterparts. It was confined mainly to Francophone West Africa (Senegal, Niger, Guinea, Chad), which enjoyed more state support than Anglophone East Africa (Ethiopia, Somalia, Kenya). The only black African filmmaker to have any significant exposure outside Africa was the Senegalese director Ousmane Sembene, who made the first indigenous black African feature film *Borom Sarret* (1963) and the first film in a native African language, *Mandabi* (1968). Sembene was a communist who learned filmmaking in Moscow. The presence of foreign distributors and the dependency of many African nations on overseas aid has probably retarded the development of African cinema since the 1970s, with the main international critical success being the South African film *Sarafina!* (1992) about a schoolgirl's struggles during apartheid; even then it relied on the presence of a well-known American actress (Whoopi Goldberg) to reach an international audience.

MANIFESTOS, POLEMICS, AVANT-GARDES

Latin American filmmakers were theorists as well as practitioners. The theoretical agenda of political filmmaking in the Third World was defined in essays by Glauber Rocha ('Aesthetics of Hunger'), Julio Garcia Espinoza ('For an Imperfect Cinema') and Fernando Solanas and Octavio Getino ('Towards a Third Cinema'). These essays, which soon acquired the status of manifestos, were published in progressive film journals in Europe and America such as *Jump Cut*, *Cineaste*, *Afterimage* and *Framework*.[17] The most widely published and translated was 'Towards a Third Cinema' and this document is worth considering in some detail as it defines the terms on which Third Cinema was understood by its practitioners.

Solanas and Getino saw Third Cinema as an alternative to what they regarded as the two dominant global modes of film practice. 'First Cinema' encompassed not only Hollywood but imitations of Hollywood in other countries, including, in the authors' minds, even some Soviet films:

> While, during the early history of the cinema, it was possible to speak of a German, an Italian, or a Swedish cinema clearly differentiated and corresponding to specific national characteristics, today such differences have disappeared. The borders were wiped out along with the expansion of US imperialism and the film model that it imposed: Hollywood movies. In our times it is hard to find a film within the field of commercial cinema, including what is known as 'author's cinema', in both the capitalist and socialist countries, that manages to avoid the models of Hollywood pictures. The latter have such a fast hold that monumental works such as the USSR's [Sergei] Bondarchuk's *War and Peace* are also monumental examples of the submission to all the propositions imposed by the US movie industry (structure, language, etc.) and, consequently, to its concepts.[18]

While, on the one hand, this is a fairly typical denunciation of Hollywood's cultural and economic imperialism, on the other hand it offers a different view of the status of national cinemas than is common in film history, suggesting that national cinemas could be identified only in the days before US hegemony of the world film market. What is most significant, however, is the assertion that even films made in socialist countries, because they use aspects of the Hollywood style, could be placed within the First Cinema paradigm.

'Second Cinema' was what Solanas and Getino referred to as 'author's cinema', and included not only European models such as the *Nouvelle Vague* but Latin American models such as *Cinema Nôvo*. While accepting that 'this alternative signified a step forward inasmuch as it demanded that the filmmaker be free to express himself in non-standard language and inasmuch as it was an attempt at cultural decolonization', Solanas and Getino nevertheless asserted that Second Cinema was limited because 'such attempts have already reached, or are about to reach, the outer limits of what the system permits'.[19] Second Cinema still operated within the institutions of national cinemas and was dependent upon the law of the market. The idea of Third Cinema, in contrast, was 'the revolutionary opening towards a cinema outside and against the System . . . a cinema of liberation'.[20]

Solanas and Getino argued that film was the most powerful instrument of political persuasion due to its peculiar formal characteristics and its didactic possibilities:

> The capacity for synthesis and the penetration of the film image, the possibilities offered by the living document and naked reality, and the power of enlightenment of audiovisual means make film far more effective than any other tool of communication. It is hardly necessary to point out that those films which achieve an intelligent use of the possibilities of the image, adequate dosage of concepts, language and structure that flow naturally from each theme, and counterpoints of audiovisual narration achieve effective results in the politicization and mobilization of cadres and even in work with the masses, where this is possible.[21]

The adoption of film in the anti-imperialist struggle had been retarded, Solanas and Getino maintained, by a range of factors, including lack of equipment, technical difficulties and the costs of film production. That a Third World political cinema emerged in the 1960s was due to such factors as lightweight cameras, rapid film stocks that allowed filming in normal light conditions (essential for non-studio based filmmaking) and, not least, the spread of technical knowledge through film magazines that 'have helped to demystify filmmaking and divest it of that almost magic aura that made it seem that films were only within the reach of "artists", "geniuses", and "the privileged"'.[22]

When 'Towards A Third Cinema' was published in English and thus became more widely disseminated, it inevitably drew comparisons with the work of Soviet theorists and filmmakers such as Eisenstein and Vertov. Willemen, for example, places the manifesto within a lineage of formalist theory that 'goes back to the Soviet avant-gardes'.[23] Yet there are significant differences in the historical contexts in which the Soviet theorists and theorists of Third Cinema were working. For one thing, Soviet cinema of the 1920s was nationally specific in a way that Third Cinema was not. And, for another, whereas the Soviet cinema was supported and sponsored by the state, Third Cinema was often on the margins of what Solanas and Getino had called 'the System'. Thus, while in Cuba cinema was adopted by the revolutionary government, in other states where the regime was less disposed towards the expression of radical ideas, political filmmaking was often an underground activity. Solanas and Getino themselves worked in a political environment much less amicable to their ideas than their Cuban counterparts. As left-wing supporters of the ousted Perón, they were outspoken critics of the military governments that ruled Argentina during the 1960s. As Solanas once put it: 'Eisenstein and Vertov had the Soviet power behind them, the Latin American filmmaker has the police behind him. That is the difference.'[24]

Where there is a parallel between Third Cinema and the Soviet school, however, is in the relationship between theory and practice. 'The existence of a revolutionary cinema is inconceivable without the constant and methodical exercise of practice, search, and experimentation,' Solanas and Getino declared.[25] The aesthetics of Third Cinema were never prescriptive; the reason why its cause was taken up by European film theorists was its formal innovation. Solanas and Getino's major film – *La Hora de los Hornos* (*Hour of the Furnaces*, 1968) – is an eclectic mix of styles and techniques, including both documentary and fiction, and both *Cinéma Vérité* and Surrealism. It employs associative montage in the manner of Eisenstein (shots of prize bulls at a cattle show in Buenos Aires are intercut with the faces of the Argentinian bourgeoisie) and

uses captioned inter-titles in the manner of Godard to break it into sections. *La Hora de los Hornos* has been described as 'a Marxist historical analysis of neo-colonialism and oppression in Argentina'.[26] The four-hour film is structured in three sections: the first part ('Neocolonialism and Violence') is dedicated to Che Guevara and shows how Argentina has been exploited not only by Europe and the United States but also by its own ruling élites; the second part ('An Act for Liberation') focuses on the Perón regime and provides an account of both its successes and its failures; and the third part ('Violence and Liberation') consists of interviews with political activists discussing the potential for revolution. While the film's ideological agenda is clearly pro-revolutionary, the film succeeds in being didactic without becoming prescriptive. It is pro-Perónist, although not unqualified in its endorsement of the ousted president. Moreover, in a manner that would have been unthinkable to Soviet filmmakers, whose montage theory was designed to impose a meaning or interpretation upon the

audience, *La Hora de los Hornos* actively encourages the participation of the spectators in political discussion and debate. At
one point the film halts and the audience is told: 'Now it is up
to you to draw conclusions, to continue the film. You have the
floor.'

Solanas and Getino maintained that the active participation
of the audience was an essential part of Third Cinema:

> Before and during the making of *La Hora de los Hornos* we
> tried out various methods for the distribution of revolu-
> tionary cinema – the little that we had made up to then.
> Each showing for militants, middle-class cadres, activists,
> workers, and university students became – without our
> having set ourselves this aim beforehand – a kind of
> enlarged cell meeting of which the films were a part but not
> the most important factor. We thus discovered a new facet
> of cinema: the participation of people who, until then, were
> considered spectators.[27]

'At times,' they added, 'security reasons obliged us to try to
dissolve the group of participants as soon as the showing was
over'. The very act of watching an underground film, they
maintained, became an act of political defiance and thus of
liberation.

There is every indication that *La Hora de los Hornos* succeeded in making political cinema accessible and popular. It
was a major critical success on the European festival circuit in
1968–9, where it coincided with a wave of popular unrest and
revolutionary fervour throughout Western Europe. In
Argentina it was shown clandestinely at first, but received a
more widespread distribution when Perón returned to power
in 1973. Solanas and Getino enjoyed a brief period of state
support – Solanas took charge of an independent filmmaking
association, Getino became the chief film censor and immediately set about liberalizing the restrictive censorship laws – but
following Perón's death in 1974 and the outbreak of a civil war
between left and right, they were forced into exile.

The Third Cinema project arose from a particular political and cultural context in which filmmakers saw themselves as part of a wider historical process. Its rallying cry was 'revolution'; its heroes were Che Guevara, Ho Chi Minh and Mao Tse-tung. Solanas and Getino, in common with so many left-wing intellectuals, believed that the 1960s had witnessed 'the development of a worldwide liberation movement whose moving force is to be found in the Third World'.[28] In the eyes of some radicals, events such as the Cuban Revolution, the Algerian War of Liberation and the Vietnam War seemed to point towards a tricontinental revolution of the oppressed and colonized peoples. In 1966 the Conference of Solidarity in Havana resolved that the peoples of Asia, Africa and Latin America should unite in their struggle against western neo-colonialism. In 1973 a conference of Third World filmmakers met in Algeria concurrent with a conference of non-aligned countries.

In hindsight, as Jonathan Buchsbaum points out, '[the] precondition for *third cinema* – the worldwide uprising of the masses – sounds like a rhetorical anachronism, soggy with Marxist internationalism'.[29] The global revolution that Third World activists (and some militants in the West) advocated never materialized. The intellectual appeal of Marxism was diminished by Mao's 'Cultural Revolution' in China that halted industrial development and retarded education and by the revelation of atrocities by the Khmer Rouge in Cambodia. Events such as the Arab-Israeli wars and the oil crisis of 1973–4 revealed tensions within the Third World. The economic downturn of the 1970s caused many Third World countries to become more inward-looking than internationalist in outlook, whilst also helping to create the circumstances in which authoritarian right-wing governments could seize power. The historical moment of Third Cinema, therefore, was short-lived. As an international cinema movement, it flourished during the period of greatest Third World militancy and declined thereafter. One of the reasons why western intellectuals have wanted to extend the Third Cinema paradigm to include oppositional films in non-Third World countries, possibly, is that Third Cinema was all but dead in the Third World by the mid-1970s.

The disappearance of Third Cinema was most apparent in the continent where it had originated. This was due in large measure to the repressive nature of the military *juntas* that held power in most Latin American countries by the mid-1970s, forcing political filmmakers either into exile or into increasingly dangerous clandestine filmmaking. Rocha and Guerra both left Brazil to work in Africa when the government became more repressive in the early 1970s (Guerra had in fact been born in Mozambique); there was a mass exodus of young filmmakers from Chile when General Augusto Pinochet came to power following a bloody coup in 1973; and the best-known Bolivian filmmaker Jorge Sanjinés (*Blood of the Condor*) was forced to continue his career in Peru following the fascist coup of 1971. In Africa, where the tradition of radical filmmaking had never been so well established, a similar pattern of military dictatorships and political repression retarded what little opportunity there had been for a militantly political African cinema to emerge.

The so-called 'return to democracy' in Latin America since the 1980s has witnessed the revival of filmmaking in the continent, though the radicalism of the Third Cinema project is no longer evident. The most successful Latin American films of recent decades were either made for the international market, such as Carlos Diegues's *Bye Bye Brazil* (1980), or were cult successes, such as Robert Rodriguez's *El Mariachi* (1992), a Colombian-produced, Mexico-set low-budget thriller that was less an imitation of the American western, as some critics have maintained, but rather an imitation of Italian imitations of the American western. The social and aesthetic concerns of Latin American filmmakers have moved on. As Stam observes: 'The anti-colonial thrust of earlier films gradually gave way to more diversified themes and aesthetic models as film-makers partially discarded the didactic model predominant in the 1960s in favour of a postmodern "politics of pleasure", incorporating music, humour and sexuality.'[30] When Fernando Solanas returned to Argentina in the mid-1980s, for example, it was to make *Tangos: The Exile of Gardel* (1985), a celebration of the place of the tango in the national culture.

Cuba has remained the main supporter of Latin American film culture, hosting the annual International Festival of Latin American Cinema since 1979 and establishing the Foundation for Latin American Cinema in 1985. Even there, however, the trend since the mid-1970s has been away from the radical style of political filmmaking and towards more mainstream commercial practices. While remaining a Communist state, Cuba was not left unaffected by economic forces and ICAIC was forced to reduce expenditure on films in the 1980s before being wound up in the early 1990s. The collapse of Communism in Eastern Europe left Cuba isolated as it relied on the Soviet bloc for film stock and equipment. At the same time censorship became more restrictive – a satirical comedy, *Alice in Wonderland*, was banned in 1991 – and some filmmakers went into exile.

The economic instability of most Third World countries has placed huge obstacles in the way of national cinemas. The once healthy Brazilian and Argentinian film industries were shadows of their former selves by the 1990s, with production limited to a handful of films a year. The Latin American market is now once again dominated by Hollywood imports, the result of the relaxation of tariffs, the abolition of quotas and the decline in domestic production. An attempt to create a common market throughout Francophone Africa in the 1980s through the Consortium Interafricain de Distribution Cinématographique failed because states did not reform their tax laws to allow it and did not pay their subsidies to support it. Burkina Faso is probably the most supportive new African state towards cinema, sponsoring the annual Pan-African Film and Television Festival in Ougadougou. Yet despite such initiatives, film production in the whole of sub-Saharan African averaged only around ten films a year throughout the 1980s and 1990s. At the time of writing, the fate of Third World cinema remains as uncertain and as precarious as it has ever been.

TWELVE

Bollywood and Beyond

India is the world's largest national cinema and the only one to represent a serious challenge to the global hegemony of Hollywood. With a domestic audience in excess of 900 million and a popular film culture in which stars are revered with a passion unknown in the West since the 1920s, India has proved resistant to the American movies that have increasingly come to dominate screens throughout much of the world. The Indian film industry, moreover, exports its products throughout Southeast Asia and, increasingly, to western countries such as Britain and America where Indian expatriates provide a large diasporic audience. Yet despite its size – India has consistently produced over 700 films per year since the 1970s – it has taken longer for Indian cinema to receive the critical and scholarly attention that has been lavished on some smaller national cinemas. It is only very recently, with the publication of both popular and academic works on popular Hindi cinema in English, that 'Bollywood' (as it is widely and, in the eyes of some, rather disparagingly known) has at last found its place in the sun. 'No one can entertain doubts any more about the growing respectability and validity that popular, mainstream Bollywood cinema has been increasingly accorded around the world, especially in the last few years', the Asian film magazine *Cinemaya* noted approvingly in 2000. 'What for decades was patronisingly considered mere popular kitsch from the world's most prolific film industry is now the new lode from London to Tokyo.'[1]

'In histories of world cinema produced in the west', one Indian film studies scholar observes, 'Indian cinema usually makes its appearance in 1956, the year in which Satyajit Ray burst on to the international film scene with *Pather Panchali*.'[2]

Basil Wright's reaction to Ray's first film typifies the response of western critics: 'I have never forgotten the private projection room at the British Film Institute during which I experienced that shock of recognition and excitement when, unexpectedly, one is suddenly exposed to a new and incontrovertible work of art.'[3] Ray's films were admired in the West, suggests M. Madhava Prasad, because they could be placed within the tradition of 'those realist/artistic products which correspond to a certain conception of true cinema'.[4] 'Bollywood', in sharp contrast, was viewed with amusement and mild condescension, with Wright, for example, dismissing it as a diet of 'endless musical films and social melodramas or comedies, all of them featuring stars whose popularity in Indian eyes is as great as was that of the Valentinos and Swansons of yesteryear in the West'.[5] He does not, however, name any of those stars.

For Indian scholars, the history of Indian cinema has tended to be written in terms of its representation of 'the biography of the nation-state'.[6] The temporal focus is largely on the post-Independence period; when attention is given to the cinema of the Raj it tends to be to claim filmmakers (such as the early pioneer D. G. Phalke) as proto-nationalists. Ray's films were again at the centre of debates around the status of film as an art form and its role in Indian cultural life. It was Ray's collaborator Chidananda Das Gupta who, in the 1960s, coined the term 'All-India Film' to describe the mainstream Hindi film industry, based in Bombay (now Mumbai), that had achieved both economic and cultural hegemony throughout the subcontinent. Since then the Hindi film has been the object of research for both Indian and western scholars.[7] It is only in the last decade or so, however, that Indian popular cinema has found its place on the agenda of film studies, and even then it has too often been discussed in terms of an 'alternative' to classical Hollywood than as the dominant mode of film practice that it is in its own right.[8]

The recent 'discovery' of Hindi cinema alongside the art cinema tradition of Ray (and a handful of others) has resulted in an over-simplistic critical paradigm of Indian national cinema, as Ashish Rajadhyaksha explains:

To a great extent, the Indian cinema megalith since 1960 has been effectively categorized in popular discourse as two things: the 'Hindi movie' and 'Satyajit Ray': the former being the song-dance-action stereotype made in over twelve languages and representing that most enviable of national possessions, a cultural mainstream, and the latter a highly generalized category involving a variety of different directors generically celebrated as being 'rooted' in their context. Both categories have been sustained as much by marketing strategies as by a committed and articulate brand of cinephilia accompanying each of them.[9]

In fact, Indian national cinema also comprises a number of regional and sub-state cinemas that fit neither the Hindi nor the art cinema paradigms. There are five major centres of film production and eight main languages: Bombay (Hindi and Marathi cinemas), Madras (Tamil and Malayalam cinemas), Calcutta (Bengali and Assamese cinemas), Hyderabad (Telugu cinema) and Bangalore (Kannada cinema). In 1993, according to official statistics, 183 films were made in Hindi, 168 in Tamil, 148 in Telugu, 78 in Kannada, 71 in Malayalam, 57 in Bengali, 35 in Marathi and ten in Assamese.[10] These regional cinemas should not be seen as existing in complete isolation from each other, as there is considerable crossover in terms of actors and personnel and there are shared conventions of story-telling between them, but they do nevertheless represent a degree of diversity and cultural difference within Indian national cinema that is unparalleled anywhere else in the world.

CINEMA AND SOCIETY FROM ORIGINS TO INDEPENDENCE

The first films were exhibited in India in 1896 and the sub-continent soon became a favourite location for western filmmakers who were keen to capture its exotic scenery for travelogues and actualities. As elsewhere, films were first treated as an attraction for élite audiences – the Cinématographe Lumière was unveiled at the posh Watson Hotel of Bombay on 7 July 1896 – but quickly became more widely disseminated through less socially exclusive and expensive venues. Early film exhibition in India took the form of travelling tent theatres, with the first purpose-built cinemas appearing from *c.* 1910. Unlike in America, where many of the nickelodeons were run by first-generation European immigrants, film exhibition in India was largely the preserve of an indigenous class of traders and entrepreneurs who invested in the entertainment industries. The most powerful exhibitor before the First World War was Jamsedjee Framjee Madan, a former actor who bought a chain of theatres and repertory companies in the early 1900s and later converted them into projection houses when he acquired the distribution rights for Pathé films. At its peak Madan Theatres amounted to 172 theatrical holdings throughout the sub-continent and is estimated to have accounted for half the national box-office.

As elsewhere in the world, early cinema in India can be seen both as a new attraction in its own right (the Cinématographe Lumière was advertised as 'the marvel of the century') and placed within existing traditions of theatrical and visual culture. India already had a thriving theatre industry by the late nineteenth century, particularly the Parsee theatre which has sometimes been placed in a direct lineage of descent to the Hindi movie. Genres such as the 'mythological' and the 'historical' were characteristic of Parsee theatre, which translated Indian myths and stories into the vernacular and included musical interludes. There was also a well-established tradition of visual culture in the form of what has come to be known as the 'Company School' of painting (Indian art produced for British and high caste Indian clients, named after the East India Company). The style of bazaar paintings and woodcuts, often used to represent mythological and religious scenes, would also feed into film. In their study of the visual culture of Hindi film, Rachel Dwyer and Divia Patel suggest that three particular arts (photography, chromolithography and theatre) 'were then taken into cinema, which was to develop its own art forms, such as backdrops and, later, sets, to create a whole *mise-en-scène*, the origins of which are interwoven with the earlier industrial art forms'.[11] It is significant in this regard that several early film pioneers came to the cinema from artistic backgrounds: D. G.

Phalke, for example, had been a painter, photographer and printer before making films. Phalke (also known as Dadasaheb Phalke) was not, as is often claimed, the first Indian film director – in fact he was a relative latecomer to cinema, not seeing his first film until 1910 – though, rather like Griffith in America, he was prolific and came to be associated with a particular type of film, the mythological (*Raja Harishchandra*, *The Life of Krishna* and *Kaliya Mardan*). It was Phalke who built the first film studio in India, in Bombay, in 1912.

The sheer size of India – which, before Partition in 1947, also encompassed modern Pakistan and Bangladesh – is the principal reason why an indigenous production sector could be more securely established than in the smaller countries of Africa or Latin America. By the 1920s an embryonic studio system was emerging: the Kohinoor Film Company in Bombay, set up by the pioneer D. N. Sampat; the Imperial Film Company, also in Bombay, founded by former exhibitor Ardeshir Irani; the Maharashtra Film Company in Kohlapur, financed by the Maharajah of Kohlapur; and the Indian Kinema Company in Calcutta. The level of film production increased significantly during the 1920s, rising from 18 features in 1920 to 40 in 1921 and 80 in 1925. In total an estimated 1,313 silent films were made in India, though this still represented a minority (approximately 15 per cent) of those exhibited. Already, in the 1920s, there is evidence of diversification within the exhibition sector as certain cinemas showed only Indian films while others specialized in American and European imports.

The popularity of cinema was soon to become a cultural and political issue. The Indian National Congress, formed originally in 1885 as an educational movement but by the interwar years becoming increasingly politicized, urged a boycott of imported goods (cultural as well as material) and promoted the concept of *swadeshi* ('own country'). Film, as an increasingly popular medium of cultural representation, became part of this movement. Phalke, for example, made a point of using Indian actors and technical personnel: 'My films are *swadeshi* in the sense that the ownership, employees and stories are *swadeshi*'.[12] Indian filmmakers turned to their own myths and legends, with many productions inspired by the epics the *Ramayana* and the

Mahabharata. It was during the silent era that the mythological, arguably the first distinctively Indian film genre, became established. The mythological has been described as 'a unique product of Indian cinema in the way that the Western is of Hollywood'.[13] These tales of gods and demons, characterized by their strong moral codes in which good triumphs over evil, 'helped to define an indigenous audience within specific distribution circuits'.[14] At the same time, however, the success of indigenous Indian films did not detract from the popularity of Hollywood movies, especially adventure films and comedies. To this extent the policy of *swadeshi* was only partially successful. As the Indian Cinematograph Committee reported in 1928:

> There is no prejudice against western films, which are much enjoyed and appreciated. There are certain types of western films which appeal to all classes and communities. The spectacular super-films and the films featuring Douglas Fairbanks, Harold Lloyd and Charlie Chaplin have a universal appeal. A film in which any of these world-famous figures of the screen appears can be sure of an enthusiastic reception in any cinema in India. The most popular film ever shown in India was *The Thief of Baghdad* [*sic*], with Douglas Fairbanks in an Oriental setting.[15]

This is further evidence of the universal appeal of silent film, which, due to its reliance on the visual image, was easily understood and assimilated regardless of linguistic and cultural differences.

The arrival of talking pictures – the first Indian 'talkie', *Alam Ara*, was produced in 1931 – was, as elsewhere, a historical turning point for Indian cinema. Most of the production companies of the silent era closed down in the early 1930s and were replaced by new studios equipped for sound, of which the 'big three' were the Prabhat Film Company of Pune, New Theatres of Calcutta and Bombay Talkies. The arrival of talking pictures, argues Prem Chowdhry, 'revolutionised the audiences' reactions to the western as well as Indian films'.[16] The audience for western films seems to have declined in the 1930s: although there is little statistical evidence, this can be deduced from the fact that western films tended to be shown in fewer cinemas, usually located in more upper-class neighbourhoods. Of the 40 cinemas in Bombay during the 1930s, for example, only two regularly screened western films. There is anecdotal evidence to suggest that Indian audiences preferred Hollywood to British films. As Satyajit Ray revealed in his autobiography:

> In the 1930s there used to be two cinemas next to each other in the heart of Calcutta's theatreland. The first one, as you came up the street that contained them, showed only British films, while the other specialised in American product. I was at school then and had already become something of a film addict. On Saturday afternoons I used to turn in at the side street and make a beeline for the second cinema, casting a contemptuous sidelong glance at the first one *en route*.[17]

The most popular foreign films with Indian audiences appear to have been action-adventures, depending on spectacle rather than dialogue, including Hollywood's Northwest Frontier epics such as *The Lives of a Bengal Lancer* and *Gunga Din*, which seem to have been popular with Indian cinema-goers if not with nationalists or intellectuals.[18] Indian producers, never slow to spot a trend, responded with a series of indigenous adventure films in the late 1930s and early 1940s, the most successful of which starred 'Fearless Nadia' (screen name of Australian-born circus performer Mary Evans) and were inspired by the Pearl White serials. Chowdhry asserts that films such as *Hunterwali*, *Miss Frontier Mail* and *Diamond Queen* 'had an unmistakable nationalist message' in their narratives of a warrior woman fighting against oppressive tyrants and argues that British-made Northwest Frontier films such as *The Drum* were produced in response 'to negate the national message'.[19]

The domestic production industry was boosted by the popularity of indigenous films in the vernacular tongue. The origins of the regional cinemas of present-day India can be identified in the 1930s as the first films were made in Bengali (*Jamai Sasthi*, 1931), Tamil (*Kalidas*, 1931), Telugu (*Bhaka Prahlada*, 1931), Marathi (*Ayodhyecha Raja*, 1932), Gujarati (*Narasinha Mehta*, 1932), Assamese (*Joymati*, 1935), Oriya (*Sita Bibaha*, 1936),

Punjabi (*Pind Di Kudi*, 1936) and Malayalam (*Balam*, 1938).[20] However, it was the Bombay-based Hindi cinema that became the dominant mode of film practice and which has ever since been equated with the national film industry of India. In fact, most 'Hindi' films are made in a language known as *filmi Hindistani*, a vernacular combination of Hindi and Urdu which is understood by both Hindu and Muslim audiences and which helps to explain why the 'Hindi' film reached the widest audience, especially in the north. According to the trade paper *Film India* the Punjab was 'the biggest market for films'.[21]

The 1930s is generally regarded as the 'first golden age' of Indian cinema (a second occurred during the 1950s). The different trends within Indian filmmaking tend to be associated with the three main studios, and, while this is probably something of an over-simplification, the notion of studio style is as relevant for the Indian film industry as it is for Hollywood during the same period. Prabhat and New Theatres embraced a tradition of realistic literary adaptations of Indian writers such as Bankim Chandra Chattopadhyay and Rabindranath Tagore. It is, perhaps, a sign of the extent to which British aesthetic values had been absorbed into Indian cultural production that this tradition of serious filmmaking should be posited on the notions of social realism and literary 'quality'. The landmark films in this tradition were P. C. Barua's *Devdas* (1935), for New Theatres, a tragic melodrama of the son of a feudal lord who descends into alcoholism and despair when caste differences prevent him from marrying his childhood sweetheart, and V. Damle and S. Fattelal's *Sant Tukaram* (1937), for Prabhat, a 'devotional' (a biographical story of a religious figure) which became the first Indian film to win a festival award (at Venice in 1937). Bombay Talkies, by contrast, has tended to be associated with 'garish imitation of Hollywood entertainment'.[22] Bombay's *Achhut Kanya* (*The Untouchable Girl*, 1936) is credited with establishing the popular screen image of rural India with its stock characterizations of landowner, peasant and innocent hero struggling against hardship. In the 1940s Bombay Talkies was superseded by Filmistan, which more than any other studio was responsible for establishing the song-and-dance fantasy film as a mainstream genre of Indian cinema.

The audience for films in India during the 1930s and 1940s was both large and socially diverse. While the number of permanent cinemas might seem small by western standards – in 1939 there were 1,265 – these were supplemented by touring and 'seasonal' cinemas for which no statistics exist. The travelling cinemas extended the reach of film into remote areas of the interior, moving from one village to another. As old western films could be purchased more cheaply than indigenous films, Hollywood movies tended to be the diet of the travelling cinemas, while Indian films would more often be shown in the permanent sites. The cinema audience swelled during the Second World War when it was the main form of entertainment for troops, including both the British and Indian armies.

The fact of British colonial rule meant that film censorship was exercised by the British authorities. Censorship had been introduced by the Cinematograph Act of 1918 which set up regional boards of censors in Bombay, Calcutta, Madras and Rangoon; a fifth board was established in Lahore in 1927. The system was at best confused, for while each regional board was empowered to certify a film for the entire country, provincial authorities retained the right to decertify a film deemed unsuitable for exhibition in the province. The ethnic composition of the boards varied (the Bombay board, for example, included representatives of the Hindu, Muslim and Parsi communities) but each board was chaired by a police commissioner who was invariably British and with whom the final decision rested. The role of the regional boards, as Chowdhry remarks, was 'to keep moral, racial, religious and political considerations in view . . . lest the British position in India be compromised'.[23] It was for this reason that, during the Second World War, imperial adventure films were withdrawn from circulation and both British and American producers shelved plans to make further Northwest Frontier epics. The genre would re-emerge only after Independence.

As far as cinema is concerned, the immediate consequences of Independence in 1947 were mixed. The creation of the new states of Pakistan and East Pakistan (later Bangladesh) meant that a substantial section of the cinema audience was lost. It could be argued, indeed, that Indian cinema lost some of its cultural diversity following Partition, as the loss of half of the Bengali-speaking market, in particular, meant that studios in Calcutta either scaled back production or turned to making films in Hindi. At the same time, however, new production centres emerged in the south to challenge the dominance of Bombay: the Udaya studios of Kerala, founded in 1947, became the leading producer of Malayalam cinema, and the popular success of S. S. Vasan's historical spectacular *Chandralekha* (1948) has been seen as marking the beginning of Tamil popular cinema. Tamil cinema, in particular, came to be associated with political and cultural regionalism due to the involvement of film personnel in the Tamil regionalist Dravida Munnetra Kazhagam (DMK) Party. Bengali cinema, which was to come to prominence in the 1950s principally due to the films of Satyajit Ray, embraced a tradition of 'art cinema' that was distinct from the mainstream Bombay film industry.

The policy of the Indian government towards the film industry was also mixed. There had been some hope in the industry in the immediate aftermath of Independence that the Nehru government would recognize film as a medium of national importance and would take an active role in promoting it as a vehicle of cultural representation. In 1950 Nehru appointed a Film Enquiry Committee under S. K. Patil, but its report, published the following year, was disappointing to the industry. The committee had been most concerned with the dramatic expansion of the industry following the Second World War – levels of production had risen from 99 features in 1945 to 199 in 1946 and 280 in 1947 – which was due in large measure to the influx of independent financier-producers who made their fortunes from the 'black economy' of the war and saw the film industry as a way of making quick returns on their investments. The government was happy to raise income by increasing the tax on ticket sales, though it was much slower to act on the committee's recommendation to establish a Film Finance Corporation to assist production (this was eventually set up in 1960) and a Film Institute (established at Pune in 1961). The government was quicker to centralize the apparatus of censorship, replacing the system of regional boards in 1952 with a Board of Censors that was empowered to certify films as either 'U' (universal) or 'A' (adult) and to insist upon such cuts or alterations it deemed fit. The new board was socially even more censorious than the previous colonial regime, banning almost all sexual content from films (including 'indecorous dancing') and thereby determining that the representation of sex in Indian film would take the form of chaste romantic love rather than sexual passion. The authority of the Board of Censors was challenged (unsuccessfully) in the Indian Supreme Court on the grounds that it contravened the constitutional right to freedom of expression.[24]

THE POLITICAL ECONOMY OF BOLLYWOOD

In the decade following Independence domestic production in India hovered between 250 and 325 feature films a year. Levels of production increased steadily during the 1960s and in 1971 India overtook Japan as the leading world producer with 431 features. A Unesco survey of 1975 found that India was the only nation in the developing world to have a larger audience for domestic films than for imported films. Production boomed during the 1970s, exceeding 700 films a year by the end of the decade. By 1983 the film industry was India's sixth-largest industry, employing 300,000 people and grossing the equivalent of $600 million annually. Film production peaked in 1990 when an astonishing 950 features were made, five times more than Hollywood. At a time when cinema-going has been in decline in most countries, India has bucked the trend: there are over 13,000 cinemas (half of them permanent, the other half touring) and an average audience of 65 million people per week.[25] The statistical evidence, at least, is suggestive of a healthy and robust industry.

Yet for a national cinema that has become the most prolific in the world, the economic base of the Indian film industry has been remarkably unstable throughout much of its history. Indian filmmaker Kumar Shahani once remarked: 'The biggest problem seems to be that we are working within a capitalist framework and we do not have a capitalist infrastructure. It is all run on highly speculative lines.'[26] Unlike the US film industry, which has been dominated by much the same oligopoly since the 1930s, the Indian film industry has been characterized by a plethora of producers and the rise and fall of many companies. The lack of vertical integration means that film production has always been a risky undertaking; economic power rests with distributors and exhibitors rather than producers. Lacking a secure economic base, the production sector has relied on unconventional sources of finance. This problem is a legacy of the 'black economy' of the Second World War. In 1951 the Patil Committee had been highly critical of the kind of people investing in the film industry:

> Within three years of the end of the War, the leadership of the industry had changed hands from established producers to a variety of successors. Leading 'stars', exacting 'financiers' and calculating distributors and exhibitors forged ahead. Film production, a combination of art, industry and showmanship, became in substantial measure the recourse of deluded aspirants to easy riches.[27]

Das Gupta suggests that the majority of film finance 'comes largely from a parallel economy lying outside the pale of the legitimate organised sector of banking and insurance and manufacturing industries'.[28] For many years, indeed, it has been alleged that film production has been a channel of money laundering for organized crime.

In his study of the relationship between economics and cultural production in Hindi cinema, M. Madhava Prasad explores tensions within that mode of film practice, arguing that 'the mode of production in the Hindi film industry is characterized by fragmentation of the production apparatus, subordination of the production process to a moment of the self-valorization of merchant capital, the consequent externality of capital to the production process, the resistance of the rentier class of exhibitors to the expansionist drive of the logic of the market, and the functional centrality of the distributor-financier to the entire process of film-making'.[29] Prasad advances a Marxist interpretation of the political economy of Hindi cinema in which the finished product indelibly bears the mark of the production process that created it and is imbued with the ideology of its financiers. The ideologies of the Hindi film, Prasad suggests, revolve around pre-capitalist values such as feudalism, servitude, the honour of the clan (*khandaan*) and institutionalized religion. He rejects the suggestion that popular Indian film responds to the tastes of the local audience and insists that films are 'works of ideology, not mirrors of reality'.[30]

What differentiates this mode of production from the Hollywood studio system, argues Prasad, is that the Hindi film is produced via a 'heterogeneous form of manufacture in which the whole is assembled from parts produced separately by specialists, rather than being centralized around the processing of a given material, as in serial or organic manufacture'.[31] Thus, separate units work independently on different aspects of the production (dialogue, songs, dances) which are then combined. Whereas in Hollywood the story or scenario is seen as the primary raw material, around which other components of the film are structured, this is not the case in the Bombay film industry where other elements, particularly the music, are of equal or even greater importance. The style of the Hindi film, with its highly conventionalized plots and stock characterizations, does not require a shooting script in the same way as a Hollywood movie: variations tend to be the work of specialists (song writers, dance choreographers and action directors). As Prasad observes: 'The different component elements have not been subsumed under the dominance of a cinema committed to narrative coherence.'[32] Only a handful of producers, such as Yash Chopra in the modern period, have been able to assert their control over the entirety of the production process.

The dependency of producers on merchant capital means that they are at the mercy of financiers who often charge interest rates of up to 60 per cent, which means that a film has to gross even more at the box-office to make a profit. Despite the high level of production, the ratio of success to failure for Indian cinema is as poor as in most other film industries. In 1989, for example, an estimated 95 per cent of theatrical releases failed to earn back their production costs.[33] It is difficult to find statistics relating to costs, though there are estimates of over £5 million for some big-budget films.[34] While this may seem small in comparison to Hollywood, the level of capital investment in relation to Gross National Product is roughly comparable to the cost of production in the West. Around 80 per cent of the budget of an average film is consumed by sets and by the high fees of stars.

Stars enjoy greater autonomy – and consequently greater economic power – than they ever did in the Hollywood studio system. This was a direct consequence of the disintegration of the Indian studio system in the 1940s (anticipating similar developments in Hollywood a decade or so later) and the shift of power within the industry away from the producers. Stars, idolized in Indian society, are able to command massive salaries; they are not tied to studio contracts and are thus able not only to choose their own roles but also to approve scripts, costumes and other aspects of production. From the early 1950s, Vijay Mishra observes, 'the "star" became the single most important aspect in the production, circulation and exhibition of films.'[35] It is significant that many of the major Indian film stars – Raj Kapoor and Dilip Kumar in the 1950s and 1960s, Amitabh Bachchan in the 1970s and 1980s – have also been involved in the production of their own films. Star power persists into the new millennium: the box-office hit *Lagaan* (2001), brainchild of unproven writer-director Ashutosh Gowariker, came to be made only through the involvement of star Aamir Khan as producer.

The relationship between the film and music industries is of central importance to the political economy of Indian cinema, though there has been little research devoted to it. Often dismissed by western commentators as mere kitsch, the musical interludes are in fact an inevitable consequence of the peculiar economic and cultural conditions of Indian cinema. Indian filmmakers started introducing songs with the arrival of sound, and this practice became so popular that very soon almost all films included musical numbers. Initially film stars sang their own songs but during the 1940s they began using so-called 'playback singers' to provide the vocals which the actors would then lip-synch. Movie songs became so popular in their own right that they were disseminated first by radio, then by record and cassette, enjoying a life of their own (and generating further income) beyond the film. The Indian film industry, indeed, was the first to recognize the commercial value of the soundtrack. In recent decades the licensing of music has become even more important to the economic fortunes of the film industry: many films are financed by the pre-sale of music rights and a film's success at the box-office might depend on the merits of its soundtrack. Thus, whereas a Hollywood movie receiving negative feedback from preview audiences would most likely have its ending rewritten, in the case of a Bollywood movie it is the songs that would be revised rather than the story. 'Indian audiences can accept repetition in storylines; they are resigned to stock characters and predictable dialogue', one critic remarks. 'But they will reject a film's music if it has no originality.'[36]

The problems faced by producers are exacerbated by the uncertainty of distribution. There is only one national distribution network in India (Rajshri); thus producers have to negotiate with regional distributors (the country is divided into five 'territories', of which Bombay and Delhi are the most lucrative). The marketing of films has expanded significantly in recent years, with television publicity and musical sales becoming increasingly important. One of the most popular genres on Indian television since the late 1980s has been the compilation programme of song sequences from films, which serves a twofold function: it raises public awareness of films before they are released and provides an indication of how well they might be expected to perform at the box-office (it is a rule of thumb that a popular soundtrack will result in good initial business for the film concerned).

What of the relationship between the film industry and the state? It is probably fair to say that the film industry has thrived despite rather than because of government policy. It is ironic that while the Patil Committee had criticized the 'deluded aspirants to easy riches' who invested in filmmaking, producers had been forced to turn to unorthodox sources of finance partly because the government refused officially to recognize film as an industry – thus denying it access to banks and insurance. Successive Indian governments have always been more interested in supporting alternative filmmaking practices than in the commercial film industry. In 1949 the Nehru government set up a Films Division to produce documentaries: inspired by the pre-war British documentary movement, the Films Division became one of the largest documentary production units in the world, producing some 200 short films a year, mostly ethno-graphic documentaries. Basil Wright, who was involved with the Films Division in the 1960s, considered – unsurprisingly – that it 'has over the years come to play an increasingly important role in Indian life'.[37] The Film Finance Corporation (FFC) was set up in 1960 with a remit to support 'the production of films of good standard': it soon became clear this meant realistic, socially aware films rather than the escapist entertainments of the Bombay studios. In 1976 the FFC was criticized for its 'art film' policy by the Committee on Public Undertakings which asserted that 'there is no inherent contradiction between artistic films of good standard and films successful at the box office'.[38] The FFC was replaced in 1980 by the National Film Development Corporation (NFDC), which helped to fund over 200 films through a system of loans and co-financing arrangements until it was wound up in 1992. The NFDC was also empowered to import foreign films and to invest in international co-productions, such as Richard Attenborough's production of *Gandhi* (1983).

The Indian film industry embodies an odd, indeed probably unique, combination of a chronically unstable economic base and an almost complete dominance of its home market. In this regard, at least, the industry has reaped some tangential benefit from government policy. When the government increased taxes on foreign films in 1960 and again in 1963, the US Motion Picture Export Association responded with a boycott of the Indian market. Although American films accounted for only three per cent of the Indian box-office, they tended to be booked into the biggest and most prestigious cinemas in urban locations, which, in the absence of new Hollywood product, then became available to Indian films.[39] No new American films were sent to India until 1975 when the MPEA signed a deal with the authorities to allow around 120 films a year to be imported. Even then, however, Indian films continued to take 95 per cent of the domestic box-office.[40] The relaxation of trade barriers in the 1990s brought about a concerted effort by the MPEA to open up the Indian market, spearheaded by *Jurassic Park*, which became the most successful western film ever shown in India. Yet even so Indian audiences have remained loyal to their home product, suggesting a strong degree of cultural resistance to Americanization. This resistance might be posited to some degree on the cultural difference of Indian and Hollywood cinema: in India, at least, it is Hollywood that represents the minority 'alternative' to a dominant national cinema.

One of the strengths of the Indian film industry, furthermore, is that it enjoys strong exports. The economic importance of exports increased significantly when the establishment of the new Republic of Bangladesh in 1971 (following the collapse of East Pakistan) brought a potential audience of 50 million people within the orbit of the Indian film industry. This partly explains the increase in production during the 1970s. It is only in the 1990s, however, that the full potential of the export market has been realized. India has one of the largest non-resident populations in the world, with large numbers of expatriates living in Britain, Europe, North America and throughout Southeast Asia. The introduction of video cassette in the 1980s opened up a previously untapped market for Indian films. In 1991–2 the overseas video market was worth over 100 million rupees (us$2.5 million); the leading markets for the export of Indian films on video are Britain, Singapore, Hong Kong, the United Arab Emirates, the United States, Canada, Nigeria, Kenya and Malaysia.[41] The expansion of multiplex cinemas has resulted in a growing theatrical presence for Indian films, which is economically significant given that higher ticket prices (in Britain and America over ten times the cost of a ticket in India) means a proportionately higher gross from those markets. It is estimated that up to 65 per cent of a film's box-office gross may come from overseas. Certain recent films have clearly been made with the diasporic audience in mind: Yash Chopra's *Dilwale Dulhaniya Le Jayenge* (1995) and Karan Johar's *Kabhi Khusi Kabhie Gham* (2001) focus on Indians living in Britain and the choices they have to make between different cultures. Diasporic films, Dwyer and Patel argue, are posited on 'celebrating a notion of Indianness that is not dependent on being an Indian citizen but on upholding "Indian values"'.[42]

Critical accounts of Indian cinema have all, to some extent, demonstrated 'the tendency to define the mainstream Indian cinema as playing a kind of default role, making Hindi the national film language and creating . . . a nationally integrated cultural domain'.[43] Hindi film is seen, following Das Gupta's categorization of the 'All-India Film', as the dominant vehicle for the promotion of national unity and social cohesion in a nation where religious, caste and linguistic differences represent fundamental problems to easy concepts of 'the national'. This has not always been the case. In the years following Independence Indian film culture was polarized, to a greater extent than before or since, between two notions of cinema: the art cinema tradition of Satyajit Ray on the one hand, the commercial world of the Hindi film on the other. As this was the period in which a national film culture was forged, and as this polarization continues to inform much writing on Indian cinema, it requires discussion.

It is ironic that the critical 'discovery' of popular Indian cinema has, to a large extent, been at the expense of the director who did most to bring international critical acclaim to the Indian film.[44] Of course there is more to Indian art cinema than just Satyajit Ray. The trend for serious literary adaptations in the 1930s could be placed in the same lineage, as could the work of the Indian Peoples' Theatre Association (IPTA), a Communist Party-backed theatre and film movement that sponsored realistic films addressing social problems. A number of important filmmakers were involved with the IPTA, including K. K. Abbas, Mehboob Khan, Bimal Roy and Guru Dutt. Basil Wright, whose view of film history was nothing if not teleological, admired Abbas's *Munna* (1953) and Roy's *Do Bigha Zamin* (*Two Acres of Land*, 1954) because they 'had a truth and sincerity about them which was almost unheard of in the world of Indian entertainment films', but still considered them 'two John the Baptists, so to speak, to prepare for Ray's coming'.[45] Such caveats aside, however, the significance of Ray's work to the cultural and aesthetic reputation of Indian cinema cannot be exaggerated. He is India's one indisputable *auteur*. His 'Apu trilogy' – *Pather Panchali* (*Song of the Road*, 1955), *Aparajito* (*The Unvanquished*, 1956) and *Apur Sansar* (*The World of Apu*, 1959) – which chronicled the youth, adolescence and early adulthood of an Indian village boy 'provided Indian cinema with its first internationally significant works of art'.[46] Ray's films were acclaimed abroad and won many festival prizes – he won the Silver Bear at Berlin two years in succession for *Mahanagar* (*The Big City*, 1964) and *Charaluta* (*The Lonely Wife*, 1965) – though his greatest commercial success in India came with a children's film, *Goopy Gyne Bagha Byne* (*The Adventures of Goopy and Bagha*, 1969).

Ray's films could not be more different from the all-singing, all-dancing stereotype of the commercial Hindi movie: they are understated, artfully crafted, both aesthetically and psychologically realistic, and, above all else, intricately concerned with the intimate drama of everyday life. Ephraim Katz, for instance, calls *Pather Panchali* '[a] human document of timeless simplicity and exquisite beauty' and admires the Apu trilogy for its 'authenticity, sincerity, beauty, and magic'.[47] A university graduate, hailing from a middle-class Bengali background, Ray was consciously part of an Indian intelligentsia that cultivated an affinity with European culture. He was one of the founders of the Calcutta Film Society in 1948 and was influenced by Italian Neo-Realist films such as De Sica's *Bicycle Thieves* as well as by the work of film theorists Rudolf Arnheim and Paul Rotha. Ray echoed the Neo-Realists in his belief that the social purpose of filmmaking should be 'the revelation of the truth of human behaviour'.[48] He preferred filming in black-and-white to the garish colour that was becoming standard for the commercial cinema by the end of the 1950s and favoured location shooting and naturalistic lighting to enhance the realism of his films.

Pather Panchali had been made with financial assistance from the West Bengal regional government, which allegedly believed it was a documentary about the road-building programme. An adaptation of a novel by Bengali author Bibhutibhushan Bandapadhaya, its literary origins and aesthetic of 'regional realism' established the criteria by which the Indian art cinema would be judged. In fact, as Derek Malcolm notes, 'Ray was constantly criticised in some Indian circles for not being Indian enough, not being radical enough in either content or style, and adhering to an old-fashioned liberal humanism that would put him in the good books of the West.'[49] Such criticisms were more than a little unfair: Ray was not an overtly political filmmaker and he preferred to work in an idiom that was accessible rather than inclined towards the avant-garde. Some of his later films did employ modernist devices such as flashbacks and freeze frames, though he admitted to being uncomfortable with this style: 'As if being modern for a film-maker consisted solely in how he juggles with his visuals and not in his attitude to life that he expressed through the film.'[50]

Ray's emergence coincided with the heyday of the Hindi social melodrama, the genre that has been the focus of much of the recent theoretical work on Indian cinema. There is still a tendency to construct Ray in opposition to the Hindi film – indeed, Ray had already done this himself in his own critical writings – though their obvious stylistic differences should not disguise the fact that the two traditions emerged from much the same cultural context. Both, for example, are concerned with the relationship between tradition and modernity, a theme that has preoccupied filmmakers throughout the Third World. The 'second golden age' of Indian cinema in the 1950s witnessed the production of a cycle of social melodramas, often made by directors involved with the IPTA such as Mehboob Khan (*Andaz*, *Amar*) and Guru Dutt (*Aar Paar*, *Pyaasa*). 'In the Bombay cinema of the 1950s', writes Ravi Vasudevan, 'the "social" film . . . was the genre which the industry understood to address the issues of modern life.'[51] Far from being entirely divorced from reality, as its critics have so often alleged, the Hindi film of the 1950s was in fact very much concerned with the examination of social problems arising from modernization, migration and urbanization.

'The epic melodrama of this period', Ashish Rajadhyaksha asserts, 'remains the closest India came to defining for itself an identifiable mass culture of nationalism.'[52] The classic foundational text in all accounts of Indian cinema is Mehboob Khan's *Mother India* (1957). Salman Rushdie later summarized the cultural and iconic significance of this film in his novel *The Moor's Last Sigh*:

The year I was born, Mehboob Productions' all-conquering movie *Mother India* – three years in the making, three hundred shooting days, in the top three all-time mega-grossing Bollywood flicks – hit the nation's screens. Nobody who saw it ever forgot that glutinous saga of peasant heroinism [sic], that super-slushy ode to the uncrushability of village India made by the most cynical urbanites in the world. And as for its leading lady – O Nargis with your shovel over your shoulder and your strand of black hair tumbling forward over your brow! – she became, until Indira-Mata supplanted her, the living mother-goddess of us all.[53]

Mother India is an epic saga of an abandoned wife Radha (played by Nargis, the foremost female star of the 1950s) who has to farm the land whilst raising her two sons. The film is rooted in the conventions of the village melodrama – Khan had explored similar themes in his 1940 film *Aurat* – which was a staple of Indian cinema both before and after Independence. *Mother India* promotes the virtue of stoicism in the face of hardship: 'As we were born to the world, we must live in it. If life is a poison, we must drink it', Radha sings as she toils in the fields. It uses melodramatic conventions to resolve social problems (through the conventional subplot of good son/bad son) and to dramatize Radha's sacrifice (at one point she prostitutes herself to the odious village moneylender in order to buy food for her sons). Yet for all the hardships and suffering endured, the film presents an ultimately positive image of a united social fabric. It maintains traditional social values (to the extent of Radha killing her 'bad' son Birju who has raped the landlord's daughter) whilst embracing modernity and progress (Radha is honoured by the state by being asked to open a new dam, thus relating the film to the ideology of technological progress embraced by the Nehru government). As Mishra observes: '*Mother India* is, quite defiantly, not a religious but a secular epic of the new, modern India where a universal moral principle transcending religious and caste differences is the dominant dharma.'[54] The figure of Nargis/Radha has been claimed both as an emblem of female empowerment and as a nationalist

statement about the strength of the Indian character in the face of social distress.[55]

The differences between Ray's films and the Hindi social melodrama, therefore, were not so much thematic (both were concerned with modernization and social change) as they were stylistic (understated realism versus melodramatic convention) and industrial-cultural (state-supported cinema for the intelligentsia versus commercial mass entertainment). It was the former school which the Film Finance Corporation preferred, supporting the production of several of Ray's films during the 1960s. Influenced to some extent by Ray's naturalism, American director James Ivory, working in association with Indian producer Ismail Merchant and German-born Polish-Jewish writer Ruth Prawer Jhabvala, was responsible for a number of intelligent, critically acclaimed social satires (*The Householder*, *Shakespeare Wallah*, *The Guru*) during the 1960s. In the early 1970s a more politicized cinema was signalled by the work of a group of directors such as Mani Kaul, Mrinal Sen and Kumar Shanani who came to be known as the New Indian Cinema. With the support of the FFC and the guidance of the veteran of Indian political cinema Ritwik Ghatak, these filmmakers adopted the conventions of political modernism (Brechtian reflexivity, direct address to the camera) characteristic of the Third Cinema paradigm. Their efforts, however, were hampered by poor distribution and their films were not widely seen. It was not until Mira Nair's powerful *Salaam Bombay!* (1987) that a critique of social deprivation reached a wide audience. Nair, a documentarist by training, used the techniques of Neo-Realism, employing real street people in preference to professional actors, to create a vivid portrait of a street urchin's perilous existence amongst the prostitutes and drug addicts of modern Bombay. The film won two prizes at the Cannes Film Festival (the Camera d'Or for first feature and the Prix de Publique) and proved that the tradition of socially realistic Indian art cinema continued alongside the garish world of the Bombay studios.

FORM AND STYLE

The critical success of Satyajit Ray's films in the West is to a very great extent due to their formal similarity to the realistic style of much European cinema. The popular Indian cinema, in contrast, is so different from conventional aesthetic assumptions of what a film should be like that it remains unfathomable to western eyes. 'Compared with the conventions of much Western cinema', Rosie Thomas remarks, 'Hindi films appear to have patently preposterous narratives, overblown dialogue (frequently evaluated by filmmakers on whether or not it is "clap-worthy"), exaggeratedly stylized acting, and to show disregard for psychological characterization, history, geography, and even, sometimes, camera placement rules.'[56] It is these elements that have caused Hindi/Indian cinema to be regarded as kitsch or claimed as an 'alternative' to classical Hollywood. In so many regards it is the antithesis of classicism: it does not conform to any regime of verisimilitude, it is highly melodramatic, it privileges performance over characterization and style over narrative. It is a cinema of spectacle, a cinema of excess, a cinema of stylization.

In order to understand Hindi cinema in its social and cultural contexts, however, it is necessary to try to see it not in terms of difference but as a coherent set of formal and stylistic practices. This claim is less absurd than it might first seem: the historical period of the Hindi movie has lasted longer than that of classical Hollywood (the most oft-cited example of film style) and is bound even more rigorously by its own rules and conventions. Hindi film has been described as a 'complete spectacle': it is an entertainment package designed for a large, impoverished, partially illiterate, culturally diverse audience.[57] Thus Hindi film affords prominence to universal themes that cross cultural and linguistic boundaries (love, death, faith, revenge) and expresses them through visual style (*mise-en-scène*, sets, costumes) rather than complex narratives. Hindi film took the form it did due to a variety of cultural, industrial and ideological determinants. Whereas classical Hollywood cinema drew upon the storytelling conventions of the nineteenth-century classic realist novel, Hindi cinema was influenced by existing cultural practices including both Sanskrit theatre (highly stylized dance dramas) and Parsee theatre (melodramatic plays which blended realism and fantasy, music and dance, and narrative and spectacle). The best way of understanding Hindi film is to see it not in terms of a cinema of narrative integration but rather, as Ravi Vasudevan suggests, as being 'loosely structured in the fashion of a cinema of attractions'.[58]

The main 'attractions' of Hindi film, according to Dwyer and Patel, 'include the sets and costumes, action sequences ("thrills"), presentation of the stars, grandiloquent dialogues, song and dance sequences, comedy interludes and special effects'.[59] Hindi films are made as vehicles for star performance rather than as character-driven dramas: performance is usually theatrical (in the case of melodramatic actors) and physical (comedians and action stars). The *mise-en-scène* is at least as important to the style of the film as the narrative (unlike classical cinema where *mise-en-scène* supports the narrative rather than distracting from it). The sets and dressings of most films are contemporary, indicative of modernity and 'westernization'. The most lavish and expensive sets, however, appear in historical costume films, which have often provided visual spectacle on a massive scale. This tradition can be dated back to *Mughal-e Azam* (*The Great Mughal*, 1960) which featured stunning sets of the Mughal emperor's palace. It reached probably its zenith in Sanjay Leela Bhansali's visually sumptuous remake of *Devdas* (2001), at 500 million rupees (around £9 million) reportedly the most expensive Indian film ever made. Critic Naman Ramachandran was in no doubt where the budget was spent, pointing out that the characters 'all live in palatial dwellings and wear designer period clothes'. One supposedly poor family 'live in a house that can only be described as a shrine to stained glass, while Chandramukhi's brothel by the lake would put most royal residences to shame'.[60]

Costume is equally important, though here there is usually a difference between male dress which emphasizes modernity (lounge suits in the 1950s, flared trousers in the 1970s, designer casuals in the 1990s) and female dress (which privileges the traditional sari, albeit styled in line with contemporary designer fashion). The 'wet sari' has become a staple of the Indian film, a discrete form of erotic spectacle 'which not only reveals the heroine's body to the point of nudity but is also associated with the erotic mood of the rainy season'.[61] As the films often come to resemble a fashion parade, it is only natural that some of the leading female stars of modern Indian cinema are models and beauty queens, foremost amongst whom is former Miss World Aishwarya Rai (*Taal, Kandukondain Kandukondain, Devdas*).

The most important attractions in defining the uniqueness of Indian film, however, are the musical numbers. Unlike other national cinemas, where the musical is a genre, the label is hardly ever used in respect of Indian film in so far as song and dance are virtually ubiquitous. There is nothing unusual in this as far as Indian audiences are concerned, as 'song and dance have traditionally played an integral role in the life of Indian peoples, whether for religious and devotional purposes or for celebrations such as birthdays and weddings'.[62] It has been said that in the 1950s the Hindi film 'froze this tendency into a formula: an average of six songs and three dances'.[63] Song and dance sequences often take up between a quarter and a third of a film's running time, thus explaining the longer running times of many features (three hours and more is not at all unusual). At first songs were included irrespective of their significance to the narrative, but over time they were increasingly used as an extension of the plot to convey mood and emotion. As in the Hollywood musical, Indian filmmakers employ different strategies to incorporate song and dance into the narrative: sometimes they are narratively motivated (for example the protagonist is a singer, a dancer or a courtesan), sometimes they are used at moments of enhanced emotion (such as a declaration of love) and at other times they represent a form of communal or social ritual. Dance also serves as a form of spectacle in its own right as filmmakers devise ever more ingenious situations: the most famous dance sequence in recent Bollywood cinema is the spectacular opening of Mani Ratnam's *Dil Se* (*With Love*, 1998), staged by choreographer Farah Khan, where the cast dances on top of a moving train. It is not unusual for characters suddenly to switch dress and even location in the middle of a dance: in *Kandukondain Kandukondain* (*I Can See It, I Can See It*, 2000), for example, a dance is staged in front of the Pyramids and Sphinx at Giza for no obvious reason (it is not narratively motivated) other than for the visual possibilities the scenery provides. Such moments again reinforce the idea of Indian film as built around attractions rather than narrative coherence.

GENRES AND STARS

In view of the lack of a stable production base and the plethora of production companies, the history of Indian popular cinema has tended to be written in terms of star-genre combinations rather than studios or producers. Critics have pointed out the difficulties of conceptualizing Indian film genres in the same terms as Hollywood: generic differentiation is far less evident in Bollywood. Indian cinema, to borrow Richard Maltby's terminology, is best understood as 'a generic cinema' rather than as 'a cinema of genres'.[64] This is not to say that there are no identifiable genres in Indian cinema. A standard taxonomy would include 'mythologicals' (fantastical versions of Indian myths and legends), 'devotionals' (stories of religious faith), 'historicals' (films with period settings) and 'socials' (a term that refers to any film with a contemporary setting ranging from crime dramas and thrillers to romances and comedies). Rosie Thomas places these, and other, genres in a historical genealogy:

> By the 1930s a number of distinctly Indian genres were well established. These included socials, mythologicals, devotionals, historicals, and stunt, costume, and fantasy films ... Although genre distinctions began to break down in the 1960s, they are still relevant, not only to an understanding of the range of films made today and in the past, but because the form of the now dominant socials has in fact integrated aspects of all earlier genres.[65]

There is a sense in which the 'social' has become a sort of meta-genre that encompasses a range of other generic forms. Prasad notes that 'the "social" has eluded a precise definition, serving simply as a label for a large quantity of films which resist more accurate differentiation ... The only element that is exclusive to the social and thus critical to its identification as a genre is its contemporary reference.'[66]

The 'social', always present in Indian cinema, became dominant during the 1950s. That was also the decade when the Indian star system in its modern form emerged. Mishra asserts that 'the star system was totally dominated by three names' (Raj Kapoor, Dilip Kumar and Dev Anand) and identifies each star as representing a different archetype that had particular resonances for contemporary society.[67] Raj Kapoor was undoubtedly India's most popular 'golden age' film star. His screen image was that of a Chaplineque 'little man' who battled against social injustice. The film that established him at the forefront of Indian popular cinema was *Awara* (*The Vagabond*, 1951), which he also directed, an oedipal melodrama about an outcast boy raised by the bandit who abducted his mother. Raj eventually avenges himself upon both the bandit and his father, a judge who threw out Raj's mother, and wins the love of the judge's ward. Kapoor played a similar role as an innocent who falls amongst bandits in *Jis Desh Men Ganga Behti Hai* (*Where the Ganges Flows*, 1960), directed by Radhu Karmakar. Kapoor's films, with their mixture of melodrama and song and their simple utopian themes of good overcoming evil and the inequality of wealth and poverty, were widely distributed throughout the Middle East and were also popular in the Soviet Union. Dilip Kumar 'played the role of the tragic hero who would rather lose his love than his duty to his friend'.[68] The film that established him was Bimal Roy's 1955 version of *Devdas*; his greatest popular success came with *Gunga Jumna* (1961), which he wrote and produced, in which he plays a police officer whose brother becomes an outlaw. It spawned a cycle of *dacoit* (rural outlaw) films throughout the 1960s. Dev Anand, whose biggest hit came with *Taxi Driver* (1954), was 'the consummate urban hero, a kind of postcolonial dandy, keeping up with whatever was the current aspiration of the Indian middle classes'.[69] This star triumvirate was dominant throughout the 1950s and much of the 1960s, challenged only by a few others such as singer-comedian Kishore Kumar and Shammi Kapoor, a sort of 'Indian Elvis Presley'. The most popular 'golden age' female stars were Nargis, who until her ground-breaking role in *Mother India* was best known as a romantic interest for Raj Kapoor (*Aag*, *Barsaat*, *Awara*), and Nutan (*Seema*, *Sujata*, *Bandini*), a former child actress who typically portrayed a heroine who suffers from social persecution before finding true love.

The crucial period of change for Indian cinema was to be the 1970s. The 'social' remained prominent throughout the 1960s, albeit following different lineages (crime drama, romantic drama, family melodrama), just as Kapoor (with 1964's romantic drama *Sangam*) and Anand (with 1967's high-tech thriller *Jewel Thief*) extended the boundaries of their star personas. The fragmentation of the 'social' as an identifiable category in the early 1970s coincided with the dislodging of the Kapoor-Kumar-Anand triumvirate. Prasad argues that in the 1970s 'the film industry faced a challenge to its established aesthetic conventions and mode of production' which it met by a strategy of segmentation. This segmentation produced 'three distinct aesthetic formations': the New Indian Cinema (state-supported artistic films), 'the middle-class cinema' (a realist cinema dependent largely upon Bengali culture for its sources and artists) and 'the populist cinema of mobilization' (featuring protagonists from the working classes and other marginalized groups).[70] The key figure in this populist cinema was Amitabh Bachchan, whom Prasad describes as 'the single most important mass cultural phenomenon of the seventies'.[71] Bachchan's emergence as the first Bollywood superstar was based on his roles in action movies such as the police thrillers *Zanjeer* and *Deewar* and the 'curry western' *Sholay*. Bachchan's films downplayed the musical numbers and kept any romantic subplot firmly in the background; instead they foregrounded action sequences and physical violence. The motorcycle-riding, gun-wielding Bachchan was the first anti-hero of Indian cinema, a star persona 'more in tune with slum aesthetics than with the staid expectations of the middle class'.[72] Bachchan's rise to superstardom coincided with a period of severe domestic crisis in India – the rise of urban crime, rampaging inflation and political corruption led to the introduction of a state of emergency by the Prime Minister Mrs Indira Gandhi in 1975 – and his popularity needs to be seen against this background. Rather like the figure of Clint Eastwood's 'Dirty Harry', Bachchan's characters provide uncompromising solutions to social disorder. In his breakthrough film *Zanjeer*, for example, Bachchan plays a police inspector who brings about the demise of a vicious crime lord: while his actions are in the public interest, they also fulfil his desire for revenge in that the villain had murdered his parents. Bachchan was to be the leading star for some two decades – when he nearly died on the set of *Coolie* in 1982 fans across the country thronged temples and mosques to pray – and was still to be found machine-gunning enemies of the state in the 1990s.

What Prasad calls the 'aesthetic of mobilization' continued to inform popular cinema into the 1980s. Increased levels of violence became a major attraction of thrillers and horror films (the Hindi horror movie tended to be a supernatural variant of the low-budget 'slasher' sub-genre that proliferated in Hollywood in the late 1970s and early 1980s). It is one of the paradoxes of Indian film censorship that it will allow all manner of gory deaths whilst maintaining a ban on sex and nudity. Violence against women featured prominently in a cycle of rape-revenge thrillers (*Scales of Justice*, *Retribution*, *Wounded Women*) whose reception sharply divides critical opinion: reviled by some for making entertainment out of misogyny and sexual violence, claimed by others as powerful texts of female empowerment and critical statements of the state's impotence in providing justice for victims of rape.[73] Dwyer and Patel explain the rise of screen violence by the introduction of colour television and the arrival of home video, suggesting, perhaps rather too simplistically, that 'the middle-class audience began watching the new television soaps and viewing films on video at home, while the cinema halls became run down and regarded as suitable only for lower-class men'.[74] The vogue for screen violence extended into the 1990s: the Tamil film *Kaadalan* (1994), a sort of MTV-style western, was one of the biggest hits of the decade.[75]

In contrast to the thrillers and horror films of the 1980s, the most popular genre of the 1990s was the romantic drama. A new generation of romantic young leading men including Shah Rukh Khan (*Dilwale Dulhaniya Le Jayenge*, *Kuch Kuch Hota Hai*) and Aamir Khan (*Rangeela*, *Ghulam*) came to the fore in this genre, which was also successful throughout the Indian diaspora. Dwyer and Patel attribute the success of the romantic drama to the return of middle-class audiences to the cinema in so far as these films 'mark the dominance of the values of the new middle classes and uphold them to the pleasure of a socially mixed audience both in India and overseas. These films revive a form of the feudal family romance in a new, stylish, yet unmistakably Hindu, patriarchal structure.'[76] The genre is not confined to Hindi cinema: *Kandukondain Kandukondain* was described by its distributors as a Tamil version of *Sense and Sensibility*. Several recent films have added an ingeniously self-referential aspect to their familiar narratives of generational conflict by casting stars of different generations: Amitabh Bachchan and Shah Rukh Khan have starred together as teacher/pupil and father/son in *Mohabbatein* and *Kabhi Khusi Kabhie Gham*.

The contemporary setting of the romantic drama would place it firmly in the category of the 'social'. Prasad observes that 'the portmanteau "social" has remained the dominant, and during certain periods, the sole genre with a contemporary signified [sic]'.[77] At the turn of the millennium, however, there was evidence of a trend back towards the 'historical' genre which had been moribund for several decades. In 2001 two of Bollywood's leading stars made epic, big-budget costume films: Shah Rukh Khan in *Asoka*, Aamir Khan in *Lagaan*. *Asoka* is a sweeping historical epic retelling the story of the warrior-emperor who embraced Buddhism after seeing the error of his bloody campaigns. Inevitably the film 'emphasises spectacle and melodramatic richness over historical accuracy'.[78] It is comparable thematically to Ridley Scott's *Gladiator* and stylistically to Akira Kurosawa's *Kagemusha*. Lavishly produced for the international market, the visually sumptuous *Asoka* was, however, not as successful as the much acclaimed *Lagaan*, which marked a major breakthrough for the Indian film industry. As Rachel Dwyer noted upon the occasion of its British release:

> On one level, the film sticks to the Bollywood 'formula' – a hero in a love triangle, a villain, songs and dances. But at the same time *Lagaan* breaks through the traditional boundaries of the Hindi film. In India the film's historical background, lack of a star heroine, village setting and folk-style music were all seen as problematic. Yet it proved one of the greatest critical and commercial successes of recent years.[79]

Lagaan (subtitled *Once Upon a Time in India* to emphasize its mythical status) combines the two foremost Indian obsessions – movies and cricket – in its fictional story of poor villagers who, unable to pay the *lagaan* (land tax) to their feudal overlord, are challenged by an arrogant British officer to settle the issue through a game of cricket. Within this simple fable, however, the ideologies of the film are clear: cricket both overcomes differences of religion and of caste (the village team includes a Sikh and an 'Untouchable') and becomes a site of ideological contestation between the people and their colonial masters (naturally the villagers win). The cricket match is choreographed as a form of spectacle in its own right and adds another form of 'attraction' to the cinema of attractions that is Bollywood.

There is evidence that, at the beginning of the twenty-first century, popular Indian cinema has at last shed its reputation for kitsch and has entered the cultural mainstream. The international success of films like *Lagaan* and *Devdas*, the Hollywood/Bollywood crossover represented in Mira Nair's *Monsoon Wedding* (2001), the acknowledged influence of the style of Indian film on Baz Luhrmann's visually sumptuous *Moulin Rouge* (2001) and the West End theatrical production of the musical *Bombay Dreams* by Andrew Lloyd Webber, suggest that audiences outside the Indian sub-continent and the diaspora have accepted this different, visually exciting, stylistically challenging form of glossy film entertainment. Whether this is a short-lived fad, or a sign of a longer-term cultural change, remains to be seen. Whatever the outcome, however, the newfound interest in all things 'Bollywood' ensures that Indian cinema is no longer seen in western eyes as comprising just the films of Satyajit Ray.

THIRTEEN

Asiatic Cinemas

The cinemas of East Asia represent a diverse and eclectic range of aesthetic traditions and stylistic practices. Ranging from, at one extreme, the 'poetics' of Japanese directors such as Yasujiro Ozu and Kenji Mizoguchi, to, at the other extreme, the kinetic action movies that have proliferated from the film industries of Hong Kong and Taiwan, Asiatic cinemas present a highly distinctive variation on the 'serious' and 'popular' paradigms that characterize film cultures around the world. In contrast to European cinemas, where various forms of realism and modernism have been the dominant aesthetic traditions, Asiatic cinemas have tended towards theatricality and stylization. Western film theorists, inevitably, have conceptualized Asiatic cinemas as 'alternatives', providing a critique of western styles of film-making, most especially classical Hollywood, and deliberately foregrounding their difference.[1] As the first western interest in Asiatic cinemas coincided with the heyday of auteurism in the 1950s and 1960s there has been a tendency to privilege the work of certain directors and thus perpetuate a predominantly aesthetic history. In the case of Japanese cinema, especially, this has led to the canonization of the 'big three' (Ozu, Mizoguchi and Akira Kurosawa) whose work has been central to critical and theoretical debates around Japanese cinema. Only more recently, however, have scholars broadened their horizons to consider the industrial and generic contexts of film production in East Asia. That Asiatic cinemas comprise a significant aspect of world film production is unquestionable. Japan was home to the world's leading film production industry for much of the 1920s (when it sometimes produced over 800 films a year) and the 1930s (when it consistently produced between 400 and 500 films a year). There was a decline in production during the

Second World War, followed by a revival in the 1950s when production again reached the levels of the 1930s. Overtaken by India in the early 1970s, Japan has nevertheless remained one of the top three world producers with between 250 and 300 films a year.[2] Japan's relative decline as a film-producing nation coincided with the rise of commercially orientated film industries in Hong Kong and Taiwan, each of which could boast a production sector in excess of 200 films a year by the 1960s. These cinemas have dominated their home markets and, in the case of Hong Kong, and to a lesser extent Taiwan, have built up strong exports throughout Southeast Asia. Indonesia, the Philippines, South Korea and Thailand also expanded significantly during the 1970s and 1980s, though have been unable to sustain this boom since the advent of the home video market severely dented cinema attendances in Asia from the mid-1980s. Of all Asiatic national cinemas, however, the one that has attracted most critical attention in recent years is China's. Although never amongst the leading producers – indeed, filmmaking almost ceased during and after the 'Cultural Revolution' – Chinese cinema has won international recognition since the mid-1980s through a number of visually exciting, formally complex films that display an ambiguous relationship with art and politics. The sheer diversity of film styles throughout East Asia makes a comprehensive survey beyond the scope of this book. As with my earlier discussion of European national cinemas, therefore, this chapter focuses on the leading countries in terms of production (Japan, Hong Kong, Taiwan) and on one aesthetically and culturally significant film movement (the New Chinese Cinema of the 1980s and 1990s).

CINEMA AND SOCIETY

It is impossible to understand the stylistic difference of Asiatic cinemas without first considering their relationship to other artistic and cultural practices. When early film shows reached the Far East – the first documented example was a variety show at Shanghai's Hsu Gardens on 11 August 1896 – they were understood within an existing tradition of visual culture of paper lanterns and puppet theatre. The Chinese, for example, described films as *dian-ying* ('electric shadows'). In Japan – the Cinématographe Lumière and Edison Vitascope both reached Osaka in February 1897 – there is evidence to suggest that early audiences were less interested in the films themselves than in the mechanical process involved in creating the illusion. There are reports that some early showmen set up their camera on one side of the stage and the screen on the other so that people could watch both the projector and the film.[3] This interest in the mechanics of the performance was not unusual: in Japanese puppet theatre (*bunraku*) the puppeteers were visible on stage rather than concealed behind screens. Throughout the silent era, indeed, film exhibition in Japan broke down the illusion of reality through the practice of using narrators (*benshi*) who stood next to the screen and told the story, long after this practice had been abandoned in the West. Akira Kurosawa, whose brother was one of these *benshi*, wrote in his autobiography: 'The narrators not only recounted the plot of the films, they enhanced the emotional content by performing the voices and sound effects and providing evocative descriptions of the events and images on the screen – much like the narrators of Bunraku puppet theatre.'[4]

It took longer for indigenous production to develop in the Far East than it had done in the West. Film exhibition was dominated by American and European films. Early Japanese producers tended to make only topicals, scenics and records of *kabuki* theatre. It was not until 1908 that the first purpose-built studio opened in Japan (in Tokyo by the Yoshizawa Company) and the production of fictional subjects began. Early Chinese filmmakers were mostly based in Shanghai, where the presence of western entrepreneurs provided a source of investment. The first major production company was the Asia Motion Picture Company, set up in 1908 by an American, Benjamin Polaski, in partnership with two Chinese businessmen. There were no Chinese-owned production interests before the overthrow of the Manchu dynasty by the Kuomintang in 1911 and not until 1916 was the first such interest founded in the form of Zhang Shichuan's Hui Xi Company.[5] It is difficult to generalize about the nature of indigenously produced films, as so few have survived, especially from China, though from what evidence there is it seems that Japanese films borrowed the theatrical distinctions of *jidai-geki* (period/costume drama) and *gendai-geki* (contemporary drama) and that Chinese filmmakers favoured a style of sentimental melodrama.

Evidence regarding the nature of cinema audiences is scant indeed. In China, where film was seen predominantly as a 'foreign' form of entertainment, exhibition practices would seem to have been directed towards the more affluent members of society (Europeans and the more cosmopolitan Chinese). In the world's most populous country there were only 120 permanent cinemas by 1925 and 275 by 1939; the majority of those were in the foreign concessions of the treaty ports (Shanghai, Nanking, Hong Kong).[6] In Japan there is also evidence to suggest that early exhibition practices were directed towards more affluent patrons with ticket prices almost the equivalent of us$1. However, the number of permanent cinemas by the 1920s and 1930s – 600 in 1920, 1,050 in 1925, 1,600 by 1935 – is suggestive of a broader social base for the cinema audience.[7]

The relationship of Far Eastern cinemas to the West during the 1920s and 1930s is, to say the least, complicated. On the one hand, American movies, in particular, were extremely popular with audiences, though us penetration was much greater in China, where some 90 per cent of films were imported and the majority of those were from Hollywood, than it was in Japan, where a stronger domestic production industry maintained a dominant share of the home market. On the other hand, there is evidence of hostility towards the representation of orientalism in western films, especially from nationalists. In China, for example, the Nationalist government of Generalissimo Chiang Kai-shek protested via its foreign consuls over the portrayal of Chinese characters in the likes of the Fu Manchu films (a number of which were produced in Britain and America during the 1920s and 1930s) and organized boycotts at home. In Japan, where the Great Kanto Earthquake of 1923 devastated studios in Tokyo and Yokahama, there was a temporary dearth of domestic product and American movies were quick to fill the gap. Some commentators have detected a 'westernization' in Japanese film during the 1920s – part of a vogue for western popular culture that also included jazz and American whiskey – though it is difficult to draw any firm conclusions. A new genre emerged in the late 1920s in the form of the *shomin-geki*, a contemporary film dealing specifically with lower-middle class life. The best-known example of this genre is probably Yasujiro Ozu's *I Was Born, But . . .* (1932), told through the eyes of a child whose father adopts western dress and mannerisms and which can be seen as a satire of social aspirations in contemporary Japan.

The control and regulation of the cinema followed a similar pattern to the West in so far as it emerged first on a local level before being centralized and brought within the orbit of the state. In Japan film exhibition initially came under the authority of local police who were empowered to grant permits for public screenings, but this practice rarely involved actually watching the films for approval. A press outcry over the film *Zingomar* in 1912 – a French production that was accused by some newspapers of promoting juvenile crime – eventually led to the introduction, five years later, of a set of Moving Picture Exhibition Regulations, including pre-screenings of films, licensing of the *benshi* and, uniquely, the designation of reserved seats in auditoria for officials to check on the films. Even so, local variations in the administration of this system resulted in the introduction of national film censorship in 1925 in response to films deemed 'harmful to public peace, morals and health'.[8] During the 1930s the right-wing military government increased the state's power over cinema through such measures as the Film Control Committee of 1934, which brought together government officials and representatives of the industry for the purpose of regulating film content, and the Film Law of 1939, modelled on the system introduced in Nazi Germany, which introduced pre-production script approval and controls over the import of foreign films (American movies, naturally, were prohibited after Pearl Harbor). A similar pattern, shifting from local regulation to state control, can be identified in China. Film exhibition was a local matter – the first formal board of censors was established in the Jiangsu province in 1923 – until the institution of a National Film Censorship Committee in 1931. As part of its attempt to establish Mandarin as the official spoken language of

China, the Nationalist government banned films in local dialects. However, the civil war between Nationalists and Communists meant that certain parts of the country, such as Guangxi and Guangdong provinces, never came fully under central control. The Japanese invasion of China in 1937 resulted in two systems of censorship, with the Chinese and Japanese authorities imposing their own rules in the areas under their control.

Censorship followed different directions after the Second World War. For four years the Japanese film industry came under the control of the Allied Occupation authorities who were mainly concerned with eradicating the cult of militarism and promoting the cause of international anti-Communism. Film censorship was handed over to the Japanese themselves in 1949 and a self-regulatory system, modelled on the US Production Code, was introduced. As the new Japanese constitution prohibited censorship, the new body was known as the Film Ethics Regulation Control Committee (Eirin) and it was empowered to inspect both scripts and finished films. This committee 'was seen by its creators as a means of maintaining the social responsibility of a powerful medium while protecting the industry from persistent calls for state censorship.'[9] In China, however, a more rigorous centralized state censorship was instituted following the Communist revolution of 1949. The film industry was nationalized: production was controlled by the Film Bureau of the Ministry of Culture, while the China Film Distribution and Exhibition Company became the controlling body for all films shown throughout the country. Most foreign films were banned (except those from the Soviet Union and Eastern Europe), while Chinese films now had to adhere to a form of Socialist Realism advocating the role of workers, peasants and soldiers in the task of national reconstruction. Examples of such films include *Victory of the Chinese People*, *New Heroes and Heroines*, *My Life* and *The Life of Wu Hsun*, though the latter was withdrawn due to the personal disapproval of Chairman Mao Tse-tung. 'During the first 40 years of the People's Republic of China', Sheila Cornelius writes, 'filmmakers were subject to the most arbitrary, inconsistent, and stringent film censorship'.[10]

The extent of state control over the cinema provides further evidence of the cultural and political importance attached to it. The People's Republic of China is home to the largest cinema audience in the world. The years following the Communist revolution of 1949 saw a quite remarkable increase in cinemagoing. The number of 'exhibition units' (including both permanent cinemas and touring projectors) increased from a mere 646 in 1949 to a massive 20,363 by 1965. Annual cinema attendances rose from 139 million to 4,600 million over the same period.[11] How can this dramatic increase be explained? As far as the Communists were concerned, they were making films with a political message that Chinese people wanted to see. A more convincing explanation, however, is that films were still a relative novelty to the vast majority of the Chinese population. Before the revolution most cinemas had been in port cities, whereas China was a predominantly rural society. The advent of touring projection units, therefore, would have introduced film to millions of people who had never set foot in a cinema. In this context it is likely that any kind of film would have been popular, especially given the absence of other mass media, radio and television, in rural areas. The fact that admission to film shows in rural areas was often free is also, surely, another significant factor in accounting for their popularity.

THE CLASSICAL JAPANESE CINEMA

The aftermath of the Kanto Earthquake was a period of instability and transition for Japan's film industry. Several studios were devastated and some were forced to relocate to Kyoto. Kyoto, the ancient capital, was the production centre for *jidai-geki* period films due to its old houses and streets, whereas the contemporary *gendai-geki* were usually set in modern Tokyo. The late 1920s was a period of experimentation in form and technique as a number of small production firms were established and Japanese filmmakers began to import ideas from other national cinemas, notably German Expressionism. In common with developments elsewhere, however, the arrival of talkies had the effect of strengthening the position of the largest companies, though the adoption of sound was slower in Japan.

The Japanese film industry in the 1930s outwardly resembled the American industry: it was an oligopoly, it had developed a studio-based mode of production and institutionalized a style that historians have since labelled 'classical'. At the beginning of the decade there were two vertically integrated companies: Nippon Katsudo Shashin (more commonly known as Nikkatsu) and the Shochiku Cinema Company. In 1934 they were joined by a third, the Tokyo Takarazuka Theatre Company (Toho). In addition to these three majors there were in the region of half a dozen smaller producers. A two-tier production sector persisted into the mid-1930s with the larger companies being the first to convert to sound whereas the smaller producers continued to make silent films. The three 'majors' were most able to afford the expense of converting to sound due to the income from their cinemas. The demand for films increased during the decade, despite the Depression, and Japanese production rose to meet it: annual production throughout the 1930s was always over 400 and reached a high of 583 in 1937. Uniquely for the period, when most national cinemas faced heavy competition from Hollywood, Japanese films maintained a dominant share of their home market. This can be explained by a combination of several factors. To some extent it was the consequence of Japan's cultural and linguistic isolation: the 'western' idiom was less easily assimilated than it was in Europe or Latin America with their greater proximity to the United States. And to some extent it was also due to the three majors' effective control of the exhibition sector, which meant they were able to keep Hollywood at bay in preference to their own films.

The organization of the Japanese film industry on studio-based, mass-production lines has inevitably drawn comparisons with Hollywood. In fact the Japanese mode of production was both like and unlike the Hollywood model. In so far as it was geared towards turning out genre films for mass consumption, there are obviously important parallels. And, in common with Hollywood, particular studio styles can also be identified in Japan. Nikkatsu, which specialized in the period *jidai-geki* following its move to Kyoto, was at something of a disadvantage when it came to the production of contemporary dramas for which it had to use studio sets rather than real locations. As Japanese film historian Hiroshi Komatsu notes: 'The studio-based *gendai-geki* produced by Nikkatsu in Kyoto were clearly distinguishable from those made in Tokyo by Shochiku and other companies.'[12] Nikkatsu was seen as embodying a more liberal production ideology in that it was inclined towards films with an element of social criticism, whereas Shochiku was on the whole more conformist, exemplified by its production in the early 1930s of a number of nationalistic films supporting Japan's policy of territorial expansion in Manchuria.

At the same time, however, there were significant organizational differences in the operating methods of the Japanese studios. Toho was closest to the Hollywood model in that it favoured a producer-unit system where one producer was in charge of several productions simultaneously. This, possibly, was why its films were seen as having a more mass-produced look and glossy visual style. Nikkatsu and Shochiku, in contrast, developed a 'cadre' system, which allowed the director and screenwriter greater control over their own films. Thus it was that 'house' directors such as Yasujiro Ozu and Hiroshi Shimizu at Shochiku, and Sadao Yamanaka and Tomu Uchida at Nikkatsu, were able to develop distinctively personal styles, as indeed were those directors such as Kenji Mizoguchi not tied to a particular studio. The Japanese studios adopted a master/apprentice system, in common with traditional practices in other arts, whereby an assistant director would be apprenticed to an established director to learn his craft. Akira Kurosawa, for example, was apprenticed to the respected Kajiro Yamamoto (whom he referred to as 'Yama-san') at Toho studios between 1936 and 1943. The apprentice (who later of course became a master himself) testified to the value of this system in fostering an individual style of filmmaking:

I learned so much about movies and the work of being a movie director from Yama-san that I couldn't begin to describe it all here. He was without question the best of teachers. The best proof of this lies in the fact that none of the work of his 'disciples' (Yama-san hated this term) resembled his. He made sure to do nothing to restrict his assistant directors, but rather encouraged their individual qualities to grow.[13]

Thus it was that the Japanese mode of production encouraged, even institutionalized, a type of auteurism that was a hard-won privilege in Hollywood and Europe.

The greater freedom for directors within the studio system notwithstanding, however, they all worked within a set of stylistic and aesthetic norms that constitute the paradigm of classical Japanese cinema. To call Japanese cinema of the 1930s 'classical' is not to imply that it was the same as classical Hollywood. Bordwell and Thompson suggest that Japan 'offers an especially interesting case of how a national cinema can both absorb and significantly modify conventions of classical Hollywood filmmaking'.[14] They argue that while most Japanese films are structurally similar to classical Hollywood films in narrative, they are stylistically different in so far as they are less bound by conventions such as the 180° rule (the invisible 'line' which the camera does not cross) or the pattern of shot/reverse shot that are fundamental principles of Hollywood narration. It is also not unusual for Japanese directors to include so-called 'empty shots' (where the camera remains on an empty diegetic space vacated by characters) in transitions between scenes – a technique adopted most extensively by Ozu – rather than conventional cuts, fades or dissolves. (This is believed to derive from the aesthetic and philosophical notion of *mu*, a space for meditation and contemplation in Buddhist art.) The result is that a greater variety of stylistic choices were available to Japanese directors, which naturally accentuated individual differences.

By common consent the two most important directors to emerge during this period were Kenji Mizoguchi and Yasujiro Ozu. Both these directors 'utilized particular norms of the Japanese cinema but also went beyond them to create a unique approach to film style'.[15] Mizoguchi, originally a graphic artist, became an assistant director at Nikkatsu in the 1920s, worked in a variety of genres (comedies, ghost stories, detective films) and in his silent films was influenced by foreign styles such as Expressionism. He came to prominence with a number of films in the mid-1930s (*The Water Magician, Osen of the Paper Cranes*,

Sisters of the Gion) that were notable for their interest in the persecution of women – a theme that has often been attributed, in a form of biographical auteurism, to the boyhood Mizoguchi's elder sister having been sold as a *geisha*. His sound films became distinctive through their use of long takes, slow camera movements and deep-focus compositions – techniques that would later lead *Cahiers du Cinéma* to compare him to the likes of Renoir and Welles. Ozu, who also worked his way up through the industry in the 1920s, came to be associated with films of delicate social observation (*I Was Born, But . . ., Woman of Tokyo, The Only Son*). His style – 'exquisite in its simplicity'[16] – is distinctive for two unique features: he places the camera at a low angle and shoots from a stationary position (approximating the eye-level of a spectator in a Japanese theatre sitting on a cushion on the floor rather than in a chair) and he shoots from all sides (creating a 360° space rather than the conventional 180° space). While film theorists disagree over the extent to which Ozu's 'poetics' were a conscious attempt to differentiate his films from the classical Hollywood style, or were rooted in traditional Japanese arts and philosophies, all are united in their admiration for the emotional beauty of his films.[17]

The formal variety of the classical Japanese cinema waned during the Second World War, when stricter government censorship and the demands of propaganda imposed greater thematic and stylistic unity on filmmakers. The military government imposed a wartime quota on the major producers – they were each allowed to release only two films a month – with the result that levels of production dropped from 497 in 1940 to 232 in 1941, 87 in 1942 and a mere 38 in 1945. The shortage of films and the effects of bombardment forced some two thirds of the nation's cinemas to close. Given the devastation wrought upon the film industry by the war, the speed of its recovery in the second half of the 1940s was remarkable. Cinema attendances in 1946 stood at 733 million (compared to a pre-war average of 400 million) and by 1950 most of the country's cinemas had reopened. Hollywood movies, seen by the Allied Occupation authorities as important in the 'democratization' of Japan, flooded into the Japanese market. The Allies purged the Japanese film industry twice, once of those charged with war crimes, and again of those deemed communists. As in Italy and Germany, where defeat in war and occupation created the conditions for Neo-Realism and *Trümmerfilme*, the theme of social reconstruction featured in a number of realist *shomin-geki* such as Ozu's *Record of a Tenement Gentleman* (1947), a possibly allegorical film in which a boy searches for his father amongst the post-war devastation, only to reject him when he is found. (The failure of the family unit to provide stability and security challenges, in a quite fundamental way, one of the central ideologies of classical Japanese cinema.) The rebuilding of post-war Japanese cinema, however, would be based principally on genre films, particularly comedies and *yakuza* (gangster) films. While the industry remained an effective oligopoly, the number of major companies by the 1950s had increased to six: Toho, Shochiku, Nikkatsu, Toei, Daiei and Shin Toho (the latter, meaning 'New Toho', was formed following a strike at Toho which resulted in one faction breaking away).

Historical accounts of post-war Japanese cinema tend to identify two distinct trends. On the one hand, filmmakers who had established themselves before the war, such as Mikio Naruse, Teinosuke Kinugasa and Heinosuke Gosho, were able to continue their careers into the post-war period. Mizoguchi and Ozu, in particular, refined the styles that had made their earlier work so distinctive. In the early 1950s Mizoguchi made a series of prestigious period films adapted from literary sources (*The Life of Oharu, A Tale of Ugetsu, Sansho Dayu*), while Ozu, in collaboration with screenwriter Kogo Noda, made a series of bittersweet films exploring family relationships, generational difference and the inevitability of ageing (*Late Spring, Early Summer, The Scent of Green Tea Over Rice, Tokyo Story, An Autumn Afternoon*). Ozu's masterpiece is generally held to be *Tokyo Story*, in which an elderly couple slowly come to realize that their grown-up children no longer have time for them. Derek Malcom calls it 'probably the best, most human film made about family relationships'.[18]

On the other hand, however, new filmmakers who came to prominence after the war were more influenced by the influx of American movies. Foremost amongst these, without any question, was Akira Kurosawa. It was Kurosawa's *Rashomon* (1951) which first brought Japanese cinema to prominence in the West, winning the Golden Lion at the Venice Film Festival and an Academy Award for Best Foreign Film. Its bold use of non-linear narrative and multiple narrators (the film is a meditation on 'truth' in which four characters each give different accounts of events leading to a murder and rape in eleventh-century Japan) were seen by western critics as placing the film within the international art cinema tradition of the post-war years. Its producer Masaichi Nagata, head of the Daiei company, however, explained its appeal in terms of its difference from other national styles: 'America was making action pictures, France had love stories, and Italy realism. So I chose to approach the world market with the appeal of Japanese historical subjects. Old Japan is more exotic than Westernized Japan is to Westerners.'[19] *Rashomon* is often credited with sparking a revival in historical costume films in Japanese cinema – a genre banned during the Occupation – which was then consolidated by Kinugasa's *Gate of Hell* and Kurosawa's *Seven Samurai* (both 1954).

Kurosawa has been described as the most 'western' of Japanese filmmakers, due in large measure to his use of montage editing techniques. Kurosawa himself acknowledged the influence of John Ford's films upon his own work. He was also critical of those who attacked his films for being 'un-Japanese': 'Japanese critics insisted that these two prizes [for *Rashomon*] were simply reflections of Westerners' curiosity and taste for Oriental exoticism, which struck me then, and now, as terrible. Why is it that Japanese people have no confidence in the worth of Japan?'[20] Such criticisms of Kurosawa's work are misplaced. His films are best understood in terms of exchange between Japanese and western cultures. Thus, on the one hand, he turned to European literature for inspiration and translated the works of Shakespeare and Dostoevsky into a Japanese idiom: *Throne of Blood* was an adaptation of *Macbeth*, *Hakuchi* of *The Idiot*. Towards the end of his career he would turn *King Lear* into the epic *Ran*. On the other hand, however, two of his samurai films (a distinctive Japanese genre) were remade as westerns: *Seven Samurai* as *The Magnificent Seven*, *Yojimbo* as *Fistful of Dollars*. As Katz argues: 'Kurosawa is a man of all genres, all periods, and all places, bridging in his work the traditional and

the modern, the old and the new, the cultures of the East and the West.'²¹ For all that he is considered 'less Japanese' than certain other directors, Kurosawa was arguably the Japanese cinema's most complete *auteur* in the sense that he collaborated on most scripts and always supervised their editing. He also established, through his frequent collaborations with Toshiro Mifune, one of the most celebrated director-star teams in cinema history.²²

The conventional account of Kurosawa's work distinguishes between his costume and samurai films on the one hand and his contemporary dramas on the other. It was the cycle of costume films of the 1950s and early 1960s (*Seven Samurai*, *The Hidden Fortress*, *Yojimbo*, *Sanjuro*) that were admired by western critics. These films promoted the *bushido* spirit of feudal Japan, characterized by values of courage, honour and sacrifice, symbolized in the figure of the samurai hero. In *Seven Samurai* and *Yojimbo* the samurai are shown to stand apart from other people, distinguished by their superior skills, their physical and moral courage and their code of honour. A Japanese critic, Tadao Sato, suggests that this type of film was not attuned to the post-war mood, arguing that 'after Japan was defeated in the Second World War *bushido* came to be regarded as an outdated, reactionary sentiment. The Japanese wanted to forget about *bushido* altogether and learn, instead, about democracy.'[23] Yet Kurosawa's films are more complex than such a reading would allow. They are equivocal in their attitude towards violence (which is depicted as harrowing but often necessary) and are not uncritical of the *bushido* code. This is most apparent in *Seven Samurai* in which a group of samurai, led by Kambei (Takashi Shimura), are hired to protect a village against a gang of ferocious bandits. The samurai are characterized as mercenaries who have different reasons for joining Kambei: for some it is a matter of pride in their skills, for others it is because they are hungry. The relationship between the villagers and their protectors is ambiguous. The peasants need the samurai but are afraid of them, fleeing when the samurai arrive in their village; later, a village elder is ashamed when he discovers that his daughter has had sexual relations with Kambei's young disciple Katsushiro (Ko Kimura). He is admonished by another villager: 'At least she was taken by a samurai. Would you rather it had been a bandit?' In one key scene, following the revelation that in the past the villagers have killed and robbed lone samurai, Kikichiyo (Toshiro Mifune) – himself a farmer's son – launches into a tirade not against the villagers but against the other samurai: 'Do you think farmers are angels? They're mean, stupid and murderous. But then, who made them such beasts? You samurai did!' Following the bloody climactic battle (brilliantly orchestrated by Kurosawa in the pouring rain), in which four of the samurai are slain, the villagers return to the fields, the closing shots indicating they have already forgotten about the samurai. Despite their victory, the surviving samurai are left no better off than when they started. Kambei remarks: 'We've lost yet again. The farmers are the victors – not us.'[24]

Recently, however, there has been renewed interest in Kurosawa's contemporary film dramas of the late 1940s and early 1950s (*Drunken Angel, The Quiet Duel, Stray Dog, Ikiru*). These films were notable for their examination of social problems affecting post-war Japan and were critical of the feudal values that had led Japan into a disastrous war. This is made most explicit in *Ikiru* in which a civil servant (Takashi Shimura), learning that he is suffering from terminal cancer, reassesses his life and spends his last days working obsessively to build a children's playground in order that he can die feeling he has done something useful. Other films were crime dramas set against realistic backgrounds, casting Mifune as a tubercular gangster living in a slum (*Drunken Angel*) and as a police detective searching the seedy Tokyo underworld for his stolen gun (*Stray Dog*). Sato testifies to the social significance of these films for post-war Japanese audiences: 'For my generation of Japanese who spent their youth in the immediate postwar years, films like *No Regrets for Our Youth*, *One Wonderful Sunday*, *Drunken Angel* and *Stray Dog*, which vividly portrayed the realities of that age and carried a strong moral message, gave us the courage to live.'[25]

Kurosawa's films – and those of other contemporaries, for example, Keisuke Kinoshita, Kon Ichikawa and Kozaburo Yoshimura – have been seen as evidence of an unmistakeable modernizing tendency in post-war Japanese cinema in so far as these younger filmmakers were more receptive to western ideas than the older generation of directors from the classical period. At the same time, however, the continued presence of the old masters during the post-war transitional period (Mizoguchi died in 1956, Ozu in 1963) ensured that Japanese cinema maintained its characteristic and unique flavour. The main stylistic trends of the period between the 1930s and the 1950s are succinctly summarized by Komatsu:

> In the Japanese cinema of the 1930s the coexistence of sound and silent film had continued for many years due to insufficient capital and special cultural circumstances. The 1940s cinema can be divided into two completely opposing periods: the Fascist ideology films of the war years and the films of democracy from the second half of the decade. The ideological changes established by the occupation did not add anything fundamentally new to the form of Japanese cinema, as the assimilation of the American cinema style had already been achieved by the 1930s. The majority of film art in post-war Japan was created by directors with an occidental vision, like Kurosawa. However, at the same time Mizoguchi and Ozu, two important, if very different, directors from the pre-war period, could carry on developing their Japanese

aesthetic in the post-war era. The war and liberation gave Japanese cinema the opportunities to foster both occidental and Japanese sensibilities.[26]

NEW CHINESE CINEMA

At the time that Japanese cinema was making its breakthrough onto the international scene in the 1950s, Chinese film remained socialist, parochial and unknown outside its own country. The adherence to Maoist political ideology created a cinema of 'mass mediocrity', consisting mostly of political films and revolutionary sagas.[27] The narratives of Chinese films tended towards 'positive heroes primarily interested in the betterment of the masses, class struggle, [and] the eventual triumph of the progressive forces over reactionary forces'.[28] The 'Hundred Flowers' movement launched by Mao in 1956 (so called after the Chinese proverb 'Let a hundred flowers blossom, let a hundred schools of thought contend') seemed, on the face of it, to invite greater independence on the part of artists and cultural producers, though this was to prove short-lived. The 'Great Leap Forward', announced in December 1957 and intended to modernize Chinese industries, brought about restructuring in the film industry as new studios were built in the provinces. By 1964 annual production had grown to 480 feature films, 3,000 newsreels, 1,400 scientific documentaries and 200 cartoons. However, a sudden halt was signalled by the 'Cultural Revolution' (1966–70) during which production all but ceased (only eleven films were completed during those years) and the film industry, in common with all aspects of Chinese life, was purged in an attempt to impose revolutionary Marxist ideology on all sections of society. The film industry became a particular target because Mao's wife Jiang Qing was a former actress with scores to settle. Production remained in single figures throughout most of the 1970s and it was not until the 1980s that it revived significantly with the advent of the so-called 'Fifth Generation' (*Diwu Dai*).

Chinese film historians have tended to categorize filmmakers into generations in line with major political events. Thus the 'First Generation' were the early pioneers during the last years of the Manchu dynasty, the 'Second Generation' were those who built up an embryonic film industry in the 1910s and 1920s, the 'Third Generation' comprised the filmmakers of the 1930s and 1940s (including Chai Chusend, whose *Song of the Fisherman* in 1935 had been the first Chinese film to win a foreign prize, at the Moscow Film Festival), while the 'Fourth Generation' were those whose careers began after the revolution of 1949. The 'Fifth Generation' refers to a group of directors (including Chen Kaige, Huang Jianxin, Tian Zhuanzhuang and Zhang Yimou) who were the first class to graduate from the Beijing Film Academy following its reopening in 1978 and who made their first films in the early and mid-1980s.[29] Chen Kaige believed that this generation benefited, albeit by accident, from a more open-minded regime at the newly reopened film academy:

I really appreciated my teachers because they didn't know how to teach us. They hadn't taught anybody for ten years. They were very open-minded. They said they would not teach the old way they used to, the old-fashioned way. We would see films, work nights, and have discussions.[30]

Whereas during the Cultural Revolution all education, such as it was, had involved a form of rote learning, Mao's death in 1976 marked the passing of unquestioning ideological dogma. The Fifth Generation filmmakers had greater freedom to express themselves and to question certain aspects of the regime, though they were still subject to strict censorship. They also had the opportunity to see imported films, including examples of European art cinema, which influenced their own filmmaking practice. That said, however, the films of the Fifth Generation – which also became known as the New Chinese Cinema – remain rooted in Chinese culture and history.

Most of the Fifth Generation filmmakers were sent to work at provincial studios, the most significant being the Xi'an Film Studio in central China whose head, Wu Tianming, was prepared to allow new filmmakers their artistic freedom. The most significant directors – in the sense that their films came to international notice – were Chen Kaige (*Yellow Earth*, *The Big Parade*, *Farewell My Concubine*, *Temptress Moon*) and Zhang Yimou (*Red Sorghum*, *Judou*, *Raise the Red Lantern*, *The Story of Qiu Ju*, *Shanghai Triad*). In common with new cinemas in other Communist countries, these films were promoted abroad as a showcase for Chinese cinema, winning festival prizes and critical acclaim, whilst often being banned, or given at most a limited distribution, in China itself. The work of the Fifth Generation, indeed, highlights a tension within official attitudes towards the cinema, for the China Film Bureau, while being uneasy about the content of some of the films, has also been keen to benefit from their cultural prestige in overseas eyes. Thus the filmmakers themselves have escaped censure even if their films have not always met with official approval. Western discourse around these films tends to see them as 'bargaining chips in the struggle for a genuine freedom of expression in China'.[31]

New Chinese Cinema represents a significant departure from previous traditions of filmmaking in Communist China. The work of the new directors was characterized by its greater psychological depth, complex narratives, thematic ambiguity and visual symbolism. The films are political in the sense that they pose questions rather than restate official dogma, though their formal and narrative complexity makes it difficult to read any straightforward political meaning from them. Indeed, meaning in New Chinese Cinema is implicit rather than explicit, expressed through form rather than through narrative. The films are notable for their highly stylized imagery and their richly textured use of colour. For example, *Yellow Earth* (1984), which dramatizes the conflict between tradition and modernization through the story of a Communist soldier who struggles to persuade a remote village community to abandon its age-old way of life, saturates the image with yellow hues and is filmed consciously in the style of the *chang'an* school of landscape painting which uses a high horizon to make the landscape seem oppressive: 'In the end, as in the beginning, the yellow land towers magnificent, terrible and ageless over all those whose lives it enfolds, seeming intractable to modern socialist mechanization.'[32]

For all their success on the 'art house' circuit – *Raise the Red Lantern* and *Farewell My Concubine*, especially, did much to raise the international profile of Chinese film in the early 1990s – many of the Fifth Generation films were criticized for being too obscure for the peasant audience that still made up 80 per cent of the Chinese population. With rare exceptions (*Red Sorghum* was the only Fifth Generation film to top audience popularity polls in China itself) Chinese audiences have preferred the less demanding genre films imported from Taiwan and Hong Kong. In 1987 a Chinese film exhibitor wrote to the film magazine *Popular Cinema* to complain that 'our Chinese films (by which I mean mainland films) are getting the cold shoulder, and what's more, the indifference also contains a certain amount of scorn!'[33] Wu Tianming summarized the problem thus: 'There are three audiences that have to be satisfied in China. One is the government, one is the art world, and one is the ordinary popular audience.'[34] There is a similarity here with the Soviet montage films of the 1920s which were also successful with intellectuals and aesthetes abroad but were considered too difficult for the masses at home to comprehend and were, moreover, regarded as aesthetically and ideologically suspect by the government. Some films were too difficult for the authorities to understand. Cornelius observes that 'it is clear that the lack of film literacy among the members of the censorship board has led to the release of films that were subsequently recalled when the audience recognized and applauded their dissident messages'.[35] The censors could never make their mind up about *Farewell My Concubine*, a visually stunning epic chronicling thirty years of change in Chinese politics and society: it was twice banned and twice unbanned before finally being shown in China in 1997, four years after winning the Palme d'Or at Cannes.

At the level of production, however, the 1990s have seen evidence of an 'opening up' of Chinese cinema to western influences. This is less a response to the worldwide outrage that greeted the brutal suppression of pro-democracy campaigners in Beijing's Tiananmen Square in 1989 and more the consequence of longer term economic reforms initiated by Mao's successor Deng Xiaoping in the 1980s. The state's monopoly on film distribution ended and China's sixteen regional film studios were required to find their own sources of finance. Private investment and co-production initiatives have been encouraged in an attempt to offset the expense of making films that perform better overseas than at home. Zhang Yimou's *The Road Home* (2000), for example, was funded largely by the Sony Corporation of Japan. At the turn of the millennium, to quote Sheldon Lu: 'China's film industry is caught in the throes of a transition from a state-controlled system to a market mechanism. National cinema suffers from a decline in funding and the audience and is in deep crisis.'[36]

ACTION, SPECTACLE AND SEX

While the interest of western critics was directed mostly to the work of directors such as Ozu, Mizoguchi, Kurosawa and the Fifth Generation filmmakers, it is only recently that attention has also been paid to the popular genres of Asiatic cinemas. As elsewhere in the world, there is a discrepancy between those films deemed artistically significant (and which represent a minority of all films produced) and those popular, often critically despised traditions of popular filmmaking that provide the commercial basis of most national cinemas. Few Asian genre films have been exported – Japanese monster movies and Hong Kong martial arts films are the rare exceptions – and thus remain unknown outside their countries of origin. It was only in the 1990s that the popular cinema of Hong Kong found a place on the agenda of film studies, while Taiwanese popular cinema has only even more recently come to prominence through the international success of Ang Lee's *Crouching Tiger, Hidden Dragon*. Yet Japanese, Hong Kong and Taiwanese cinemas have all produced highly distinctive popular genres which represent unique cultural responses to specific local entertainment needs.

In Japan, for example, there is a case to make that the most significant film of 1954 – commercially if not artistically – was neither *Seven Samurai* nor *Sansho Dayu* but *Godzilla* (known in Japan as *Gojira*). This monster movie, produced at the Toho Studios, needs to be seen as part of an international trend in the early 1950s for apocalyptic science-fiction films, commonly attributed to anxieties arising from the advent of the atom bomb (used, of course, against the Japanese cities of Hiroshima and Nagasaki in 1945). On one level *Godzilla* might be derided (indeed has been) as nothing more than low-budget rubbish featuring a large man in a baggy monster suit stamping over an unconvincing studio model of Tokyo. On another level, however, it has been interpreted as an allegory of the 'monster' unleashed by nuclear power: Godzilla, a prehistoric beast, is awakened from hibernation by an American atomic test. As John Brosnan remarks: 'It seems oddly masochistic of the Japanese that they would, a mere nine years after experiencing the real thing, take so much pleasure in watching on their cinema screens a vast monster, with radioactive breath, systematically levelling their cities.'[37] It may have been that the film was intended to prick the conscience of the victors – additional scenes were filmed with American actor Raymond Burr as a reporter offering a moralizing commentary when the film was picked up for US distribution – though any such intent was neutered by the way in which Japanese audiences took Godzilla to their hearts. The film's box-office success led to a wave of sequels (*Son of Godzilla, Godzilla's Revenge*) and imitations (*Gigantis the Fire Monster, Dogora the Space Monster, Ebirah, Horror of the Deep, Matanga, Fungus of Terror*) which lasted for the next twenty years.

The quality of the films aside, the proliferation of monster movies between the mid-1950s and the 1970s simply exemplified the commercial logic of the film industry. 'The yearly repetition of a dramatic spectacle generally assured large box-office receipts,' writes Komatsu. 'The plot of each film in a cycle was almost identical, but their popularity ensured that they were used as a last resort by the big companies to defend cinema audiences from erosion by television.'[38] Whereas American westerns in the 1960s responded to the decline of audiences by teaming stars, Japanese monster movies teamed monsters, resulting in the likes of *King Kong versus Godzilla* and culminating in *Destroy All Monsters* (1968) which brought all Toho's terrible creatures together to counter an invasion from outer space. By this time a substantial ideological realignment within the genre had taken place: Godzilla itself, once the destroyer of Tokyo, had now became its defender against all manner of other beasts (*Godzilla versus Hedorah, Godzilla versus the Sea Monster, Godzilla versus the Smog Monster* – the latter an early 1970s allegory of the perils of unchecked industrial pollution). Despite – or perhaps because of – their risible special effects, Japanese monster movies also found a cult audience overseas. And, rather like Hollywood B-movies, they provided inspiration for New Hollywood filmmakers: *Godzilla* was remade in 1998 as a multi-million dollar summer blockbuster with state-of-the-art special effects.

By the time the monster cycle petered out in the 1970s, Japanese popular cinema was undergoing fundamental changes. As elsewhere audiences were in decline (attendances by the early 1970s were only a sixth of what they had been in the 1950s) and by 1975 imported films (American movies especially) surpassed Japanese films at the box-office. Daiei went bankrupt in 1971 and other studios were forced into a strategy of retrenchment. A new genre emerged in the form of the *roman poruno* ('romantic pornography'). Nikkatsu, for example, concentrated on the production of sex films from 1971, 'resulting in the unique phenomenon of a major studio turning exclusively to the production of pornography'.[39] The emergence of the sex film as a major genre was made possible by the relaxation of censorship as Eirin was forced to respond to the industry's changing circumstances. As a self-regulatory organization paid for by the film industry and whose membership included industry representatives, it was perhaps only to be expected that Eirin would act in accordance with the industry's interests. This was to bring Eirin into confrontation with the Japanese police, who were at the forefront of a crusade against sex films. In 1972 Eirin's offices were raided by police and three of its film inspectors were indicted under the obscenity laws, alongside six filmmakers; all were acquitted on trial. A charge of obscenity was also brought against Nagisa Oshima's *In the Realm of the Senses* (1976), an 'artistic' sex film that climaxes, notoriously, in the castration of the male protagonist by his lover. The courts found in the film's favour, though definitions of obscenity remained a matter of interpretation in Japan.[40]

Sex was one ingredient used by filmmakers in an attempt to win back dwindling audiences; violence, predictably, was another. In 1976 an 'R' rating (prohibiting exhibition to children under 15) was introduced in response to the wave of violent *yakuza* films. In the mid-1980s another new genre emerged in the form of the animated film featuring 'realistic' sex and violence. This genre is often referred to as *manga* after the comic books on which the films are based; it is more correctly known, however, as *anime*. Although not the first of its type, Katsushiro Otomo's *Akira* (1987), a violent, dystopian, post-apocalyptic science-fiction *anime*, was the most critically acclaimed of this new genre and became a cult success abroad. The films are characterized by a style of rapid editing similar to Hong Kong action movies; they generate much of their revenue through videocassette sales. The arrival of home video impacted particularly severely in Japan: video rental fees were much lower than ticket prices for cinemas (Japan has probably the highest admission prices in the world). At a time when the Japanese entertainment giants Sony and Matsushita were buying Hollywood studios, the Japanese film industry had lost out to Hollywood movies at home. Nikkatsu, Japan's oldest film company, went bankrupt in 1993.

The declining fortunes of the Japanese film industry are in sharp contrast to those of Hong Kong, which boasts healthy production, distribution and exhibition sectors and which has succeeded in beating off Hollywood competition in its home market. The origins of the Hong Kong film industry extend back to the 1920s, though it was in the post-war period that this British Crown Colony became a mass-production film industry as firms and filmmakers relocated to Hong Kong from Shanghai and a studio system developed through the efforts of entrepreneurs such as Li Zuyong (who founded the Yonghua Company in 1947) and the Shaw brothers (who built the large Movietown studio complex in 1958). Hong Kong soon became the third leading film producer in the world behind Japan and the United States, averaging around 250 films a year during the 1950s and 1960s (the high point was 1956 when 311 films were produced), though the annual level of production fluctuated considerably during those decades. With mainland China effectively isolated after 1949, Hong Kong became the major exporter of films in East Asia, producing films both in Cantonese and in Mandarin for local and regional consumption. Two vertically-integrated companies emerged to dominate the industry in the 1960s – Shaw Brothers and the Motion Picture & General Investment (MP & GI) Company – and were joined in the 1970s by a third when Raymond Chow, a former production chief for Shaw Brothers, left to set up Golden Harvest Pictures and also built up his own chain of cinemas. The level of production declined from the mid-1960s, falling below 200 in 1966 and stabilizing at an average of 130 films a year during the 1970s (though there were still fluctuations, exemplified by the 201 films produced in 1973 at the height of the kung-fu craze). This decline was due not to any diminishing in the popularity of cinema as it was in Japan – indeed, the size of the potential cinema-going audience in Hong Kong grew in the 1970s as post-war baby-boomers reached adolescence – but rather to a deliberate strategy on the part of the major producers (especially Shaw Brothers) to concentrate on fewer films with higher production values.

Like Indian cinema, Hong Kong cinema is a multi-lingual cinema. The differences between Cantonese and Mandarin became institutionalized industrially as well as culturally. 'The often cut-throat business competition, cultural conflicts, and artistic interflow between Cantonese-speaking and Mandarin-speaking filmmaking created an especially rich and complex tradition in Hong Kong cinema', observe Poshek Fu and David Desser.[41] Cantonese films were produced primarily for the domestic market (some 80 per cent of Hong Kong's population were Cantonese speakers), while Mandarin films, produced in lesser quantity during the 1950s and early 1960s, had a larger overseas market (including Taiwan and the diasporic Chinese audience throughout the Pacific region). That Mandarin films were to displace Cantonese films towards the end of the 1960s (Cantonese production declined from 200 in 1960 to a mere handful of films in the early 1970s) was due to a number of related cultural and industrial factors. Cantonese films came to be seen as parochial, Mandarin films as more cosmopolitan; Mandarin films had higher production values; and, crucially, the major vertically integrated companies were Mandarin.

Cantonese cinema revived in the late 1970s, but by the 1980s the differences were no longer institutionalized in the same way as there no longer existed separate exhibition sectors for the two languages. In modern Hong Kong cinema the dichotomy between Cantonese and Mandarin sub-cinemas has virtually disappeared.

For a mass-production industry, Hong Kong cinema has a small domestic market (the colony's population stood at 2.3 million in 1950 and 6.8 million in 1997). Film production therefore has to be run on an economical basis; Hong Kong filmmakers cannot afford the profligacy of Hollywood. Production costs are kept low: in the 1960s the average cost was about HK$500,000, in the 1990s around HK$10 million (equivalent to US$1.2 million).[42] The theatrical 'life' of a film is very short (a major success might play for only a month) and the profit margins are small, though more Hong Kong films are likely to break even than is the case for either Hollywood or Bollywood. With local films produced in such large numbers they have successfully beaten off competition from imported films in the domestic market.

The major genres of Hong Kong cinema include comedies, romances, costume films, and (in the 1950s and 1960s) *huangei* opera films. However, the genre that is widely seen as being synonymous with Hong Kong cinema is the martial arts action film. The *wuxia pan* ('martial chivalry') film has a long pedigree in East Asian cinema that extends back to the silent era, though it was in the 1960s that it emerged as a major genre in Hong Kong through the popular success of a cycle of swordfight films (*One-Armed Swordsman*, *The Assassin*, *Dragon Inn*, *The Wandering Swordsman*). These films were an eclectic mixture of styles and influences, including Japanese samurai films, spaghetti westerns and Peking Opera (from which the films borrowed their gravity-defying acrobatic 'flying swordsmen'). A new type of martial arts film arose in the early 1970s, however, in the form of the kung-fu film. What made the kung-fu film distinctive was that it had a modern rather than a period setting and that it used performers who had authentic martial arts techniques. The kung-fu film is yet another example of a popular genre disparaged by critics (who dubbed them 'chop-sockies') but which possesses a cultural significance regardless of its perceived quality. Stephen Teo argues that the kung-fu film 'ultimately set the tone for the modernization of Hong Kong cinema as the genre reflected the dynamic qualities of Hong Kong society and the fast developing economy itself'.[43] It occupies a place in Hong Kong film culture comparable to the films of Amitabh Bachchan in India, representing a populist cinema identifying with working-class values. In contrast to the noble warriors of swordfight films, the heroes of kung-fu films tended to be cynical and self-interested, usually motivated either by personal gain (hence the frequency of the plot device of the martial arts tournament) or by revenge.

The kung-fu film came to be associated with one studio (Golden Harvest) and, pre-eminently, with one star: Bruce Lee. Lee, born in San Francisco and raised in Hong Kong, had first demonstrated his martial arts skills in the American television series *The Green Hornet* (as Oriental houseboy Cato). He became a cult hero through a series of Hong Kong martial arts films in the early 1970s that showcased his remarkable athletic prowess (*The Big Boss*, *Fist of Fury*, *The Way of the Dragon*, *Game of Death*). These films not only broke box-office records in Hong Kong but were picked up for distribution in America where they were shown to popular acclaim in urban cinemas catering for predominantly working-class and/or Asian audiences. Lee called his style of fighting *jeet kun-do* ('way of the intercepting fist') though the more general term *kung-fu* was adopted to describe a genre also including films without Lee (*Five Fingers of Death*, *Deep Thrust*, *The Invisible Fist*, *Shanghai Killers*). The kung-fu craze peaked in 1973, explaining that year's increase in production output, and reached its commercial high point with the Hollywood-backed *Enter the Dragon*, teaming Lee with two minor American action stars (John Saxon and Jim Kelly), though Lee's death from a brain haemorrhage in the same year marked the beginning of the end for the genre. Enterprising Hong Kong filmmakers tried to exploit Lee's popularity through lookalikes with similar-sounding names (Bruce Li, Bruce Leh, Bruce Lei) but they never matched the success of the genuine article. Other martial arts stars have emerged who match Lee in box-office success (Jackie Chan, Jet Li and – to include a female example – Michelle Yeoh), but the pure kung-fu film has been displaced by action comedies and triad thrillers. The 1990s witnessed a revival of the costume martial arts film exemplified by Tsui Hark's *Once Upon a Time in China* and its numerous sequels and imitators.

The popular cinema of Hong Kong represents a triumph of style and spectacle over narrative and characterization. This is deliberate on the part of filmmakers. As the director King Hu once remarked: 'If the plots are simple, the stylistic delivery will be even richer.'[44] Bordwell describes the style of Hong Kong cinema since the 1970s as one of a 'breathlessly accelerated tempo – whirlwind action sequences, conversations ever on the move, rapidly changing angles, constantly mobile camera . . . In these movies virtually nobody stays still unless he or she is dying.'[45] This breathless, kinetic style reached its height in the action movies of director John Woo in the 1980s and early 1990s (*A Better Tomorrow*, *The Killer*, *Hard-Boiled*). Woo's films, usually starring Chow Yun Fat as a gangster or a policeman, are based around themes of loyalty and betrayal and are character-ized by their graphic, cathartic violence: the climax of *Hard-Boiled* is an extended shoot-out in a hospital where dozens of heavies (and, in a manner reminiscent of Sam Peckinpah's *The Wild Bunch*, several innocent bystanders) are blown away. Censorship in Hong Kong, controlled by an official govern-ment agency, has always been quite permissive in the level of violence it will allow. It was only in 1988 that a classification system was introduced: Category I (suitable for all), Category II (unsuitable for children) and Category III (forbidden to viewers under eighteen). Category III tends to be reserved for porno-graphic and gore-horror films, many of which are now released straight to video. Hong Kong censors have historically been more sensitive about political issues (especially the question of the colony's relations with China) than moral concerns.

Hong Kong cinema continued to flourish throughout the 1980s and into the mid-1990s. Some of the old producers ceased operations (Shaw Brothers closed down in the mid-1980s) but the basic structure of the industry remained much the same. The exhibition sector remained strong despite com-petition from home video and film production actually increased in the early 1990s before the Asian economic crisis later in the decade signalled a relapse. At the same time, however, a shadow hung over Hong Kong cinema in the form of its reversion to mainland rule in 1997 when the colony became a 'Special Administrative Region' under the control of Beijing. Some Hong Kong filmmakers began to make plans for a future outside Hong Kong: Raymond Chow established a base in Canada, John Woo moved to Hollywood and stars like Jackie Chan and Chow Yun Fat developed Hollywood careers in parallel with their Hong Kong movies. Others looked to develop closer relations with Taiwan, which remained a Chinese territory outside mainland control.

The island of Taiwan became the refuge of Chiang Kai-shek's Nationalists following the Communist victory of 1949. Film production was initially controlled by the authoritarian government, which established the Central Motion Picture Corporation to produce anti-Communist propaganda. The most popular films with Taiwanese audiences, however, were genre imports from Hong Kong. The Taiwanese production sector expanded rapidly in the late 1950s – annual output in the middle of the decade was barely two dozen films a year, by the decade's end it was over a hundred – and reached 200 by the end of the 1960s. Despite the regime's policy of promoting 'wholesome realism', the bulk of Taiwanese production consisted of imitations of Hong Kong genre films. Some Hong Kong filmmakers established studios in Taiwan – Lee Han-Hsiang left Shaw Brothers to set up the Grand Movie Company, Hu Chin Chuan founded the International Motion Picture Studio – and imported genres such as the romance and the swordfight film. Taiwanese producers shifted from Amoy (Taiwanese dialect) to Mandarin language films – the number of Mandarin films rose from a mere 10 in 1964 to 116 in 1968 and 163 by 1970 – and even, for a brief period at the end of the 1960s, exported Mandarin films to Hong Kong. Taiwanese popular cinema enjoyed its 'golden age' in the 1960s, but it was short-lived. Production declined in the 1970s and, unlike Hong Kong, box-office revenues declined.[46]

To what extent was Taiwanese popular cinema an imitation of that of Hong Kong? It has been suggested that the two cinemas exemplify 'a history of difference' with Hong Kong specializing in action-oriented genres and Taiwan inclining more towards sentiment and melodrama: 'These differences in Hong Kong and Taiwanese films helped establish demographic differentiation among film audiences, with the swordplay films of Hong Kong appealing to men, and the Taiwanese weepies appealing to women.'[47] The extent of these differences should not, however, be exaggrated. Hong Kong produced its share of romantic dramas and Taiwan has turned out myriad martial arts films. Indeed, it is from Taiwan that perhaps the two most critically acclaimed *wuxia pan* have originated. The Hong Kong director King Hu made *A Touch of Zen* (1971) in Taiwan; combining the characteristic flying swordsmen of the genre with Buddhist philosophy, the film was shown at the Cannes Film Festival in 1975 and subsequently became an 'art house' success in the West. An even more successful commercial/art house crossover came in the form of Ang Lee's *Crouching Tiger, Hidden Dragon* (2000), a visually stunning US-Taiwanese-Chinese co-production that won four Oscars (for Best Foreign Film, Best Cinematography, Best Art Direction and Best Music). Lee's film takes the basic ingredients of the genre (the quest for a mystical object, a secret martial arts society, a young woman disguised as a swordsman) but adds a greater level of psychological depth than is usual to the narrative. *Crouching Tiger, Hidden Dragon* is a self-conscious aestheticization of the genre: the fight choreography has a balletic quality as the protagonists glide up walls and across rooftops with a grace that would not ashame Astaire and Rogers. Indeed, as one critic remarked, the climactic duel between master swordsman Li Mu Bai (Chow Yun Fat) and Jen (Zhang Ziyi) is 'more a swooning seduction than a fight as such'.[48] Its aesthetic qualities aside, however, *Crouching Tiger, Hidden Dragon* represents a significant landmark in film history as a commercially successful collaboration between Hollywood (Sony/Columbia) and East Asian film industries. Its worldwide grosses of over $100 million would seem to indicate that it has 'paved the way for large international audiences to accept a Chinese-language revival of the old genre'.[49]

Other Asiatic cinemas that deserve mention are Indonesia and the Philippines. In both archipelagos a large domestic market was fed by a combination of indigenous production (which peaked in the 1970s and 1980s) and imports. Indonesia, with a total population in excess of 190 million, had a fluctuating history of film production following independence in 1950 (there had been a small production sector in the Dutch East Indies during the 1930s, but this ceased during the Japanese occupation in the Second World War). An immediate rise in production in the first half of the 1950s, peaking at 64 features in 1955, was followed by a decline in the second half of the decade which continued throughout the next decade to single figures at the end of the 1960s. The decline coincided with the period of so-called 'Guided Democracy' (1957–65) when the Communist-aligned government of President Sukarno was in the ascendancy. A military coup leading to the establishment of a right-wing government under General Suharto, known as New Order, helped to bring about conditions in which domestic production could revive by introducing subsidies for the industry and a quota on imports. Indonesian film production increased again during the 1970s, peaking at 124 features in 1977 and averaging between sixty and seventy a year throughout the 1970s and 1980s. Indonesian films accounted for approximately 40 per cent of the domestic market; the rest was divided between American, Indian and Hong Kong imports (Indonesia has large Indian and Chinese minorities). The popular genres of Indonesian cinema are local variants on genres established elsewhere, such as the Indonesian musical (*dangdut*), the Indonesian martial arts film (*silat*) and the Indonesian teen film (*remaja*). Some Indonesian films were exported to Singapore and Malaysia, where indigenous production was negligible. The Philippines, with a population of 75 million, has a larger production sector than Indonesia. Again, the Second World War halted production, which then revived in the 1950s and stabilized in the 1960s and 1970s at around 150 features per year; a peak of 253 was reached in 1971, over fifty films more than in any other year. The popular genres of Filipino cinema, again representing local variations on international forms, include romantic dramas, comedies and the musical (*zarzuela*). A more permissive censorship regime – at least with regard to sex and violence – enabled the vampire film and a violent form of pornography known as *bomba* to emerge as dominant genres.

In both Indonesia and the Philippines, however, political censorship is quite stringent, even after the fall of Suharto and Marcos, respectively, seemed to offer prospects of more democratic governments. Other East Asian national cinemas that witnessed relative production booms were South Korea in the early 1970s and Thailand in the mid-1980s, again dominated by genre films produced primarily for domestic consumption.[50]

Despite efforts to promote a more serious, socially committed cinema in the Far East – there were 'new wave' movements in Japan in the 1960s, Hong Kong in the late 1970s and Taiwan in the 1980s – the bulk of film production remains focused around popular genres. It is for this reason that, other than the classical Japanese cinema and the New Chinese Cinema, much East Asian cinema remains outside the orbit of western interest. Yet, in terms of sheer levels of production, if not necessarily aesthetic quality, the popular genres of Asian cinemas represent one of the most culturally significant aspects of world film history. The martial arts film, especially, is a distinctive example of an indigenous regional genre that has its own culturally specific codes and conventions. Its production exceeds that of more familiar genres like the American western and the Hollywood musical and its cultural and historical roots are much older. The current academic interest in the genre, combined with the international success of *Crouching Tiger, Hidden Dragon*, suggests that the popular cinema of the Far East is about to find its long overdue place in the sun.

FOURTEEN

Middle Eastern Cinemas

The Middle East accounts for approximately five per cent of the world's film production and is host to a variety of national cinemas that remain almost unknown beyond their own states. Notwithstanding the example of Egypt, which, as we have seen, had a small studio system by the 1930s and exported films throughout the Arab world, it took longer for significant film industries to emerge in the Middle East. The history of cinema throughout most of the Middle East, therefore, is essentially a post-war development. A number of factors can be advanced to explain cinema's relatively late entry into the region. In a global context, cinema developed fastest in the countries with the highest level of industrialization and urbanization (the United States, Western Europe, Japan) and slowest in regions where predominantly pre-industrial, rural societies remained the norm (China, Africa, the Middle East). As a secular, commercial form of entertainment, cinema was entirely unrelated to traditional forms of Arab leisure activity. Political instability in the Middle East, furthermore, especially between Israel (established in 1948) and its Arab neighbours, has meant that conditions in the region have not been conducive to large-scale production. Unlike in Africa, however, where economic underdevelopment has been the major impediment to indigenous film production, these conditions are not replicated in the Middle East. The wealth of the 'oil sheiks' has made little difference: the leading film-producing nations in the Middle East (Egypt, Turkey) are amongst some of the poorer states, while the wealthiest (Saudi Arabia, Kuwait, the United Arab Emirates) do not produce films in any significant numbers. It was not really until the 1960s and 1970s that distinctive national cinemas could be identified. Some states, such as Algeria, aligned themselves with the Third Cinema paradigm; others, such as Iran, have developed a national film culture 'with both ethical substance (as defined by the Islamic state) and artistic merit'.[1] The diversity of film cultures that can be identified in the region makes the label 'Arab cinema' that some commentators have applied to a broad geographical diaspora from the Maghreb to the Persian Gulf problematic as a theoretical construct; the presence of Israeli cinema, moreover, also makes it technically inaccurate.

CINEMA AND SOCIETY

The introduction of cinema to the Middle East, as in the Far East, took place under the aegis of foreign entrepreneurs and showmen. Although there are documented examples of public film shows in Algiers, Cairo and Alexandria in 1896, these were for foreign residents rather than for locals. It took longer for cinema to extend into the Ottoman Empire. It was not until 1908, for example, that the first films were shown in Aleppo (Syria), and only in 1909 did they reach Baghdad. Film production, similarly, tended to be the work of foreigners, usually making scenics and topicals. It was not for several decades that the first indigenous feature films were produced in Egypt (1927), Syria (1928), Tunisia (1928), Lebanon (1929), Iran (1932) and Morocco (1934). Thus, as two historians of Arab cinema observe, 'the cinema's appearance was fragmentary – the result more of exceptional endeavour by isolated individuals than of any underlying necessity'.[2] Throughout most of the Middle East, indeed, cinema as a social institution was hardly established at all by the time the first talkies arrived in the region in the early 1930s.

What reasons can be advanced to explain cinema's relatively late entry into the Middle East? It cannot be explained simply in terms of cultural difference, for, as we have seen, by the 1920s cinema had become established in societies as different from the West as India and Japan. Nor can the linguistic diversity of spoken Arabic be considered a satisfactory explanation in its own right when the success of cinema in multi-lingual India is taken into account. There is evidence to suggest that film exhibition was intended primarily for foreign residents rather than for the local populations. In Libya, for example, where only about twenty cinemas were built between the Italian annexation of 1911 and independence in 1951, imported films were shown without Arabic subtitles suggesting that their audiences were Italian speakers rather than locals.[3] Cinemas in most Middle Eastern countries tended to be concentrated in cities with large European populations and there was differentiation within the exhibition sector, with comfortable, air-conditioned and more expensive cinemas catering for an audience of Europeans and more prosperous members of the bourgeoisie, and rudimentary, cheaper cinemas (often with wooden bench seating) for local audiences.

A more general explanation for the cultural resistance to cinema throughout most of the Middle East arises from the unique characteristics of the Islamic faith. In western eyes Islam has become almost synonymous with censorship and social and religious oppression; in its defence could be cited the argument that it is probably no more censorious and oppressive than other major religions, including Christianity and Judaism, have been at particular times in their history. Cinema has, at best, an uneasy relationship with Islam, arising in large measure from the religion's ambiguous attitude towards the representation of images of any kind. 'Islam is said to forbid pictures, and to condemn all pictorial representation of the human face,' one Islamic scholar has observed, and, while then proceeding to expose this assumption as a fallacy, concedes, nevertheless, that as 'a pictorial art [cinema] . . . is liable, in the eyes of the stricter rite, to such condemnation as strikes all arts of the image'.[4] The first public cinema in Tehran, opened in 1905 by European-educated entrepreneur Ebrahim Sahaf-Bashi, was forced to close following a public outcry when it was rumoured that films were shown featuring shots of unveiled women.[5] Foreign distributors have always had to be alert to the fact that many American and European films, especially those featuring any form of sexual display or indecorous female dress, would be likely to upset local sensibilities. As so much Hollywood cinema, especially, has been posited on sexual spectacle – already apparent in the silent melodramas of the 1920s and in the dance routines of 1930s musicals – it is unsurprising that such films should not find a large audience in the Islamic world.

Behrad Najafi's study of the history of cinema in Iran, for example, argues that 'social, cultural, and political circumstances in general militated against the development of a film culture in the country'.[6] Religious leaders put up strong opposition to the cinema as a social practice. The Ulema (clerical interpreters of the Hadith, considered by many an authority almost on a par with the Koran) conducted a campaign against cinema both via the mosque and in print, arguing that it had a detrimental effect on the morals of the masses. The Islamic newspaper *Homoyun* declared in 1935:

> When that lust-seeking capricious man and that nubile young girl sit side-by-side in front of the movie-screen and view the nude men and women embracing and taking long warm kisses from each other's mouths, will not the fire of lust inflame in them, preparing the grounds for all sorts of moral corruption which will burn up the harvest of their lives? Yes, it will burn, burn like fire burning dry thistle.[7]

On one level this echoes the views of moral reformers in western countries who also viewed cinemas as dens of iniquity that encouraged sexual licentiousness and moral impropriety. On another level, however, there was an explicitly religious dimension to this opposition arising from the fact that imported western films, which accounted for the majority of those shown, manifested (either directly or indirectly) Christian values and were thus regarded as offensive to the Islamic faith. The Ulema did their most to curtail the influence of cinema and declared it *tahrim* (forbidden); consequently millions of Iranians would not visit a cinema. Filmmakers in Iran often had to work under the patronage of the Shah and films themselves were a luxury entertainment for the royal court, foreign nationals and the local *bourgeoisie*.

The fact that before the Second World War much of the Middle East came under European colonial rule or mandates also needs to be taken into consideration. Political and economic factors militated against the development of indigenous production as European powers were naturally reluctant to encourage any form of cultural expression that might inflame nationalist sentiment and European producers and distributors naturally wanted to ensure it was their films which were shown. It is significant in this regard that the only country in either the Arab world or Africa to develop a substantial film production industry during the interwar period was Egypt, which had become a sovereign independent state in 1922 (though even so the British maintained a military presence in the Suez Canal Zone until 1956). The emergence of national film industries in the Middle East tended to coincide with political independence. Thus it was not until the 1950s and 1960s that any significant level of indigenous film production can be identified.

Political independence in the Middle East and North Africa signalled a change in the social acceptance of cinema. Hitherto both nationalists and religious leaders had been united in their opposition to this 'westernized' medium. However, while religious groups continued to voice their opposition – the Pan-Islamic Congress, meeting in Karachi in 1952, called upon Islamic governments to close all cinemas – politicians were now more inclined to look favourably upon cinema as a vehicle for promoting the ideology Arab pan-nationalism. This movement was supported by intellectuals who recognized the cultural value of film for promoting unity within the newly independent Arab world. One such intellectual in the United Arab Republic (the short-lived union between Egypt and Syria from 1958 until 1961) articulated this view:

> In order to build a new Arab society based upon solid foundations of understanding between peoples and co-operation in the struggle against poverty, disease, and ignorance, we must use all the resources of the cinema and so direct our films that they may help us to bring about the victory of Arab nationalism. The actors of the Arab cinema should have a deep faith in the important task which is entrusted to them by the nation, the people, humanity, and life . . . We may wish that common effort, and co-operation between producers, may increase more and more, in order to make Arabic films in

common, which will raise the level of spiritual and human values, encourage peace and virtuous conduct and spread affection and understanding amongst the Arab nations.[8]

There have been various initiatives to promote Arab filmmaking, including the establishment of film festivals at Damascus and Carthage, though in the immediate post-independence period it was Egyptian cinema that became the dominant force in the Arab world.

The ascendancy of Egyptian cinema was due to both cultural and economic factors. Egypt remained the leading film-producing and exporting nation in the Middle East, consistently producing around 40–50 films a year between the 1940s and the 1970s, when it was overtaken by Pakistan. Rather like Hindi cinema in India, which developed colloquial *Hindistani* as the language for films, Egyptian filmmakers adopted a form of colloquial Arabic that is widely understood. As Lebanese scholar Farid Jabre explains: 'The audiences in the Arab countries, without understanding every word of the Egyptian dialect, have got used to it and feel uncomfortable when faced with another Arabic dialect.'[9] In 1961 the Egyptian film industry became the first in the region to be nationalized when the government of Colonel Nasser set up the General Organization of Egyptian Cinema. This body was responsible for the production of three-quarters of Egyptian films over the next decade and followed a policy of supporting the cause of Arab pan-nationalism. Egyptian filmmakers came to look back on the 1960s as 'a golden age of nationalized, protected cinema . . . dedicated to Egypt and Arabs in the name of land, and to solidarity and integrity in the name of the family'.[10] The Egyptian example provided a model for other Arab countries, including Syria and Iraq where similar state organizations were established, even though by the early 1970s the Egyptian industry had been denationalized because so few of the films made by the General Organization had been commercially successful.

Egypt was overtaken as the leading regional producer by Pakistan in the 1970s. At the time of Partition in 1947, most of the filmmakers based in Lahore left for Bombay so that Pakistan inherited production facilities but a dearth of talent. Pakistani film production was negligible during the 1950s but took off during the 1960s, rising from 38 films a year at the beginning of the decade to 90 by its end. In the early 1970s Pakistan was producing over a hundred films annually and, while this level has since dipped, its average annual production of around 80 features still ranks it amongst the leading world film producers. The majority of films made in 'Lollywood', as the Lahore-based film industry is disparagingly known, are generic imitations of Bollywood. Although the exhibition of Indian films has been restricted in Pakistan since the 1960s, there is a thriving black market in video cassettes of Indian films. Pakistani films are an object of derision in their own country – the veteran director W. Z. Ahmed recently called them 'a national disgrace'[11] – and, in contrast to Indian cinema, have not built up an overseas audience. The Pakistani film industry has suffered through the dismantling of the protectionist legislation introduced shortly after independence and by a lack of modern equipment. The most prestigious Pakistani film of recent years was *Jinnah* (1998), a biopic of Muhammed Ali Jinnah, the Pakistani patriot and first governor-general, though ironically this film was the work of a director (Jamil Dehlavi) exiled in Britain and starred a British actor (Christopher Lee) in the title role.

The nature and extent of state control over the cinema varies enormously within the Middle East, though nowhere could censorship be described as liberal by western standards. Film censorship tends to be the responsibility of government departments or boards of censors comprised of government officials. Censorship policies and regulations, however, do vary. In prerevolutionary Iran, for instance, the official censor was less concerned with sex (it sanctioned commercial films including nudity and erotic imagery) than it was with social and political matters (insisting, for example, that royalty must always be portrayed in a positive light). The first example of censorship in Iran, indeed, had been in 1934 when head of state Shah Reza Pahlavi intervened personally to insist that a film biopic of the Persian poet Firdawsi was changed to portray the then king as a just ruler and a patron of the arts.[12] In Egypt the functions of political and moral censorship are divided between an official state censorship authority (the Ministry of Culture) that scrutinizes scripts and has censors present during the shooting of films, and an unofficial body (the Islamic Research Council based at al-Azhar University) which examines cultural products for religious orthodoxy and moral propriety. Egypt's most acclaimed filmmaker, Youssef Chahine, has suffered at the hands of both parties. His *The Sparrow* (1971), a critical examination of the reasons for Egypt's defeat by Israel in the Six-Day War of 1967, had to be made elsewhere (Lebanon) and was banned by the government of President Sadat, while his *The Emigrant* (1994), despite having been a popular success, was withdrawn from distribution when the Islamic Research Council objected to its portrayal of a character taken to be the Jewish patriarch Joseph, though on this occasion Chahine appealed successfully against the ban in the courts.[13] The Taliban regime, which came to power in Afghanistan in the mid-1990s, had the most consistent censorship policy of any Islamic government: it simply imposed a blanket ban on all films and videos.

Islamic law is frequently cited as a justification for censorship, though in practice it is a combination of religious and political factors which motivate the regulation of cinema. The far-reaching nature of censorship is exemplified by the Iraqi Law on the Censorship of Foreign Films of 1973 which prohibits 'the propagation of reactionary, chauvinistic, populist, racialist or regionist ideas, of favouring the spirit of defeatism, serving imperialism and Zionism and their supporters . . . defaming the Arab nation and its goals and causes of destiny, or brotherly and friendly countries, or defaming or offending the national liberation movements of the world'.[14] Effectively this empowered the Ba'athist regime to ban any film it disliked for any reason. The subject most likely to inflame opinion even in moderate Islamic states is any favourable representation of Israel and Judaism. It was for this reason that Steven Spielberg's much-acclaimed *Schindler's List* (1993), which the director insisted should be shown uncut or not at all, was widely banned throughout the Islamic world. Jordan, Lebanon, Egypt, Dubai and the United Arab Emirates all refused to show it, as did Far Eastern countries with large Muslim populations, such as Indonesia and Malaysia. While the official reason often given was that the film contained nudity and a sex scene, this was little more than a convenient excuse for governments hostile to the Jewish faith.[15] In contrast, the Nazi propaganda film *Jud Süss* was shown in some Arab states in the 1950s.

Given its unique status as the world's only Jewish state, it is only to be expected that cinema in Israel has followed a divergent path from its Arab neighbours. Israeli cinema has always been more closely aligned with the West than others in the Middle East. At first this was a practical necessity, as in the years immediately following its foundation in 1948 Israel had to import overseas filmmakers, including Britain's Thorold Dickinson who directed *Hill 24 Doesn't Answer* (1954), the first Israeli feature film, a surprisingly anti-heroic war film set during the first Arab-Israeli War in 1948. Domestic production has rarely risen above the teens but Israel has been open to western films in a way that other Middle Eastern countries have not and film attendance per head of population is amongst the highest in the world. The first Israeli filmmakers to achieve commercial success, if not critical acclaim, were cousins Menahem Golan and Yoram Globus who turned out popular genre films, including spy films, musicals and a type of Israeli romantic comedy known as *boureka*. In 1979 they bought Cannon Pictures, an independent production company which under their guidance came to specialize in low-budget action films such as the *Missing in Action* and *Delta Force* series (dubbed 'Cannon-fodder' by critics). In the 1980s the Cannon Group also acquired cinema chains and existed as a sort of 'mini-major' on the periphery of the US film industry until it was brought to its knees by the combination of an overly ambitious expansion programme and financial irregularities.

In common with so many other new states (including Islamic states), the Israeli government was quick to recognize the political and cultural value of film and took measures to support its fledgling industry. The Israeli Film Law of 1954 provided official assistance and tax benefits for films made in Israel. Israeli technicians thus gained experience by working on American productions such as *Exodus* (1960) and *Cast a Giant Shadow* (1966). In 1979 the Ministry of Education and Culture introduced a subsidy scheme to encourage 'quality film' which has supported various young Israeli filmmakers such as Daniel Wachsmann, Dalia Hager and Ayaleth Menahemi. The Israeli Theatre and Film Censorship Board, appointed by the Ministry of the Interior, consists of a mixture of officials, journalists, jurists, teachers and police officers. It has been on the whole more even-handed than Islamic censors, being sensitive to films that might be deemed offensive to all religions – *The Passover Plot* (1976) was banned because it might be upsetting to Christians – though its main concern, naturally, is any suggestion of anti-Semitism. There is, however, one uncanny parallel with Islamic states. In 1991 the right-wing political party, Likud, campaigned to close all cinemas east of the main Haifa-Tel Aviv highway on the Jewish Sabbath. Although the campaign was unsuccessful, it provides evidence that religious opposition to the cinema exists in Israel just as it does in the Islamic states.

Film production in the Middle East has been hampered by political instability, war and terrorism. The Arab-Israeli Wars of 1967 and 1973–4, the Iran-Iraq War of 1980–88, the Gulf War of 1991 and continued tension between Israel and the Palestinian Authority have all disrupted production. The distribution of films between countries is also subject to change. While, obviously, no Israeli films are permitted in Islamic countries, political differences within the Arab world can also lead to bans. Egyptian films were temporarily prohibited in Jordan following the conclusion of the Camp David Peace between Egypt and Israel in 1979. Iraq has been more or less isolated since the end of the Gulf War, whereas Iran, isolated following the Islamic Revolution of 1979, has slowly opened up again. The tensions within the Middle East are such, however, that the pan-Arab cinema envisioned by some intellectuals in the 1960s now seems a much more remote possibility.

NEW IRANIAN CINEMA

The most significant movement in Middle Eastern cinema in recent years, both culturally and aesthetically, has been the emergence of the New Iranian Cinema. Roy Armes dates the start of this movement quite precisely: '1970 [saw] the appearance of a New Iranian Cinema . . . created by a fairly heterogeneous group of young intellectuals, many of them foreign-educated, and receiving some support from the Ministry of Culture and the state television service.'[16] Twenty-two years later, at the 1992 Toronto International Film Festival, Iranian cinema was referred to as 'one of the pre-eminent national cinemas in the world today'; and in 1999 the *New York Times* called it 'one of the world's most vital national cinemas'.[17] The emergence of a distinctive national cinema in Iran is remarkable not only because it has attracted a sustained level of critical interest (in contrast to many new cinemas which flower and fade all too quickly), but also because its history spans two very different political regimes, the absolutist monarchy of Shah Muhammad Reza Pahlavi and the equally autocratic Islamic Republic created after 1979 by followers of Ayatollah Khomeini.

Until the end of the 1960s the state-controlled Iranian film industry had produced mostly genre films of no great merit – melodramas, comedies and *luti* (tough-guy) films – and had imported song-and-dance films from India and Egypt. The Shah's ambition to modernize Iran along western lines meant that American films and television programmes were widely available. The birth of the New Iranian Cinema is usually identified with two films made in 1969 and released in 1970: Massoud Kimiai's *Quaisar* and Dariush Mehrjui's *The Cow*. These films were seen as marking a return to traditional cultural values: *Quaisar* was a *luti* in which the villain is associated with westernization, *The Cow* was a social realist film about village life. In common with new cinemas under authoritarian regimes elsewhere in the world, it was the critical prestige that these films garnered overseas that led the government to support the filmmakers even though it did not necessarily approve of what they were trying to do and say. *The Cow*, for example, 'embodied a contradiction that became the hallmark of the New Wave movement: it was sponsored by the state (Ministry of Culture and Art, MCA) and was censored and banned (for one year) by the state (the same Ministry)'.[18]

The early 1970s saw the emergence of a state-sponsored film culture in Iran, with the founding of the Tehran Film Festival,

the establishment of a film school and the sponsorship of young filmmakers. The MCA and the National Iranian Television and Radio (NIRT), both run by relatives of the Shah, invested in the production of documentaries and fictional films. Najafi describes the style of the films as one of 'passive realism':

> The majority of the films in the Iranian New Wave were characterized by a certain mood which was their most common feature. I propose the term 'passive realism' to designate this mood. In brief, such films are 'passive' because the main characters are resigned to undesirable, gloomy circumstances which breed frustration, pessimism, acceptance and inaction; they are 'realistic' because they focus on Iranian social reality, drawing attention to the isolation, alienation and repression which became facts of life during the reigns of the Pahlavi Shahs.[19]

Among the filmmakers whose work can be included in this movement were Bahram Bayzai (*Downpour*, *The Crow*) and Amir Naderi (*Goodbye My Friend*) who had trained abroad and who forged links with the Writers' Guild (*Kanun-e Nevisandegan*), a centre of intellectual opposition to the regime. Their efforts were hampered, however, by government censorship, which regulated the amount of social criticism allowed in the films. It was due to excessive state intervention that a group of filmmakers tried to set up an independent collective, the New Film Group, in the mid-1970s, but their attempt to evade censorship by employing more avant-garde techniques obscured the meaning of the films which did not find much of an audience.

The Iranian film industry peaked in the early 1970s when it produced around 90 films a year, but the increasing costs of production and the uncertainty of box-office success (ticket prices were deliberately kept low by the regime) meant that the industry was already facing a crisis before the Islamic Revolution of 1979 forced the Shah into exile and ushered in a period of even greater uncertainty. Unlike the Ulema or the Taliban, however, Khomeini and his followers were not opposed to cinema itself, but rather to what they saw as its misuse under the Shah. Khomeini himself declared:

> We are not opposed to cinema, to radio or to television . . . The cinema is a modern invention that ought to be used for the sake of educating the people, but as you know, it was used to corrupt our youth. It is the misuse of cinema that we are opposed to, a misuse caused by the treacherous policies of our rulers.[20]

Thus, while film production was severely curtailed following the revolution, it was never intended that cinema would be banned entirely. Instead it was to be employed in support of the new Islamic Republic. The Ayatollah's regime set out to 'purify' and 'Islamize' cinema. In some instances this purification was taken literally either by burning cinemas or by performing a ceremonial ritual of ablution. The industry was purged of filmmakers who were deemed to have been responsible for supporting the policies of the Shah, surviving cinemas were renamed to remove any western associations, and imports of western films, especially American movies, were severely reduced. In 1982 film censorship was brought under the control of the Ministry of Culture and Islamic Guidance, and in 1983 the Farabi Cinema Foundation was set up to subsidize production and promote an Iranian film culture on Islamic principles. The major components of Islamic culture, as understood in post-revolutionary Iran, were nativism (a return to traditional values) and independence (both political and economic). The regime promoted *towhid* (monotheism), *velayat-e faqih* ('rule of the supreme jurisprudent'), *mostaz'afan* (defence of the disinherited) and *estekbar-e jahani* (opposition to imperialism, usually referring to the United States).[21]

'Over the two decades after the establishment of the Islamic Republic,' writes Hamid Naficy, 'a new cinema has emerged which is markedly different from the one that had existed previously.'[22] The difference was not necessarily due to new personnel, as several of the directors who had been active in the pre-revolutionary cinema (Bahram Bayzai, Massoud Kimiai, Amir Naderi) continued into the post-revolutionary period; they were joined by a new generation of filmmakers recruited by the Farabi Foundation (Kianoush Ayyari, Abbas Kiarostami, Mohsen Makhmalbaf). It was, rather, a different cinema in terms of its industrial structure and its ideological orientation. Post-revolutionary Iranian cinema is unique in a number of respects. For one thing, it has never been an entirely monolithic or doctrinaire cinema. For all that they continue to operate under strict state censorship, Iranian filmmakers have never had to adhere to a totalizing political and aesthetic doctrine in the manner of Socialist Realism. The government has supported different filmmaking practices that ensure diversity and variation. Thus, a 'populist cinema' of genre films, funded by the private sector, has co-existed with an 'art cinema' or 'quality cinema' funded by the state. The populist cinema included family melodramas, comedies and war films (a genre that was prominent during the war against Iraq in the 1980s when it could be used to promote national solidarity in the wake of the revolution). The art cinema comprises more serious, realist films which examine social problems. While these films account for a relatively small proportion of all those made, they have been critically acclaimed at home and abroad. They range in style from the semi-documentary films of Abbas Kiarostami (*Where Is My Friend's Home*, *Close Up*, *And Life Goes On*) to the semi-surrealist fables of Mohsen Makhmalbaf (*The Peddler*, *The Cyclist*).

A feature of contemporary Iranian cinema that has attracted much attention of late is the space it allows for women. This 'space' is both industrial and aesthetic. In spite of all the obstacles posed by a patriarchal society in which women are treated as second-class citizens, a number of women directors have actually come to prominence in Iran in the 1990s, such as Puran Derakhshandeh (*The Little Bird of Happiness*) and Tahmineh Milani (*What's New*). It is in the work of women directors that Iranian films have addressed hitherto taboo subjects such as divorced working mothers (Rakhshan Bani-Etemad's *May Lady*) and emancipation (Samirah Makhmalbaf's *The Apple*). Samirah, daughter of Mohsen Makhmalbaf, summed up the difficulties faced by women directors: 'There are laws that are written and laws that are unwritten, but which people really believe in: our problem more than anything is one of cultural tradition . . . [But] once I'd finished *The Apple* I travelled with it all over the world, and I found that everywhere women's prospects are worse than men's.'[23] One commentator even suggests that post-revolutionary Iranian cinema has demonstrated 'an attitude to women that is far more progressive than attitudes before the Revolution'.[24] At the same time, however, the 'space' for women on-screen is regulated by strict censorship. For example, women are not allowed to share the same diegetic space as men and the female gaze must be 'averted'. In order to negotiate such restrictions, Iranian filmmakers have had to develop a different sort of film grammar that is quite distinctive, with shot composition and point-of-view used to position women. Critics disagree over the ideological effect of this alternative film grammar. Thus, on the one hand, one critic highlights the 'ridiculous' nature of the restrictions imposed on actors by analysing a scene from *The Apple*: 'Though Forugh [the female protagonist] is supposed to be close to her son, they cannot touch because the actors playing the roles are not really parent and child'.[25] Laura Mulvey, on the other hand, suggests that 'the taboos imposed erase many established conventions and ways of seeing, and create a new challenge for the cinema'.[26] Mulvey sees Iranian film as an 'alternative' to the voyeuristic and fetishistic tendencies of the classical cinema: rather than being presented as 'objects of to-be-looked-at-ness' women become 'objects of *not*-to-be-looked-at-ness'.

Yet perhaps the difference of Iranian film from other national cinemas should not be exaggerated. While not denying the unique circumstances in which it emerged, there are historical parallels in other national cinemas. Agnès Devictor observes: 'Although they were established in a very specific political and cultural frame, the post-revolutionary Iranian state's interventions in the cinema sector can be compared, to a certain extent, with cinema regulations observed in other places and at other times.'[27] Thus, Iranian officials often cite the example of France to justify their protectionist, even isolationist, measures. The House of Cinema, created in 1993, performs the same sort of role as the French Centre National de la Cinématographie in regulating relations between the government and the film industry. And, for all the apparent absurdity of censorship regulations, they are not too different from the US Production Code which similarly regulated on-screen relations between the sexes (married couples, for example, had to sleep in separate beds). In any case, the restrictions imposed on film content are, in some measure, the price paid by filmmakers for generous levels of state support of a sort that is increasingly being denied to filmmakers elsewhere (including, as we have seen, in the People's Republic of China). For most of the 1980s and throughout the 1990s Iran has consistently produced between 40 and 50 films a year. Its presence on the international festival circuit, moreover, some thirty years after it first came to the attention of western critics, is evidence of 'the continuing vigour and conviction of Iranian cinema'.[28]

FIFTEEN

Anglophone Cinemas

The final group of national cinemas that can be examined in a comparative context are the cinemas of the English-speaking countries other than Great Britain. These consist principally of the cinemas of the self-governing dominions (Canada, Australia, New Zealand) and Irish cinema. These national cinemas have been amongst the last to attract academic attention and consequently to find their place in the histories of film. One of the reasons for this neglect is simply that none of these cinemas has ever had a particularly large production sector; indeed, only Australia could be considered a significant film-production nation in numerical terms. Another reason for their neglect is that unlike the cinemas of the Far East or the Middle East, these cinemas do not immediately stand out in terms of their cultural difference and hence have not been seized upon by film theorists as 'alternatives' to Hollywood. Elizabeth Jacka's description of Australian cinema – 'not metropolitan enough to be in the international mainstream of either intellectual or artistic life, and not marginal enough to be exotic' – could equally be applied to the other Anglophone cinemas mentioned above.[1] Yet despite their absence from the historical map of the world's cinemas, and regardless of the actual volume of production, these countries have given rise to intellectually exciting film cultures which have contributed significantly to debates within film studies around concepts of 'the national'. The histories of Australian, New Zealand, Canadian and Irish cinemas all highlight questions of nationhood and cultural identity, the relationship between the local and the global, and the nature and extent of state support for a national cinema and an indigenous film culture. While each of these cinemas has its own unique characteristics, its own particular genres and archetypes, it is possible to identify common themes and even, to some extent, parallel histories in the development of film both as a social practice and as a means of national expression. At the risk of over-simplifying, the history of these cinemas has been essentially one of transition from the 'colonial' to the 'postcolonial'.

FROM COLONIAL CINEMAS TO POSTCOLONIAL CINEMAS

It should be relatively uncontentious to suggest that at the beginning of the twentieth century Ireland, Canada, Australia and New Zealand were, to all intents and purposes, still essentially colonial countries. Canada (1867), Australia (1901) and New Zealand (1907) had all been accorded the status of self-governing dominions within the British Empire (strictly speaking Australia was a commonwealth rather than a dominion), but their political ties with the 'mother country' remained strong, exemplified by the fact that all three countries entered both world wars alongside Britain. Ireland, of course, was part of the United Kingdom until the creation of the Irish Free State (1922) gave dominion status to the island except for six of the nine counties of Ulster in the north east which remained within the United Kingdom as the province of Northern Ireland. The Irish Free State adopted the name Éire under a new constitution in 1937 and remained in the British Commonwealth, though observing neutrality during the Second World War, until the proclamation of the Irish Republic in 1949.

It might have been expected that political, cultural and economic ties within the British Empire and Commonwealth would have privileged the distribution of British films. However, this was not so. By the 1920s American movies were estimated to comprise 90 per cent of all the films shown in the dominions. Lord Newton, a vocal supporter of the British film industry, complained to the House of Lords that:

> The Colonial market, especially in Australia, is completely dominated by American films so that it is almost impossible to show a British film at all. I am told that even when Lord

Jellicoe was Governor of New Zealand it was only with the utmost difficulty – I am not even sure that they succeeded – that the Jutland film could be shown. There was a film called 'Armageddon', which was produced for the purpose of showing what the Australians had done in the war. I believe it was impossible to find a cinema in Australia which would produce [*sic*] that film because they were all booked up with American films.[2]

The dominance of American movies is quite easily explained. The British production sector was in the doldrums for much of the 1920s whereas the US film industry had been pursuing an aggressive foreign policy ever since the First World War had created the circumstances in which it could displace Europe as the world's leading exporter of films. The arrival of talking pictures made the English-speaking markets even more important to Hollywood. Although the dominions had relatively small exhibition sectors – Canada had 1,200 cinemas by the late 1930s, Australia had 1,400 and New Zealand 700 – their predominantly English-speaking audiences and the almost complete absence of a domestic production industry meant that demand for American movies was high.[3] Canada was considered part of the 'domestic' North American market as far as the US film industry was concerned, while Australia and New Zealand were grouped together as 'Australasia'. The pattern of American dominance was replicated in Ireland, where Anglo-American distribution interests held sway (British distributors, of course, handled American as well as British movies).[4]

Domestic feature film production was negligible in Canada and New Zealand until the 1970s and in Ireland until the 1980s. A relatively buoyant production sector had been established in Australia during the silent period, but the arrival of talking pictures saw many producers collapse. Cinesound emerged as the main Australian production company in the 1930s, producing two or three films a year, consisting mostly of so-called 'backblocks' rural comedies, but the company discontinued feature production during the Second World War. It was not until the 1970s that Australian production revived. Yet the scarcity of feature film production does not mean that there was no activity at all. For one thing, there is a history of documentary production in the dominions. John Grierson's appointment as head of the newly established National Film Board of Canada in 1939 was instrumental in the emergence of the Canadian non-fiction film during the Second World War through documentary series such as *The World in Action* and *Canada Carries On*; the Commonwealth Film Unit, modelled on the Canadian example, was established in Australia during the war and was soon producing around 50 films a year in association with the Australian National Film Board; and pioneer New Zealand filmmakers such as Rudall Hayward and John O'Shea concentrated principally on documentaries with occasional forays into features. And, for another thing, these countries have served as locations for overseas productions. Britain's Ealing Studios made a number of Australian-set features in the late 1940s (*The Overlanders, Eureka Stockade, Bitter Springs*); and John Ford (*The Quiet Man*, 1952) and David Lean (*Ryan's Daughter*, 1970) were the two most prominent directors to make films in Ireland. In the 1980s and 1990s Vancouver became a favourite location for economy-conscious American productions ostensibly set in New York, while at the turn of the millennium New Zealand locations were used to stand in for 'Middle Earth' in an epic three-part production of *The Lord of the Rings*.

One of the consequences of the dearth of indigenous production was that filmic representations of the Irish and Australians, especially, were for many years left in the hands of others – principally Hollywood and Britain. For British cinema audiences, Arthur Lucan's comic washerwoman 'Old Mother Riley' was probably the most familiar screen image of Irishness in the 1930s and 1940s, just as Chips Rafferty symbolized the archetypal Australian in films of the 1940s and 1950s. The response of the Irish and the Australians themselves to their representation in films is ambiguous. On the one hand, caricatures of brawling, drunken 'Oirishmen' were so commonplace in the 1930s that the *Dublin Evening Mail* could claim with some legitimacy that 'no race has suffered more at the hands of American and English film and stage productions than has ours'.[5] On the other hand, however, this sort of response ignores the fact that the Irish themselves had been complicit in the creation of stereotypes and have even, in certain circumstances, celebrated them. There is no more 'Oirish' film than *The Quiet Man* in which John Wayne and Victor McLaglen engage in cinema's most famous comic brawl. Yet, as Jeffrey Richards observes, for all its stereotypes and caricatures, *The Quiet Man* 'is far and away the most popular representation of Ireland and Irishness in America, Britain and Ireland itself'.[6] In Australia, where there was also concern in intellectual circles over the representation of Australian society and the Australian character, the beginning of a cultural debate was signalled when Tom Fitzgerald, editor of the *Nation*, declared in 1958: 'It is typical of the undeveloped personality of our people that we have practically no indigenous films . . . The daydreams we get from celluloid are not Australian daydreams. Our kingdom is not of this world.'[7] Yet the most commercially successful Australian film ever made – both in Australia itself and worldwide – remains Paul Hogan's *'Crocodile' Dundee* (1986), which positively celebrates the image of the Australian male as an easy-going, self-reliant, chauvinistic 'ocker'. The film was criticized by Australian intellectuals on the grounds that it shows 'what the world thinks we do best – cracking jokes, eating bush tucker and being basically naive to technology and the culture of the rest of the world'.[8] However, the massive popular success of *'Crocodile' Dundee* illustrates, as Richards has reminded us, that 'intellectuals are notoriously not "real" people'.[9]

It was in the second half of the twentieth century, as the dominions loosened their ties with Britain – Canada was granted full national sovereignty in 1982, Australia is currently in the process of holding a referendum on its constitutional link with Britain – that intellectual and political interest in the question of national cinemas came to the fore. There is a parallel of sorts here with other postcolonial cinemas in India, Africa and Latin America, though the Anglophone cinemas were never to embrace the political radicalism of Third Cinema. One of the unique features of the history of Anglophone cinemas is that several of them gave rise to an intellectual national film culture without the presence of an established national film production industry. Fitzgerald's article of 1958 marked the beginning of a debate over the importance of a national cinema that resulted, argues Graeme Turner, in the recognition of 'film as the most desirable medium for projecting an image of new confidence and maturity seen to mark contemporary Australian culture and society'.[10] There was similar interest in Canada in the 1960s and 1970s in the question of defining a national culture and in the place of cinema within that culture. Intellectual interest in the creation of an 'English-Canadian' cinema – as opposed to the '*Cinéma Canadien*' associated with the predominantly Francophone province of Québec – was exemplified in the appearance of a number of critical film journals such as *Cinema Canada*, *Take One* and *Cine Action*.

Yet despite this intellectual investment in the notion of national cinemas, there were significant barriers in the way of establishing domestic film production industries. None of the countries has a domestic market of sufficient size for anything other than the cheapest of films to stand any chance of recouping their costs at home. At the same time, however, they face an unequal challenge against Hollywood in the world market. Tom O'Regan explains the dilemma for Australian cinema in these terms:

> Servicing 18 million people, Australian cinema is not large enough to support an extensive film production industry, nor the scale of local production in higher budgeted movie and limited episode serial television. As a medium-sized producer, it cannot as easily differentiate itself through either producing a sufficient volume of product or readily occupying a market niche as can the larger French, Italian or British cinemas (these are readily known in their own right). In part because of the difficulties of delivering a 'brand name', diverse Australian product circulates locally and internationally.[11]

The problem is even more acute for New Zealand and Ireland, each with a population under four million. Roger Donaldson, an Australian-born director raised in New Zealand, observed: 'In a country of only three million people that can give you back at best a tenth or a fifth of the budget, you've got to look to an international market.'[12]

The odd one out in this context is Canada, which has a population in excess of 30 million, but which has still been unable to sustain a sizeable production sector. The problem for Canada is a peculiar one, arising from its geographical proximity to the United States and its economic dependency upon its neighbour. Film distribution in Canada is monopolized by American companies and free-trade agreements between Canada and the United States have militated against the introduction of a quota for indigenous films. The fact that Canada's population, although large, is spread over such a vast area with fewer large cities than in the United States means that the potential cinema audience is dissipated. As Christopher Gittings observes: 'Another major obstacle to feature production is the nature of the Canadian domestic market: small and scattered, it could not support a profit-making feature-film industry, therefore the prohibitive expense of foreign distribution would have been necessary for financial success.'[13]

That Anglophone national cinemas were able to develop a domestic production base at all has been due in large measure to state support for the film industry. It is significant that the increase in domestic production that occurred in Canada and Australia in the 1970s and in New Zealand in the early 1980s coincided with efforts by their governments to provide practical support and positive encouragement for their national cinemas. The Canadian Film Development Corporation was established in 1967 to support feature film production and to provide loans and prizes for filmmakers. As a result of its efforts film production in Canada increased from only 10 features in 1966 and 11 in 1967 to 25 in 1969 and 46 in 1970.[14] The CFDC was followed by provincial organizations: the Ontario Film Development Corporation, the Institut Québécois du Cinéma, and other similar bodies in British Columbia, Alberta, Nova Scotia and Saskatchewan. In Australia the Australian Film Development Corporation (1971) was succeeded by the Australian Film Commission (1975) and the Australian Film Finance Corporation (1988). These official bodies invested in productions deemed to contain 'significant' Australian content and which were produced wholly or substantially in Australia; they were inevitably criticized by filmmakers for their 'random and unsatisfactory' decisions as to which films to support.[15] In fact Australian film officials have proved very catholic in their tastes, with the films supported ranging from outback 'ocker' comedies produced for domestic consumption (*The Adventures of Barry McKenzie*) to national epics intended for the international market (*Gallipoli*). Again the national body was followed by regional equivalents as individual states set up their own film commissions: South Australia (1972), New South Wales, Victoria, Queensland, Tasmania (all 1977) and Western Australia (1978). The New Zealand Film Commission was set up in 1978 to assist indigenous production. Favourable tax laws also attracted some international co-productions to New Zealand in the early 1980s (*Merry Christmas Mr Lawrence*, *The Bounty*) until the loophole was closed.

The history of state support for a national cinema in Ireland is both longer and yet at the same time more *ad hoc* than in other Anglophone countries. Ireland was in fact the first of these countries to introduce economic measures in support of a national cinema as the government of Taoiseach Eamon de Valera changed from a *laissez-faire* outlook in the 1930s to pro-tectionism and subsidy after the Second World War. In the late 1940s the Irish Minister of Finance, Frank Aitken, opposed the development of Ireland as a production base for overseas film-makers, urging instead that '[if] this country is going to spend money on the film business, it should be spent on the produc-tion of Irish films by Irish organisations and not in the provision of facilities which at present suit foreigners but which might well be far too elaborate for the requirements of domestic pro-ducers.'[16] The election of Sean Leamass, a known supporter of cinema, as Taoiseach in 1959 signalled the start of state support through the creation of the Irish Film Finance Corporation (1960) and government investment in the Ardmore Studios. Yet despite these efforts there was little indigenous production; Ardmore – renamed the National Film Studios of Ireland in 1975 – was used more by overseas producers than by Irish film-makers, just as Aitken had feared, and went into receivership in the 1980s. The IFFC was succeeded by the Irish Film Board (1981) which controversially invested its first budget in Neil Jordan's *Angel* (1981), produced by board member John Boorman. Writing in 1987, however, Kevin Rockett welcomed the formation of the IFB and suggested other measures that were necessary to develop a healthy production sector in Ireland:

> The establishment of the Irish Film Board has encouraged
> new developments in Irish film culture as well as providing a
> focus for the gradual evolution of an indigenous film indus-
> try. Its future success will as likely be determined by the avail-
> ability of a sympathetic tax regime for private investment as
> by the cash allocations from the state. Its future will ulti-
> mately be measured by the commitment and quality of
> indigenous film production.[17]

Ironically the IFB was wound up in 1987 – the victim of 'a short-
sighted government anxious for immediate profit and with little
interest in sustained development for cultural reasons'[18] – only
to be reconstituted in 1993, exemplifying the Irish government's inconsistent approach to supporting the film industry.
The most successful 'Irish' films of the 1990s, Alan Parker's *The
Commitments* (1991) and Neil Jordan's *The Crying Game* (1992),
were made entirely by commercial investment from British and
American sources.

Anglophone cinemas illustrate the theoretical limitations of
traditional models of national cinemas in which cinema is seen as
a reflection of national identity and national culture. Nowhere is
this better demonstrated than in Ireland, where the fact of partition within 'the island of Ireland' makes the very concept of
'Irishness' a fiercely contested subject. Political and religious differences between Ireland and Northern Ireland, as well as within
Northern Ireland itself, raise questions about whose identity is
being represented in 'Irish' cinema. The fact that so many 'Irish'
films are in fact Anglo-Irish co-productions further problematizes the constitution of a national cinema. In Canada, Australia
and New Zealand the question of nationhood involves relationships not only between the colonists and the 'mother country' (in
which the colonists assert their independence from British rule
and therefore from British culture) but also between colonists
and indigenous native populations (the Native North American,
Aborigine and Maori populations who regard their own culture
as having been displaced by the white European settlers).

The theoretical discourse that attempts to articulate these

problems is that of postcolonialism. Like postmodernism, another widely misunderstood and misused term, postcolonialism has come to mean different things in different contexts. Most theorists now accept the differentiation between hyphenated 'post-colonialism' (a historical condition that comes after colonialism) and unhyphenated 'postcolonialism' (an interdisciplinary discourse that theorizes relations between colonizers and colonized). Postcolonialism (unhyphenated) involves the study of cultural, political and economic relations within both colonial and post-colonial (hyphenated) societies. As Lance Pettitt has remarked in his study of Irish film and television: 'A postcolonial consciousness comes into being as the result of a colonised individual critically recognising their place in the historical structure called colonialism.'[19] Anglophone cinemas are postcolonial cinemas in so far as they give expression to a postcolonial consciousness. This has involved both the projection of a 'national' culture for overseas consumption (most explicit in the case of Australian cinema) and also the critical interrogation of the place of minorities and marginalized groups within society.

NEW WAVES AND POSTCOLONIALITY

The first Anglophone national cinema to come to international prominence was Australia in the 1970s. Uniquely, the New Australian Cinema, as it became known, encompassed both the paradigms of art cinema and commercial cinema. The Australian 'period film' that emerged in the 1970s – exemplified by Ken Hannan's *Sunday Too Far Away* (1975), Peter Weir's *Picnic at Hanging Rock* (1975) and Gillian Armstrong's *My Brilliant Career* (1979) – was a mode of film practice that aligned itself with other nationally specific art film traditions. These films were supported by the Australian Film Commission (AFC) which saw the art film as a way of establishing its cultural credentials in recognition of the criticism directed at its predecessor the Australian Film Development Corporation (AFDC) for supporting low-brow genres such as the 'ocker' comedy and the sex film. The aim of the AFC was 'to encourage a more culturally sensitive cinema' and thus it was that 'the period genre had the firm imprimatur of the new statutory body'.[20]

The Australian period film combined a number of international influences – the polite gentility of British television costume drama, the narrative ambiguity of European art cinema – with specifically Australian characteristics, especially in their use of landscape:

> Camera movement and *mise-en-scène* languorously exposed Australian light, land, flora and fauna, and period costume and décor. Aestheticizing the uncanny desolation of the Australian landscape, often in the manner of the Heidelberg school of painting, the cinematography presented within Australia a sense of national cultural definition, of homeland.[21]

The most acclaimed of these films were *Picnic at Hanging Rock* and *My Brilliant Career*: the former (schoolgirls on a picnic go missing and are never found) has been interpreted variously as an allegory of sexual awakening or of colonial repression, while the latter (bush farmer's daughter seeks to make a living as a writer) has been seen as a statement about career feminism. Both films were notable for their slow pacing and psychological characterizations; they brought a cultural respectability to Australian film that justified the AFC's policy.

If the period film represented the artistic maturity of Australian cinema, then its commercial breakthrough was signalled by the success of George Miller's *Mad Max* (1979) and Weir's *Gallipoli* (1981) and *The Year of Living Dangerously* (1982). *Mad Max*, a violent post-apocalyptic road movie, was about as far removed from the genteel period film as could be imagined; its unexpected box-office success at home and abroad gave rise to two sequels (*Mad Max 2: The Road Warrior*, *Mad Max Beyond Thunderdome*). *Mad Max* was a 'sleeper' hit (it cost $350,000 and grossed over $100 million internationally); *Gallipoli*, in contrast, was a calculated money-spinner and the closest that Australian cinema has come to producing a national epic. O'Regan observes that the film 'was valued and devalued in Australia as a social document recreating popular memory'.[22] The star of both *Mad*

Max and *Gallipoli* – and of *The Year of Living Dangerously*, a political drama set in 1960s Indonesia – was Mel Gibson, an American-born, Australian-raised actor who was to become one of the leading Hollywood box-office stars of the next two decades.

The history of Australian cinema since the early 1980s has revolved around the same two poles of commercial and art film (the fact that a director like Weir could traverse the two with such ease suggests that the institutional differences should not be exaggerated). Thus, on the one hand there has been 'a crassly commercial cinema, recycling possibly regressive notions and ideals' (*Mad Max*, '*Crocodile' Dundee* and their sequels), while on the other hand there has been 'a quirky, eccentric cinema to one side of the international norm as a means of establishing international attractiveness' (*Strictly Ballroom, The Adventures of Priscilla, Queen of the Desert, Muriel's Wedding*).[23] Australia faces a problem common to many national cinemas, however, in so far as its commercially most successful filmmakers have moved on: Weir, Miller, Bruce Beresford, Fred Schepisi and Phillip Noyce have all become expatriate directors plying their trade in Hollywood.

New Zealand has been less successful than its neighbour in achieving international recognition. This is due both to its smaller production base (annual production rarely exceeds single figures) and to its geographical and cultural proximity to Australia. The emergence of New Zealand cinema was due mainly to the early films of two directors – Roger Donaldson (*Sleeping Dogs, Smash Palace*) and Geoff Murphy (*Wild Man, Goodbye Pork Pie*) – that were critically successful overseas. *Smash Palace*, a gritty, hard-edged 'crisis of masculinity' drama, was shown at the New Directors/New Films Festival in New York in 1982 (as, too, was *Mad Max 2*) and was greeted by one critic as a welcome change from 'the costumed, well-mounted, period dramas that have traveled best so far from the Pacific side of the Southern Hemisphere'.[24] New Zealand cinema is too small to identify any dominant genres; critical attention focuses instead on directors of whom the most successful in recent years are Peter Jackson (*Heavenly Creatures, The Frighteners*) and Jane Campion (*An Angel at my Table, The Piano*). *The Piano*, one of the biggest 'art house' successes of the 1990s, again problematizes the question of national cinema as it was supported by script development money from the Australian Film Commission. O'Regan suggests that *The Piano* 'represents Australasian filmmaking and a growing convergence and integration of the Australian and New Zealand film-making, exhibition and distribution sectors in the 1990s'.[25]

The Piano exemplified a trend in both Australian and New Zealand cinemas that 'urged the dominant national self towards reconciliation with its repressed black and female others'.[26] In Australia there had been occasional films focusing on black protagonists (*The Chant of Jimmie Blacksmith*, 1978), but it was only in the 1990s that Aboriginal filmmakers such as Kevin Lucas

(*Black River*) and Tracey Moffatt (*Bedevil*) were able to direct features. In 1993 the Australian Film Commission sponsored an investigation into filmmaking by and about Aboriginal people; the report (by Aboriginal scholar Marcia Langton) concluded that 'film and television are the main way in which non-Aboriginal Australians know about Aborigines'.[27] Some Aboriginal critics have argued that the campaign for sex equality has overshadowed the campaign for racial equality in Australia; at least this charge could not be levelled against *The Piano* which presents both the mute woman (Holly Hunter) and her Maori protector (played by a white actor, Harvey Keitel) as victims of white, male, colonial oppression (in the form of landowner Sam Neill). This willingness to examine the place of the indigenous populations in society – also apparent in Lee Tamahori's *Once Were Warriors* (1994), which dramatizes the problems faced by a modern, urban-dwelling Maori family – is one of the characteristics of a postcolonial cinema.

With occasional exceptions such as Ted Kotcheff's *The Apprenticeship of Duddy Kravitz* (1974), Canadian cinema before the 1980s was 'generally characterized by creative timidity and often by mediocrity'.[28] Canadian cinema from the 1980s has displayed the commercial/art cinema dichotomy evident in Australian cinema, though these paradigms are associated more with the work of particular directors rather than with any generic patterns. The commercial face of Canadian cinema is represented pre-eminently by the films of David Cronenberg, who has specialized in horror films (*Rabid, Scanners, The Fly*) but who has also won critical acclaim for psychological dramas (*Dead Ringers, Naked Lunch, M. Butterfly*). The art cinema tradition is exemplified by the work of Denys Arcand (*The Decline of the American Empire, Jesus of Montreal*) and Atom Egoyan (*The Adjuster, Exotica*). Both the commercial and the art cinema sectors have been supported financially by the National Film Board of Canada – again displaying extremely catholic taste in its choices – and by Telefilm Canada, a body set up in the 1980s to invest in film and television with Canadian content.

Canadian film policy also actively promoted the cause of women filmmakers. In 1974 the National Film Board set up Studio D, the first publicly funded women's film production unit in the world. Its wide-ranging remit encompassed production ('Studio D provides an opportunity for women to develop and express their creativity in film, and to move into filmmaking occupations that have been dominated by men'), education ('Studio D brings the perspective of women to all social issues through the medium of film, promoting personal, social and political awareness') and exhibition ('Studio D expresses the specific information needs of women audiences').[29] Under the direction of documentarist Kathleen Shannon, Studio D specialized in the production of socially conscious, politically aware documentaries by filmmakers such as Beverly Schaeffer, Terri Nash and Cynthia Scott. It was criticized, however, for representing women's issues as monolithic without taking due account of race, class and sexuality. Studio D was restructured in the 1990s as part of the New Initiatives in Film programme 'by making representations of the ethnic and racial diversity of women's culture in Canada a major component of the studio's production'.[30]

Irish 'new wave' filmmakers in the 1980s such as Joe Comerford (*Traveller, Reefer and the Model*) and Pat Murphy (*Maeve, Ann Devlin*) also focused on the plight of characters on the margins of society. These films all adopt a distinctly critical perspective towards the representation of social relations. *Traveller*, for example, 'implied that the disintegration of family and marriage could be seen as a metaphor for Irish political problems'.[31] Neil Jordan, dividing his time between Ireland, Britain and America, is the one Irish filmmaker who has returned consistently to the theme of the 'Troubles' in films such as *Angel* and *The Crying Game*. In order to render the divisions within Irish politics acceptable for a mass audience, however, Jordan has tended to use the Troubles as topical background to a revenge thriller plot (*Angel*) and an unusual transsexual romance (*The Crying Game*). The latter film has been the focus of much critical debate and polemic: condemned as pro-IRA propaganda by some and as anti-IRA propaganda by others, praised for its progressive representation of gender issues by some and criticized for reactionary portrayal of women by others.[32] It was the success of *The Crying Game* that brought Jordan back to the attention of Hollywood and allowed him to make *Michael Collins* (1996), a biopic of the IRA founder starring

Irish-born Hollywood actor Liam Neeson. This time the little doubt about the film's politics.

The promise of an end to the Troubles – a peace process ated by the Downing Street Declaration of December 199 affirmed by the Good Friday Agreement of 1998 – would s to have made filmmakers distance themselves from overt po cal comment. Instead there has been a vogue for sentimen nostalgic, whimsical films portraying Ireland as a rural, folk cu ture in the best tradition of *The Quiet Man*. Films such as *He My Song*, *The Playboys*, *Into the West* and *Circle of Friends* (the firs two British-made) 'constitute a new distinct trend which can be usefully considered as an Irish heritage cinema'.[33] This is part of a process that Ruth Barton has called 'the Ballykissangelization of Ireland' (after the popular BBC comedy drama of the 1990s, *Ballykissangel*) and which involves the commodification of Irish culture for overseas (especially British) consumers:

> It is ironic that a country which established its national identity largely through recourse to historical and mythical narratives has now, with equal fervour, adopted a policy of commodifying those narratives for the purposes of develop-ing its second largest industry, tourism. It is a further irony that the major consumers of Irish heritage tourism are the former colonizers, the British.[34]

What these films reveal is 'the complex relationship between former colonizer and former colonized'. The Irish heritage films reveal similar tensions over the representation – indeed the natu-ralization – of national stereotypes as *'Crocodile' Dundee* did in Australia. To some extent, indeed, Irish filmmakers seem to have come full circle in so far as the Irish stereotypes once propagated by the British have been reclaimed as part of a cultural strategy to promote safe, tourist-friendly images of Ireland to British audi-ences. These are questions that face all postcolonial cinemas: whose identity (or identities) are being represented, and for whom? These issues seem set likely to dominate critical dis-course around Anglophone cinemas for some time to come.

PART VI: CONCLUSION

SIXTEEN

Cinema Without Frontiers

Cinema celebrated its centenary in 1995. During its first century of existence cinema grew from a cottage industry to become a global business enterprise, established itself as a social institution throughout most of the world and legitimated itself as a popular art form. Cinema has the distinction of being the first truly mass medium: more widely disseminated than newspapers, preceding radio, television and the internet. For much of its first century the cinema was the pre-eminent form of popular entertainment for people throughout the Americas, Europe and Asia. Its appeal crosses boundaries of nation, gender, class, culture, language and religion. To that extent cinema is a social institution 'without frontiers'.

How does cinema, at the start of the twenty-first century, compare with cinema at the end of the nineteenth? To modern eyes, early cinema seems unfamiliar, primitive, remote, alien – proof that the past is indeed a foreign country where things are done differently. What do the *actualités* of the Lumière brothers have in common with the postmodern, special effects-driven comic-book fantasy of the Wachowski brothers (*The Matrix*)? And there would seem to be little in common between the nickelodeons of popular legend, with their wooden bench seating and primitive projection equipment, and the modern multiplex cinema with its surgically clean auditoria, comfortable seating and digital projection. The fact that films are now seen more widely on television, video and DVD than in the cinema itself, moreover, is indicative of a fundamental difference between 1900 and 2000.

Yet, on closer inspection, perhaps the differences between the past and the present are not so great as might first appear. For all the technological advances that have occurred since the

419

Lumières and other pioneers unveiled their films to the public, the medium of film is still essentially the same. It is posited on creating an illusion of reality. The techniques used to create the illusion have changed, but the illusion itself remains at the heart of the experience of watching a film. The pictures of workers leaving a factory and of a train entering a station that enthralled early spectators were just as much an illusion in their own right as the virtual reality world of *The Matrix* was to the science-fiction enthusiasts of 1999. And if, on one level, the Cinématographe Lumière represents the 'birth' of cinema as popular entertainment, on another level it also marks the beginning of cinema as a global institution. There is a quite striking similarity in the international marketing of the Cinématographe, as the Lumières sent operators around the world in 1896 to exploit its commercial value before the novelty waned, and the global release strategies of major blockbusters a century later.

The two most successful modes of film practice at the start of the twentieth-first century – the New Hollywood corporate blockbuster and the Bollywood song-and-dance spectacular – have both been described as a 'cinema of attractions'. They afford greater prominence to visual spectacle than to narrative coherence and they appeal to audiences of diverse national and cultural backgrounds. In the last decade or so the use of computer-generated imaging in blockbusters such as *Jurassic Park*, *Titanic* and *Gladiator* has led, perhaps for the first time since the trick films of Méliès, to the effects behind the illusion becoming as much of an attraction as the illusion itself. The inclusion of song and dance numbers in the Bollywood movie is reminiscent of early cinema exhibition when films were included in variety shows alongside other attractions including singers, dancers and other 'turns'.

As a social institution, moreover, cinema serves much the same purpose today as it did at the beginning. It is, first and foremost, a medium of entertainment. For all the artistic ambitions of some filmmakers, they are working in a popular medium. Cinema is popular not in the old-fashioned sense of a folk culture (what Raymond Williams has defined as 'made by the people for themselves') but rather in the modern sense of a mass-produced culture (one that is 'setting out to win favour').[1] Cinema has a broader-based popular appeal than other forms of communal entertainment such as theatre or opera. What began as a novelty attraction for the bourgeoisie became entertainment for the masses. It is no coincidence that cinema's period of greatest popularity in the first half of the twentieth century coincided with the emergence of 'mass society': population growth, urbanization, industrialization, increasing levels of consumerism and leisure activity were all factors that helped to create the social conditions in which cinema could flourish. Cinema was to prove especially responsive to the needs of the masses. It was able to connect with the mass public, to respond to people's hopes and aspirations, their dreams and desires. It is significant that cinemas were often referred to as 'dream palaces'. That the appeal of cinema arises from its provision of escapism and entertainment is eloquently proved by the fact that around the world the preferences of cinema audiences have been for fictional drama and popular genres; only rarely have 'serious' films also become popular successes.

As soon as it became clear that film was more than a novelty attraction, the film industry was organized on a mass-production basis. The emergence of the narrative feature film within the first two decades of the medium's existence established the dominant form of filmmaking that has remained in place ever since. The fictional feature film is the staple product of all national cinemas; the classical narrative film, institutionalized in Hollywood by the late 1910s, became the dominant international film form. As Thompson and Bordwell observe: 'American studio directors standardized an approach to cinematic storytelling that became the basis of the commercial film style.'[2] It is this style of film that has the widest popular appeal and, therefore, the widest social acceptance. Many histories of cinema set up an opposition between Hollywood on the one hand (categorized as populist, formulaic, socially and aesthetically conservative) and 'alternatives' to Hollywood on the other (cinemas either of formal innovation or displaying a commitment to 'serious' filmmaking). Thus it is that certain national film movements have been privileged in the aesthetic history of cinema: German Expressionism, Soviet montage, Poetic

Realism, Italian Neo-Realism, the *Nouvelle Vague*, the Czech New Wave, New Iranian Cinema, New Chinese Cinema. It is a largely artificial distinction. All feature films are part of the social institution of cinema; the stylistic differences between them are considerable, but all are posited to a greater or a lesser degree on character-driven narratives, psychologically oriented motivation and verisimilitude (film characters behave and act like 'real' people).

Any history of world cinemas has to address the relationship between Hollywood and other film industries. Critics of globalization allege that American movies have imposed American cultural values on the rest of the world. Intellectuals outside America, Marxists especially, see Hollywood as being instrumental in what Eric Hobsbawm describes as 'the global triumph of the United States and its way of life'.³ It cannot be denied that the US film industry has been the most successful in building up its worldwide production, distribution and exhibition interests, or that the American style of filmmaking has proved remarkably durable throughout the world since the 1920s. American movies have the dominant market share in most European, Latin American and African countries; they have also made significant inroads into Southeast Asia. The increasingly rare instances of European films that perform well at the box-office are greeted with choruses of patriotic chauvinism regardless of their quality. It is a point of honour amongst French commentators, for example, that home-grown films such as *Les Visiteurs* and *Astérix et Obélix contre César* outperform Hollywood juggernauts like *Jurassic Park* and *The Phantom Menace* at the French box-office.

Why have American films been so successful? The Marxist view would be that they have triumphed by imposing a homogenized form of mass entertainment on audiences and by exploiting the weaknesses of other national film industries. An empiricist response would be that audiences have consciously chosen American movies in preference to others and that Hollywood is merely responding to market conditions rather than creating them. There is probably an element of truth in both arguments, but neither is entirely convincing by itself. The conditions that brought about the hegemony of the US film industry were established during and after the First World War when other leading national film industries were fatally weakened by the reduction of resources and the disruption of international trade. Hollywood did not create these circumstances, but it certainly benefited from them. Having established its hegemony, moreover, the US film industry has naturally sought to maintain it. Recent research has demonstrated how the Motion Picture Export Association, the overseas branch of the US film industry's cartel formed at the end of the Second World War, has pursued an aggressive foreign policy both to protect its share of existing markets and to expand into new territories.[4] At the same time, however, Hollywood's historical dominance of the world's screens needs to be nuanced. Two of the world's most populous countries have been resistant to American imports for cultural and political reasons. The US film industry has identified India and China as its two main growth markets for the twenty-first century, but the evidence of past experience is that it is unlikely to make much inroad into either without adapting to local conditions. And even in those territories where American movies have been in the ascendancy, their popularity does not mean that other films were necessarily unpopular. Film historians have only recently begun to realize the economic and cultural vitality of other national cinemas (beyond the traditions of art cinema associated with some countries). Popular genres such as musicals, comedies, romances and thrillers have been staples of most national cinemas, produced in the local idiom for domestic consumption. Yet these indigenous traditions of popular cinema have been written out of film history due to the continuing prevalence of aesthetic assumptions about 'art' and 'quality' and cultural prejudices against 'the popular'.

Relations between Hollywood and other national cinemas are better understood in terms of economic and cultural exchange rather than as straightforward economic and cultural imperialism. Thus, while American films have dominated cinema screens throughout much of the world, American investment has also supported production sectors in other countries. Most of the successful British films since the 1960s, including the James Bond series (which celebrated its fortieth anniversary with the release of *Die Another Day* in 2002) have been made with financial support from Hollywood. The two worldwide blockbuster successes of 2001 arose from Hollywood investment in what were both distinctly 'non-American' projects. AOL Time Warner financed the production of *Harry Potter and the Philosopher's Stone* in Britain, the first in what looks set to be a highly lucrative franchise based on J. K. Rowling's indisputably British children's stories. And independent producer New Line Cinema risked financial ruin by bankrolling New Zealand director Peter Jackson's adaptation of J.R.R. Tolkein's *The Lord of the Rings*. These films blur the distinction between 'American' cinema on the one hand and 'British' and 'New Zealand' cinema on the other. Their worldwide success (the first *Harry Potter* film grossed over $900 million worldwide; *The Fellowship of the Ring*, the first instalment of the Jackson/Tolkein trilogy, grossed some $500 million) suggests that they are, perhaps, best described as 'international' films. Their success arises from a combination of the economic might of Hollywood and the cultural resources of the British and New Zealand film industries in terms of acting and writing talent as well as production facilities.

What for the future of cinema? Historians should always be wary of making predictions; knowledge of the past provides no special insight into the future. Yet there are a few general observations that are, perhaps, worth making. It would seem unlikely that either the global hegemony of Hollywood or its production strategy geared around the blockbuster is likely to change significantly in the immediate future. It would also seem unlikely that, in those countries where once-flourishing domestic production industries have been reduced to shadows of their former selves, there will be any significant revival. The decline of European film industries means that Asia has now become the centre of world production. The popular success of Indian cinema, both at home and abroad, is the most significant economic and cultural development in cinema over the last thirty years. At the turn of the millennium it looks to be on the verge of establishing itself as a major international presence alongside the US film industry. The increasing importance of the global marketplace – itself a consequence of escalating production costs and diminishing audiences – would seem likely to make film, once again, the truly international medium that it was before the arrival of sound. The advent of new technologies whose potential is only just being realized (digitization, the internet) opens up exciting new possibilities for cinema. Some commentators predict that these new technologies will mean the end of cinema as we have known it: films such as *Toy Story* and *Final Fantasy* suggest that human actors may no longer be necessary, while the possibility of delivering movies over the Internet might fundamentally alter the nature of exhibition. I would expect that, on the evidence of its history to date, the film industry is more likely to assimilate these new technologies than be radically altered by them. Many commentators predicted that first television and then video would spell the end of cinema, but it survived both. Whatever the prognosis for its future, however, cinema has an exceptionally rich, varied and diverse past.

References

ONE · FILM HISTORY: SOURCES, METHODS, APPROACHES

1 British Universities Film Council, *Film and the Historian* (London, 1968), p. 44.
2 Jeffrey Richards, *Visions of Yesterday* (London, 1973), p. XVI.
3 Ernest Lindgren, 'The Importance of Film Archives', *The Penguin Film Review*, 5 (1945), p. 47.
4 Derek Malcolm, *A Century of Films* (London, 2000), p. 1.
5 Quoted in Robert Sklar, *Film: An International History of the Medium* (London, 1993), p. 12
6 David Robinson, *World Cinema: A Short History* (London, 1973), p. 1.
7 Robert C. Allen and Douglas Gomery, *Film History: Theory and Practice* (New York, 1985), pp. 37–8.
8 Kristin Thompson and David Bordwell, *Film History: An Introduction* (New York, 1994), p. XL.
9 Malcolm, *A Century of Films*, p. 1.
10 Steve Jenkins, 'The BBC 100', *Sight and Sound*, New Series V/1 (1995), p. 16.
11 David Bordwell, Janet Staiger and Kristin Thompson, *The Classical Hollywood Cinema: Film Style & Mode of Production to 1960* (London, 1985), p. 10.
12 Raymond Fielding, 'The Technological Antecedents of the Coming of Sound', in Evan W. Cameron, ed., *Sound and the Cinema* (Pleasantville, NY, 1980), p. 2.
13 Allen and Gomery, *Film History: Theory and Practice*, p. 132.
14 Kerry Segrave, *American Films Abroad: Hollywood's Domination of the World's Movie Screens from the 1890s to the Present* (Jefferson, NC, 1997), p. 282.
15 Nick Roddick, *A New Deal in Entertainment: Warner Brothers in the 1930s* (London, 1983), p. 14.
16 Allen and Gomery, *Film History: Theory and Practice*, pp. 36–7.
17 Siegfried Kracauer, *From Caligari to Hitler: A Psychological History of the German Film* (Princeton, 1947), p. 6.
18 Paul Monaco, *Cinema and Society: France and Germany during the Twenties* (New York, 1976), p. 160.
19 Kristin Thompson, *Exporting Entertainment: America in the World Film Market 1907–1934* (London, 1985), p. 168.
20 John Houseman, 'Today's Hero: A Review', *Hollywood Quarterly*, II/2 (1947), p. 161.
21 Lester Asheim, 'The Film and the Zeitgeist', *Hollywood Quarterly*, II/4

(1947), p. 415.

22 Robert B. Ray, *A Certain Tendency of the Hollywood Cinema, 1930–1980* (Princeton, 1985), p. 141.

23 Arthur Marwick, *Class: Image and Reality in Britain, France and the United States since 1930* (London, 1980), p. 22.

24 Richards, *Visions of Yesterday*, p. xv.

25 Robert Sklar, *Movie-Made America: A Cultural History of American Movies* (New York, 1975), p. 316.

26 Richards, *Visions of Yesterday*, p. xv.

27 Prem Chowdhry, *Colonial India and the Making of Empire Cinema: Image, Ideology and Identity* (Manchester, 2000), p. 3.

28 Segond's comments were made in a review of Richards's *Visions of Yesterday* in the British film studies journal *Monogram*, 6 (1975), pp. 43–4.

29 Graeme Turner, *Film as Social Practice* (London, 1988), p. 129.

30 David Bordwell, 'Textual analysis etc.', *Enclitic*, 10–11 (1981–2), p. 135.

31 Liliana Cavani, *The Night Porter* (Turin, 1974), p. xiv.

32 John Belton, *American Cinema/American Culture* (New York, 1994), p. xxi.

33 Elizabeth Grottle Strebel, 'Jean Renoir and the Popular Front', in K.R.M. Short, ed., *Feature Films as History* (London, 1981), p. 92.

34 The 'Gramscian turn' in film studies is exemplified in Marcia Landy's books *British Genres: Cinema and Society, 1930–1960* (Princeton, 1991), *Film, Politics and Gramsci* (Minneapolis, 1994) and *Cinematic Uses of the Past* (Minneapolis, 1996).

35 Tony Aldgate, 'Ideological Consensus in British Feature Films, 1935–1947', in Short, ed., *Feature Films as History*, p. 111.

36 Molly Haskell, *From Reverence to Rape: The Treatment of Women in the Movies* (Chicago, 2nd edn 1987), p. 2.

TWO · WORLD CINEMAS: THEORETICAL AND HISTORICAL PERSPECTIVES

1 *The Guinness Book of Film Facts and Feats*, ed. Patrick Robertson (London, 1985), pp. 17–21.

2 David Bordwell, Janet Staiger and Kristin Thompson, *The Classical Hollywood Cinema: Film Style & Mode of Production to 1960* (London, 1985), p. xiv.

3 *Ibid.*, p. 9.

4 *Ibid.*, p. 10.

5 *Ibid.*, p. 367.

6 In the second edition of *The Cinema Book*, ed. Pam Cook and Mieke Bernink (London, 1999), for example, early cinema, New Hollywood, Hindi cinema and East Asian cinema are grouped together, rather uncomfortably, in a section entitled 'Alternatives to Classic Hollywood', along with more legitimate contenders for the 'alternative' label, art cinema, avant-garde cinema and Third World/postcolonial cinema.

7 Paul Rotha, *The Film Till Now: A Survey of World Cinema* (London, 1949 edn), p. 313.

8 Ginette Vincendeau, 'Issues in European Cinema', in John Hill and Pamela Church Gibson, eds, *World Cinema: Critical Approaches* (Oxford, 2000), p. 56.

9 Peter Wollen, *Readings and Writings: Semiotic Counter-Strategies* (London, 1982), p. 132.

10 Noël Burch, *Life to Those Shadows*, trans. Ben Brewster (London, 1990), p. 198.

11 Rosie Thomas, 'Indian Cinema: Pleasures and Popularity', *Screen*, xxvi/3–4 (1985), p. 131.

12 Andrew Higson, *Waving the Flag: Constructing a National Cinema in Britain* (Oxford, 1995), p. 6.

13 Stephen Crofts, 'Reconceptualising National Cinema/s', *Quarterly Review of Film and Video*, xiv/3 (1993), p. 50. Interestingly, Crofts's taxonomies have no place for American cinema, which, because of its global presence, is rarely described as a national cinema. In a revised version of his table, Crofts includes the category of 'United States cinema' ('so called to include the recent medium-budget "independent" films associated with, say, the Sundance Institute as well as Hollywood'). 'Concepts of National Cinema', in Hill and Gibson, eds, *World Cinema: Critical Approaches*, p. 6.

14 Quoted in Nick Roddick, '"If the United States spoke Spanish, we would have a film industry"', in Martyn Auty and Nick Roddick, eds, *British Cinema Now* (London, 1985), p. 5.

15 Lindsay Anderson, 'Alfred Hitchcock', *Sequence*, 9 (1949), p. 113.

16 'Introduction' to Richard Dyer and Ginette Vincendeau, eds, *Popular European Cinema* (London, 1992), p. 1.

17 David Bordwell, 'The Art Cinema as a Mode of Film Practice', *Film Criticism*, iv/1 (1979), pp. 56–64.

18 Steve Neale, 'Art Cinema as Institution', *Screen*, xii/1 (1981), p. 14.

19 Quoted in Richard Taylor, *Film Propaganda: Soviet Russia and Nazi Germany* (London, 1979), p. 29.

20 Fernando Solanas and Octavio Getino, 'Towards a Third Cinema' [1969], in Bill Nichols, ed., *Movies and Methods Volume I* (Berkeley, 1976), p. 47.

21 Paul Willemen, 'The Third Cinema Question: Notes and Reflections', in Jim Pines and Paul Willemen, eds, *Questions of Third Cinema* (London, 1989), p. 3.

22 Examples of a comparative approach to film history include: Keith Reader, *Cultures on Celluloid* (London, 1981), an impressionistic discussion of American, British, French and Japanese films; Jeffrey Richards, *Visions of Yesterday* (London, 1973), a comparison of the ideologies of 'the cinema of Empire', 'the cinema of National Socialism' and 'the cinema of Populism'; and Pierre Sorlin, *European Cinemas, European Societies 1939–1990* (London, 1991), which the author describes as 'a research into comparative social history which draws its material from a still popular means of entertainment – cinema' (p. 5). Recent additions to this scarce literature include Lucy Mazdon, *Encore Hollywood: Remaking French Cinema* (London, 2000), which offers an illuminating comparison between American remakes of French films and the French originals, and Martin Stollery, *Alternative Empires: European Modernist Cinemas and Cultures of Imperialism* (Exeter, 2001), exploring the representation of colonialism in German, Soviet and British cinema of the interwar years.

23 Peter Besas, *Behind the Spanish Lens: Spanish Cinema under Fascism and Democracy* (Denver, 1985), p. 262.

24 Tom O'Regan, *Australian National Cinema* (London, 1996), p. 45.

25 Andrew Higson and Richard Maltby, '"Film Europe" and "Film America": An Introduction', *"Film Europe" and "Film America": Cinema, Commerce and Cultural Exchange 1920–1939* (Exeter, 1999), p. 25.
26 Robert C. Allen and Douglas Gomery, *Film History: Theory and Practice* (New York, 1985), p. 132.
27 Tytti Soila, Astrid Söderbergh Widding and Gunnar Iversen, *Nordic National Cinemas* (London, 1998), p. 2
28 For example, Geoffrey Nowell-Smith, ed., *The Oxford History of World Cinema* (Oxford, 1996), includes chapters by Roy Armes on 'The Arab World', pp. 661–7, and by P. Vincent Magombe on 'The Cinemas of Sub-Saharan Africa', pp. 667–72.
29 Sorlin, *European Cinemas, European Societies*, p. 5.

THREE · EARLY CINEMA

1 See Thomas Elsaesser, ed., *Early Cinema: Space, Frame, Narrative* (London, 1990), which is a reader bringing together the work of these and other scholars.
2 Kevin Brownlow, *The Parade's Gone By . . .* (London, 1968); Barry Salt, *Film Style and Technology: History and Analysis* (London, 1983).
3 *The Last Machine* was the title of a BBC documentary series marking the centenary of cinema in 1995.
4 Eric Rhode, *A History of the Cinema from its Origins to 1970* (London, 1978), p. 3.
5 Geoffrey Nowell-Smith, 'The Loop and the Maltese Cross', in Nowell-Smith, ed., *The Oxford History of World Cinema* (Oxford, 1996), p. 7.
6 Kristin Thompson and David Bordwell, *Film History: An Introduction* (New York, 1994), p. 15.
7 Charles Musser, *History of the American Cinema Volume 1. The Emergence of Cinema: The American Screen to 1907* (New York, 1990), p. 159.
8 André Bazin, 'The Ontology of the Photographic Image', in *What Is Cinema? Volume I*, ed. and trans. Hugh Gray (Berkeley, 1967), p. 12.
9 David Bordwell, 'Citizen Kane', *Film Comment*, VII/2 (1971), p. 39.
10 Andrew Sarris, *The American Cinema: Directors and Directions 1929–1968* (New York, 1996 edn), p. 51.
11 Noël Burch, *Life to Those Shadows*, trans. Ben Brewster (London, 1990), pp. 186–201.
12 André Gaudreault, 'Temporality and Narrative in Early Cinema, 1895–1908', in John Fell, ed., *Film Before Griffith* (Berkeley, 1984), p. 322.
13 Tom Gunning, 'The Cinema of Attractions: Early Film, Its Spectator and the Avant-Garde', in Elsaesser, ed., *Space, Frame, Narrative*, pp. 56–62.
14 Thompson and Bordwell, *Film History*, p. 51.
15 There is an extensive critical and historical literature on Griffith. The 'old' view is exemplified by *The Man Who Invented Hollywood: The Autobiography of D.W. Griffith*, ed. James Hart (Louisville, KY, 1972) and the anecdotal accounts by Karl Brown, *Adventures with D.W. Griffith* (New York, 1973) and Lillian Gish, *The Movies, Mr Griffith and Me* (New York, 1970). Revisionist assessments include Mike Allen, *Family Secrets: The Feature Films*

of *D.W. Griffith* (London, 1999), Tom Gunning, *D.W. Griffith and the Origins of American Narrative Film* (Urbana, IL, 1991) and Scott Simmon, *The Films of D.W. Griffith* (Cambridge, 1993)

16 Eileen Bowser, *History of the American Cinema Volume 2. The Transformation of Cinema 1907–1915* (New York, 1990), p. 43. See also William Uricchio and Roberta E. Pearson, *Reframing Culture: The Case of the Vitagraph Quality Films* (Princeton, 1993).

17 F. Dubrez Fawcett, *Dickens the Dramatist* (London, 1952), p. 193.

18 Bowser, *The Transformation of Cinema*, pp. 42–3.

19 S.M. Eisenstein, 'Dickens, Griffith, and the Film Today' [1944], *Film Form*, ed. and trans. Jay Leda (New York, 1949), p. 195.

20 *Ibid.*, pp. 196–7.

21 Robert C. Allen, 'From Exhibition to Reception: Reflections on the Audience in Film History', in Annette Kuhn and Jackie Stacey, eds, *Screen Histories: A Reader* (Oxford, 1998), p. 13.

22 Robert C. Allen and Douglas Gomery, *Film History: Theory and Practice* (New York, 1985), p. 156.

23 Quoted in *Chronicle of the Cinema*, ed. Robyn Karney (London, 1995), p. 22.

24 *Ibid.*, p. 36.

25 Musser, *The Emergence of Cinema*, p. 183.

26 Bowser, *The Transformation of Cinema*, pp. 4–7.

27 *Moving Picture World*, 11 March 1911, p. 539.

28 The 'nickelodeon debate' can be traced through local studies such as Robert C. Allen, 'Motion Picture Exhibition in Manhattan: Beyond the Nickelodeon', *Cinema Journal*, XVIII/2 (1979), pp. 2–15; Douglas Gomery, 'The Growth of Movie Monopolies: The case of Balaban & Katz', *Wide Angle*, III/1 (1979), pp. 54–63; and Burnes St. Patrick Hollyman, 'The First Picture Shows: Austin, Texas, 1894–1913', *Journal of the University Film Association*, XXIX/3 (1977), pp. 3–8.

29 See Kathy Peiss, *Cheap Amusements: Working Women and Leisure in Turn-of-the-Century New York* (Philadephia, 1986).

30 Thompson and Bordwell, *Film History*, p. 33.

31 Rachael Low, *The History of the British Film 1906–1914* (London, 1949), p. 13.

32 *Ibid.*, p. 25.

33 Terry Ramsaye, *A Million and One Nights: A History of the Motion Picture through 1925* (London, 1954 edn), p. 431.

34 Quoted in Bowser, *The Transformation of Cinema*, p. 3.

35 *The Guinness Book of Film Facts and Feats*, pp. 169–70

36 Quoted in Richard Taylor and Ian Christie, eds, *The Film Factory: Russian and Soviet Cinema in Documents*, trans. Richard Taylor (London, 1988), p. 13.

37 Quoted in Rhode, *A History of the Cinema from its Origins to 1970*, p. 31.

38 Richard Maltby, 'Censorship and Self-Regulation', in *The Oxford History of World Cinema*, p. 236.

39 *Chronicle of the Cinema*, p. 20.

40 Quoted in Gregory D. Black, *Hollywood Censored: Morality Codes, Catholics, and the Movies* (Cambridge, 1994), pp. 9–10.

41 *Chronicle of the Cinema*, p. 94.

42 Bowser, *The Transformation of Cinema*, p. 48.

43 Quoted in Greg Garrett, 'Film', *Censorship: A World Encyclopedia*, ed. Derek

Jones (London, 2001), p. 798.

44 Jeffrey Richards, 'British Film Censorship', in Robert Murphy, ed.,
    The British Cinema Book (London, 1997), p. 168.

45 Maltby, 'Censorship and Self-Regulation', p. 238.

46 Thompson and Bordwell, *Film History*, p. 49.

47 Richard Abel, *The Red Rooster Scare: Making Cinema American, 1900–1910*
    (Berkeley, 1999), p. 118.

48 *Ibid.*, p. 179.

49 See Bowser, *The Transformation of Cinema*, pp. 21–31.

50 See David Bordwell, Janet Staiger and Kristin Thompson, *The Classical
    Hollywood Cinema: Film Style & Mode of Production to 1960* (London, 1985),
    pp. 121–41.

51 John Belton, *American Cinema/American Culture* (New York, 1994), pp. 96–7.

52 The first film trade journals were *Le Bulletin Phonographique et
    Cinématographique* (France, from 1899) and *The Optical Lantern and
    Cinematograph Journal* (Britain, from 1904). While the US entertainment
    trade journal *Variety* included items on film from the 1890s, the first trade US
    journal devoted entirely to the medium was *Moving Picture World* (beginning
    in 1907). The first fan magazines included *Il Cinematagrafo* (Italy, from 1907),
    Motion Picture Story Magazine (America, from 1911) and *Picturegoer* (Britain,
    from 1913).

53 Quoted in Rhode, *A History of the Cinema from its Origins to 1970*, p. 29.

FOUR · THE EMERGENCE OF NATIONAL CINEMAS

1 Kristin Thompson, *Exporting Entertainment: America in the World Film
   Market 1907–1934* (London, 1985), p. 71.

2 Rachael Low, *The History of the British Film 1914–1918* (London, 1950), p. 14.

3 Kristin Thompson and David Bordwell, *Film History: An Introduction* (New
   York, 1994), pp. 56–60.

4 Quoted in Nicholas Reeves, 'Cinema, Spectatorship and Propaganda: *Battle
   of the Somme* (1916) and its Contemporary Audience', *Historical Journal of
   Film, Radio and Television*, XIII/1 (1997), p. 9.

5 Quoted in Peter Jelavich, 'German Culture in the Great War', in Aviel
   Roshwald and Richard Stites, eds, *European Culture in the Great War: The Arts,
   Entertainment, and Propaganda, 1914–1918* (Cambridge, 1999), p. 42.

6 See Klaus Kreimeier, *The Ufa Story: A History of Germany's Greatest Film
   Company 1918–1945*, trans. Robert and Rita Kimber (Berkeley, 1999),
   pp. 29–60.

7 Thompson, *Exporting Entertainment*, p. 100.

8 Ronald Bergan, *The United Artists Story* (London, 1986), pp. 21, 23;
   The Guinness Book of Film Facts and Feats, ed. Patrick Robertson (London,
   1985), p. 38.

9 Quoted in Richard Abel, *French Cinema: The First Wave, 1915–1929*
   (Princeton, 1984), p. 10

10 A.J.P. Taylor, *English History 1914–1945* (Oxford, 1965), p. 181.

11 Quoted in Kristin Thompson, 'The Rise and Fall of Film Europe',
    in Andrew Higson and Richard Maltby, eds, *"Film Europe" and "Film*

America": Cinema, Commerce and Cultural Exchange 1920–1939 (Exeter, 1999), p. 60.

12 Andrew Higson, 'Polyglot Films for an International Market: E. A. Dupont, the British Film Industry, and the Idea of a European Cinema, 1926–1930', in Higson and Maltby, eds, "Film Europe" and "Film America", p. 284.

13 For a summary discussion of the formative tradition, see J. Dudley Andrew, The Major Film Theories: An Introduction (London, 1976), pp. 11–101.

14 Paul Rotha, The Film Till Now: A Survey of World Cinema (London, 1949 edn), p. 252.

15 On the cinema of German Expression, see Siegfried Kracauer, From Caligari to Hitler: A Psychological History of the German Film (Princeton, 1947), Lotte H. Eisner, The Haunted Screen: Expressionism in the German Cinema and the Influence of Max Reinhardt (Berkeley, 1973), and Thomas Elsaesser, Weimar Cinema and After: Germany's Historical Imaginary (London, 2000).

16 Rotha, The Film Till Now, p. 251.

17 Anatoli Lunacharsky, 'The Tasks of the State Cinema in the RSFSR' [1919], in Ian Christie and Richard Taylor, eds, The Film Factory: Russian and Soviet Cinema in Documents 1896–1939, trans. Richard Taylor (London, 1988), pp. 47–9.

18 Ephraim Katz, The Macmillan International Film Encyclopedia (London, 1994), p. 412.

19 Richard Taylor, The Battleship Potemkin (London, 2000), p. 35.

20 Ibid., p. 65.

21 Pavel Petrov-Bytov, 'We have no Soviet cinema' [1929], in Christie and Taylor, eds, The Film Factory, p. 261.

22 Quoted in Annette Kuhn, 'Soviet Cinema', in Pam Cook and Mieke Bernink, eds, The Cinema Book (London, 2nd edn 1999), p. 74.

23 Katz, The Macmillan International Film Encyclopedia, p. 503.

24 Rotha, The Film Till Now, pp. 298, 297.

25 Thompson and Bordwell, Film History, p. 186.

26 Quoted in Robert C. Allen and Douglas Gomery, Film History: Theory and Practice (New York, 1985), p. 98

27 Lucy Fischer, Sunrise: A Song of Two Humans (London, 1998), p. 20.

28 Robert C. Allen, 'William Fox Presents Sunrise', Quarterly Review of Film Studies, II/3 (1977), p. 327.

29 For a case study of the production and reception of the film, see Allen and Gomery, Film History, pp. 91–104.

30 The 'old' view of the coming of sound is exemplified by Benjamin B. Hampton, History of the American Film Industry (New York, 1931).

31 See two articles by Douglas Gomery: 'The Coming of the Talkies: Invention, Innovation and Diffusion', in Tino Balio, ed., The American Film Industry (Madison, 1976), pp. 193–211, and 'Towards an Economic History of the Cinema: The Coming of Sound to Hollywood', in Teresa de Laurentis and Stephen Heath, eds, The Cinematic Apparatus (New York, 1980), pp. 38–46. Gomery's research into the coming of sound is summarized in Allen and Gomery, Film History, pp. 115–24.

32 Donald Crafton, History of the American Cinema Volume 4. The Talkies: American Cinema's Transition to Sound 1926–1931 (New York, 1997), p. 4.

33 David Bordwell, Janet Staiger and Kristin Thompson, The Classical Hollywood

Cinema: Film Style & Mode of Production to 1960 (London, 1985), p. 306.

34 Quoted in François Truffaut, with Helen G. Scott, *Hitchcock* (London, 1986 edn), p. 73.

35 H. Mark Glancy, *When Hollywood Loved Britain: The Hollywood 'British' Film 1939–45* (Manchester, 1999), pp. 10–12.

FIVE · THE DREAM FACTORY

1 Hortense Powdermaker, *Hollywood the Dream Factory: An Anthropologist Looks at the Movie-Makers* (London, 1951), p. 39.

2 Tino Balio, *History of the American Cinema Volume 5. Grand Design: Hollywood as a Modern Business Enterprise 1930–1939* (New York, 1993), pp. 30–32; Colin Shindler, *Hollywood in Crisis: Cinema and American Society 1929–1939* (London, 1996), p. 4.

3 Robert Sklar, *Movie-Made America: A Cultural History of American Movies* (New York, 1975), p. 269.

4 Margaret Thorp, *America at the Movies* (New Haven, CT, 1939), p. 17.

5 *Ibid.*, p. 9.

6 Garth Jowett, *Film: The Democratic Art* (Boston, 1976), p. 7

7 Thorp, *America at the Movies*, p. 17.

8 Richard Maltby, *Harmless Entertainment: Hollywood and the Ideology of Consensus* (Metuchen, NJ, 1983), p. 13.

9 *New York Times*, 29 January 1942, p. 25.

10 Sklar, *Movie-Made America*, p. 195.

11 The history of the Legion of Decency is documented in Gregory D. Black's authoritative studies, *Hollywood Censored: Morality Codes, Catholics, and the Movies* (Cambridge, 1994) and *The Catholic Crusade Against the Movies, 1940–1975* (Cambridge, 1997).

12 The window of opportunity afforded filmmakers between the introduction and the enforcement of the Production Code is discussed in Thomas Docherty's informative *Pre-Code Hollywood: Sex, Immorality, and Insurrection in American Cinema 1930–1934* (New York, 1999).

13 From his obituary in *Variety*, 8 December 1965, p. 2.

14 Quoted in Doherty, *Pre-Code Hollywood*, p. 361.

15 Quoted in Shindler, *Hollywood in Crisis*, p. 27.

16 John Douglas Eames, *The MGM Story* (London, 1979), p. 79; John Douglas Eames, *The Paramount Story* (London, 1985), pp. 37–8; Clive Hirschhorn, *The Warner Bros. Story* (London, 1979), p. 84; Richard B. Jewell, with Vernon Harbin, *The RKO Story* (London, 1983), p. 24.

17 Quoted in Shindler, *Hollywood in Crisis*, p. 27.

18 Balio, *Grand Design*, p.15; Shindler, *Hollywood in Crisis*, pp. 27–8; Jewell, *The RKO Story*, pp. 32, 44; Hirschhorn, *The Warner Bros. Story*, pp. 100, 112; Eames, *The MGM Story*, pp. 74, 82.

19 Mae D. Huttig, 'The Motion Picture Industry Today' [1944], in Tino Balio, ed., *The American Film Industry* (Madison, 1976), p. 248.

20 Shindler, *Hollywood in Crisis*, p. 213.

21 See Douglas Gomery, 'Hollywood, the National Recovery Administration, and the Question of Monopoly Power', *Journal of the University Film*

Association, XXVIII/2 (1976), pp. 47–52.

22 F.D. Klingender, 'The New Deal and the American Film', *Cinema Quarterly*, III/4 (1935), pp. 197–8.

23 Basil Wright, *The Long View: A Personal Perspective on World Cinema* (London, 1974), p. 102.

24 Edward Buscombe, 'Walsh and Warner Bros.', in Phil Hardy, ed., *Raoul Walsh* (Edinburgh, 1974), p. 54.

25 Nick Roddick, *A New Deal in Entertainment: Warner Brothers in the 1930s* (London, 1983), p. 73.

26 F. D. Klingender and Stuart Legg, *Money Behind the Screen* (London, 1937), p. 79.

27 Sklar, *Movie-Made America*, p. 165.

28 Balio, *Grand Design*, p. 25.

29 Neal Gabler, *An Empire of Their Own: How the Jews Invented Hollywood* (New York, 1988), p. 5.

30 Richard Maltby, 'The Political Economy of Hollywood: The Studio System', in Philip Davies and Brian Neve, eds, *Cinema, Politics and Society in America* (Manchester, 1981), p. 54.

31 David Bordwell, Janet Staiger and Kristin Thompson, *The Classical Hollywood Cinema: Film Style & Mode of Production to 1960* (London, 1985), p. XIII.

32 Thomas Schatz, *The Genius of the System: Hollywood Filmmaking in the Studio Era* (New York, 1988), p. 162.

33 Clive Hirschhorn, *The Universal Story* (London, 1983), p. 96.

34 Theodor Adorno and Max Horkheimer, *Dialectic of Enlightenment*, trans. John Cumming (London, 1973), p. 123.

35 Larry Swindell, '1939: A Very Good Year', *American Film*, I/3 (1975), p. 28.

36 André Bazin, 'On the *politique des auteurs*' [1957], *Cahiers du Cinéma Vol. 1. The 1950s: Neo-Realism, Hollywood, New Wave*, ed. Jim Hillier (London, 1985), p. 258.

37 Leo Rosten, *Hollywood: The Movie Colony* (New York, 1941), p. 242.

38 Andrew Sarris, *The American Cinema: Directors and Directions 1929–1968* (New York, 1996 edn), pp. 30–31.

39 Studies of directors and their relationships with the studios, based on archival research, include Peter Baxter, *Just Watch! Sternberg, Paramount and America* (London, 1993), Joseph McBride, *Frank Capra: The Catastrophe of Success* (London, 1992), Robert Sklar and Vito Zagarrio, eds, *Frank Capra: Authorship and the Studio System* (Philadelphia, 1998) and James C. Robertson, *The Casablanca Man: The Cinema of Michael Curtiz* (London, 1993).

40 Sarris, *The American Cinema*, p. 78.

41 Thomas Schatz, *History of the American Cinema Volume 6. Boom and Bust: American Cinema in the 1940s* (New York, 1997), p. 90.

42 For an authoritative account of the film's production history based on the studio archives, see Robert M. Carringer, *The Making of Citizen Kane* (Berkeley, 1985).

43 Schatz, *Boom and Bust*, p. 131.

44 *Ibid.*, p. 170.

45 *Ibid.*, p. 172.

46 American film propaganda during the Second World War is the subject of three admirable monographs: Thomas Docherty, *Projections of War:*

Hollywood, *American Culture and World War II* (New York, 1993); Clayton R. Koppes and Gregory D. Black, *Hollywood Goes to War: How Politics, Profits, and Propaganda Shaped World War II Movies* (New York, 1987); and Colin Shindler, *Hollywood Goes to War: Films and American Society 1939–52* (London, 1979).

47 Aljean Harmetz, *Round Up the Usual Suspects: The Making of Casablanca – Bogart, Bergman, & World War II* (London, 1993), p. 347.

48 See David Culbert, 'Our Awkward Ally: *Mission to Moscow* (1943)', in John E. O'Connor and Martin A. Jackson, eds, *American History/American Film: Interpreting the Hollywood Image* (New York, 1979), pp. 121–45.

49 Schatz, *Boom and Bust*, p. 370.

50 Herman G. Weinberg, 'The Dreams that Money Can Buy', *Sight and Sound*, XV/60 (1947), p. 140.

51 Abraham Polonsky, '"The Best Years of Our Lives": A Review', *Hollywood Quarterly*, II/3 (1947), p. 259.

52 Robert B. Ray, *A Certain Tendency of the Hollywood Cinema, 1930–1980* (Princeton, 1985), p.145. For a contextual history of the film in its social context, see Martin A. Jackson, 'The Uncertain Peace: *The Best Years of Our Lives* (1946)', in O'Connor and Jackson, eds, *American History/American Film*, pp. 147–65.

53 Quoted in Lary May, *The Big Tomorrow: Hollywood and the Politics of the American Way* (Chicago, 2000), p. 177.

54 Brian Neve, *Film and Politics in America: A Social Tradition* (London, 1992), p. 93; Richard Maltby, 'Made for Each Other: The Melodrama of Hollywood and the House Committee on Un-American Activities, 1947', in Davies and Neve, eds, *Cinema, Politics and Society in America*, pp. 76–96.

55 The 'Hollywood Ten' were Edward Dmytryk, Dalton Trumbo, John Howard, Sam Ornitz, Lester Cole, Adrian Scott, Herbert Biberman, Alvah Bessie, Ring Lardner Jr and Albert Maltz.

56 Dan Georgakas, 'Don't call him Gadget: A Reconsideration of Elia Kazan', *Cineaste*, XVI/4 (1988), p. 5

57 *The Nation*, 10 January 1953, p. 21.

58 John Belton, *American Cinema/American Culture* (New York, 1994), p. 253.

59 Schatz, *Boom and Bust*, p. 291; Richard Maltby, *Hollywood Cinema: An Introduction* (Oxford, 1995), p. 67.

60 Belton, *American Cinema/American Culture*, p. 258.

61 Bordwell, Staiger and Thompson, *The Classical Hollywood Cinema*, pp. 332–3.

62 Schatz, *The Genius of the System*, p. 440.

SIX · NEW HOLLYWOOD

1 David Bordwell, Janet Staiger and Kristin Thompson, *The Classical Hollywood Cinema: Film Style & Mode of Production to 1960* (London, 1985), p. 10.

2 Robert B. Ray, *A Certain Tendency of the Hollywood Cinema, 1930–1980* (Princeton, 1985), p. 68.

3 Jim Hillier, *The New Hollywood* (London, 1992), p. 18.

4 John Belton, *American Cinema/American Culture* (New York, 1994), p. 257.

5 Roy Pickard, *The Hollywood Story* (London, 1986), p. 216.

6 Douglas Gomery, 'Transformation of the Hollywood System', in Geoffrey Nowell-Smith, ed., *The Oxford History of World Cinema* (Oxford, 1996), p.450.

7 David A. Cook, *History of the American Cinema Volume 9. Lost Illusions: American Cinema in the Shadow of Watergate and Vietnam 1970–1979* (New York, 2000), p. 16.

8 Quoted in Tag Gallagher, *John Ford: The Man and His Films* (Berkeley, 1986), p. 437.

9 Peter Biskind, *Easy Riders, Raging Bulls: How the Sex' n' Drugs 'n' Rock 'n' Roll Generation Saved Hollywood* (London, 1998), p. 15.

10 David Thomson, 'Why Dirty Harry Beats Harry Potter', *Observer Review*, 13 January 2002, p. 8.

11 Thomas Elsaesser, 'The Pathos of Failure: Notes on the Unmotivated Hero', *Monogram*, 6 (1975), p. 14.

12 Thomson, 'Why Dirty Harry Beats Harry Potter', p. 8.

13 Cook, *Lost Illusions*, p. XVII.

14 Thomas Schatz, 'The New Hollywood', in Jim Collins, Hilary Radner and Ava Preacher Collins, *Film Theory Goes to the Movies* (London, 1993), p. 10.

15 William Goldman, *Adventures in the Screen Trade: A Personal View of Hollywood and Screenwriting* (London, 1985 edn), p. 215.

16 *Quo Vadis?* ($8.25 million), *The Ten Commandments* ($13.5 million) and *Ben-Hur* ($15 million) each set a new record for the most expensive film ever made. *The Ten Commandments*, *Ben-Hur* and *The Robe* were, respectively, the second, fourth and seventh highest-grossing films at the North American box-office in the 1950s, with grosses of $85.4 million, $73.2 million and $45.2 million. *The Variety Almanac 2000*, ed. Peter Cowie (London, 2000), p. 71.

17 Quoted in Schatz 'The New Hollywood', p. 13.

18 Cook, *Lost Illusions*, p. 34.

19 *Ibid*, p. 51; John Douglas Eames, *The Paramount Story* (London, 1985), p. 267; Clive Hirschhorn, *The Warner Bros. Story* (London, 1979), p. 429.

20 Schatz, 'The New Hollywood', p. 17.

21 Timothy Corrigan, *A Cinema Without Walls: Movies and Culture After Vietnam* (London, 1991), p. 12.

22 *The Variety Almanac 2000*, p. 71.

23 J. Hoberman, 'Ten Years That Shook the World', *American Film*, x/8 (1985), p. 58.

24 Goldman, *Adventures in the Screen Trade*, pp. 151–2. For a defence of the blockbuster movie, see Geoff King, *Spectacular Narratives: Hollywood in the Age of the Blockbuster* (London, 2000).

25 Noël Carroll, 'The Future of Allusion: Hollywood in the Seventies (and Beyond)', *October*, 20 (1982), p. 56.

26 Schatz, 'The New Hollywood', p. 35.

27 Cook, *Lost Illusions*, p. 37.

28 Schatz, 'The New Hollywood', p. 27.

29 Ray, *A Certain Tendency of the Hollywood Cinema*, p. 254.

30 Michael Medved, *Hollywood vs. America* (New York, 1992), p. 227.

31 See Robin Wood, *Hollywood from Vietnam to Reagan* (New York, 1989).

32 Belton, *American Cinema/American Culture*, p. 322.

33 Fredric Jameson, 'Postmodernism and Consumer Society', in Ann Gray and Jim McGuigan, eds, *Studying Culture: An Introductory Reader* (London,

1997), p. 198.

34 Medved, *Hollywood vs. America*, p. 3.

35 Leslie Felperin Sharman, 'Forrest Gump', *Sight and Sound*, New Series, IV/10 (1994), p. 43.

36 Quoted in Dave Kehr, 'Who Framed Forrest Gump?', *Film Comment*, XXXI/2 (1995), p. 45.

37 See Toby Miller, Nitin Govil, John McMurria and Richard Maxwell, *Global Hollywood* (London, 2001).

38 Hillier, *The New Hollywood*, p. 23.

39 Richard Maltby, *Hollywood Cinema: An Introduction* (Oxford, 1995), p. 75. *Batman* earned North American grosses of $251 million, *Batman Returns* (1992) grossed $162 million, *Batman Forever* (1995) $184 million and *Batman and Robin* (1997) $107 million. Overall, therefore, the series was subject to the law of diminishing returns that affects most franchises. The first two films were directed by Tim Burton, the third and fourth by Joel Schumacher.

40 Hillier, *The New Hollywood*, p. 25.

41 *Screen International*, 17 October 1997, p. 5.

42 Maltby, *Hollywood Cinema*, p. 482.

43 Quoted in Hillier, *The New Hollywood*, p. 28.

44 Tom Gunning, 'The Cinema of Attractions: Early Film, its Spectator and the Avant-Garde', in Thomas Elsaesser, ed., *Space, Frame, Narrative* (London, 1990), p. 61.

45 Peter Krämer, 'Women First: *Titanic* (1997), Action-adventure Films and Hollywood's Female Audience', *Historical Journal of Film, Radio and Television*, XVIII/4 (1998), p. 612.

46 Goldman, *Adventures in the Screen Trade*, p. 49.

47 These grosses represent a modest profit margin against a negative cost of $153 million.

48 Miller, Govil, McMurria and Maxwell, *Global Hollywood*, p. 5.

49 Stephen Price, *History of the American Cinema Volume 10. A New Pot of Gold: Hollywood under the Electronic Rainbow, 1980–1989* (New York, 2000), p. 246.

50 Arthur Marwick, *The Arts in the West since 1945* (Oxford, 2002), p. 324.

SEVEN · AMERICAN GENRES, AMERICAN SOCIETY

1 Barry Keith Grant, 'Introduction', *Film Genre Reader II* (Austin, 1995), p. xv.

2 Robert Warshow, *The Immediate Experience* (New York, 1970), p. 129.

3 Thomas Schatz, *Hollywood Genres: Formulas, Filmmaking, and the Studio System* (New York, 1981), p. 261.

4 John Belton, *American Cinema/American Culture* (New York, 1994), p. 116.

5 André Bazin, 'The Western: or the American film *par excellence*', in *What Is Cinema? Vol. II*, ed. and trans. Hugh Gray (Berkeley, 1971), pp. 140–48.

6 Michael Coyne, *The Crowded Prairie: American National Identity in the Hollywood Western* (London, 1997), p. 2.

7 Jim Kitses, *Horizons West: Studies of Authorship within the Western* (London, 1969), p. 19.

8 Will Wright, *Sixguns and Society: A Structural Study of the Western* (Berkeley, 1975), p. 32. For a balanced assessment and critique of Wright's book, see

Christopher Frayling, 'The American Western and American Society', in Philip Davies and Brian Neve, eds, *Cinema, Politics and Society in America* (Manchester, 1981), pp. 136–62.

9 Alan Lovell, 'The Western', *Screen Education*, 41 (1967), p. 97.

10 For a full listing of the major westerns released between 1939 and 1941, see Coyne, *The Crowded Prairie*, p. 18.

11 André Bazin, 'The Evolution of the Western', *What is Cinema? Vol. II*, p. 149.

12 For an account of the production history of the film and its reception, see the BFI 'Film Classic' by Edward Buscombe, *Stagecoach* (London, 1992).

13 Lindsay Anderson, *About John Ford* (London, 1981), p. 14.

14 Schatz, *Hollywood Genres*, p. 67; Coyne, *The Crowded Prairie*, p. 40.

15 Quoted in Coyne, *The Crowded Prairie*, p. 42.

16 Bazin, 'The Evolution of the Western', p. 151.

17 See Edward Buscombe, *The Searchers* (London, 2000), for an assessment of the film's critical reputation and a discussion of its complex and multi-layered narrative.

18 Robin Wood, *Howard Hawks* (London, 1968), p. 39.

19 Ed Buscombe, 'The Idea of Genre in the American Cinema', *Screen*, XI/2 (1970), p. 44.

20 Belton, *American Cinema/American Culture*, p. 227.

21 Colin McArthur, *Underworld USA* (London, 1972), p. 18.

22 Andrew Tudor, *Image and Influence* (London, 1974), p. 196.

23 Warshow, 'The Gangster as Tragic Hero', *The Immediate Experience*, p. 136.

24 *Ibid.*, p. 132.

25 Schatz, *Hollywood Genres*, p. 89.

26 Richard Maltby, *Hollywood Cinema: An Introduction* (Oxford, 1995), p. 111.

27 Schatz, *Hollywood Genres*, p. 95.

28 *Ibid.*, p. 84.

29 Nick Roddick, *A New Deal in Entertainment: Warner Brothers in the 1930s* (London, 1983), p. 99.

30 John Raeburn, 'The Gangster Film', in W.D. Gehring, ed., *Handbook of American Film Genres* (Westport, CT, 1988), p. 55.

31 Jack Shadoian, *Dreams and Dead Ends: The American Gangster/Crime Film* (Cambridge, MA, 1977), p. 11.

32 Quoted in Schatz, *Hollywood Genres*, p. 111.

33 John Houseman, 'Today's Hero: A Review', *Hollywood Quarterly*, II/2 (1947), pp. 161–3.

34 For a concise critical overview of the writing on *film noir*, see Steve Neale, *Genre and Hollywood* (London, 2000), pp. 151–77.

35 Paul Schrader, 'Notes on *film noir*', *Film Comment*, VIII/1 (1972), p. 13.

36 Belton, *American Cinema/American Culture*, p. 187.

37 Neale, *Genre and Hollywood*, pp. 155–6; Alain Silver and Elizabeth Ward, eds, *Film Noir: An Encyclopedic Reference Guide to the American Style* (London, 2nd edn 1991), pp. 393–7.

38 Richard Winnington, *Drawn and Quartered* (London, 1949), p. 93.

39 Schatz, *Hollywood Genres*, p. 113.

40 David A. Cook, *A History of Narrative Film* (London, 2nd edn 1990), p. 471.

41 Schrader, 'Notes on *film noir*', p. 13.

42 Robert B. Ray, *A Certain Tendency of the Hollywood Cinema, 1930–1980*

(Princeton, 1985), p. 160.

43 J. A. Place and L. S. Pearson, 'Some Visual Motifs of *film noir*', *Film Comment*, x/1 (1974), p. 31.

44 Paul Kerr, 'Out of what past? Notes on the B *film noir*', in Paul Kerr, ed., *The Hollywood Film Industry* (London, 1986), p. 242.

45 Ralph Willett, 'The Nation in Crisis: Hollywood's Response to the 1940s', in Davies and Neve, eds, *Cinema, Politics and Society in America*, p. 67.

46 Belton, *American Cinema/American Culture*, p. 191.

47 Janey Place, 'Women in film noir', in E. Ann Kaplan, ed., *Women in Film Noir* (London, 1980), p. 35

48 Sylvia Harvey, 'Woman's Place: The Absent Family of film noir', in Kaplan, ed., *Women in Film Noir*, p. 33.

49 Neale, *Genre and Hollywood*, p. 154.

50 Belton, *American Cinema/American Culture*, p. 203.

51 Roger Manvell, *The Film and the Public* (Harmondsworth, 1955), p. 174.

52 Jane Feuer, *The Hollywood Musical* (London, 1982), p. VII.

53 Schatz, *Hollywood Genres*, p. 186.

54 For a discussion of 'Judy Garland and Gay Men', see Richard Dyer, *Heavenly Bodies: Film Stars and Society* (London, 1987), pp. 141–94.

55 Tino Balio, *History of the American Cinema Volume 5. Grand Design: Hollywood as a Modern Business Enterprise 1930–1939* (New York, 1993), p. 211.

56 Neale, *Genre and Hollywood*, p. 105.

57 Mark Roth, 'Some Warners Musicals and the Spirit of the New Deal', *The Velvet Light Trap*, 17 (1977), p. 7; Feuer, *The Hollywood Musical*, p. 42.

58 See John Mueller, 'Fred Astaire and the Integrated Musical', *Cinema Journal*, XXIV/1 (1984), pp. 28–40.

59 See Hugh Fordin, *The Movies' Greatest Musicals* (New York, 1984), which, despite its somewhat celebratory title, is actually a history of the Freed Unit based on archival sources.

60 Jane Feuer, 'The Self-reflective Musical and the Myth of Entertainment', in Rick Altman, ed., *Genre: The Musical* (London, 1981), p. 213.

61 Rick Altman, 'The Musical', in Geoffrey Nowell-Smith, ed., *The Oxford History of World Cinema* (Oxford, 1996), p. 303.

62 The best overview of the critical writing on melodrama is again to be found in Neale, *Genre and Hollywood*, pp. 179–204.

63 *Variety*, 25 May 1937.

64 Molly Haskell, *From Reverence to Rape: The Treatment of Women in the Movies* (Chicago, 2nd edn 1987), p. 214.

65 Maria LaPlace, 'Producing and Consuming the Woman's Film: Discursive Struggle in *Now, Voyager*', in Christine Gledhill, ed., *Home Is Where the Heart Is: Studies in Melodrama and the Woman's Film* (London, 1987), p. 148.

66 Haskell, *From Reverence to Rape*, p. 220.

67 *Ibid.*, p. 222.

68 Thomas Elsaesser, 'Tales of Sound and Fury: Observations on the Family Melodrama', in Gledhill, ed., *Home Is Where the Heart Is*, p. 51.

69 *Ibid.*, p. 68.

70 Schatz, *Hollywood Genres*, p. 225.

71 Annette Kuhn, 'Women's Genres: Melodrama, Soap Opera and Theory', *Screen*, XXV/1 (1984), p. 18.

72 Laura Mulvey, *Visual and Other Pleasures* (London, 1989), p. 39.
73 Quoted in Maltby, *Hollywood Cinema*, p. 137.
74 Peter Krämer, 'Women First: *Titanic* (1997), Action-adventure Films and Hollywood's Female Audience', *Historical Journal of Film, Radio and Television*, XVIII/4 (October 1998), p. 614.

EIGHT · EUROPEAN CINEMAS IN PEACE AND WAR

1 Pierre Sorlin, *European Cinemas, European Societies 1939–1990* (London, 1991), p. 20.
2 *The Guinness Book of Film Facts and Feats*, ed. Patrick Robertson (London, 1985), pp. 17–21.
3 Jeffrey Richards, *The Age of the Dream Palace: Cinema and Society in Britain 1930–1939* (London, 1984), p. 11; Linda Wood, ed., *British Film Industry* (London, 1980).
4 A.J.P. Taylor, *English History 1914–1945* (Oxford, 1965), p. 313.
5 David Welch, *Propaganda and the German Cinema, 1933–1945* (Oxford, 1983), pp. 31, 35.
6 Susan Hayward, *French National Cinema* (London, 1993), p. 48.
7 Colin Crisp, *The Classic French Cinema, 1930–1960* (London, 1997 edn), p. 14.
8 *The International Motion Picture Almanack 1939–1940*, ed. Terry Ramsaye (New York, 1940), p. 944.
9 Quoted in Richards, *The Age of the Dream Palace*, p. 58.
10 *The International Motion Picture Almanack 1939–1940*, p. 829.
11 John Sedgwick, *Popular Filmgoing in 1930s Britain: A Choice of Pleasures* (Exeter, 2000), pp. 251–2.
12 Kevin Rockett, 'Protecting the Family and the Nation: The Official Censorship of American Cinema in Ireland, 1923–1954', *Historical Journal of Film, Radio and Television*, XX/3 (2000), p. 284.
13 Quoted in Mira Liehm, *Passion and Defiance: Film in Italy from 1942 to the Present* (Berkeley, 1984), p. 3.
14 Sabine Hake, *German National Cinema* (London, 2002), p. 53.
15 For a case history of the censorship of *Love on the Dole*, see Sarah Street, *British Cinema in Documents* (London, 2000), pp. 23–38.
16 Richards, *The Age of the Dream Palace*, p. 323.
17 *Ibid.*, p. 324.
18 Quoted in Richard Maltby and Ruth Vasey, '"Temporary American Citizens": Cultural Anxieties and Industrial Strategies in the Americanization of European Cinema', in Andrew Higson and Richard Maltby, eds, *"Film Europe" and "Film America": Cinema, Commerce and Cultural Exchange 1920–1939* (Exeter, 1999), p. 38.
19 Quoted in Richards, *The Age of the Dream Palace*, pp. 62–3.
20 Quoted in Kevin Rockett, Luke Gibbons and John Hill, *Cinema and Ireland* (New York, 1988), p. 38.
21 Julian Petley, *Capital and Culture: German Cinema 1933–1945* (London, 1979), p. 1.
22 *Ibid.*, p. 3.

23 Ginette Vincendeau, 'In the name of the father: Marcel Pagnol's "Trilogy": *Marius* (1931), *Fanny* (1932), *César* (1936)', in Susan Hayward and Ginette Vincendeau, eds, *French Film: Texts and Contexts* (London, 1990), p. 71.

24 Ginette Vincendeau, *Pépé le Moko* (London, 1998), p. 38.

25 There is a scarcity of good historical material on Renoir: the most recent study is Martin O'Shaughnessy, *Jean Renoir* (Manchester, 2000). See also Leo Braudy, *Jean Renoir: The World of His Films* (London, 1977) and Raymond Durgnat, *Jean Renoir* (Berkeley, 1974).

26 Eric Rhode, *A History of the Cinema from its Origins to 1970* (London, 1978), p. 360.

27 Elizabeth Grottle Strebel, 'Jean Renoir and the Popular Front', in K.R.M. Short, ed., *Feature Films as History* (London, 1981), p. 78.

28 Quoted in John W. Martin, *The Golden Age of French Cinema 1929–1939* (London, 1983), p. 119.

29 Peter Wollen, '*La Règle du jeu* and Modernity', *Film Studies: An International Review*, 1 (1999), p. 13.

30 Hayward, *French National Cinema*, p. 118.

31 Quoted in Graham Roberts, *Forward Soviet! History and Non-fiction Film in the* USSR (London, 1999), p. 127.

32 John Grierson, *Grierson on Documentary*, ed. Forsyth Hardy (London, 1946), pp. 35–37, 41.

33 The Arts Enquiry, *The Factual Film* (Oxford, 1947), p. 11. There is an extensive critical and historical literature on the documentarists, ranging from the anecdotal history of Elizabeth Sussex, *The Rise and Fall of British Documentary* (Berkeley, 1975), the formal and aesthetic history of Alan Lovell and Jim Hillier, *Studies in Documentary* (London, 1972), the ideological and cultural history of Ian Aitken, *Film and Reform: John Grierson and the Documentary Film Movement* (London, 1990), and the political and institutional history of Paul Swann, *The British Documentary Film Movement, 1926–1946* (Cambridge, 1989).

34 Brian Winston, *Claiming the Real: The Griersonian Documentary and Its Legitimations* (London, 1995), p. 60.

35 Swann, *The British Documentary Film Movement*, p. 84.

36 See, for example, Richard Taylor, *Film Propaganda: Soviet Russia and Nazi Germany* (London, 1979). A useful synthesis of recent research on the subject is Nicholas Reeves, *Film Propaganda: Myth or Reality?* (London, 1999).

37 Geoffrey Nowell-Smith, 'Introduction to Part 2: Sound Cinema', in Nowell-Smith, ed, *The Oxford History of World Cinema* (Oxford, 1996), p. 209.

38 Welch, *Propaganda and the German Cinema*, p. 42.

39 Hake, *German National Cinema*, p. 59.

40 Quoted in Welch, *Propaganda and the German Cinema*, p. 91.

41 *Ibid.*, p. 158.

42 Steve Neale, 'Propaganda', *Screen*, XVIII/3 (1977), p. 25.

43 *Ibid.*, p. 32.

44 K.R.M. Short, ed., *Catalogue of Forbidden German Feature and Short Film Productions* (Trowbridge, 1996), p. 147.

45 The intriguing censorship history of this film – unique as the only one to have been banned by both the Nazis and the Allies – is documented in Robert E.

Peck, 'The Banning of *Titanic*: A Study of British Postwar Film Censorship in Germany', *Historical Journal of Film, Radio and Television*, xx/3 (2000), pp. 427–44.

46 There is a growing body of work on the the popular cinema of the Third Reich, including Jo Fox, *Filming Women in the Third Reich* (Oxford, 2000), Sabine Hake, *Popular Cinema of the Third Reich* (Austin, 2001), Erich Rentschler, *The Ministry of Illusion: Nazi Cinema and its Afterlife* (Cambridge, MA, 1996) and Linda Schulte-Sasse, *Entertaining the Third Reich: Illusions of Wholeness in Nazi Cinema* (Durham, 1996). For an over-view of the revisionist tendency in reclaiming the popular, see chapter seven ('Nazi cinema at the intersection of the classical and the popular') of Patrice Petro, *Aftershocks of the New: Feminism and Film History* (New Brunswick, NJ, 2002), pp. 124–35.

47 Rentschler, *The Ministry of Illusion*, p. 190.

48 *Ibid.*, p. 207.

49 Paul Rotha, *Rotha on the Film: A Selection of Writings about the Cinema* (London, 1958), p. 234.

50 Quoted in Sussex, *The Rise and Fall of British Documentary*, p. 119.

51 See James Chapman, *The British at War: Cinema, State and Propaganda, 1939–1945* (London, 1998). Case studies of selected films can be found in Anthony Aldgate and Jeffrey Richards, *Britain Can Take It: British Cinema in the Second World War* (Edinburgh, 2nd edn 1994).

52 Roger Manvell, *Films and the Second World War* (London, 1974), p. 101.

53 Michael Balcon, *A Lifetime of Films* (London, 1969), p. 133.

54 Charles Barr, *Ealing Studios* (London, 1977), p. 35.

55 There is an abundant critical literature on Gainsborough's costume melodramas: see in particular Sue Aspinall and Robert Murphy, eds, *Gainsborough Melodrama* (London, 1983), Sue Harper, *Picturing the Past: The Rise and Fall of the British Costume Film* (London, 1994), pp. 119–35, and Pam Cook, ed., *Gainsborough Pictures* (London, 1997).

56 James Chapman, '*The Life and Death of Colonel Blimp* (1943) Reconsidered', *Historical Journal of Film, Radio and Television*, xv/1 (1995), pp. 19–54.

57 Quoted in Taylor, *Film Propaganda*, p. 216.

58 'Introduction', Ulrike Sieglohr, ed., *Heroines Without Heroes: Reconstructing Female and National Identities in European Cinema, 1945–51* (London, 2000), p. 1.

59 Quoted in Margaret Dickinson and Sarah Street, *Cinema and State: The Film Industry and the British Government, 1927–84* (London, 1985), p. 176.

60 Crisp, *The Classic French Cinema*, p. 75.

61 Quoted in Dickinson and Street, *Cinema and State*, p. 180.

62 Crisp, *The Classic French Cinema*, p. 76.

63 Thomas Elsaesser, *New German Cinema: A History* (New Brunswick, NJ, 1989), pp. 13–17.

64 Hake, *German National Cinema*, p. 87.

65 Kristin Thompson and David Bordwell, *Film History: An Introduction* (New York, 1994), p. 412.

66 *Ibid.*, p. 414.

67 Ephraim Katz, *The Macmillan International Film Encyclopedia* (London, 1994), p. 220.

68 Dilys Powell, *The Dilys Powell Film Reader*, ed. Christopher Cook

(Manchester, 1991), p. 346.

69 Quoted in Millicent Marcus, *Italian Film in the Light of Neorealism* (Princeton, 1986), p. 14.

70 André Bazin, '*Umberto D*: A Great Work', in *What Is Cinema Volume II*, ed. and trans. Hugh Gray (Berkeley, 1971), pp. 79–80.

71 Cesare Zavattini, 'A Thesis on Neo-realism', in David Overbey, ed., *Springtime in Italy: A Reader on Neo-realism* (London, 1978), pp. 77–8.

72 Quoted in Marcus, *Italian Film in the Light of Neorealism*, p. 26.

73 See Robert R. Shandley, *Rubble Films: German Cinema in the Shadow of the Third Reich* (New York, 2001).

74 Crisp, *The Classic French Cinema*, p. 68.

75 Elsaesser, *New German Cinema*, p. 17.

76 Sorlin, *European Cinemas, European Societies*, p. 81.

77 Asa Briggs, *The History of Broadcasting in the United Kingdom Volume V: Competition 1955–1975* (Oxford, 1995), p. 1005; Crisp, *The Classic French Cinema*, p. 71; Pierre Sorlin, *Italian National Cinema 1896–1996* (London, 1996), pp. 116–17.

NINE · NEW WAVES, NEW CINEMAS

1 Raymond Durgnat, *A Mirror for England: British Movies from Austerity to Affluence* (London, 1970), p. 151.

2 See Arthur Marwick, *The Sixties: Cultural Revolution in Britain, France, Italy and the United States, c.1958–c.1974* (Oxford, 1998).

3 Colin Crisp, *The Classic French Cinema, 1930–1960* (London, 1997), p.68; Thomas Elsaesser, *New German Cinema: A History* (New Brunswick, NJ, 1989), p. 36; Linda Wood, ed., *British Film Industry* (London, 1981); Pierre Sorlin, *Italian National Cinema 1896–1996* (London, 1996), p. 118.

4 Crisp, *The Classic French Cinema*, p. 70.

5 Sorlin, *Italian National Cinema*, p. 119.

6 Jacques Siclier, 'New Wave and French Cinema', *Sight and Sound*, XXX/3 (1961), p. 117.

7 Lindsay Anderson, 'Get Out and Push!', in Tom Maschler, ed., *Declaration* (London, 1957), p. 157.

8 François Truffaut, 'A Certain Tendency of the French Cinema' [1954], in Bill Nichols, ed., *Movies and Methods Volume 1: An Anthology* (Berkeley, 1976), p. 233

9 Roger Manvell, *New Cinema in Europe* (London, 1966), p. 7

10 David Bordwell, *Narration in the Fiction Film* (London, 1985), pp. 230–31.

11 Marwick, *The Sixties*, p. 18.

12 Manvell, *New Cinema in Europe*, p. 18.

13 The negotiation between censors and filmmakers is impressively documented in Anthony Aldgate, *Censorship and the Permissive Society: British Cinema and Theatre 1955–1965* (Oxford, 1995).

14 'Introduction', Peter Graham, ed., *The New Wave* (London, 1968), p. 7.

15 James Monaco, *The New Wave: Truffaut, Godard, Chabrol, Rohmer, Rivette* (New York, 1976), p. VII.

16 Arthur Marwick, *The Arts in the West since 1945* (Oxford, 2002), p. 145.

17 Quoted in Philip French, ed., *Malle on Malle* (London, 1993), pp. 30–31.

18 Kristin Thompson and David Bordwell, *Film History: An Introduction* (New York, 1994), p. 528.

19 Jean Domarchi, Jacques Doniol-Valcroze, Jean-Luc Godard, Pierre Kast, Jacques Rivette, Eric Rohmer, 'Hiroshima, notre amour' [1959], in *Cahiers du Cinéma Volume 1. The 1950s: Neo-Realism, Hollywood, New Wave*, ed. Jim Hillier (Cambridge, MA, 1985), p. 59.

20 Emma Wilson, *French Cinema since 1950: Personal Histories* (London, 1999), p. 22.

21 Quoted in Tom Milne, ed., *Godard on Godard* (London, 1972), p. 173.

22 François Truffaut, 'Evolution of the New Wave' [1967], in *Cahiers du Cinéma Volume 2. 1960–1968: New Wave, New Cinema, Reevaluating Hollywood*, ed. Jim Hillier (Cambridge, MA, 1986), p. 106.

23 Quoted in Marwick, *The Arts in the West since 1945*, p. 152.

24 'Introduction', Geoffrey Nowell-Smith, with James Hay and Giuseppe Volpi, *The Companion to Italian Cinema* (London, 1996), p. 5.

25 Penelope Houston, *The Contemporary Cinema* (Harmondsworth, 1963), p. 27.

26 Mira Liehm, *Passion and Defiance: Film in Italy from 1942 to the Present* (Berkeley, 1984), pp. 188–9.

27 C.B. Thomsen, 'Interview with Marco Bellocchio', *Sight and Sound*, XXXVII/1 (1967/8), p. 15.

28 Durgnat, *A Mirror for England*, p. 129.

29 Dilys Powell, *The Dilys Powell Film Reader*, ed. Christopher Cook (Manchester, 1991), p. 202.

30 Roy Armes, *A Critical History of the British Cinema* (London, 1978), p. 264.

31 John Hill, *Sex, Class and Realism: British Cinema 1956–1963* (London, 1986), pp. 132–3.

32 Arthur Marwick, '*Room at the Top, Saturday Night and Sunday Morning* and the "Cultural Revolution" in Britain', *Journal of Contemporary History*, XIX/1 (1984), p. 148.

33 Quoted in Julia Knight, *Women and the New German Cinema* (London, 1992), pp. 29–30.

34 Elsaesser, *New German Cinema*, p. 2.

35 Anton Kaes, 'The New German Cinema', in Geoffrey Nowell-Smith, ed., *The Oxford History of World Cinema* (Oxford, 1996), p. 616.

36 Thompson and Bordwell, *Film History: An Introduction*, p. 660.

37 Quoted in Thomas Elsaesser, *Fassbinder's Germany* (Amsterdam, 1996), pp. 20–21.

38 Elsaesser, *New German Cinema*, p. 3.

39 Peter Hames, *The Czechoslovak New Wave* (Berkeley, 1985), p. 2.

40 Quoted in Manvell, *New Cinema in Europe*, p. 18.

41 Basil Wright, *The Long View: A Personal Perspective on World Cinema* (London, 1974), p. 599.

42 Hames, *The Czechoslovak New Wave*, p. 279.

43 Thompson and Bordwell, *Film History: An Introduction*, p. 475.

44 Jacek Fuksiewicz, *Polish Cinema* (Warsaw, 1973), p. 51.

45 Jill Forbes and Sarah Street, *European Cinemas: An Introduction* (London, 2000), p. 21

46 Thompson and Bordwell, *Film History: An Introduction*, p. 725.

47 See Peter Giles, 'History with Holes: Channel Four Television Films of the
1980s', in Lester Friedman, ed., *British Cinema and Thatcherism: Fires Were
Started* (London, 1993), pp. 70–91. Hanif Kureishi was the writer of *My
Beautiful Laundrette*, though, characteristically for British film culture, is generally acknowledged as its 'author' rather than director Stephen Frears. See
also Christine Geraghty, *My Beautiful Laundrette:
A British Film Guide* (London, forthcoming).

48 Jill Forbes, *The Cinema in France: After the New Wave* (London, 1992),
pp. 62–72.

49 *Blue* was joint winner of the Golden Lion at the Venice Film Festival (with
Robert Altman's *Short Cuts*) and *White* won Kieslowski the Silver Bear for
Best Director at the Berlin Film Festival. Only *Red*, premiered at Cannes,
failed to win a major festival prize. Geoff Andrew suggests this was 'a political
move designed to deny the director the first ever "grand slam" of major
awards at Europe's three most prestigious film festivals'. Andrew, *The 'Three
Colours' Trilogy* (London, 1998), p. 77.

50 Peter Wollen, 'The Last New Wave: Modernism in the British Films of the
Thatcher Era', in Friedman, ed., *British Cinema and Thatcherism*, p. 49.

TEN · POPULAR GENRES, POPULAR PLEASURES

1 'Introduction' to Richard Dyer and Ginette Vincendeau, eds, *Popular
European Cinema* (London, 1992), p. 1.

2 André Bazin, Jacques Doniol-Valcroze, Pierre Kast, Roger Leenhardt,
Jacques Rivette, Eric Rohmer, 'Six characters in search of *auteurs*: a discussion
about the French cinema', in *Cahiers du Cinéma Volume 1. The 1950s: Neo-
Realism, Hollywood, New Wave*, ed. Jim Hillier (Cambridge, MA, 1985), p. 32.

3 Julian Petley and Alan Burton, 'Introduction', *Journal of Popular British
Cinema*, 1 (1998), p. 4.

4 On the British war film of the 1950s see James Chapman, 'Our Finest Hour
Revisited: The Second World War in British Feature Films since 1945',
Journal of Popular British Cinema, 1 (1998), pp. 63–75; Robert Murphy, *British
Cinema and the Second World War* (London, 2000); and John Ramsden,
'Refocusing "The People's War": British War Films of the 1950s', *Journal of
Contemporary History*, XXXIII/1 (1998), pp. 35–63.

5 William Whitebait, 'Bombardment', *New Statesman*, 5 April 1958, p. 432.

6 Roy Armes, *A Critical History of the British Cinema*, (London, 1978), p. 179.

7 Andy Medhurst, '1950s War Films', in Geoff Hurd, ed., *National Fictions:
World War Two in British Films and Television* (London, 1985), pp. 35, 38.

8 Christine Geraghty, *British Cinema in the Fifties: Gender, Genre and the 'New
Look'* (London, 2000), p. 189.

9 Ramsden, 'Refocusing "The People's War"', pp. 49–51.

10 Murphy, *British Cinema and the Second World War*, p. 233.

11 Pierre Sorlin, *European Cinemas, European Societies 1939–1990* (London,
1991), pp. 76–7.

12 *Monthly Film Bulletin*, II/580 (1982), p. 81.

13 Susan Hayward, *French National Cinema* (London, 1993), p. 260.

14 Quoted in Philip French, ed., *Malle on Malle* (London, 1993), p. 103.

15 Guy Austin, *Contemporary French Cinema* (Manchester, 1996), p. 32.

16 Chris Darke, 'Lucie Aubrac', *Sight and Sound*, New Series, VIII/2 (1998), p. 47.

17 David Robinson, 'Comedy', in Geoffrey Nowell-Smith, ed., *The Oxford History of World Cinema* (Oxford, 1996), p. 81.

18 Sabine Hake, *German National Cinema* (London, 2002), p. 69.

19 Jeffrey Richards, *The Age of the Dream Palace: Cinema and Society in Britain, 1930–1939* (London, 1984), pp. 169–206.

20 Pierre Sorlin, 'From *The Third Man* to *Shakespeare in Love*: Fifty Years of British Success on Continental Screens', in Justine Ashby and Andrew Higson, eds, *British Cinema, Past and Present* (London, 2000), p. 84.

21 Dilys Powell, *The Dilys Powell Film Reader*, ed. Christopher Cook (Manchester, 1991), pp. 22–3.

22 The definitive study of the studio and its films is Charles Barr's *Ealing Studios* (London, 1977).

23 Michael Balcon, *A Lifetime of Films* (London, 1969), pp. 158–9.

24 John Ellis, 'Made in Ealing', *Screen*, XVI/1 (1975), p. 116.

25 Ephraim Katz, *The Macmillan International Film Encyclopedia* (London, 1994), p. 1330.

26 Hayward, *French National Cinema*, p. 185.

27 Andy Medhurst, 'Carry On Camp', *Sight and Sound*, New Series, II/4 (1992), p. 16.

28 Arthur Marwick, *The Arts in the West since 1945* (Oxford, 2002), p. 318.

29 Martine Danan, 'Revisiting the Myth of the French Nation: *Les Visiteurs* (Poiré, 1993)', in Phil Powrie, ed., *French Cinema in the 1990s: Continuity and Difference* (Oxford, 1999), p. 92.

30 *Ibid.*

31 Sorlin, *European Cinemas, European Societies*, p. 40.

32 Michael Denning, *Cover Stories: Narrative and Ideology in the British Spy Thriller* (London, 1987), p. 6.

33 *Ibid.*, p. 34.

34 On Hitchcock's British thrillers of the 1930s see Charles Barr, *English Hitchcock* (Moffat, 1999), and Tom Ryall, *Alfred Hitchcock and the British Cinema* (London, 1986), pp. 115–40.

35 Hayward, *French National Cinema*, p. 152.

36 Sorlin, *European Cinemas, European Societies*, p. 40.

37 Powell, *The Dilys Powell Film Reader*, p. 22.

38 C.A. Lejeune, *The C.A. Lejeune Film Reader*, ed. Anthony Lejeune (Manchester, 1991), p. 241.

39 British Cold War spy films are discussed in Tony Shaw, *British Cinema and the Cold War: The State, Propaganda and Consensus* (London, 2001).

40 See James Chapman, *Licence To Thrill: A Cultural History of the James Bond Films* (London, 1999).

41 'Young Romantic', *Films and Filming*, XIII/5 (1967), p. 58.

42 Jeffrey Richards, *Films and British National Identity: From Dickens to 'Dad's Army'* (Manchester, 1997), p. 163.

43 Quoted in Chapman, *Licence To Thrill*, p. 6.

44 Robin Wood, *Hitchcock's Films* (London, 1977 edn), p. 96.

45 Armes, *A Critical History of the British Cinema*, p. 257.

46 Quoted in Marwick, *The Arts in the West since 1945*, p. 151.

47 Martin Rubin, *Thrillers* (Cambridge, 1999), p. 136.
48 Morando Morandini, 'Italy: Auteurs and After', in Geoffrey Nowell-Smith, ed., *The Oxford History of World Cinema* (Oxford, 1996), p. 592.
49 Michèle Lagny, 'Popular Taste: The Peplum', in Dyer and Vincendeau, eds, *Popular European Cinema*, p. 167.
50 See Christopher Frayling, *Spaghetti Westerns: Cowboys and Europeans from Karl May to Sergio Leone* (London, 1981).
51 *Ibid.*, p. 191.
52 Christopher Wagstaff, 'A Forkful of Westerns: Industry, Audiences and the Italian Western', in Dyer and Vincendeau, eds, *Popular European Cinema*, p. 257.
53 *Ibid.*, p. 253.
54 Quoted in Tom Johnson and Deborah Del Vecchio, *Hammer Films: An Exhaustive Filmography* (Jefferson, NC, 1996), p. 122.
55 Quoted in Peter Hutchings, *Hammer and Beyond: The British Horror Film* (Manchester, 1993), p. 6.
56 Armes, *A Critical History of the British Cinema*, p. 250.
57 David Pirie, *A Heritage of Horror: the English Gothic Cinema 1946–1972* (London, 1973), p. 9.
58 There are several books on Fisher, including Peter Hutchings, *Terence Fisher* (Manchester, 2001), and Wheeler Winston Dixon, *The Charm of Evil: The Life and Films of Terence Fisher* (Metuchen, NJ, 1994).
59 Vivian Sobchack, 'The Fantastic', in Nowell-Smith, ed., *The Oxford History of World Cinema*, p. 320.
60 Armes, *A Critical History of British Cinema*, p. 147.
61 Carol Jenks, 'The Other Face of Death: Barbara Steele and *La maschera del demonio*', in Dyer and Vincendeau, eds, *Popular European Cinema*, pp. 152–3.
62 Entry in *The Aurum Film Encyclopedia: Horror*, ed. Phil Hardy (London, 1985), p. 147.
63 Hutchings, *Hammer and Beyond*, p. 145.
64 *The Aurum Film Encyclopedia: Horror*, p. 241.
65 Quoted in Katz, *The Macmillan International Film Encyclopedia*, p. 124.
66 Hayward, *French National Cinema*, p. 245.
67 *Ibid.*, p. 246; David McGillivray, *Doing Rude Things: The History of the British Sex Film 1957–1981* (London, 1992), p. 13.

ELEVEN · THE CHALLENGE OF THIRD CINEMA

1 Robert Stam, 'Third World and Postcolonial Cinema', in Pam Cook and Mieke Bernink, eds, *The Cinema Book* (London, 1999), p. 120.
2 Paul Willemen, 'The Third Cinema Question: Notes and Reflections', in Jim Pines and Paul Willemen, eds, *Questions of Third Cinema* (London, 1989), p. 28.
3 Teshome H. Gabriel, 'Towards a Critical Theory of Third World Films', in Pines and Willemen, eds, *Questions of Third Cinema*, p. 31
4 H. Mark Glancy, *When Hollywood Loved Britain: The Hollywood 'British' Film* (Manchester, 1999), p. 18.
5 *Ibid.*, pp. 19–20
6 Quoted in Lizbeth Malkmus and Roy Armes, *Arab and African Film Making*

(London, 1991), p. 18.

7 Gabriel, 'Towards a Critical Theory of Third World Films', p. 32.
8 Quoted in Roberta Stam and Randal Johnson, 'The Cinema of Hunger: Nelson Pereira dos Santos', in Randal Johnson and Robert Stam, eds, *Brazilian Cinema* (Austin, 1982), p. 70.
9 Gabriel, 'Towards a Critical Theory of Third World Films', p. 33.
10 *Ibid.*
11 Kristin Thompson and David Bordwell, *Film History: An Introduction* (New York, 1994), p. 606.
12 *Ibid.*, p. 610.
13 Gabriel, 'Towards a Critical Theory of Third World Films', p. 34.
14 Thompson and Bordwell, *Film History: An Introduction*, p. 620.
15 *Ibid.*, p. 618.
16 Mike Wayne, *Political Cinema: The Dialectics of Third Cinema* (London, 2001), p. 9.
17 Jonathan Buchsbaum, 'A Closer Look at Third Cinema', *Historical Journal of Film, Radio and Television*, XXI/2 (2001), p. 153.
18 Fernando Solanas and Octavio Getino, 'Towards a Third Cinema' [1969], in Bill Nichols, ed., *Movies and Methods Volume I* (Berkeley, 1976), p. 51.
19 *Ibid.*, pp. 51–2.
20 *Ibid.*, p. 52.
21 *Ibid.*, p. 53.
22 *Ibid.*, p. 54.
23 Willemen, 'The Third Cinema Question', p. 12.
24 Quoted in Buchsbaum, 'A Closer Look at Third Cinema', p. 161.
25 Solanas and Getino, 'Towards a Third Cinema', p. 57.
26 'Third World on Screen', in Ann Lloyd, ed., *The History of the Movies* (London, 1988), p. 351.
27 Solanas and Getino, 'Towards a Third Cinema', p. 61.
28 *Ibid.*, p. 47.
29 Buchsbaum, 'A Closer Look at Third Cinema', p. 161.
30 Stam, 'Third World and Postcolonial Cinema', p. 123.

TWELVE · BOLLYWOOD AND BEYOND

1 Meenakshi Shedde, 'Making a Song & Dance about Two Cultures', *Cinemaya*, 47 (2000), p. 8.
2 M. Madhava Prasad, *Ideology of the Hindi Film: A Historical Construction* (Oxford, 1998), p. 14.
3 Basil Wright, *The Long View: A Personal Perspective on World Cinema* (London, 1974), p. 460.
4 Prasad, *Ideology of the Hindi Film*, p. 14.
5 Wright, *The Long View*, p. 459.
6 For a concise summary of nationalist film theory, see Ashish Rajadhyaksha, 'Indian Cinema', in John Hill and Pamela Church Gibson, eds, *World Cinema: Critical Approaches* (Oxford, 2000), pp. 151–6.
7 The first major English language history of Indian cinema was by one American and one Indian scholar, Erik Barnouw and S. Krishnaswamy, *Indian*

Film (New York, 1963; rev. edn 1980).

8 For example, the section on 'Hindi Cinema' (by Ashish Rajadhyaksha) in *The Cinema Book*, ed. Pam Cook and Mieke Bernink (London, 2nd edn 1999) is placed under 'Alternatives to Classic Hollywood', pp. 130–34. Prasad's *Ideology of the Hindi Film* counters this position by claiming Hindi cinema as a dominant mode of film practice in the Bordwell-Staiger-Thompson manner.

9 Ashish Rajadhyaksha, 'India: Filming the Nation', in Geoffrey Nowell-Smith, ed., *The Oxford History of World Cinema* (Oxford, 1996), p. 678.

10 K. Moti Gokulsing and Wimal Dissanayake, *Indian Popular Cinema: A Narrative of Cultural Change* (Stoke on Trent, 1998), p. 123.

11 Rachel Dwyer and Divia Patel, *Cinema India: The Visual Culture of Hindi Film* (London, 2002), p. 43.

12 Quoted in Rajadhyaksha, 'Hindi Cinema', p. 131.

13 Gokulsing and Dissanayake, *Indian Popular Cinema*, p. 13.

14 Rajadhyaksha, 'Hindi Cinema', p. 131.

15 Quoted in Prem Chowdhry, *Colonial India and the Making of Empire Cinema: Image, Ideology and Identity* (Manchester, 2000), p. 14.

16 *Ibid.*, p. 13.

17 Satyajit Ray, *Our Films, Their Films* (Bombay, 1976), p. 144.

18 Chowdhry, *Colonial India and the Making of Empire Cinema*, p. 15.

19 *Ibid.*, p. 98.

20 Gokulsing and Dissanayake, *Indian Popular Cinema*, p. 22.

21 Quoted in Chowdhry, *Colonial India and the Making of Empire Cinema*, p. 17.

22 Ephraim Katz, *The Macmillan International Film Encyclopedia* (London, 1994), p. 674.

23 Chowdhry, *Colonial India and the Making of Empire Cinema*, p. 19.

24 Soli J. Sorabjee, "India since 1947: Legal Aspects', in *Censorship: A World Encyclopedia*, ed. Derek Jones (London, 2001), p. 1164.

25 Gokulsing and Dissanayake, *Indian Popular Cinema*, p. 49.

26 Quoted in Prasad, *Ideology of the Hindi Film*, p. 29.

27 Quoted in Rajadhyaksha, 'India: Filming the Nation', p. 679.

28 Quoted in Gokulsing and Dissanayake, *Indian Popular Cinema*, p. 50.

29 Prasad, *Ideology of the Hindi Film*, pp. 31–2.

30 *Ibid.*, p. 237.

31 *Ibid.*, p. 32.

32 *Ibid.*, p. 45.

33 Kristin Thompson and David Bordwell, *Film History: An Introduction* (New York, 1994), p. 774.

34 Dwyer and Patel, *Cinema India*, p. 26.

35 Vijay Mishra, *Bollywood Cinema: Temples of Desire* (London, 2002), p. 126.

36 Nasreen Munni Kabir, 'Playback Time: A Brief History of Bollywood "Film Songs"', *Film Comment*, XXXVIII/3 (2002), p. 43.

37 Wright, *The Long View*, p. 458.

38 Quoted in Rajadhyaksha, 'India: Filming the Nation', p. 688.

39 Kerry Segrave, *American Films Abroad: Hollywood's Domination of the World's Movie Screens from the 1890s to the Present* (Jefferson, NC, 1997), p. 217.

40 *Ibid.*, p. 256.

41 Gokulsing and Dissanayake, *Indian Popular Cinema*, p. 114.

42 Dwyer and Patel, *Cinema India*, p. 217.

43 Rajadhyaksha, 'Hindi Cinema', p. 133.
44 'Given the current vogue for all things Bollywood, it's perhaps not
    surprising that Satyajit Ray's films have slipped slightly off the critical
    map', notes Philip Kemp. 'Ray himself rarely doubted that his movies and
    Indian popular cinema were antithetical; his ideal was always simplicity
    and understatement, where lavishness and large gestures are the essence
    of the Mumbai style.' 'Mitra man', *Sight and Sound*, New Series, XII/8
    (2002), p. 4.
45 Wright, *The Long View*, p. 460.
46 Rajadhyaksha, 'Hindi Cinema', p.132. On Ray's films, see Chidananda Das
    Gupta, *The Cinema of Satyajit Ray* (New Delhi, 1980) and Andrew Robinson,
    Satyajit Ray: The Inner Eye (London, 1989).
47 Katz, *The Macmillan International Film Encyclopedia*, p. 1126.
48 Quoted in Chidananda Das Gupta, ed., *Satyajit Ray: An Anthology of
    Statements on Ray and by Ray* (New Delhi, 1981), p. 136.
49 Derek Malcolm, *A Century of Films* (London, 2000), p. 141.
50 Quoted in Marie Seton, *Portrait of a Director: Satyajit Ray* (Bloomington,
    1971), p. 283.
51 Ravi S. Vasudevan, 'Shifting Codes, Dissolving Identities: The Hindi Social
    Film of the 1950s as Popular Culture', in Vasudevan, ed., *Making Meaning in
    Indian Cinema* (Oxford, 2000), p. 105
52 Rajadhyaksha, 'India: Filming the Nation', p. 683.
53 Salman Rushdie, *The Moor's Last Sigh* (London, 1995), p. 138.
54 Mishra, *Temples of Desire*, p. 77.
55 For a detailed study of the film, incoporating materials from the Mehboob
    studio archives, see Gayatri Chatterjee, *Mother India* (London, 2002), in the
    BFI 'Film Classics' series.
56 Rosie Thomas, 'Indian Cinema: Pleasures and Popularity', *Screen*, XXVI/3–4
    (1985), p. 131.
57 Thompson and Bordwell, *Film History*, p. 482.
58 Ravi Vasudevan, 'The Politics of Cultural Address in a "Transitional" Cinema:
    A Case Study of Popular Indian Cinema', in Christine Gledhill and Linda
    Williams, eds, *Reinventing Film Studies* (London, 2000), p. 131.
59 Dwyer and Patel, *Cinema India*, p. 30.
60 Naman Ramachandran, 'Devdas', *Sight and Sound*, New Series, XII/9 (2002),
    p. 58.
61 Dwyer and Patel, *Cinema India*, p. 91.
62 Gokulsing and Dissanayake, *Indian Popular Cinema*, p. 97.
63 Thompson and Bordwell, *Film History*, p. 482.
64 Richard Maltby, *Hollywood Cinema: An Introduction* (Oxford, 1995), p. 107.
65 Rosie Thomas, 'Mythologies and Modern India', in William Luhr, ed., *World
    Cinema since 1945* (New York, 1987), p. 304.
66 Prasad, *Ideology of the Hindi Film*, pp. 135–6.
67 Mishra, *Temples of Desire*, p. XIII.
68 *Ibid.*
69 *Ibid.*
70 Prasad, *Ideology of the Hindi Film*, p. 118.
71 *Ibid.*, p. 131.
72 Mishra, *Temples of Desire*, p. XIV.

73 See Lalitha Gopalan, 'Avenging Women in Indian Cinema',
    in Vasudevan, ed., *Making Meaning in Indian Cinema*, pp. 215–37.
74 Dwyer and Patel, *Cinema India*, p. 22.
75 See Vivek Dhareshwar and Tejaswini Niranjana, '*Kaadalan* and the Politics of
    Resignification: Fashion, Violence and the Body', in Vasudevan, ed., *Making
    Meaning in Indian Cinema*, pp. 191–214.
76 Dwyer and Patel, *Cinema India*, p. 22.
77 Prasad, *Ideology of the Hindi Film*, p. 136.
78 Rachel Dwyer, 'Asoka', *Sight and Sound*, New Series, xxi/11 (2001), p. 40.
79 Rachel Dwyer, 'Lagaan', *Sight and Sound*, New Series, i/10 (2001), p. 52.

THIRTEEN · ASIATIC CINEMAS

 1 See, for example, Noël Burch, *To the Distant Observer: Forms and Meaning in
    the Japanese Cinema* (Berkeley, 1979), David Bordwell, *Ozu and the Poetics of
    Cinema* (Princeton, 1988), and David Kirihara, *Patterns of Time: Mizoguchi
    and the 1930s* (Madison, wi, 1992).
 2 *The Guinness Book of Film Facts and Feats*, ed. Patrick Robertson (London,
    1985), pp. 18–21.
 3 Joseph L. Anderson and Donald Richie, *The Japanese Film: Art and Industry*
    (Princeton, rev. edn 1982), p. 47.
 4 Akira Kurosawa, *Something Like an Autobiography*, trans. Audie E. Brock (New
    York, 1982), p. 74.
 5 'Appendix 2: Chronology', in Chris Berry, ed., *Perspectives on Chinese Cinema*
    (London, 1991), p. 204.
 6 Jay Leda, *Dianying: An Account of Films and the Film Audience in China*
    (Cambridge, ma, 1972), pp. 24–5.
 7 *The Guinness Book of Film Facts and Feats*, p. 170.
 8 Quoted in Aaron Gerow, 'Japan: Film', in *Censorship: A World Encyclopedia*, ed.
    Derek Jones (London, 2001), p. 1267.
 9 *Ibid.*, p. 1268.
10 Sheila Cornelius, 'China: Film, Communist China', *Censorship: A World
    Encyclopedia*, p. 509
11 Chris Berry, 'China after the Revolution', in Geoffrey Nowell-Smith, ed.,
    The Oxford History of World Cinema (Oxford, 1996), p. 694.
12 Hiroshi Komatsu, 'The Classical Cinema in Japan', in Nowell-Smith, ed.,
    The Oxford History of World Cinema, p. 414.
13 Kurosawa, *Something Like an Autobiography*, pp. 100–101.
14 David Bordwell and Kristin Thompson, *Film Art: An Introduction*
    (New York, 2nd edn 1986), p. 367.
15 *Ibid.*, p. 369.
16 Ephraim Katz, *The Macmillan International Film Encyclopedia* (London, 1994),
    p. 1047.
17 See Bordwell, *Ozu and the Poetics of Cinema*, and Donald Richie, *Ozu:
    His Life and Films* (Berkeley, 1974).
18 Derek Malcolm, *A Century of Films* (London, 2000), p. 1.
19 Quoted in Kristin Thompson and David Bordwell, *Film History:
    An Introduction* (New York, 1994), p. 463. The critics' response to the film is

analysed by Greg M. Smith, 'Critical Reception of *Rashomon* in the West', *Asian Cinema*, XIII/2 (2002), pp. 115–28.

20 Kurosawa, *Something Like an Autobiography*, p. 187.

21 Katz, *The Macmillan International Film Encyclopedia*, p. 769.

22 Donald Richie, *The Films of Akira Kurosawa* (Berkeley, 1965), was the first auteurist study of the director in English.

23 Tadao Sato, 'Akira Kurosawa: Tradition in a Time of Transition', *Cinemaya*, 42 (1998), p. 30.

24 For a close analysis of the film see Joan Mellen, *Seven Samurai* (London, 2001), in the BFI 'Film Classics' series.

25 Sato, 'Akira Kurosawa', p. 30.

26 Komatsu, 'The Classical Cinema in Japan', p. 422.

27 Katz, *The Macmillan International Film Encyclopedia*, p. 249.

28 Kwok-Kan Tam and Wimal Dissanayake, *New Chinese Cinema* (Hong Kong, 1998), pp. 3–4.

29 However, Sheila Cornelius suggests the Fifth Generation were so called 'because they were mainly comprised of members from the fifth class to graduate from the school's Directing Department'. *New Chinese Cinema: Challenging Representations* (London, 2002), p. 35.

30 Chen Kaige, 'Breaking the Circle: The Cinema and Cultural Change in China', *Cineaste*, XVII/3 (1990), p. 3.

31 Tony Rayns, 'The Days', *Sight and Sound*, New Series, V/3 (March 1995), p. 79.

32 Jerome Silbergeld, *China into Film: Frames of Reference in Contemporary Chinese Cinema* (London, 1999), p. 18.

33 Mo Zhong, 'A Reader's Letter that will Make People Think', in Berry, ed., *Perspectives on Chinese Cinema*, p. 125.

34 Quoted in Chris Berry, 'Market Forces: China's "Fifth Generation" Faces the Bottom Line', in Berry, ed., *Perspectives on Chinese Cinema*, p. 122.

35 Cornelius, 'China: Film, Communist China', *Censorship: A World Encyclopedia*, p. 509.

36 'Introduction', Sheldon H. Lu, ed., *Transnational Chinese Cinemas: Identity, Nation, Gender* (Honolulu, 1997), p. 9.

37 John Brosnan, *Future Tense: The Cinema of Science Fiction* (London, 1978), p. 98.

38 Hiroshi Komatsu, 'The Modernization of Japanese Film', in Nowell-Smith, ed., *The Oxford History of World Cinema*, p. 719.

39 *Ibid.*, p. 719.

40 Gerow, 'Japan: Film', *Censorship: A World Encyclopedia*, p. 1269.

41 'Introduction', Poshek Fu and David Desser, eds, *The Cinema of Hong Kong: History, Arts, Identity* (Cambridge, 2000), p. 2

42 David Bordwell, *Planet Hong Kong: Popular Cinema and the Art of Entertainment* (Cambridge, MA, 2000), p. 119.

43 Stephen Teo, 'The 1970s: Movement and Transition', in Fu and Desser, eds, *The Cinema of Hong Kong*, p. 99.

44 Quoted in Thompson and Bordwell, *Film History*, p. 603.

45 Bordwell, *Planet Hong Kong*, p. 162.

46 Li Cheuk-To, 'Popular Cinema in Hong Kong', in Nowell-Smith, ed., *The Oxford History of World Cinema*, p. 708.

47 Chiao Hsiung-Ping, 'The Distinct Taiwanese and Hong Kong Cinemas', in

Berry, ed., *Perspectives on Chinese Cinema*, p. 156.
48 Tony Rayns, 'Crouching Tiger, Hidden Dragon', *Sight and Sound*, New Series, xi/1 (2001), p. 46.
49 *Ibid.*, p. 45.
50 See Salim Said, *Shadows on the Silver Screen: A Social History of the Indonesian Film* (Jakarta, 1991). There is to date no scholarly study of Filipino cinema in English.

FOURTEEN · MIDDLE EASTERN CINEMAS

1 Ephraim Katz, *The Macmillan International Film Encyclopedia* (London, 1994), p. 677.
2 Lizbeth Malkmus and Roy Armes, *Arab and African Film Making* (London, 1991), p. 28.
3 *Ibid.*, p. 5
4 Salah Stetie, 'Islam and the Image', in Georges Sadoul, ed., *The Cinema in the Arab Countries* (Beirut, 1966), pp. 13–22.
5 Behrad Najafi, *Film in Iran 1900 to 1979: A Political and Cultural Analysis* (Stockholm, 1986), p. 28.
6 *Ibid.*, p. 23.
7 *Ibid.*, pp. 29–30.
8 Hilmi Halim, 'The Cultural Influence of Arabic Films', in Sadoul, *The Cinema in the Arab Countries*, pp. 402.
9 Farid Jabre, 'The Industry in Lebanon 1958–65', in Sadoul, *The Cinema in the Arab Countries*, p. 177.
10 Malkmus and Armes, *Arab and African Film Making*, p. 51.
11 Quoted in Conan Elphicke, 'Lollywood Babylon', *Sight and Sound*, New Series, xi/4 (2001), p. 8.
12 Ali Shahabi, 'Iran: Film', in *Censorship: A World Encyclopedia*, ed. Derek Jones (London, 2001), p. 1208.
13 Karim Alrawi, 'Egypt – Since 1798', in *Censorship: A World Encylopedia*, p. 728.
14 Quoted in Greg Garrett, 'Film', in *Censorship: A World Encyclopedia*, p. 808.
15 Simone Clark, 'Steven Spielberg – *Schindler's List*', in *Censorship: A World Encyclopedia*, pp. 2326–8.
16 Roy Armes, *Third World Film Making and the West* (Berkeley, 1987), p. 191.
17 Hamid Naficy, 'Iranian Cinema', in Oliver Leaman, ed., *Companion Encyclopedia of Middle Eastern and North African Film* (London, 2001), p. 175.
18 Hamid Naficy, 'Iranian Cinema', in Geoffrey Nowell-Smith, ed., *The Oxford History of World Cinema* (Oxford, 1996), p. 674
19 Najafi, *Film in Iran*, p. 143.
20 Quoted in Hamid Naficy, 'Islamizing Film Culture in Iran', in Richard Tapper, ed., *The New Iranian Cinema: Politics, Representation and Identity* (London, 2002), p. 29.
21 Naficy, 'Iranian Cinema', *Companion Encyclopedia of Middle Eastern and North African Film*, p. 161.
22 Naficy, 'Islamizing Film Culture in Iran', p. 29.
23 Quoted in Sheila Johnston, 'Quietly Ruling the Roost', *Sight and Sound*, New Series, ix/1 (1999), p. 20.

24 Shahla Lahiji, 'Chaste Dolls and Unchaste Dolls: Women in Iranian Cinema since 1979', in Tapper, ed., *The New Iranian Cinema*, p. 225.
25 *Sight and Sound*, New Series, IX/1 (1999), p. 20.
26 Laura Mulvey, 'Afterword', in Tapper, ed., *The New Iranian Cinema*, p. 259.
27 Agnès Devictor, 'Classic Tools, Original Goals: Cinema and Public Policy in the Islamic Republic of Iran', in Tapper, ed., *The New Iranian Cinema*, p. 71.
28 Sheila Whitaker, 'A Woman's Touch', *Sight and Sound*, New Series, XI/5 (2001), p. 10.

FIFTEEN · ANGLOPHONE CINEMAS

1 Elizabeth Jacka, 'Australian Cinema', in John Hill and Pamela Church Gibson, eds, *World Cinema: Critical Approaches* (Oxford, 2000), p. 132.
2 Quoted in Margaret Dickinson and Sarah Street, *Cinema and State: The Film Industry and the British Government 1927–84* (London, 1985), p. 16.
3 *The Motion Picture Almanac 1939–1940*, ed. Terry Ramsaye (New York, 1940), p. 944.
4 Kevin Rockett, Luke Gibbons and John Hill, *Cinema and Ireland* (New York, 1988), p. 39.
5 *Ibid.*, p. 56.
6 Jeffrey Richards, *Films and British National Identity: From Dickens to Dad's Army* (Manchester, 1997), p. 233.
7 Quoted in Jacka, 'Australian Cinema', pp. 132–3.
8 Quoted in Tom O'Regan, *Australian National Cinema* (London, 1996), p. 225.
9 Richards, *Films and British National Identity*, p. 176.
10 Quoted in Jacka, 'Australian Cinema', p. 133.
11 O'Regan, *Australian National Cinema*, p. 90.
12 Interview with Roger Donaldson, *Films in Review*, XXXIII/8 (1982), p. 496.
13 Christopher E. Gittings, *Canadian National Cinema* (London, 2002), p. 78.
14 *The Guinness Book of Film Facts and Feats*, ed. Patrick Robertson (London, 1985), p. 21.
15 Quoted in Brian McFarlane, *Australian Cinema 1970–1985* (London, 1987), p. 21.
16 Quoted in Rockett, Gibbons and Hill, *Cinema and Ireland*, p. 97.
17 *Ibid.*, p. 122.
18 Lance Pettitt, *Screening Ireland: Film and Television Representation* (Manchester, 2000), p. 39.
19 *Ibid.*, p. 9.
20 Stephen Crofts, 'New Australian Cinema', in Geoffrey Nowell-Smith, ed., *The Oxford History of World Cinema* (Oxford, 1996), pp. 723–4.
21 *Ibid.*, p. 724.
22 O'Regan, *Australian National Cinema*, p. 19.
23 *Ibid.*, p. 54.
24 Tom Allen, 'Journals', *Film Comment*, XVIII/4 (1982), p. 2.
25 O'Regan, *Australian National Cinema*, p. 72.
26 Crofts, 'New Australian Cinema', p. 730.
27 Jacka, 'Australian Cinema', p. 135.
28 Ephraim Katz, *The Macmillan International Film Encyclopedia* (London,

1994), p. 213.

9 Quoted in Gittings, *Canadian National Cinema*, p. 91.
30 *Ibid.*, p. 92.
31 Pettitt, *Screening Ireland*, p. 109.
32 See Jane Giles, *The Crying Game* (London, 1997), in the BFI 'Modern Classics' series.
33 Ruth Barton, 'The Ballykissangelization of Ireland', *Historical Journal of Film, Radio and Television*, XX/3 (2000), p. 417.
34 *Ibid.*, p. 413.

SIXTEEN · CINEMA WITHOUT FRONTIERS

1 Raymond Williams, *Keywords* (London, 1983), p. 237.
2 Kristin Thompson and David Bordwell, *Film History: An Introduction* (New York, 1994), p. 797.
3 Quoted in Toby Miller, Nitin Govil, John McMurria and Richard Maxwell, *Global Hollywood* (London, 2001), p. 3
4 Kerry Segrave, *American Films Abroad: Hollywood's Domination of the World's Movie Screens from the 1890s to the Present* (Jefferson, NC, 1997).

Select Bibliography

I. GENERAL HISTORIES, REFERENCE WORKS AND ENCYCLOPÆDIAS

Banerjee, Shampa, and Anil Srivastava, *One Hundred Indian Feature Films: An Annotated Filmography* (New York, 1988)

Barnard, Timothy, and Peter Rist, eds, *South American Cinema: A Critical Filmography 1915–1994* (Austin, 1996)

Buscombe, Edward, ed., *The BFI Companion to the Western* (London, 1988)

Cook, David A., *A History of Narrative Film* (London, 2nd edn 1990)

Dickinson, Thorold, *A Discovery of Cinema* (London, 1971)

Ellis, Jack, *History of Film* (Englewood Cliffs, NJ, 1979)

Elsaesser, Thomas, with Michael Wedel, eds, *The BFI Companion to German Cinema* (London, 1999)

Hardy, Phil, ed., *The Aurum Film Encyclopedia: Horror* (London, 1985)

—, ed., *The Aurum Film Encyclopedia: The Western* (London, 1983)

Karney, Robyn, ed., *Chronicle of the Cinema* (London, 1995)

Katz, Ephraim, *The Macmillan International Film Encyclopedia* (London, 1994)

Leaman, Oliver, ed., *Companion Encyclopedia of Middle Eastern and North African Film* (London, 2001)

Luhr, William, ed., *World Cinema since 1945* (New York, 1987)

McFarlane, Brian, Geoff Mayer and Ian Bertrand, eds, *The Oxford Companion to Australian Film* (Oxford, 1999)

McLintock, Marsha Hamilton, *The Middle East and North Africa on Film: An Annotated Filmography* (New York, 1982)

Mast, Gerald, *A Short History of the Movies* (Indianapolis, 1981)

Newman, Kim, ed., *The BFI Companion to Horror* (London, 1996)

Nowell-Smith, Geoffrey, ed., *The Oxford History of World Cinema* (Oxford, 1996)

—, with James Hay and Gianni Volpi, eds, *The Companion to Italian Cinema* (London, 1996)

Pendergast, Tom and Sara, eds, *International Dictionary of Films and Filmmakers Volume 1: Films* (Detroit, 4th edn 2000)

—, eds, *International Dictionary of Films and Filmmakers Volume 2: Directors* (Detroit, 4th edn 2000)

Rajadhyaksha, Ashish, and Paul Willemen, eds, *Encyclopædia of Indian Cinema* (London, 1999)

Ramsaye, Terry, *A Million and One Nights: A History of the Motion Picture* (London, 1954 edn; first published in New York, 1926).

Rhode, Eric, *A History of the Cinema from its Origins to 1970* (Harmondsworth, 1976)

Robinson, David, *World Cinema: A Short History* (London, 1973)

Rotha, Paul, *The Film Till Now* (London, 1930; 1949 edition revised by Richard Griffith)

Sklar, Robert, *Film: An International History of the Medium* (London, 1993)

Taylor, Richard, Nancy Wood, Julian Graffy and Dina Iordanova, eds, *The BFI Companion to Eastern European and Russian Cinema* (London, 2001)

Thompson, Kristin, and David Bordwell, *Film History: An Introduction* (New York, 1994)

Thomson, David, *A Biographical Dictionary of Film* (London, 1994; originally published as *A Biographical Dictionary of the Cinema* in 1975)

Vincendeau, Ginette, ed., *The Companion to French Cinema* (London, 1996)

Wright, Basil, *The Long View: A Personal Perspective on World Cinema* (London, 1974)

Zhang Yingjin, ed., *Encyclopedia of Chinese Film* (London, 1998)

2 . CRITICAL, METHODOLOGICAL AND HISTORIO-GRAPHICAL ISSUES

Allen, Robert C., and Douglas Gomery, *Film History: Theory and Practice* (New York, 1985)

Andrew, J. Dudley, *The Major Film Theories: An Introduction* (Oxford, 1976)

Bordwell, David, and Kristin Thompson, *Film Art: An Introduction* (New York, 1979)

British Universities Film Council, *Film and the Historian* (London, 1969)

Cherchi Usai, Paolo, *Burning Passions: An Introduction to the Study of Silent Cinema*, trans. Emma Sansone Rittle (London, 1994)

Collins, Jim, Hilary Radner and Ava Preacher Collins, eds, *Film Theory Goes to the Movies* (London, 1993)

Cook, Pam, and Mieke Bernink, eds, *The Cinema Book* (London, 2nd edn 1999)

Gledhill, Christine, and Linda Williams, eds, *Reinventing Film Studies* (London, 2000)

Grenville, J.A.S., *Film as History: The Nature of Film Evidence* (Birmingham, 1971)

Haskell, Molly, *From Reverence to Rape: The Treatment of Women in the Movies* (Chicago, rev. edn 1987)

Hill, John, and Pamela Church Gibson, eds, *World Cinema: Critical Approaches* (Oxford, 2000)

Kuhn, Annette, and Jackie Stacey, eds, *Screen Histories: A Screen Reader* (Oxford, 1998)

Lapsley, Robert, and Michael Westlake, *Film Theory: An Introduction* (Manchester, 1988)

Mast, Gerald, Marshall Cohen and Leo Braudy, eds, *Film Theory and Criticism* (Oxford, 1974)

Petro, Patrice, *Aftershocks of the New: Feminism and Film History* (New York, 2002)

Pines, Jim, and Paul Willemen, eds, *Questions of Third Cinema* (London, 1989)

Sarris, Andrew, *The American Cinema: Directors and Directions 1929–1968* (New York, 1968)

Smith, Paul, ed., *The Historian and Film* (Cambridge, 1976)

Staiger, Janet, *Interpreting Films: Studies in the Historical Reception of American Cinema* (Princeton, 1992)

Turner, Graeme, *Film As Social Practice* (London, 1988)

Wayne, Mike, *Political Film: The Dialectics of Third Cinema* (London, 2001)

Wollen, Peter, *Signs and Meanings in the Cinema* (London, 1969; rev. edn 1972)

3 . NATIONAL CINEMAS AND FILM INDUSTRIES

Abel, Richard, *The Red Rooster Scare: Making Cinema American, 1900–1910* (Berkeley, 1999)

Aldgate, Anthony, *Censorship and the Permissive Society: British Cinema and Theatre 1955–1965* (Oxford, 1995)

—, and Jeffrey Richards, *Best of British: Cinema and Society from 1930 to the Present* (London, rev. edn 1999)

—, and Jeffrey Richards, *Britain Can Take It: The British Cinema in the Second World War* (Edinburgh, 2nd edn 1994)

Anderson, Joseph L., and Donald Richie, *The Japanese Film: Art and Industry* (Princeton, rev. edn 1982)

Armes, Roy, *A Critical History of British Cinema* (London, 1977)

—, *French Cinema* (London, 1985)

—, *Third World Film Making and the West* (Berkeley, 1987)

Austin, Guy, *Contemporary French Cinema: An Introduction* (Manchester, 1996)

Balio, Tino, *History of the American Cinema Volume 5. Grand Design: Hollywood as a Modern Business Enterprise, 1930–1939* (New York, 1993)

—, ed., *The American Film Industry* (Madison, WI, 1976)

Barlet, Olivier, *African Cinemas: Decolonizing the Gaze*, trans. Chris Turner (London, 2000)

Barnouw, Erik, and S. Krishnaswany, *Indian Film* (Oxford, 2nd edn 1980)

Barr, Charles, ed., *All Our Yesterdays: 90 Years of British Cinema* (London, 1986)

Belton, John, *American Cinema/American Culture* (New York, 1994)

Bergfelder, Tim, Erica Carter and Deniz Göktürk, eds, *The German Cinema Book* (London, 2002)

Bergman, Andrew, *We're in the Money: Depression America and Its Films* (New York, 1971)

Berry, Chris, ed., *Perspectives on Chinese Cinema* (London, 1991)

Besas, Peter, *Behind the Spanish Lens: Spanish Cinema under Fascism and Democracy* (Denver, 1985)

Biskind, Peter, *Easy Riders, Raging Bulls: How the Sex'n'Drugs'n'Rock'n'Roll Generation Saved Hollywood* (London, 1998)

—, *Seeing Is Believing: How Hollywood Taught Us to Stop Worrying and Love the Fifties* (London, 1984)

Black, Gregory D., *The Catholic Crusade Against the Movies, 1940–1975* (Cambridge, 1997)

—, *Hollywood Censored: Morality Codes, Catholics, and the Movies* (Cambridge, 1994)

Blake, Richard A., *Screening America: Reflections on Five Classic Films* (New York, 1991)

Bondanella, Peter, *Italian Cinema: From Neorealism to the Present* (New York, 1983)

Bordwell, David, *Planet Hong Kong: Popular Cinema and the Art of Entertainment* (Cambridge, MA, 2000)

Bordwell, David, Janet Staiger and Kristin Thompson, *The Classical Hollywood Cinema: Film Style & Mode of Production to 1960* (London, 1985)

Bowser, Eileen, *History of the American Cinema Volume 2. The Transformation of Cinema 1907–1915* (New York, 1990)

Browne, Nick, Paul G. Pickowicz, Vivian Sobchack and Esther Yau, eds, *New Chinese Cinemas: Forms, Identities, Politics* (Cambridge, 1994)

Burns, E. Bradford, *Latin American Cinema: Film and History* (Los Angeles, 1975)

Burns, J.M., *Flickering Shadows: Cinema and Identity in Colonial Zimbabwe* (Ohio, 2002)

Chakravarty, Sumita, *National Identity in Indian Popular Cinema 1947–1987* (Austin, 1993)

Chapman, James, *The British at War: Cinema, State and Propaganda, 1939–1945* (London, 1998)

Clark, Paul, *Chinese Cinema: Culture and Politics since 1949* (Cambridge, 1987)

Cook, David A., *History of the American Cinema Volume 9. Lost Illusions: American Cinema in the Shadow of Watergate and Vietnam 1970–1979* (New York, 2000)

Cowie, Peter, *Scandinavian Cinema* (London, 1992)

Crafton, Donald, *History of the American Cinema Volume 4. The Talkies: American Cinema's Transition to Sound, 1926–1931* (New York, 1997)

Craven, Ian, ed., *Australian Cinema in the 1990s* (London, 2001)

Cripps, Thomas, *Hollywood's High Noon: Moviemaking and Society before Television* (Baltimore, 1997)

Crisp, Colin, *The Classic French Cinema 1930–1960* (London, 1993)

Curran, James, and Vincent Porter, eds, *British Cinema History* (London, 1983)

Davies, Philip, and Brian Neve, eds, *Cinema, Politics and Society in America* (Manchester, 1981)

Diawara, Manthia, *African Cinema* (Bloomington, 1992)

Dickinson, Margaret, and Sarah Street, *Cinema and State: The Film Industry and the British Government 1927–84* (London, 1985)

Docherty, Thomas, *Pre-Code Hollywood: Sex, Immorality and Insurrection in American Cinema 1930–1934* (New York, 1999)

—, *Projections of War: Hollywood, American Culture, and World War II* (New York, 1993)

Dwyer, Rachel, and Divia Patel, *Cinema India: The Visual Culture of Hindi Film* (London, 2002)

Dyer, Richard, and Ginette Vincendeau, eds, *Popular European Cinema* (London, 1992)

Eisner, Lotte H., *The Haunted Screen: Expressionism in the German Cinema and the Influence of Max Reinhardt*, trans. Roger Greaves (Berkeley, 1969)

Eleftheriotis, Dimitris, *Popular Cinema of Europe: Studies of Texts, Contexts and Frameworks* (New York, 2001)

Elsaesser, Thomas, ed., *Early Cinema: Space, Frame, Narrative* (London, 1990)

—, *New German Cinema: A History* (New Brunswick, NJ, 1989)

—, *Weimar Cinema and After: Germany's Historical Imaginary* (London, 2000)

Evans, Peter William, ed., *Spanish Cinema: The Auteurist Tradition* (Oxford, 1999)

Forbes, Jill, *The Cinema in France: After the New Wave* (London, 1992)

—, and Sarah Street, eds, *European Cinema: An Introduction* (Basingstoke, 2000)

Fox, Jo, *Filming Women in the Third Reich* (Oxford, 2000)

Friedman, Lester, ed., *British Cinema and Thatcherism: Fires Were Started* (London, 1993)

Fu, Poshek, and David Desser, eds, *The Cinema of Hong Kong: History, Arts, Identity* (Cambridge, 2000)

Fuksiewicz, Jacek, *Polish Cinema* (Warsaw, 1973)

Gazdar, Mushtaq, *Pakistan Cinema 1947–1990* (Oxford, 1997)

Geraghty, Christine, *British Cinema in the Fifties: Gender, Genre and the 'New Look'* (London, 2000)

Gittings, Christoper E., *Canadian National Cinema* (London, 2002)

Gokulsing, K. Moti, and Wimal Dissanayake, *Indian Popular Cinema: A Narrative of Cultural Change* (Stoke on Trent, 1998)

Gomery, Douglas, *The Hollywood Studio System* (London, 1986)

Goulding, Daniel J., ed., *Post New Wave Cinema in the Soviet Union and Eastern Europe* (Bloomington, 1989)

Guback, Thomas H., *The International Film Industry: Western Europe and America since 1945* (Bloomington, 1969)

Hake, Sabine, *German National Cinema* (London, 2002)

—, *Popular Cinema in the Third Reich* (Austin, 2002)

Hames, Peter, *The Czechoslovak New Wave* (Berkeley, 1985)

Hansen, Miriam, *Babel and Babylon: Spectatorship in American Silent Film* (Cambridge, MA, 1991)

Harper, Sue, *Women in British Cinema: Mad, Bad and Dangerous to Know* (London, 2000)

Hay, James, *Popular Film Culture in Fascist Italy* (Bloomington, 1987)

Hayward, Susan, *French National Cinema* (London, 1993)

—, and Ginette Vincendeau, eds, *French Film: Texts and Contexts* (London, 1990)

Higson, Andrew, *Waving the Flag: Constructing a National Cinema in Britain* (Oxford, 1995)

—, and Richard Maltby, eds, *'Film Europe' and 'Film America': Cinema, Commerce and Cultural Exchange 1920–1939* (Exeter, 1999)

Hill, John, *British Cinema in the 1980s: Issues and Themes* (Oxford, 1999)

—, *Sex, Class and Realism: British Cinema 1956–1963* (London, 1986)

Hillier, Jim, *The New Hollywood* (London, 1993)

Hjort, Mette, and Scott MacKenzie, eds, *Cinema and Nation* (London, 2000)

Jordan, Barry, and Rikki Morgan-Tamosunas, *Contemporary Spanish Cinema* (Manchester, 1998)

Kenez, Peter, *Cinema and Soviet Society, 1917–1953* (Cambridge, 1992)

Kerr, Paul, ed., *The Hollywood Film Industry: A Reader* (London, 1986)

King, Geoff, *Spectacular Narratives: Hollywood in the Age of the Blockbuster* (London, 2000)

—, *New Hollywood: An Introduction* (London, 2001)

King, John, *Magical Reels: A History of Cinema in Latin America* (London, 1990)

Knight, Julia, *Women and the New German Cinema* (London, 1992)

Koppes, Clayton R., and Gregory D. Black, *Hollywood Goes to War: How Politics, Profits and Propaganda Shaped World War II Movies* (London, 1988)

Koszarski, Richard, *History of the American Cinema Volume 3. An Evening's Entertainment: The Age of the Silent Feature Picture, 1915–1928* (New York, 1990)

Kracauer, Siegfried, *From Caligari to Hitler: A Psychological History of the German Film* (Princeton, 1947)

Krämer, Peter, *The Big Picture: Hollywood Cinema from Star Wars to Titanic* (London, 2003)

Kuhn, Annette, *Cinema, Censorship and Sexuality 1909–1925* (London, 1988)

Kuosho, Harry, *Celluloid China: Cinematic Encounters with Culture and Society* (Chicago, 2002)

Landy, Marcia, *British Genres: Cinema and Society, 1930–1960* (Princeton, 1991)

—, *Italian Film* (Cambridge, 2000)

Lawton, Anna, *Kinoglasnost: Soviet Cinema in Our Time* (Cambridge, 1992)

—, *The Red Screen: Politics, Society and Art in Soviet Cinema* (London, 1992)

Lee, Hyangjin, *Contemporary Korean Cinema: Identity, Culture, Politics* (Manchester, 2000)

Lent, John A., ed., *The Asian Film Industry* (London, 1990)

Leyda, Jay, *Kino: A History of Russian and Soviet Film* (Princeton, 3rd edn 1983)

—, *Dianying: An Account of Films and the Film Audience in China* (Cambridge, MA, 1972)

Liehm, Mira, *Passion and Defiance: Film in Italy from 1942 to the Present* (Berkeley, 1984)

McFarlane, Brian, *Australian Cinema 1970–1985* (London, 1987)

McLoone, Martin, *Irish Film: The Emergence of a Contemporary Cinema* (London, 2000)

Malkmus, Lizbeth, and Roy Armes, *Arab and African Film Making* (London, 1991)

Maltby, Richard, *Harmless Entertainment: Hollywood and the Ideology of Consensus* (Metuchen, NJ, 1983)

—, *Hollywood Cinema: An Introduction* (Oxford, 1995)

Marcus, Millicent, *Italian Film in the Light of Neorealism* (Princeton, 1986)

—, *Filmmaking by the Book: Italian Cinema and Literary Adaptation* (Baltimore, 1993)

Martin, John W., *The Golden Age of French Cinema 1929–1939* (London, 1983)

May, Lary, *The Big Tomorrow: Hollywood and the Politics of the American Way* (Chicago, 2000)

Mazdon, Lucy, ed., *France on Film: Reflections on Popular French Cinema* (London, 2000)

Mishra, Vijay, *Bollywood Cinema: Temples of Desire* (London, 2002)

Monaco, Paul, *History of the American Cinema Volume 8. The Sixties: 1960–1969* (New York, 2001)

Murphy, Robert, *British Cinema and the Second World War* (London, 2000)

—, *Realism and Tinsel: Cinema and Society 1939–1948* (London, 1989)

—, *Sixties British Cinema* (London, 1992)

Musser, Charles, *History of the American Cinema Volume 1. The Emergence of Cinema: The American Screen to 1907* (New York, 1990)

Naficy, Hamid, *Cinema and National Identity: A Social History of the Iranian Cinema* (Austin, 2003)

Najafi, Behrad, *Film in Iran 1900 to 1979: A Political and Cultural Analysis* (Stockholm, 1986)

Neupert, Richard, *A History of the French New Wave Cinema* (Madison, WI, 2002)

Neve, Brian, *Film and Politics in America: A Social Tradition* (London, 1992)

Nolleti, Arthur, and David Desser, eds, *Reframing Japanese Cinema: Authorship, Genre, History* (Bloomington, 1992)

Nowell-Smith, Geoffrey, and Steven Ricci, eds, *Hollywood and Europe: Economics, Culture, National Identity 1945–1995* (London, 1998)

O'Connor, John E., and Martin A. Jackson, eds, *American History/American Film: Interpreting the Hollywood Image* (New York, 1979)

O'Regan, Tom, *Australian National Cinema* (London, 1996)

Paranagua, Paulo Antonio, ed., *Mexican Cinema* (London, 1996)

Petley, Julian, *Capital and Culture: German Cinema 1933–45* (London, 1979)

Petrie, Graham, *Hollywood Destinies: European Directors in America, 1922–1931* (London, 1985)

Pettitt, Lance, *Screening Ireland: Film and television representation* (Manchester, 2000)

Powrie, Phil, *French Cinema in the 1980s: Nostalgia and the Crisis of Masculinity* (Oxford, 1997)

—, ed., *French Cinema in the 1990s: Continuity and Difference* (Oxford, 1999)

Prasad, M. Madhava, *Ideology of the Hindi Film: A Historical Construction* (Oxford, 2000)

Price, Stephen, *History of the American Cinema Volume 10. A New Pot of Gold: Hollywood Under the Electronic Rainbow, 1980–1989* (New York, 2000)

Quart, Leonard, and Albert Auster, *American Film and Society since 1945* (New York, rev. edn 1991)

Ray, Robert B., *A Certain Tendency of the Hollywood Cinema, 1930–1980* (Princeton, 1985)

Rayns, Tony, ed., *Eiga: 25 Years of Japanese Cinema* (Edinburgh, 1984)

—, and Scott Meek, ed., *Electric Shadows: 45 Years of Chinese Cinema* (London, 1980)

Reader, Keith, *Cultures on Celluloid* (London, 1981)

Reeves, Nicholas, *The Power of Film Propaganda: Myth or Reality?* (London, 1999)

Rentschler, Eric, *The Ministry of Illusion: Nazi Cinema and its Afterlife* (Cambridge, MA, 1996)

Roberts, Graham, *Forward Soviet! History and Non-fiction Film in the USSR* (London, 1999)

Robinson, David, ed. and trans., *Cinema in Revolution: The Heroic Era of the Soviet Film* (London, 1973)

Rockett, Kevin, Luke Gibbons and John Hill, *Cinema and Ireland* (New York, 1987)

Roddick, Nick, *A New Deal in Entertainment: Warner Bothers in the 1930s* (London, 1983)

Rollins, Peter C., ed., *Hollywood as Historian: American Film in a Cultural Context* (Lexington, KY, rev. edn 1998)

Richards, Jeffrey, *The Age of the Dream Palace: Cinema and Society in Britain 1930–1939* (London, 1984)

—, *Films and British National Identity: From Dickens to 'Dad's Army'* (Manchester, 1997)

Robertson, James C., *The British Board of Film Censors: Film Censorship in Britain, 1896–1950* (London, 1985)

—, *The Hidden Cinema: British Film Censorship in Action, 1913–1972* (London, 1989)

Rockett, Kevin, Luke Gibbons and John Hill, *Cinema and Ireland* (New York, 1987)

Roddick, Nick, *A New Deal in Entertainment: Warner Brothers in the 1930s* (London, 1983)

Sadoul, George, *The Cinema in the Arab Countries* (Beirut, 1966)

Said, Salim, *Shadows on the Silver Screen: A Social History of the Indonesian Film* (Jakarta, 1991)

Schatz, Thomas, *History of the American Cinema Volume 6. Boom and Bust: American Cinema in the 1940s* (New York, 1997)

—, *The Genius of the System: Hollywood Filmmaking in the Studio Era* (New York, 1988)

—, *Hollywood Genres: Formulas, Filmmaking and the Studio System* (New York, 1981)

Segrave, Kerry, *American Films Abroad: Hollywood's Domination of the World's Movie Screens* (Jefferson, NC, 1997)

Shindler, Colin, *Hollywood Goes to War: Film and American Society 1939–52* (London, 1979)

—, *Hollywood in Crisis: Cinema and American Society 1929–1939* (London, 1996)

Shohat, Ella, *Israeli Cinema: East/West and the Politics of Representation* (Austin, 1989)

Sieglohr, Ulrike, ed., *Heroines Without Heroes: Reconstructing Female and National Identities in European Cinema 1945–51* (London, 2000)

Silbergeld, Jerome, *China into Film: Frames of Reference in Contemporary Chinese Cinema* (London, 1999)

Sklar, Robert, *Movie-made America: A Cultural History of American Movies* (New York, 1975)

Soila, Tytti, Astrid Söderbergh and Gunnar Iversen, *Nordic National Cinemas* (London, 1998)

Sorlin, Pierre, *European Cinemas, European Societies 1939–1990* (London, 1991)

—, *Italian National Cinema 1896–1996* (London, 1996)

Staiger, Janet, ed., *The Studio System* (New Brunswick, NJ, 1995)

Stam, Robert, and Randal Johnson, eds, *Brazilian Cinema* (Austin, 1982)

Stead, Peter, *Film and the Working Class: The Feature Film in British and American Society* (London, 1989)

Stollery, Martin, *Alternative Empires: European Modernist Cinemas and the Culture of Imperialism* (Exeter, 2001)

Stone, Rob, *Spanish Cinema* (Harlow, 2002)

Street, Sarah, *British National Cinema* (London, 1997)

Tam, Kwok-Kon, and Wimal Dissanayake, *New Chinese Cinema* (Hong Kong, 1998)

Tapper, Richard, ed., *The New Iranian Cinema: Politics, Representation and Identity* (London, 2002)

Taylor, Richard, *Film Propaganda: Soviet Russia and Nazi Germany* (London, rev. edn 1998)

—, and Ian Christie, eds, *Inside the Film Factory: New Approaches to Russian and Soviet Cinema* (London, 1991)

Teo, Stephen, *Hong Kong Cinema: The Extra Dimension* (London, 1997)

Thompson, Kristin, *Exporting Entertainment: America in the World Film Market 1907–34* (London, 1985)

Tomaselli, Keyan, *The Cinema of Apartheid: Race and Class in South African Film* (London, 1989)

Vasudevan, Ravi S., ed., *Making Meaning in Indian Cinema* (Oxford, 2000)

Welch, David, *Propaganda and the German Cinema 1933–1945* (Oxford, 1983)

Whyte, Alistair, *New Cinema in Eastern Europe* (London, 1971)

Wilson, Emma, *French Cinema since 1950: Personal Histories* (London, 1999)

Wood, Robin, *Hollywood from Vietnam to Reagan* (New York, 1989)

Yau, Esther C.M., ed., *At Full Speed: Hong Kong Cinema in a Borderless World* (Minneapolis, 2001)

4. GENRES, CYCLES AND TRENDS

Aitken, Ian, *Film and Reform: John Grierson and the Documentary Film Movement* (London, 1990)

Altman, Rick, *The American Film Musical* (Bloomington, 1987)

—, ed., *Genre: The Musical* (London, 1981)

Barnouw, Erik, *Documentary: A History of the Non-Fiction Film* (New York, rev. edn 1993)

Barr, Charles, *Ealing Studios* (London, 1977)

Byers, Jackie, *All that Hollywood Allows: Re-Reading Genre in 1950s Melodrama* (London, 1991)

Cameron, Ian, ed., *The Movie Book of Film Noir* (London, 1992)

—, and Douglas Pye, eds, *The Movie Book of the Western* (London, 1996)

Cawelti, John G., *Adventure, Mystery and Romance: Formula Stories as Art and Popular Culture* (Chicago, 1976)

Chapman, James, *Licence To Thrill: A Cultural History of the James Bond Films* (London, 1999)

Chibnall, Steve, and Robert Murphy, eds, *British Crime Cinema* (London, 1999)

— and Julian Petley, eds, *British Horror Cinema* (London, 2002)

Chowdhry, Prem, *Colonial India and the Making of Empire Cinema: Image, Ideology and Identity* (Manchester, 2000)

Clover, Carol J., *Men, Women and Chainsaws: Gender in the Modern Horror Film* (London, 1992)

Coates, Paul, *The Gorgon's Gaze: German Cinema, Expressionism, and the Image of Horror* (Cambridge, 1991)

Cook, Pam, ed., *Gainsborough Pictures* (London, 1997)

Coyne, Michael, *The Crowded Prairie: American National Identity in the Hollywood Western* (London, 1997)

Elley, Derek, *The Epic Film: Myth and History* (London, 1984)

Feuer, Jane, *The Hollywood Musical* (London, 1982)

Frayling, Christopher, *Spaghetti Westerns: Cowboys and Europeans from Karl May to Sergio Leone* (London, 1981)

French, Philip, *Westerns: Aspects of a Movie Genre* (London, 1973)

Glancy, H. Mark, *When Hollywood Loved Britain: The Hollywood 'British' Film 1939–45* (Manchester, 1999)

Gledhill, Christine, ed., *Home Is Where the Heart Is: Studies in Melodrama and the Women's Film* (London, 1987)

Gopalan, Lalitha, *Cinema of Interruptions: Action Genres in Contemporary Indian Cinema* (London, 2002)

Grant, Barry Keith, ed., *Film Genre Reader* (Austin, 1986)

Harper, Sue, *Picturing the Past: The Rise and Fall of the British Costume Film* (London, 1994)

Hunter, I.Q., ed., *British Science Fiction Cinema* (London, 1999)

Hutchings, Peter, *Hammer and Beyond: The British Horror Film* (Manchester, 1993)

Jancovich, Mark, *Rational Fears: American Horror in the 1950s* (Manchester, 1996)

Kaplan, E. Ann, ed., *Women in Film Noir* (London, rev. edn 1998)

Kitses, Jim, *Horizons West: Studies of Authorship within the Western* (London, 1969)

Krutnik, Frank, *In a Lonely Street: Film Noir, Genre, Masculinity* (London, 1991)

Lenihan, John, *Showdown: Confronting Modern America in the Western Film* (Urbana, IL, 1980)

Lovell, Alan, and Jim Hillier, *Studies in Documentary* (London, 1972)

McArthur, Colin, *Underworld USA* (London, 1972)

McGillivray, David, *Doing Rude Things: The History of the British Sex Film 1957–1981* (London, 1992)

Mazdon, Lucy, *Encore Hollywood: Remaking French Cinema* (London, 2000)

Munby, Jonathan, *Public Enemies, Public Heroes: Screening the Gangster from Little Caesar to Touch of Evil* (Chicago, 1999)

Neale, Steve, *Genre and Hollywood* (London, 2000)

Palmer, R. Barton, *Hollywood's Dark Cinema: The American Film Noir* (New York, 1994)

Paris, Michael, *From the Wright Brothers to Top Gun: Aviation, Nationalism and Popular Cinema* (Manchester, 1995)

Pirie, David, *A Heritage of Horror: The English Gothic Cinema 1946–1972* (London, 1973)

Richards, Jeffrey, *Visions of Yesterday* (London, 1973)

Rubin, Martin, *Thrillers* (Cambridge, 1999)

Shadoian, Jack, *Dreams and Dead Ends: The American Gangster/Crime Film* (Cambridge, MA, 1977)

Silver, Alain, *The Samurai Film* (South Brunswick, NJ, 1977)

Slotkin, Richard, *Gunfighter Nation: The Myth of the Frontier in Twentieth Century America* (New York, 1992)

Swann, Paul, *The British Documentary Film Movement, 1926–1946* (Cambridge, 1989)

Tasker, Yvonne, *Spectacular Bodies: Gender, Genre and the Action Cinema* (London, 1993)

Telotte, J.P., *Voices in the Dark: The Narrative Patterns of Film Noir* (Urbana, 1989)

Tudor, Andrew, *Monsters and Mad Scientists: A Cultural History of the Horror Movie* (Oxford, 1989)

Uricchio, William, and Roberta E. Pearson, *Reframing Culture: The Case of the Vitagraph Quality Films* (Princeton, 1993)

Wright, Will, *Sixguns and Society: A Structural Study of the Western* (Berkeley, 1975)

Wyke, Maria, *Projecting the Past: Ancient Rome, Cinema and History* (London, 1997)

5. A NOTE ON FILM JOURNALS

There is a wide and eclectic range of scholarly film journals, reflecting the different methods and approaches to the study of film within the academy. The specialist film history journals, all adhering to the tried and trusted empiricist approach, are *Film History*, *Film & History* and the *Historical Journal of Film, Radio and Television*. However, historical articles on film topics are also to be found in film studies journals such as *Cinema Journal*, *Quarterly Review of Film Studies*, *Screen* and *Wide Angle*. More inclined towards 'alternative' and avant-garde filmmaking are *Cineaste*, *Framework* and *Jump Cut*. There are numerous critical magazines covering all aspects of world cinema, including *Film Comment*, *Film International* (the English language version of the Swedish *Filmhäftet*), *Films in Review* and *Sight & Sound*. *Cinemaya* is a specialist English-language magazine devoted to Asian film, while *Asian Cinema* is a more scholarly journal on the same subject.

List of Illustrations

The author and publishers wish to express their thanks to the above sources of illustrative material and/or permission to reproduce it.

General Index

Guerra, Ruy 310, 320
Guy, Alice 72

Haggar, William 58
Haley, Bill 189
Hammer horror 270, 298–300
Harlan, Veit 226, 230
Hawks, Howard, 114, 117, 168, 182
Hayes, Richard 200
Hays, Will H. 99
Hayward, Rudall 405
Hayworth, Rita 117, 182, 184
Hepworth, Cecil 58–9, 70
Herzog, Werner 256–7
Historical Journal of Film, Radio and Television 18
Hitchcock, Alfred 22, 81, 88, 89, 93, 114, 286, 287, 289
'Hollywood Ten' 123
Hollywood vs America 150
Hopper, Dennis 135–6, 138
horror films 49, 88, 100, 270, 297–301, 350–51
Houseman, John 28, 177
HUAC (House UnAmerican Activities Committee) 121–5
Hugenberg, Alfred 78, 206
Hughes, Howard 100–1, 127, 171
Hui Xi Company 356
Hunter, Tim, 149
Huston, John 117, 123, 182

Imperial Film Company 326
Ince, Thomas 73
Independent Motion Pictures 73–4
Indian Kinema Company 326
Indian Peoples' Theatre Association 339, 341
Institut des Hautes Etudes Cinématographiques (France) 230
Instituto Cubano del Arte e Industria Cinematograficos (Cuba) 312
Instituto Nacional do Cinema (Brazil) 309
'intellectual montage' 85
International Association for Media and History 17
International Federation of Film Archives 51, 236
International Festival of Latin American Cinema 321
International Movie Studio 382
InterUniversity History Film Consortium 17
Irish Film Board 409–10

Irish Film Finance Corporation 409
Islamic Research Council (Egypt) 393
Ivory, James 343–4

Jaekin, Just 303
'James Bond' films 154, 288–90, 423–4
Jameson, Fredric 149
Jarman, Derek 36, 268–9
Jarmusch, Jim 144
Johnson, Nunnally 105
Johnston, Eric 122
Jolson, Al 91, 186
Jordan, Neil 416–7

Kaige, Chen 371–72
Kapoor, Raj 335, 348–9
Käutner, Helmut 230
Kaye, Danny 123
Kazan, Elia 124
Keaton, Buster 93, 282
Kerkorian, Kirk 133–4
Khan, Aamir 335, 351, 352
Khan, Mehboob 339, 341–2
Khan, Shah Rukh 351, 352
Kiarostami, Abbas 399
Kieslowski, Krzysztof 42, 268
Kinetograph 53
Kinetoscope 53
Kluge, Alexander 256
Kohinoor Film Company 326
Korda, Alexander 207, 208
Krasker, Robert 287
Kuleshov, Lev 82
Kumar, Dilip 335, 348, 349
kung-fu films (Hong Kong), 379–80
Kuratorium Junger Deutscher Film 241
Kurosawa, Akira 22, 38, 352, 354, 356, 362, 365–9

L'Herbier, Marcel 87
Laemmle, Carl 64, 73, 74, 107
Lang, Fritz 83, 181
Lattuada, Alberto 200
Lawrence, Florence 74
Le Prince, Augustin-Louis 53
Le Roy, Mervyn 174
Lee, Bruce 380
Legion of Decency 98–9
Lenin, Vladimir Ilyich 43
Leone, Sergio 295–6
Levine, Joseph E. 293
Lewton, Val 111
Liberty Pictures 117
Linder, Max 72, 279

Schwarzenegger, Arnold 150, 293
Scorsese, Martin 135–6, 176
Scott, Randolph 169, 170
Screen 18
Selig Polyscope Company 73
Selznick, David O. 102, 112, 117
Sembene, Ousmane 313
Sequence 236
sex films, 200, 271, 301–3, 376
Shaw Brothers 378, 381
Shochiku Cinema Company 49, 361–2
Shub, Esther 86
Shumyatsky, Boris 204–5
Siclier, Jacques 241
Siegel, Don 174
Siodmark, Robert 181
Sirk, Douglas 192
Sjöstrom, Victor 79
Skladonowsky, Max & Emil 53
Slade Film History Register 16
Smell-O-Vision 24
Smith, G. A. 55
Socialist Realism 87, 194, 205, 213–15, 230, 245, 359
Société Générale de Films 87
Solanas, Fernando 44, 314–18, 320
Sony Corporation 153–4
sound 35, 90–94, 186, 327–8
Soyuzkino, 204
'spaghetti westerns' 42, 270, 294–9, 379
spy thrillers, 271, 285–92
Spielberg, Steven 135–6, 138, 140–43
Stallone, Sylvester 144, 148, 293
Stanwyck, Barbara 182, 191
Staudte, Wolfgang 230
Stewart, James 117, 127–8, 164, 166, 170
Straub, Jean–Marie 42
Stromberg, Hunt 186
studio system
    Egypt 307
    India 327–9, 334
    Hollywood 24, 74, 96, 109–15, 130–34
    Hong Kong 377–9
    Japan 361–4
Sturges, Preston 98
Svensk Filmindustri (Sweden) 207
Svenska Biografteatern (Sweden) 79

talking pictures; *see* sound
Tarantino, Quentin 145, 176
Tati, Jacques 282–3
Tehran Film Festival 396
television 125–6, 193–4, 237, 264–5
Thalberg, Irving 111

Third Cinema 32, 36, 44, 305–21
3-D film 24
thrillers 49; *see also film noir*; gangster films; spy thrillers
Time Warner 153, 424
Todd, Mike 128
Tokyo Takarazuka Theatre Company (Toho) 49, 361, 374–5
Toland, Gregg 115
'topicals' 55
Toronto International Film Festival 396
Trevelyan, John 243
Truffaut, François 212, 242, 246, 248–9, 250, 267
Trumbo, Dalton 123, 125
Trümmerfilme 235
Twentieth Century-Fox Film Corporation 49, 101–3, 139, 141, 152

Ufa (Universum Film Aktiengesellschaft) 49, 78, 81, 206
United Artists, 102, 131, 133, 288, 296
Universal Pictures, 102, 107, 112, 127, 140, 153
University Historians' Film Committee 16–17

Vadim, Roger 241, 246–7
Valentino, Rudolph 89
Varda, Agnès 247–8
Variety 68, 102–3, 191, 193
Vasiliev, Sergei & Georgi 213
Venice Film Festival 205, 366
vertical integration 49, 101–2
Vigo, Jean 209–10
Visconti, Luchino 42, 232, 233, 241, 250

Wajda, Andrzej 261
Walsh, Raoul 111, 174
Wanger, Walter 102, 117
war film 49, 119, 271, 272–8
Warner Bros. 25, 91–2, 97, 101–3, 105–6, 133, 173–4, 186–7
Warner, Jack 108
Warshow, Robert 160, 172
Warwick Trading Company 55
Watt, Harry 215
Wayne, John 122, 133, 147, 163, 164, 167, 169, 170
Weir, Peter 412–13
Welles, Orson 22, 26, 114–5, 180, 364
Wellman, William 111, 174
Wenders, Wim 256, 267
westerns 49, 132, 137, 161–71

Film Index